SEVENTH EDITION

PUBLICATION
Manual

of the American Psychological Association

SEVENTH EDITION **7**

PUBLICATION
Manual

of the American Psychological Association

THE OFFICIAL GUIDE TO APA STYLE

AMERICAN PSYCHOLOGICAL ASSOCIATION
Washington, DC

For information on APA's permission policy, see https://www.apa.org/about/contact/copyright/

Published by
American Psychological Association
750 First Street, NE
Washington, DC 20002
https://www.apa.org

Order Department
https://www.apa.org/pubs/books
order@apa.org

For additional ordering information, including international distributors, see https://www.apa.org/pubs/ordering

Typeset in Aria and Avenir

APA Style Director: Emily L. Ayubi
APA Style Content Development Managers: Chelsea L. Bromstad Lee, Hayley S. Kamin, and Timothy L. McAdoo
APA Style Editors: Anne T. Woodworth and Ayanna A. Adams
Director, Print & Electronic Book Production: Jennifer M. Meidinger
Printer: RR Donnelley, Houston, TX
Cover and Interior Designer: Debra Naylor, Naylor Design, Inc., Washington, DC
Indexer: WordCo Indexing Services, Inc., Norwich, CT

The correct reference for this book is as follows:

American Psychological Association. (2020). *Publication manual of the American Psychological Association* (7th ed.). https://doi.org/10.1037/0000165-000

ISBN 978-1-4338-3215-4 (Hardcover)
ISBN 978-1-4338-3216-1 (Paperback)
ISBN 978-1-4338-3217-8 (Spiral)

Library of Congress Cataloging-in-Publication Data applied for

https://doi.org/10.1037/0000165-000

Printed in the United States of America

10 9 8 7 6 5 4 3 2 1

CONTENTS

133538

LIST OF TABLES AND FIGURES

Tables

Figures

EDITORIAL STAFF AND CONTRIBUTORS

Project Director

Emily L. Ayubi

APA Style Team

Chelsea L. Bromstad Lee

Hayley S. Kamin

Timothy L. McAdoo

Anne T. Woodworth

Ayanna A. Adams

***Publication Manual* Revision Task Force**

James Campbell Quick, *Chair*

Mark Appelbaum

Jacklynn Mary Fitzgerald

Scott Hines

Heidi M. Levitt

Arthur M. Nezu

Pamela Reid

APA Publications and Communications Board Task Force on Journal Article Reporting Standards

APA Working Group on Quantitative Research Reporting Standards

Mark Appelbaum, *Chair*

Harris Cooper

Rex B. Kline

Evan Mayo-Wilson

Arthur M. Nezu

Stephen M. Rao

James Campbell Quick, *Publications and Communications Board Liaison*

APA Working Group on Reporting Standards for Qualitative Research

Heidi M. Levitt, *Chair*

Michael Bamberg

John W. Creswell

David M. Frost

Ruthellen Josselson

Carola Suárez-Orozco

James Campbell Quick, *Publications and Communications Board Liaison*

APA Public Interest Bias-Free Language Committees

Committee on Aging

Walter R. Boot

Brian Carpenter

Erin E. Emery-Tiburcio

Margaret Norris

Patricia A. Parmelee

Maggie L. Syme

Deborah A. DiGilio, *Staff Liaison*

Committee on Disability Issues in Psychology

Erin E. Andrews

Susan D'Mello

Jennifer J. Duchnick

ACKNOWLEDGMENTS

The precursor to the *Publication Manual of the American Psychological Association* was published in 1929 as a seven-page article in *Psychological Bulletin* describing a "standard of procedure, to which exceptions would doubtless be necessary, but to which reference might be made in cases of doubt" (Bentley et al., 1929, p. 57). Since then, the scope and length of the *Publication Manual* have grown in response to the needs of researchers, students, and educators across the social and behavioral sciences, health care, natural sciences, humanities, and more; however, the spirit of the original authors' intentions remains.

To address changes in scholarly writing and publishing since the release of the sixth edition, we consulted many professional groups and experts (each recognized individually in the Editorial Staff and Contributors list). We thank members of the *Publication Manual* Revision Task Force for their vision for the manual and for ensuring that our guidance reflects current best practices. We also thank the APA Working Group on Quantitative Research Reporting Standards for updating the original journal article reporting standards (JARS) for quantitative research and the APA Working Group on Reporting Standards for Qualitative Research for their groundbreaking work in establishing the first set of qualitative and mixed methods JARS in APA Style. We are indebted to members of the APA Public Interest Directorate committees and other advocacy groups who revised the bias-free language guidelines on age, disability, race and ethnicity, sexual orientation and gender diversity, and socioeconomic status. We are also grateful to the reviewers who provided valuable perspectives while representing psychology, nursing, education, business, social work, ethics, and writing instruction.

The important work of the *Publication Manual* Revision Task Force, JARS working groups, APA bias-free language committees, and other experts builds on efforts from previous groups. Thus, we also acknowledge the significant contributions of prior task forces, working groups, and APA staff members who revised previous editions of the *Publication Manual*.

For their guidance on writing about older adults with respect and dignity, we thank Nancy Lundebjerg and Dan Trucil from the American Geriatrics Society. For her contribution to the sections on race and ethnicity, we thank Karen Suyemoto from the University of Massachusetts Boston. For their insights on sexual orientation, gender, and disability, we thank reviewers from the Human Rights Campaign: Jay Brown, Katalina Hadfield, Ellen Kahn, and Sula Malina. We also thank lore m. dickey, Mira Krishnan, and Anneliese A. Singh, members of APA Division 44: Society for the Psychology of Sexual Orientation and Gender Diversity, for their expertise in revising the sections on sexual orientation and gender diversity. For his suggestions regarding substance use language, we thank William W. Stoops from the University of Kentucky College of Medicine. They all shared their wisdom and passion for their communities to help people write with respect and inclusivity.

This edition of the *Publication Manual* is more accessible thanks in large part to the enthusiastic, detailed, and thoughtful contributions from David Berman Communications—in particular, David Berman, Michael E. Cooper, Hannah Langford Berman, and Krisandra Ivings. They helped refine our recommendations for fonts, headings, reference style, color contrast, and more to benefit all people who will use the manual.

For their guidance on presenting findings in tables and figures, we thank Adelheid A. M. Nicol and Penny M. Pexman. We also thank Gilad Chen, Anne M. Galletta, Roger Giner-Sorolla, Kevin Grimm, Lisa L. Harlow, Wendy Rogers, and Nadine Michele Weidman for their insights into publishing. We thank Steve W. J. Kozlowski, Open Science and Methodology Chair, for his expertise on replication and publication ethics. For their valuable expertise on legal references, we thank David DeMatteo and Kirk Heilbrun from Drexel University.

We also thank the many APA staff and consultants who contributed their feedback and expertise. These staff work across APA Publishing, the Education Directorate, the Executive Office, Information Technology Services, the Office of General Counsel, the Public Interest Directorate, and the Science Directorate: Joe Albrecht, Emma All, Ida Audeh, David Becker, Cara Bevington, Martha Boenau, Marla Bonner, Liz Brace, Dan Brachtesende, Dan Brown, Ann Butler, Kerry Cahill, Brenda Carter, Lindsay Childress-Beatty, Alison Cody, Lyndsey Curtis, Chris Detzi, Katie Einhorn, Andy Elkington, Kristine Enderle, Elise Frasier, Rob Fredley, Dana Gittings, Hannah Greenbaum, Rachel Hamilton, Sue Harris, Beth Hatch, Annie Hill, Sue Houston, Shelby Jenkins, Robert Johnson, Lois Jones, Shontay Kincaid, Kristen Knight, Kristin Walker Kniss, Marla Koenigsknecht, David Kofalt, George Kowal, J.J. Larrea, Stefanie Lazer, Katy Lenz, Glynne Leonard, Kathryn Hyde Loomis, Tim Meagher, Jennifer Meidinger, Claire Merenda, Necco McKinley, Debra Naylor, David Nygren, Sangeeta Panicker, Amy Pearson, Steph Pollock, Lee Rennie, Natalie Robinson, Kathleen Sheedy, Jasper Simons, Rose Sokol-Chang, Ann Springer, Elizabeth Stern, Amber Story, Daniya Tamendarova, Nina Tandon, Ron Teeter, Karen Thomas, Jenna Vaccaro, Purvi Vashee, Chi Wang, Jason Wells, Sarah Wiederkehr, Angel Williams, Kimberly Williams, Aaron Wood, and Sherry Wynn.

Last, we thank our many users who contributed their feedback via emails, surveys, interviews, focus groups, and social media. Your insights into what worked for you and what more you needed from APA Style have been invaluable in revising and creating content for this edition of the manual.

INTRODUCTION

Excellence in writing is critical for success in many academic and professional pursuits. APA Style is a set of guidelines for clear and precise scholarly communication that helps authors, both new and experienced, achieve excellence in writing. It is used by millions of people around the world in psychology and also in fields ranging from nursing to social work, communications to education, business to engineering, and other disciplines for the preparation of manuscripts for publication as well as for writing student papers, dissertations, and theses. The *Publication Manual of the American Psychological Association* is the authoritative resource for APA Style, and we are proud to deliver its seventh edition.

Why Use APA Style?

APA Style provides a foundation for effective scholarly communication because it helps authors present their ideas in a clear, concise, and organized manner. Uniformity and consistency enable readers to (a) focus on the ideas being presented rather than formatting and (b) scan works quickly for key points, findings, and sources. Style guidelines encourage authors to fully disclose essential information and allow readers to dispense with minor distractions, such as inconsistencies or omissions in punctuation, capitalization, reference citations, and presentation of statistics.

When style works best, ideas flow logically, sources are credited appropriately, and papers are organized predictably and consistently. People are described using language that affirms their worth and dignity. Authors plan for ethical compliance and report critical details of their research protocol to allow readers to evaluate findings and other researchers to potentially replicate the studies. Tables and figures present data in an engaging, consistent manner.

Whether you use APA Style for a single class or throughout your career, we encourage you to recognize the benefits of a conscientious approach to writing. Although the guidelines span many areas and take time and practice to learn, we hope that they provide a balance of directiveness and flexibility and will eventually become second nature.

APA Style for Students

The *Publication Manual* has long been an authoritative source for scholarly writing, and this edition provides more targeted guidance and support for students. All students, no matter what career they pursue, can benefit from mastering scholarly writing as a way to develop their critical thinking skills and hone the precision and clarity of their communication.

Most guidelines in the *Publication Manual* can be applied to both student papers and professional manuscripts. The manual also has elements specifically designed for students, including a student title page; guidance on citing classroom or intranet sources; and descriptions of common types of student papers such as annotated bibliographies, response papers, and dissertations and theses. Journal article reporting standards (JARS) are intended primarily for authors seeking publication but may be helpful for students completing advanced research projects.

Utility and Accessibility

We have created the seventh edition of the *Publication Manual* with the practical needs of users in mind. Within chapters, content is organized using numbered sections to help users quickly locate answers to their questions. This ease of navigability and depth of content mean that the manual can be used as both a reference work and a textbook on scholarly writing.

This edition promotes accessibility for everyone, including users with disabilities. In consultation with accessibility experts, we ensured that the guidelines support users who read and write works in APA Style through a variety of modalities, including screen readers and other assistive technologies. For example, we present a streamlined format for in-text citations intended to reduce the burden of both writing and reading them. We provide guidance on how to use adequate contrast in figures to meet Web Content Accessibility Guidelines (Web Accessibility Initiative, 2018). We also support the use of a variety of fonts and default settings in common word-processing programs, meaning that users need to make fewer adjustments to their systems to be ready to write in APA Style. Above all, our aim is to support the many ways in which people communicate. We encourage authors to be conscientious and respectful toward both the people about whom they are writing and the readers who will benefit from their work.

What's New in the Seventh Edition?

Brief descriptions of new and updated content are provided next on a chapter-by-chapter basis. For a more comprehensive overview of content changes, see the APA Style website (https://apastyle.apa.org).

Chapter 1: Scholarly Writing and Publishing Principles

Chapter 1 addresses types of papers and ethical compliance.

- New guidance addresses quantitative, qualitative, and mixed methods articles as well as student papers, dissertations, and theses.

- Information on planning for and ensuring ethical compliance reflects best practices.
- Guidance on data sharing, including in qualitative research, reflects open practice standards.

Chapter 2: Paper Elements and Format

Chapter 2 is designed to help novice users of APA Style select, format, and organize paper elements.

- The title page is updated for professionals, and a new student title page is provided.
- For all papers, the byline and affiliation format on the title page aligns with publishing standards.
- The author note includes more information, such as ORCID iDs, disclosure of conflicts of interest or lack thereof, and study registration information.
- The running head format has been simplified for professional authors and is not required for students.
- Font specifications are more flexible to address the need for accessibility.
- An updated heading format for Levels 3, 4, and 5 improves readability and assists authors who use the heading-styles feature of their word-processing program.
- Two new sample papers are provided: a professional paper and a student paper, with labels to show how specific elements appear when implemented.

Chapter 3: Journal Article Reporting Standards

Chapter 3 orients users to journal article reporting standards (JARS) and includes tables outlining standards for reporting quantitative, qualitative, and mixed methods research.

- JARS for quantitative research has been significantly expanded and updated (see Appelbaum et al., 2018; Cooper, 2018).
- The updated JARS now cover qualitative and mixed methods research (see Levitt, 2019; Levitt et al., 2018).

Chapter 4: Writing Style and Grammar

Chapter 4 provides guidance on writing style and grammar.

- The singular "they" is endorsed, consistent with inclusive usage.
- More detailed guidance helps writers avoid anthropomorphism.

Chapter 5: Bias-Free Language Guidelines

Chapter 5 presents bias-free language guidelines to encourage authors to write about people with inclusivity and respect.

- Existing guidance on age, disability, gender, racial and ethnic identity, and sexual orientation has been updated to reflect best practices.

- New guidance is provided on participation in research, socioeconomic status, and intersectionality.

Chapter 6: Mechanics of Style

Chapter 6 covers the mechanics of style, including punctuation, capitalization, abbreviations, numbers, and statistics in text.

- Updated guidance answers a common question: Use one space after a period at the end of a sentence, unless an instructor or publisher requests otherwise.
- Formatting of linguistic examples has changed; quotation marks are now used around examples, rather than italics, to promote accessibility.
- Expanded guidance is provided on the capitalization of proper nouns, job titles, diseases and disorders, and more.
- Guidelines for the presentation of abbreviations address common questions, such as how to include a citation with an abbreviation.
- Guidelines for the presentation of numbers have been updated to be consistent throughout a work (e.g., there is no longer an exception for presenting numbers in an abstract).
- New guidance is given on how to write gene and protein names.
- Updated guidelines allow greater flexibility for lettered, numbered, and bulleted lists.

Chapter 7: Tables and Figures

Chapter 7 presents guidance on creating tables and figures.

- More than 40 new sample tables and figures are presented, in dedicated sections, covering a variety of research types and topics.
- The presentation of tables and figures in text is more flexible (either after the reference list on separate pages or embedded in the text).
- Formatting of tables and figures is parallel, including consistent styles for numbers, titles, and notes.
- The accessible use of color in figures is addressed.

Chapter 8: Works Credited in the Text

Chapter 8 addresses appropriate levels of citation as well as plagiarism, self-plagiarism, and other unethical writing practices.

- In-text citations have been simplified; all in-text citations for works with three or more authors are shortened to the name of the first author plus "et al." (except where this would create ambiguity).
- New guidance is provided on how to cite recorded or unrecorded Traditional Knowledge and Oral Traditions of Indigenous Peoples.
- Examples of paraphrasing demonstrate how to achieve clear attribution without overcitation.
- New guidance is provided on how to format quotations from research participants.

Chapter 9: Reference List

Chapter 9 examines the four elements of a reference list entry (author, date, title, and source).

- The number of authors included in a reference entry has changed; up to 20 authors are now included before names are omitted with an ellipsis.
- The presentation of digital object identifiers (DOIs) and URLs has been standardized. Both are presented as hyperlinks; the label "DOI:" is no longer used, and the words "Retrieved from" are used only when a retrieval date is also needed.
- Updated guidance explains when to include DOIs and URLs for works retrieved from most academic research databases as well as from proprietary databases such as ERIC or UpToDate.
- New formatting guidance is provided for annotated bibliographies.

Chapter 10: Reference Examples

Chapter 10 provides more than 100 examples of APA Style references, each with accompanying parenthetical and narrative in-text citations.

- Templates are provided for every reference category.
- References are streamlined; for example, journal article references always include the issue number, and book references now omit the publisher location.
- Audiovisual materials receive expanded coverage, with new examples for YouTube videos, PowerPoint slides and lecture notes, TED Talks, and more.
- Social media, webpages, and websites are addressed in new categories. For consistency and ease of formatting, blogs and other online platforms that publish articles are part of the periodicals category.

Chapter 11: Legal References

Chapter 11 presents expanded and updated legal reference examples.

- Guidelines from *The Bluebook: A Uniform System of Citation* continue to be the foundation for APA Style legal references, with some modifications.
- New, relevant legal reference examples are provided (e.g., the Every Student Succeeds Act).

Chapter 12: Publication Process

Chapter 12 provides guidance on the publication process.

- New content helps early career researchers adapt a dissertation or thesis into a journal article or articles, select a journal for publication, avoid predatory or deceptive publishers, and navigate journal submission.
- Improved guidance on the journal publication process reflects current processes and policies authors need to be aware of when preparing a manuscript for submission.
- New guidance addresses how authors can share and promote their work following publication.

APA Style Online

The APA Style website (https://apastyle.apa.org) is the premier and authoritative online destination for APA Style. In addition to numerous free resources and instructional aids, it contains supplemental content that is referred to throughout the manual, including additional reference examples, sample papers, and guidance on using color effectively and accessibly in figures.

The JARS website (https://apastyle.apa.org/jars) contains the full repository of information about journal article reporting standards for a wide range of research designs; it is freely available to complement the orienting information in Chapter 3.

The APA Style blog (https://apastyle.apa.org/blog) and related social media accounts will continue to answer questions about and share insights into APA Style with the publication of the seventh edition, providing authoritative content from members of the APA Style team.

Academic Writer (https://digitallearning.apa.org/academic-writer) is APA's cloud-based tool for teaching and learning effective writing. Developed by the creators of APA Style, this product helps both student and professional authors compose research papers and master the application of seventh-edition APA Style.

Notes to Users

The *Publication Manual* refers to numerous products and services that are not affiliated with the American Psychological Association but that our readers may encounter or use during the process of research, writing, and publication. The trademarks referenced in the *Publication Manual* are the property of their respective owners. The inclusion of non-APA products is for reference only and should not be construed as an endorsement of or affiliation between APA and the owners of these products and their respective brands.

Finally, some eagle-eyed users have asked why every aspect of APA Style is not applied throughout this manual. The manual is a published work, whereas the guidelines for APA Style are meant to be applied to manuscripts being submitted for publication or to student papers. Considerations for published works such as this book (e.g., typesetting, line spacing, length, fonts, use of color, margins) differ from those of draft manuscripts or student papers and thus necessitate deviations from APA Style formatting. Also, in this manual—in which we are writing about writing—it is often necessary to distinguish between explanatory text and examples through the use of font, color, and other design elements. Wherever possible, however, we have endeavored to demonstrate APA Style while writing about it and to present the information in a way that is accessible for our many users around the world.

1

SCHOLARLY WRITING AND
PUBLISHING PRINCIPLES

Contents

1

SCHOLARLY WRITING AND PUBLISHING PRINCIPLES

Research is complete only when scholars share their results or findings with the scientific community. Although researchers may post articles on scholarly collaboration sites or preprint servers or share them informally by email or in person, the most widely accepted medium for formal scholarly communication continues to be the published article in a peer-reviewed, scientific journal. Scientific journals contain our primary research literature and thus serve as repositories of the accumulated knowledge of a field.

Students are also important members of the scholarly community. Although most student work is not formally published, by writing papers students engage in critical thinking, thoughtful self-reflection, and scientific inquiry and thereby prepare to make unique contributions to the repository of knowledge. Therefore, student writing deserves the same level of care and attention to detail as that given to professional writing.

In this chapter, we provide important principles that professional and student authors should consider before writing their paper or, in many cases, before embarking on a research study. We begin with overviews of the different types of articles and papers professional and student authors write. This is followed by a discussion of ethical, legal, and professional standards in publishing that all authors of scholarly work, regardless of the type of paper they are writing or their level of experience, must be mindful of and abide by. For example, research conducted with human participants or nonhuman animal subjects must be approved by an institutional review board (IRB), institutional animal care and use committee (IACUC), or another ethical committee. Similarly, an author writing about human participants must protect their confidentiality while following best practices for data sharing. Moreover, any written work, from a course paper to a published manuscript, should represent an original contribution and include appropriate citations to the work of others. Thus, scholarly writing and publishing, in all forms, are inherently embedded in and guided by an ethical context.

Types of Articles and Papers

Many types of articles are published in scientific journals, including quantitative, qualitative, and mixed methods empirical articles and replications. These journal articles report *primary*, or original, research—that is, research that has not been previously formally published. Theoretical articles and methodological articles do not present research but describe advancements in theories or methods. Journal articles that review or synthesize findings from primary research include literature reviews and quantitative and qualitative meta-analyses. By understanding the characteristics of different types of articles and the types of information they most efficiently convey, you will be able to select an article type that fits your research and to follow the appropriate journal article reporting standards (discussed in Chapter 3). Students may write the same kinds of articles that are published in journals, as well as student papers (including course assignments, dissertations, and theses) not intended for publication in a journal (see Section 1.10). Sample papers are included at the end of Chapter 2 and on the APA Style website (https://apastyle.apa.org).

1.1 Quantitative Articles

In *quantitative articles*, authors report original, empirical, quantitative research. *Quantitative research* refers to a set of approaches commonly used in the behavioral and social sciences and related fields in which the observed outcomes are numerically represented. The results of these studies are typically analyzed using methods (statistics, data analyses, and modeling techniques) that rely on the numerical properties of the measurement system. Quantitative research studies use a variety of experimental designs and a range of analytic techniques. Some quantitative articles present novel hypotheses and data analyses not considered or addressed in previous reports of related data. Within the article, authors should describe elements of their study in the first person (see Section 4.16). Researchers who used a quantitative approach should follow the quantitative journal article reporting standards to report their findings (see Sections 3.5–3.12).

Quantitative articles typically include distinct sections that reflect the stages of the research process and appear in the following sequence:

- **Introduction:** a statement of the purpose of the investigation, a review of the background literature, and an explicit statement of the hypotheses being explored (see Section 3.4)

- **Method:** a full description of each step of the investigation, including details about the materials used and the procedures followed (which should be sufficient to enable replication), a full statement of the research design, statements on the protection of human participants or nonhuman animal subjects and informed consent, and a description (in words and/or a figure) of the flow of participants through the study (see Section 3.6)

- **Results:** data analysis and a report of the findings (see Section 3.7)

- **Discussion:** a summary of the study, including any interpretation, limitations, and implications of the results (see Section 3.8)

Reports of Multiple Studies. Authors of quantitative articles often report the findings of several conceptually linked studies in one manuscript. These authors should make the rationale, logic, order, and method of each study clear to readers. Headings should be used to label each study—for instance, "Experiment 1," "Experiment 2," and so forth. This format organizes the sections and makes them easier to discuss in the manuscript or in later research articles. Method and Results subsections can appear under each study heading. If appropriate, the authors can include a short subsection titled "Discussion" in which they explore the implications of the results of each study, or they can combine the discussion with the description of results under a heading such as "Results and Discussion." Authors should always include a comprehensive general discussion of all the studies at the end of the article, which often has the heading "General Discussion."

1.2 Qualitative Articles

In *qualitative articles*, authors report original, empirical, qualitative research. *Qualitative research* refers to scientific practices that are used to generate knowledge about human experience and/or action, including social processes. Qualitative approaches tend to share four sets of characteristics:

- Researchers analyze data consisting of natural language (i.e., words), researcher observations (e.g., social interactions), and/or participants' expressions (e.g., artistic presentations) rather than collecting numerical data and conducting mathematical analyses. Reports tend to show the development of qualitative findings using natural language (although numbers may be used adjunctively in describing or exploring these findings).

- Researchers often use an iterative process of analysis in which they reexamine developing findings in light of continued data analysis and refine the initial findings. In this way, the process of analysis is self-correcting and can produce original knowledge.

- Researchers recursively combine inquiry with methods that require researchers' reflexivity about how their own perspectives might support or impair the research process and thus how their methods should best be enacted.

- Researchers tend to study experiences and actions whose meaning may shift and evolve; therefore, they tend to view their findings as being situated within place and time rather than seeking to develop laws that are expected to remain stable regardless of context.

Researchers who used a qualitative approach should follow the qualitative journal article reporting standards to report their findings (see Sections 3.13–3.17).

Case Studies and Other Types of Qualitative Articles. A variety of methods are reported in qualitative articles, and the structure of qualitative articles varies depending on the nature of the study. For example, in *case studies* researchers report analyses or observations obtained while working closely with an individual, group, community, or organization. Case studies illustrate a problem in depth; indicate a means for solving a problem; and/or shed light on needed research, clinical applications, or theoretical matters. Qualitative articles also describe studies with multiple participants, groups, communities, or organizations that identify commonalities and/or differences across these entities. Such research can have a systemic focus, examining the ways in which social processes, actions, or discourses are structured.

Regardless of the qualitative research approaches they use, when writing reports, authors should carefully consider the balance between providing important illustrative material and using confidential participant data responsibly (see Sections 1.18–1.19 for more on confidentiality; see also Section 1.15). Qualitative reports may be organized thematically or chronologically and are typically presented in a reflexive, first-person style, detailing the ways in which the researchers arrived at questions, methods, findings, and considerations for the field.

1.3 Mixed Methods Articles

In *mixed methods articles*, authors report research combining qualitative and quantitative empirical approaches. Mixed methods research should not be confused with *mixed models research*, which is a quantitative procedure, or with *multimethods research*, which entails using multiple methods from the same approach. Mixed methods research involves the following:

- describing the philosophical assumptions or theoretical models used to inform the study design (Creswell, 2015);
- describing the distinct methodologies, research designs, and procedures in relation to the study goals;
- collecting and analyzing both qualitative and quantitative data in response to research aims, questions, or hypotheses; and
- integrating the findings from the two methodologies intentionally to generate new insights.

The basic assumption of a mixed methods approach is that the combined qualitative findings and quantitative results lead to additional insights not gleaned from the qualitative or quantitative findings alone (Creswell, 2015; Greene, 2007; Tashakkori & Teddlie, 2010). Because there are many ways to design a mixed methods study, the structure of mixed methods articles varies depending on the specific nature of the study and the balance between the two methodologies. Researchers who used a mixed methods approach should follow the mixed methods journal article reporting standards to report their findings (see Section 3.18).

1.4 Replication Articles

In *replication articles*, authors report the results of work intended to verify or reproduce findings from previous investigations. The aim of a *replication study* is to examine whether the conclusions from an earlier study remain the same or similar over variations in the conduct of the original study. There are internal and external forms of replication; only external replications are addressed in APA journal article reporting standards (see Section 3.10). An *external replication* occurs when researchers obtain a new sample and duplicate, insofar as is possible or desirable, the features of the original study being replicated. New design, measures, and/or data-analysis methods can also be used to test whether a finding has generality beyond the particular situation studied in the original work, but any such variations must be clearly specified in the report.

Researchers conducting an external replication should report sufficient information to allow readers to determine whether the study was a direct (exact, literal) replication, approximate replication, or conceptual (construct) replication. In a *direct replication*, researchers repeat a study collecting data from a new sample in a way that duplicates as far as possible the conditions of the earlier study.

A direct replication is called an *exact replication* or a *literal replication* when researchers use procedures that are identical to the original experiment or duplicated as closely as possible (e.g., with variations only in the location of the study and the investigators conducting the study). These forms of replication are useful for establishing that the findings of the original study are reliable. In an *approximate replication* (or a *modified replication*), researchers incorporate alternative procedures and additional conditions into the features of the original study; such replications usually contain the original study design along with some additional study features. The purpose of an approximate or modified replication may be not only to replicate a study but also to determine whether some factors not included in the original formulation have an influence on the outcome. In a *conceptual replication*, researchers introduce different techniques and manipulations to gain theoretical information; it is possible that no features of the initial study are retained. Researchers may use other labels for or descriptions of replications (for further exploration of this issue, see National Academies of Sciences, Engineering, and Medicine, 2019); the descriptions provided in this section were adapted from the *APA Dictionary of Psychology* (https://dictionary.apa.org).

1.5 Quantitative and Qualitative Meta-Analyses

Meta-analysis refers to a collection of techniques in which researchers use the findings from a group of related studies to draw a general conclusion (synthesis) based on the extant research on a topic. Individual participant or subject data are not used in meta-analyses because the data analyzed are at the study level.

Just as the reporting standards for quantitative and qualitative studies vary by study design, those for meta-analyses vary by the particular questions asked in the study and the approaches used to answer those questions. Because the study is the input unit for a meta-analysis, the studies included are provided in the reference list and marked with an indicator that shows they were part of the meta-analysis. This indicator distinguishes studies included in a meta-analysis from other references. For example, in APA Style articles, references used in a meta-analysis are preceded by an asterisk (see Section 9.52).

Quantitative Meta-Analysis. Within quantitative approaches, meta-analyses generally stipulate a technique in which effect-size estimates from individual studies are the inputs to the analyses. Meta-analysis is also used to determine factors that may be related to the magnitude of the outcome in quantitative studies—for example, design factors (e.g., randomized vs. nonrandomized), demographic factors (e.g., percentage of the study sample below the poverty line), and so forth. Meta-analytic reports usually follow the same basic structure as quantitative studies (see Section 1.1) and contain an introduction and Method, Results, and Discussion sections. Researchers who use a quantitative meta-analytic approach should follow the reporting standards for quantitative meta-analysis (see Section 3.12).

Qualitative Meta-Analysis. Within qualitative research, there are a variety of approaches to meta-analysis, including qualitative metasynthesis, metaethnography, metamethod, and critical interpretive synthesis. These approaches often use strategies from primary qualitative analyses to synthesize findings across studies. Qualitative meta-analyses can be used to highlight methodological trends, identify common findings and gaps, develop new understandings, and propose future directions for an area of research. Qualitative meta-analytic reports have a structure similar to that of qualitative primary reports, with the addition of a description of the perspectives and situatedness of the authors of the primary works included in the analysis. Qualitative meta-analyses do not entail a singular procedure but rather an aggregating function common to meta-analytic approaches. Qualitative meta-analyses are not to be confused with *quantitative reviews*, in which authors generate a narrative description of a quantitative literature base. We recommend referring to those studies as *literature reviews* or *narrative literature reviews* to avoid confusion with qualitative meta-analyses (see Section 1.6). Researchers who used a qualitative meta-analytic approach should follow the reporting standards for qualitative meta-analysis (see Section 3.17).

1.6 Literature Review Articles

Literature review articles (or *narrative literature review articles*) provide narrative summaries and evaluations of the findings or theories within a literature base. The literature base may include qualitative, quantitative, and/or mixed methods research. Literature reviews capture trends in the literature; they do not engage in a systematic quantitative or qualitative meta-analysis of the findings from the initial studies.

In literature review articles, authors should

- define and clarify the problem;
- summarize previous investigations to inform readers of the state of the research;
- identify relations, contradictions, gaps, and inconsistencies in the literature; and
- suggest next steps in solving the problem.

The components of literature review articles can be arranged in various ways— for example, by grouping research on the basis of similarity in the concepts or theories of interest, methodological similarities among the studies reviewed, or the historical development of the field.

1.7 Theoretical Articles

Theoretical articles draw from existing research literature to advance theory. Theoretical articles present empirical information only when it advances the theoretical issue being explicated. Authors of theoretical articles trace the development of a theory to expand and refine its constructs, present a new theory, or analyze an existing theory. Typically, they point out flaws or demonstrate the advantage(s) of one theory over another. Authors also may examine a theory's internal consistency and external validity. The order of sections in a theoretical article can vary.

1.8 Methodological Articles

Methodological articles present new approaches to research or practice, modifications of existing methods, or discussions of quantitative and/or qualitative data analysis. These articles use empirical data (quantitative, qualitative, or both) only as a means to illustrate an approach to research. Some use simulated data to demonstrate how methods work under varying conditions (e.g., different sample sizes, number of variables, level of nonnormality, size of coefficients).

Methodological articles provide sufficient detail for researchers to assess the applicability of the methodology and its feasibility for the type of research problem it is designed to study. Further, these articles allow readers to compare proposed methods with those in current use. In methodological articles, highly technical materials (e.g., derivations, proofs, data generation, computer code, extensive details of simulations) should be presented in appendices or as supplemental materials to improve overall article readability. When having detailed information (e.g., parameters used in a simulation) is necessary for readers to understand the major points being made, those details should be presented in the text of the article.

1.9 Other Types of Articles

Additional types of published articles include brief reports, comments on and replies to previously published articles, book reviews, obituaries, and letters to the editor. Authors should consult the editors or author guidelines of individual journals for specific information regarding these kinds of articles.

1.10 Student Papers, Dissertations, and Theses

Although the *Publication Manual* originated as a guide for authors seeking publication in scholarly journals, it has been widely adopted by academic instructors, departments, and institutions that require students to use APA Style when writing scholarly papers. Students may write the same types of papers that are professionally published (e.g., literature review articles) or assignments that fall outside that scope (e.g., dissertations, theses, essays, response or reaction papers, annotated bibliographies). Likewise, this manual has historically addressed researchers working in the field of psychology; however, students and researchers use APA Style in other fields and disciplines, including social work, nursing, communications, education, and business. Some journals in these fields require APA Style, and others do not. Other field-specific requirements may also apply (e.g., nurses may have to adhere to a nurse's code of ethics rather than a psychologist's code of ethics).

Student assignments commonly written at the undergraduate level include annotated bibliographies, many types of essays, and response or reaction papers. The descriptions that follow are generally representative of these types of papers; check with your assigning instructor or institution for specific guidelines.

- **Annotated bibliographies** consist of reference list entries followed by short descriptions of the work called *annotations*. Instructors generally set most requirements for these papers, but many APA Style guidelines still apply (see Section 9.51).

- **Cause-and-effect essays** report how specific events lead to particular results or advocate for a specific position. A clear and strong thesis provides a solid foundation for this type of essay. The paragraphs are generally structured by describing each cause and its collateral effect, with logical transitions between them.

- **Comparative essays** compare and contrast two (or more) items with the goal of linking disparate items under a central thesis. The paper structure can be organized to focus on Topic 1 and then Topic 2, or the topics may be interwoven.

- **Expository essays** follow a multiparagraph structure (e.g., five paragraphs) and explain or provide information on a specific topic. The paper structure includes an introduction, body, and a conclusion. Evidence should be provided to reinforce the written claims detailed in the paper.

- **Narrative essays** convey a story from a clear point of view and include a beginning, middle, and end. Narrative essays should have a clearly defined purpose and focus and include concise, evocative language.

- **Persuasive essays** are intended to convince readers to adopt a certain viewpoint or take a particular action. They present clear arguments, include logical transitions, and have a similar paper structure to the expository essay.

- **Précis** are concise summaries in students' own words of essential points, statements, or facts from a single work; the length of a précis is typically about a quarter of the length of the original work. The précis structure includes a brief thesis and sections that mirror the sections of the original work, such as Method, Results, and Discussion.

- **Response or reaction papers** summarize one or more works and describe students' personal reactions or responses to them, including how the work or works impacted them, are relevant to their life, and so forth. This type of paper is typically short (e.g., three pages or so). The first person is used in describing personal reactions (see Section 4.16).

Dissertations or theses are typically required of graduate students, but undergraduate students completing advanced research projects may write similar types of papers. Academic institutions or departments have detailed guidelines for how to format and write dissertations and theses, and the requirements and acceptable format vary by discipline. Some dissertations and theses are hundreds of pages long and contain thorough literature reviews and exhaustive reference lists, whereas others follow a multiple-article format consisting of several shorter, related papers that are intended for individual publication. See Section 12.1 for guidance on adapting a dissertation or thesis into a journal article.

   As mentioned in the introduction to this manual, most of the guidelines in the *Publication Manual* can be applied to student papers. However, because the scope of what constitutes a student paper is broad and flexible, and because students submit papers to their academic institutions rather than to an APA journal, we do not designate formal requirements for the nature or contents of an APA Style student paper. Thus, questions about paper length, required sections, and so forth are best answered by the instructor or institution setting the assignment. Students should follow the guidelines and requirements developed by their instructors, departments, and/or academic institutions when writing papers, including dissertations and theses; these guidelines and requirements may entail adaptations of or additions to the APA Style guidelines described in this manual. We encourage writers, instructors, departments, and academic institutions using APA Style outside of the journal publication context to adapt APA Style to fit their needs.

Ethical, Legal, and Professional Standards in Publishing

In addition to abiding by standards specific to writing and publishing, authors of scholarly research should also follow ethical standards (e.g., Section 8, Research and Publication, of the APA *Ethical Principles of Psychologists and Code of Conduct*, hereinafter referred to as the APA Ethics Code; APA, 2017a; see also https://www.apa.org/ethics/code) and broader professional standards when conducting a research study. Moreover, individuals engaged in conducting, analyzing, or reporting any type of research should have acquired the requisite skills and experience to do so competently (e.g., Section 2, Competence, of the APA Ethics Code; see also the *Multicultural Guidelines: An Ecological Approach to Context, Identity, and Intersectionality*; APA, 2017b).

Ethical and legal principles underlie all scholarly research and writing. These long-standing principles are designed to achieve the following goals:

- ensuring the accuracy of scientific findings,
- protecting the rights and welfare of research participants and subjects, and
- protecting intellectual property rights.

Writers in the social and behavioral sciences work to uphold these goals and to follow the principles that have been established by their professional disciplines. The guidance in this section is drawn from the APA Ethics Code (APA, 2017a), which applies to all APA members regardless of where they publish and contains standards that address the reporting and publishing of scientific data. The APA Ethics Code is not a static document—it is revised over time to reflect shifts or changes in the understanding and conception of the principles of beneficence and nonmaleficence, fidelity and responsibility, integrity, justice, and respect by the scientific community relative to advances in science and technology and evolving cultural norms. Revised or new versions of the APA Ethics Code appear on the APA website after adoption by the APA Council of Representatives.

Ensuring the Accuracy of Scientific Findings

1.11 Planning for Ethical Compliance

Regardless of the type of article, attention to ethical concerns should begin long before any manuscript is submitted for publication. Among the issues to carefully consider while research is in the planning stages are those related to institutional approval, informed consent, deception in research, participant protections, and data sharing. Most journals, including APA journals, require authors submitting a manuscript for publication to also submit forms affirming their compliance with ethical standards for research and publication and disclosing their conflicts of interest, if any (see Section 12.13 for more information and a link to the APA ethical compliance form). We encourage all authors, whether or not they will submit their manuscript to an APA journal, to consult these ethics resources before beginning their research project and at regular intervals throughout the research process. To ensure that they meet ethical standards, before starting a research project, authors should contact the appropriate IRB or ethical review group for their institution or country for information on the kinds of research that require ethics approval, procedures for obtaining ethics approval, ethical and research requirements, and so forth. Authors not affiliated with a university, hospital, or other institution with an IRB are still expected to follow ethical standards in conducting their research and should consult an external IRB if necessary. For more information on IRBs, see the APA website (https://on.apa.org/2FuiPJ1).

Authors are encouraged to report in the text of the manuscript the institutional approvals the study received, as described in the APA journal article reporting standards in Chapter 3 (see Sections 3.6 and 3.14 and Tables 3.1–3.3). Authors should also be prepared to answer potential questions related to these issues from editors or reviewers during the review process (see Section 12.13). As a final step prior to manuscript submission, authors should also consult the ethical compliance checklist in Section 1.25.

1.12 Ethical and Accurate Reporting of Research Results

The essence of ethics in all scientific reporting is that authors report the methods and results of their studies fully and accurately. Therefore, the ethical and professional issues discussed in this section apply equally to quantitative, qualitative, and mixed methods research (see Chapter 3 for additional reporting standards).

Authors must not fabricate or falsify data (APA Ethics Code Standard 8.10a, Reporting Research Results). Modifying results, including visual images, to support a theory or hypothesis and omitting troublesome observations from a report to present a more convincing story are also prohibited (APA Ethics Code Standard 5.01b, Avoidance of False or Deceptive Statements). Similarly, representing data-generated hypotheses (post hoc) as if they were preplanned is a violation of basic ethical principles.

The practice of "omitting troublesome observations" includes

- selectively failing to report studies (e.g., in the introduction or Discussion section) that, although methodologically sound and relevant to the hypothesis, theory, or research question at hand, had results that do not support the preferred narrative (i.e., that contrast with results obtained in the current study);
- selectively omitting reports of relevant manipulations, procedures, measures, or findings within a study, for similar reasons; and
- selectively excluding participants or other individual data observations, without a valid methodological reason, in order to achieve desired results.

To clarify expectations for reporting and help safeguard scientific integrity, APA (like other scientific organizations) has issued a series of reporting standards (Appelbaum et al., 2018; Cooper, 2018; Levitt, 2019; Levitt et al., 2018). These standards, which are discussed in Chapter 3, address many aspects of the ethical reporting of experiments. They include expectations for describing all measured variables, for tracking participant flow through a study (with an accompanying prototype figure; see Figure 7.5 in Section 7.36) so that no participant is selectively excluded without mention, and for reporting special classes of studies such as clinical trials.

Reporting standards, like the APA Ethics Code, are not static; changes are continually made to improve how researchers report results. One of the more recent and important changes for quantitative research reporting is that hypotheses should now be stated in three groupings: preplanned–primary, preplanned–secondary, and exploratory (post hoc). Exploratory hypotheses are allowable, and there should be no pressure to disguise them as if they were preplanned. Similarly, qualitative researchers should transparently describe their expectations at the outset of the research as part of their research reporting.

1.13 Errors, Corrections, and Retractions After Publication

Careful preparation of manuscripts for publication is essential, but errors can still appear in the final published article. When errors are substantive enough to affect readers' understanding of the research or their interpretation of the results, authors are responsible for making such errors public.

Corrections. When a correction is needed, the first step is to inform the editor and the publisher of the journal so that a formal correction notice (erratum) can be published. The goal of such a notice is to openly and transparently correct the knowledge base for current and future users of the information in the published article. A correction notice is usually appended to the original article's record in research databases so that readers will retrieve it when they access either the article or a database's record for the article; at times, the article itself may also be corrected. See also APA Ethics Code Standard 8.10b, Reporting Research Results, as well as Section 12.22 of this manual for further information on when and how to write a correction notice.

Retractions. Occasionally, the problems with an article are so great (e.g., plagiarism, fabrication or falsification of data, belatedly discovered calculation or measurement errors that change the interpretation of the findings) that the entire article is retracted by the author or authors, their institution, or the publisher. Whatever the reason for the retraction, the intent is to remove the information from the scientific literature and thus avoid wasting the time and resources of other scientists who might rely on or attempt to replicate the compromised results. The retracted article may still be available in databases; however, a retraction notice will accompany it to notify readers of its status. Authors should avoid citing retracted articles unless the citation is essential; if authors do cite a retracted article, its reference list entry should reflect that the article has been retracted (see the APA Style website at https://apastyle.apa.org for an example).

1.14 Data Retention and Sharing

Data Retention. Authors are expected to retain the data associated with a published article in accordance with institutional requirements; funder requirements; participant agreements; and, when publishing in an APA journal, the APA Ethics Code (Standard 8.14, Sharing Research Data for Verification). When planning a research study and before beginning data collection, authors are encouraged to consider how the data will be retained (and shared) and to outline clear data-handling procedures in the study protocol submitted to an IRB or other ethics committee. During the informed consent process, authors should describe to study participants the data they intend to collect, save, and/ or share with other researchers and obtain their approval. In qualitative studies, data sharing may not be appropriate because of confidentiality, consent, and other limitations (see Section 1.15).

Data Sharing. The APA Ethics Code prohibits authors from withholding data from qualified requesters for verification through reanalysis in most circumstances (see Standard 8.14, Sharing Research Data for Verification), as long as the confidentiality of the participants is protected. The APA Ethics Code permits psychologists to require that a requester be responsible for any costs associated with the provision of the data. Increasingly, funders are also requiring that data be shared in an open- or secured-access repository or that a data-management plan otherwise be spelled out. Authors publishing in an APA journal are invited to share their data on APA's portal on the Open Science Framework (https://osf.io/view/apa/).

Notably, incentives are offered to researchers who wish to share their data, such as Open Science Badges offered through the Center for Open Science. Open Science Badges are awarded for the open sharing of *materials* used by researchers in the process of data collection and analysis (e.g., instructions, stimuli, blank questionnaires, treatment manuals, software, interview protocols, details of procedures, code for mathematical models); *source data*, meaning the original written, electronic, or audiovisual records of the study participants' responses (e.g., paper questionnaires, transcripts, output files, observational notes, video recordings); and *analysis data*, meaning the processed version of the source data used to produce the analyses reported in the paper.

Sharing During Review. Subject to the conditions and exceptions discussed next, authors are expected to share data, analyses, and/or materials during the review and publication process if questions arise with respect to the accuracy of the report. On request, the authors should share the raw data with the journal's editor and (if approved by the editor) with reviewers to verify the reported analyses and data and to assess their rigor. If questions arise about the integrity or processing of the source data, authors should also share access to them with the editor on request. Costs of sharing data requested during the review process should be borne by the authors. Similarly, students should expect to provide raw data to faculty reviewing their dissertation, thesis, or research project. A journal editor has the right to deny publication if the authors refuse to share requested materials or data during the review process. In the case of student work, refusal to share requested materials or data may result in a failing grade or defense. See Section 1.15 for additional considerations when sharing access to data from qualitative studies.

Sharing After Publication. Authors must make their data available after publication, subject to conditions and exceptions, within the period of retention specified by their institution, journal, funder, or other supporting organization. This permits other competent professionals to confirm the reported analyses using the data on which the authors' conclusions are based or to test alternative analyses that address the article's hypotheses (see APA Ethics Code Standard 8.14a, Sharing Research Data for Verification, and Standard 6.01, Documentation of Professional and Scientific Work and Maintenance of Records). *Competent professionals* are those who are currently accountable to a research institution or an educational employer and who demonstrate sufficient training and credentials to understand the research study's background, methods, and analyses. The journal editor may be asked to determine who qualifies as a competent professional given the topic of the research. See Section 1.15 for additional considerations when sharing qualitative research data.

Typically, any additional costs of complying with a request for data beyond the general standards of internal data maintenance (e.g., anonymization, transfer of data, translation) should be borne by the requester, and these costs should be assessed at a reasonable local rate for the necessary services and materials. If it emerges that authors are unwilling or unable to share data for verification within the retention period, the journal's current editor may retract the article or issue an Expression of Concern about its findings according to the policy of the publisher.

Data and materials may sometimes be requested after publication for purposes beyond the ones outlined previously. Regardless of why the data and materials are requested, to avoid misunderstanding, it is important that the researcher requesting data and the researcher providing it come to a written agreement about the conditions under which the data are to be shared (see APA Ethics Code Standard 8.14b, Sharing Research Data for Verification). Generally, such an agreement specifies the limits on how the shared data may be used (e.g., for verification of already published results, for inclusion in meta-analytic studies, for secondary analysis), who may have access to the data (e.g., only the requester, the requester and direct supervisees, anyone interested with no limits on further sharing), and how the requester will store and dispose of the data. Furthermore, the agreement should specify any limits on the dissemination of the results of analyses performed on the data (e.g., whether they can be published in conference presentations, internal reports, journal articles, or book chapters) and any expectations for authorship of publications based on shared data. Data-sharing arrangements must be entered into with proper consideration of the rights of the copyright owner (see Section 12.20), participants' consent, requirements of funding agencies, requirements of IRBs and other ethics committees that provided permission to conduct the study, and rules promulgated by the employer of the holder of the data.

Authors may choose or be required to share data and/or materials openly by posting them online. Journal editors may set a policy to encourage open sharing, to require it, and/or to require authors to give a reason why data and materials cannot be shared (e.g., risk to participant privacy). A permanent link to any data or materials to be shared openly should be included in the article, such as in an Open Practices section in the author note (see Section 2.7); the reference for the data set should also be included in the reference list of the article (see Section 10.9 for how to cite). Federally funded or grant-funded research is often subject to requirements for data sharing; see, for example, the data-sharing policies of the National Institutes of Health (n.d.).

Conditions and Exceptions to Data Sharing. Before sharing or posting data and materials for any purpose, researchers must remove any personally identifiable information or code that would make it possible to reestablish a link to an individual participant's identity. Sometimes, a unique combination of demographic or other public information can be used to establish a participant's identity, and this possibility must be kept in mind and avoided as well. Researchers should consult the relevant policies of their institution or country (e.g., the European Union General Data Protection Regulation [GDPR], the Health Insurance Portability and Accountability Act [HIPAA]) for regulations and guidance on conditions for sharing data and deidentifying protected health information.

In addition to protecting the confidentiality of research participants, some proprietary arrangements may prohibit the sharing of data and materials (e.g., data provided in confidence by a business entity, a coding scheme developed commercially by the authors). Editors are responsible for setting policy for their journal about the acceptability for publication of research resting on proprietary arrangements, given that its accuracy and veracity cannot be checked in the usual way. This policy may depend on the availability of alternative ways to satisfy concerns about scientific integrity. For example, research using a proprietary personality scale may be acceptable if enough qualified researchers subscribe to it that someone can be found to help with independent verification.

1.15 Additional Data-Sharing Considerations for Qualitative Research

The sharing of qualitative data with editors, peers, and other researchers has distinct considerations in addition to those described in Section 1.14. The APA Committee on Human Research and numerous qualitative researchers have expressed concerns about sharing qualitative research data (Data Sharing Working Group, 2015; DuBois et al., 2018; Guishard, 2018). Although consensus on how to navigate this issue has not yet been established, this section highlights several points that contraindicate or suggest alternates to data sharing.

Presentation of Raw Data in Research Reports. Data are typically reproduced in qualitative research reports. Segments of data (e.g., quotations from interviews) are presented to exemplify the process of analysis and to demonstrate the grounding of the findings in the data. Because these raw data are available for examination in the text of the article, they provide a basis by which readers, as well as editors and reviewers during the manuscript review process, can evaluate (and perhaps question) the appropriateness of the conclusions reached.

Confidentiality Limitations. The obligation to protect participants' confidentiality can present special ethical issues for qualitative data sharing. For instance, raw data from a qualitative study involving multiple detailed stories about participants' lives may contain details that are necessary to make the data meaningful but that can be revealing in compromising ways when triangulated. Qualitative research may also involve intensive case studies of people who were selected because of their unique attributes. Although the researchers may try to mask participants' identities within a manuscript, it may not be possible to retain all that is meaningful to evaluate an analysis and at the same time protect participants' confidentiality if the complete data set is shared. The high burden on the researchers to remove all information that can lead to the identification of a participant is unjustifiable if it produces a set of data that is stripped of meaning. As a result, the researchers may instead need to withhold data to ensure participant confidentiality (see McCurdy & Ross, 2018, on the sometimes prohibitive complications of this process).

Consent Limitations. There is also the consideration that participants may give consent to participate in a study to a specific group of researchers and may not extend that consent to other researchers. This may be of particular concern with vulnerable populations. For instance, lesbian participants may consent to have their data analyzed by researchers who are in their community and who seek to support their rights, but that consent may not apply to other researchers with different motivations. Likewise, some researchers spend years developing the trust to collect and analyze data from a community, and community members may not extend that trust to other groups of researchers. Indeed, communities may be owners or co-owners of the data themselves and may refuse to share the data (DuBois et al., 2018; Tuck & Yang, 2014). As a result, the relationship between the researchers and the participants is an important ethical consideration and one that may contraindicate data sharing.

Researchers' Perspective Limitations. Many qualitative researchers view their own history and epistemological perspectives as legitimate influences on the process of inquiry. Thus, when sharing data from qualitative research, the researchers' perspectives and experiences must be taken into account. Research can be compromised if researchers are unreflective or not purposeful or explicit about this influence. However, when researchers are aware, they can deliberately elaborate on the investigative attitudes (e.g., phenomenological bracketing), personal experiences (e.g., ethnographic study), research teams (e.g., including researchers from the communities under analysis), or analytic lenses (e.g., critical theories) that enrich their research and thereby deepen the acuity they bring to the analytic task (Guishard et al., 2018). These qualitative researchers would not necessarily expect editors or external researchers to interpret their research in the same way when evaluating their analysis because they may not share their perspectives.

In qualitative inquiry, the researchers are the analytic tool, so those who have developed an intimate understanding of a data set or who have developed a perspective to enhance their sensitivity to the data typically are better attuned to nuances, implicit meanings, and systemic connections. This means that an editor or external researcher should not expect replication of the findings and should articulate an appropriate purpose and rationale for review of the shared data prior to the data being shared. Also, the approach to investigation selected may signify epistemological commitments of researchers and their participants, and these values need to be considered and honored in data-sharing efforts. In any case, a review of the data would need to be conducted with a keen awareness of the distinct epistemological positions and analytic processes within qualitative research.

1.16 Duplicate and Piecemeal Publication of Data

Reports in the literature must accurately reflect the independence of separate research efforts. Both duplicate and piecemeal publication of data misrepresent the amount of original research in the repository of scientific knowledge. *Duplicate publication* is the publication of the same data or ideas in two separate works. *Piecemeal publication* is the unnecessary splitting of the findings from one research effort into multiple works.

Duplicate Publication. Misrepresentation of data as original when they have been published previously is specifically prohibited by the APA Ethics Code (Standard 8.13, Duplicate Publication of Data). Duplicate publication distorts the knowledge base by making it appear that more information is available than actually exists. It also wastes scarce resources (journal pages and the time and efforts of editors and reviewers). The prohibition against duplicate publication is especially critical for the cumulative knowledge of the field. Duplicate publication can give the erroneous impression that findings are more replicable than is the case or that particular conclusions are more strongly supported than is warranted by the cumulative evidence. Duplicate publication can also lead to copyright violations; authors cannot assign the copyright for the same material to more than one publisher. When submitting a manuscript for publication, authors are obligated to disclose whether they have posted the manuscript online, either in full or in substantial part; some editors may consider such posting to be prior publication.

Examples of and Exceptions to Duplicate Publication. Authors should not submit manuscripts that have been published in whole or in substantial part elsewhere, including manuscripts with substantially similar form or content to their previously published works. This policy also applies to translations; authors are not permitted to publish research in one language and then translate the article into another language and publish it again. Authors in doubt about what constitutes prior publication should consult the editor of the journal to which they are submitting their manuscript.

The policy regarding duplicate publication also means that the same or overlapping material that has appeared in a publication offered for public sale, such as conference proceedings or a book chapter, should not be republished elsewhere because these sources are considered widely available. For example, a brief report is published in an APA journal with the understanding that an extended report will not be published elsewhere because APA brief reports include sufficient descriptions of methodology to allow for replication; the brief report is the archival record for the work.

The policy regarding duplicate publication has some exclusions. Manuscripts previously published in abstracted form (e.g., in conference proceedings) or in a periodical with limited circulation or availability (e.g., report by a university department or government agency, dissertation) can be published again in a venue of wide circulation (e.g., in a journal). Consult a journal editor to determine whether a study reported in a dissertation or thesis or posted in a preprint repository could benefit from peer review and publication as a journal article.

Similarly, it is not considered duplicate publication to reanalyze already published data in light of new theories or methodologies, if the reanalysis is clearly labeled as such and provides new insights into the phenomena being studied. The policy also does not apply to follow-up studies; for example, researchers may first report the initial findings from a clinical trial and subsequently report results of a follow-up assessment 2 years after the trial's completion.

Acknowledging and Citing Previous Work. Authors sometimes want to publish what is essentially the same material in more than one venue to reach different audiences. Such duplicate publication can rarely be justified, given the ready accessibility of published works online. If authors think it is justified, the article must include a reference to the original report—both to inform editors, reviewers, and readers and to fulfill the authors' obligations to the copyright holder of the previous work.

If it is deemed scientifically necessary to re-present previously published material—for instance, to report new analyses or to frame new research that follows up on previous work from the authors' laboratory—the following conditions must be met:

1. The amount of duplicated material must be small relative to the total length of the text.

2. The authors must clearly acknowledge in the author note and in all relevant sections of the article (e.g., Method, Results) that the information was reported previously, and the previous work must be cited.

3. The authors must provide a copyright attribution for any reprinted or adapted tables and figures and may need to secure permission from the copyright holder as well (see Sections 12.14–12.18).

4. The original work must be clearly and accurately cited in the reference list (see also the discussion on self-plagiarism in Sections 1.17 and 8.3).

When the original work has multiple authors and the authorship of the new work is not identical, all authors of the original work must provide appropriate copyright permission (see Section 12.20) and receive agreed-upon credit (e.g., in an author note; see Section 2.7) for their contributions in the later publication.

Piecemeal Publication. Authors are obligated to present work as parsimoniously and completely as possible within the space constraints of journal articles. Data that can be meaningfully combined within a single article should be presented together to enhance effective communication.

Piecemeal, or fragmented, publication of research findings can be misleading if multiple reports appear to represent independent instances of data collection or analyses; distortion of the scientific literature, especially in reviews or meta-analyses, may result. Piecemeal publication of the results from a single study is therefore undesirable unless there is a clear reason for doing so. It may be quite difficult to determine whether a valid reason exists; therefore, authors who submit manuscripts based on studies or data presented in other published or submitted works should inform the journal editor of the source and extent of the overlap, and they should detail how their submission builds on the previous reports. Whether the publication of two or more reports based on the same or on closely related research constitutes fragmented publication is a matter of editorial judgment.

Multiple Publications From Large-Scale, Longitudinal Projects and Qualitative and Mixed Methods Research. There are times when it is both necessary and appropriate to publish multiple reports. Multidisciplinary projects often address diverse topics and answer different questions; thus, publishing the results in a single article may be inappropriate. Similarly, researchers sometimes design studies with the purpose of addressing distinct theoretical questions using the same instruments; if written as separate research reports, each report should make a unique contribution and not overlap substantially with the others or with previously published material. Researchers should consider at the outset of data collection how the data will be presented (e.g., in one report vs. multiple reports); although new research questions or analyses may arise in the process of analyzing the data, researchers should not fish through the data for the sole purpose of extracting additional studies. Although all reports stem from the same overall project, the introduction, Results, and Discussion sections of each report would be unique, and at least some aspects of the Method section would be unique as well.

Longitudinal or large-scale studies are another instance when multiple publications are often appropriate because the data at different time points make independent scientific contributions. Further, useful knowledge should be made available to others as soon as possible, which is precluded if publication is delayed until all the studies are complete.

Multiple reports may be needed in some qualitative and mixed methods research when qualitative data collection and analysis produce volumes of findings that are not appropriate for publication in a single article—for instance, when investigators conduct interviews to explore questions that have distinct purposes and are meaningful in relation to separate literatures and concerns. With mixed methods studies, authors might publish multiple articles, such as a qualitative study, a quantitative study, and a mixed methods overview study, each focusing on new insights based on findings across the methods.

When authors create multiple reports from studies of this sort, they are obligated to cite prior reports on the project to help readers understand the work accurately. For example, in the early years of a longitudinal study, the authors might cite all previous publications from it. For a well-known or long-term longitudinal study, the authors might cite the original publication, a more recent summary, and earlier articles that focused on the same or related scientific questions addressed in the current report. It is useful to distinguish between data sets that are complete and data sets that are still in collection. It is not necessary to repeat the description of the design and methods of prior reports in their entirety; authors may refer readers to an earlier publication for this detailed information. It is important, however, to provide sufficient information so that readers can evaluate the current report. It is also important to clarify the degree of sample overlap in multiple reports from large studies. Again, authors should inform and consult with the journal editor before submitting a manuscript of this type.

Whether the publication of two or more reports based on the same or closely related research constitutes piecemeal publication is a matter of editorial judgment, as is the determination of whether the manuscript meets other publication criteria. Authors should note in the manuscript all prior works related to the study by including them in the reference list and citing them in the text (see the previous section on acknowledging and citing previous work). When submitting the manuscript, authors must inform the journal editor in a cover letter of any similar manuscripts that have already been published, accepted for publication, or submitted for concurrent consideration to the same journal or elsewhere. The editor can then make an informed judgment as to whether the submitted manuscript includes sufficient new information to warrant consideration. If the authors' identities are masked for review, references to previous work should be concealed as well until after the review process.

If, during the review or production process, a manuscript is discovered to be in violation of duplicate or piecemeal publication policies and the authors failed to inform the editor of the potential for violation, then the manuscript can be rejected without further consideration. If such a violation is discovered after publication in an APA journal, appropriate action, such as retraction by the publisher or notice of duplicate publication, can be taken.

Republication of an Article as a Book Chapter. Journal articles sometimes are revised for publication as book chapters. Authors have a responsibility to reveal to readers that portions of the new work were previously published and to cite and reference the source. If copyright is owned by a publisher or by another person, authors must obtain permission to reprint or adapt the work and include a copyright attribution in the chapter (see Sections 12.14–12.18).

1.17 Implications of Plagiarism and Self-Plagiarism

Plagiarism is the act of presenting the words, ideas, or images of another as one's own; it denies authors credit where credit is due. Whether deliberate or unintentional, plagiarism violates ethical standards in scholarship (see APA Ethics Code Standard 8.11, Plagiarism) and has profound real-world effects. Authors who try to publish plagiarized work face rejection from publication, as well as possible sanction by professional bodies, censure in their place of employment, and/or exclusion from applying for federal funding. Students who turn in a plagiarized assignment face a failing grade, as well as possible censure from a student or university honor board, suspension, or expulsion. *Self-plagiarism* is the act of presenting one's own previously published work as original; it misleads readers and falsely inflates the number of publications on a topic. Like plagiarism, self-plagiarism is unethical. To learn more about what constitutes plagiarism and self-plagiarism and how to avoid both, see Sections 8.2 and 8.3.

Protecting the Rights and Welfare of Research Participants and Subjects

1.18 Rights and Welfare of Research Participants and Subjects

The APA Ethics Code (Sections 3 and 8) specifies the standards psychologists are to follow when conducting research with human participants and nonhuman animal subjects. Both humans and nonhuman animals in research studies have the right to ethical and humane treatment. Research with human participants involves additional rights and welfare protections; for example, researchers are required to

- obtain informed consent, assent, or permission, as appropriate, using language that is reasonably understood by research participants;
- avoid or minimize participants' exposure to
  - physical, emotional, or psychological harm;
  - exploitative relationships;
  - undue influence based on the researchers' status, power, or authority;
  - excessive or inappropriate inducements to participate; and
  - unjustified or unduly delayed deception or debriefing procedures; and
- take adequate measures to prevent unauthorized access to or release of participant data to the public or other researchers not specified in the informed consent (e.g., by obtaining prior written agreement for sharing of research data).

Nonhuman animal subjects are to be cared for humanely and provided with healthful conditions during their stay in research facilities. The protocol for research with nonhuman animals must be reviewed by an appropriate animal care committee (e.g., an IACUC) before it is conducted to ensure that the procedures are appropriate and humane (APA, 2012a).

Researchers who are APA members, regardless of field, are required to certify that they have followed ethical standards as a precondition of publishing their articles in most journals, including APA journals (see Section 12.13). We encourage authors to include in the text of their manuscripts certifications that their research followed ethical and institutional guidelines, as described in the APA journal article reporting standards in Chapter 3. For instance, if research participants consented to having their identifying information disclosed (e.g., their name), the authors should indicate in the Method section of the article that consent was given. Failure to follow these standards can be grounds for rejecting a manuscript for publication or for retracting a published article.

1.19 Protecting Confidentiality

When authors describe their research, they are prohibited from disclosing "confidential, personally identifiable information concerning their clients/patients, students, research participants, organizational clients, or other recipients of their services" (APA Ethics Code Standard 4.07, Use of Confidential Information for Didactic or Other Purposes) unless participants give documented consent to disclose their identities. The exact requirements for documentation vary depending on the nature of the consent obtained and the type of study.

Confidentiality in case studies can, at times, be difficult to achieve. For example, the researcher might obtain written consent from the subject of the report to publish the study. The researcher must be careful not to exploit the subject—for example, when the researcher has supervisory, evaluative, or other authority over them, as in the case of a client, patient, supervisee, employee, or organizational client (see APA Ethics Code Standard 3.08, Exploitative Relationships, and Standard 3.05, Multiple Relationships).

In some types of qualitative research (e.g., participatory action research, autoethnography), the participants may be investigators and authors, meaning they will be personally identifiable. Participant-authors or participant-investigators should retain control over what information about them is presented in the report (see Section 1.15 for more on sharing data from qualitative research).

Strategies to Disguise Identifying Material. Researchers can protect confidentiality by disguising some aspects of the data so that neither the subject nor third parties (e.g., family members, employers) are identifiable. Four main strategies are used: (a) altering specific characteristics, (b) limiting the description of specific characteristics, (c) obfuscating case detail by adding extraneous material, and (d) using composite descriptions. Disguising identifying information must be done carefully because it is essential not to change variables in a way that would lead readers to draw false conclusions (Sweeney et al., 2015). For example, altering a person's gender in a case illustrating a promising therapy for sexual assault trauma might compromise its educative value if the person's gender played a significant role in the treatment. Subject details should be omitted only if they are not essential to the phenomenon being described. Confidentiality, however, should never be sacrificed for clinical or scientific accuracy. Reports that cannot adequately disguise identifiable subject information should not be submitted for publication. For examples of how to incorporate case material (e.g., quotations from research participants) into the text, see Section 8.36.

Data Deidentification. Extra steps may be needed to protect participants' confidentiality when working with data sets containing multiple forms of data or protected health information. The HIPAA website provides guidance on deidentifying data (see https://www.hhs.gov/hipaa/for-professionals/privacy/special-topics/de-identification/index.html). Researchers have also developed methods for deidentifying various kinds of data; see, for example, the work of the Data Privacy Lab (https://dataprivacylab.org/projects/index.html).

1.20 Conflict of Interest

In the APA Ethics Code (Standard 3.06, Conflict of Interest), *conflict of interest* is defined broadly as involving "personal, scientific, professional, legal, financial, or other interests or relationships" that could negatively affect professional conduct or cause harm to persons with whom a professional interacts (see also Sections 2.7 and 12.13). Thus, the main concerns when a conflict of interest arises in publishing are the impairment of objectivity in both performing and evaluating research and the potential for harm to or exploitation of research participants.

Author Interest. In all scientific disciplines, professional communications are presumed to be based on objective and unbiased interpretations of evidence. Transparency about researchers' positions in relation to their evidence and interpretations is central. For example, authors' economic and commercial interests in products or services used in a study or discussed in a manuscript may color their ability to collect evidence and interpret it with fidelity. Although the presence of such interests does not necessarily constitute an unethical conflict of interest per se, the integrity of the field requires open and honest disclosure of the possibilities of such influences when they may exist. In general, an author's safest and most transparent course of action is to disclose in an author note activities and relationships that, if known to others, might be viewed as a conflict of interest, even if the author does not believe that any conflict or bias exists.

Whether an interest is significant depends on individual circumstances and cannot be defined by a threshold amount. Holdings in a company through a mutual fund are not ordinarily sufficient to warrant disclosure, whereas salaries, research grants, consulting fees, and personal stock holdings should be disclosed. Participation on a board of directors or any other relationship with an entity that is in some way part of the research project should also be carefully considered for possible disclosure.

In addition to disclosing possible influences that might lead authors to support certain findings, authors should also consider disclosing when circumstances could influence them against a product, service, facility, or person. For example, having a copyright or royalty interest in a competing psychological test or assessment protocol might be seen as a possible source of negative bias against another test instrument (American Educational Research Association et al., 2014).

Editor and Reviewer Interest. For editors and reviewers who evaluate a given manuscript for publication, conflicts of interest are defined more broadly than economic interests and are usually dealt with by recusal rather than disclosure. It is the responsibility of editors and reviewers to recognize their conflicts of interest, disclose these conflicts to the person who assigned them the manuscript, and either decline the request or ask the assigning person to make a decision.

For editors and reviewers, conflicts of interest may be economic, as described previously for authors. If the main topic of an article has direct implications for a commercial interest of the editor or reviewer, that individual should decline the request to review the article. Any other economic conflicts that bear on the review are for the person who assigned the manuscript to decide.

Conflicts of interest for editors and reviewers may also take the form of personal connections. Having a family tie, marital relationship, close friendship, or romantic connection with an author is generally seen as a conflict of interest. Professional relationships also may constitute a conflict of interest if, for example, one of the authors is a coauthor, past or current collaborator, past doctoral student or supervisor, or current colleague of the editor or reviewer. Editors-in-chief should set policy for their journal about whether collaboration-based conflicts extend for a lifetime or elapse after a certain number of years have passed. If an editor or reviewer guesses the identity of an anonymized author, and there is potential for a personal conflict, the editor or reviewer should make the assigning person aware of this.

Although differences of scientific or political opinion may influence evaluation of a manuscript, it is impractical to define any opinion-based agreement or disagreement as constituting a disqualifying conflict of interest. However, if an editor or reviewer finds that their point of view is fundamentally opposed to the rationale or approach of a manuscript, they should let the assigning person know this. For their part, editors should seek opinions from reviewers with a variety of positions when evaluating a manuscript known to be controversial.

Protecting Intellectual Property Rights

1.21 Publication Credit

Authorship is reserved for persons who make a substantial contribution to and who accept responsibility for a published work. Individuals should take authorship credit only for work they have performed or to which they have substantially contributed (APA Ethics Code Standard 8.12a, Publication Credit). Authorship encompasses, therefore, not only persons who do the writing but also those who have made substantial scientific contributions to a study. Substantial professional contributions may include formulating the problem or hypothesis, structuring the experimental study design, organizing and conducting the analysis, or interpreting the results and findings. Those who so contribute are listed as authors in the byline. Lesser contributions, which do not constitute authorship, may be acknowledged in the author note (see Section 2.7; see also a taxonomy of authorship in the natural sciences called CRediT at https://casrai.org/credit). Lesser contributions may include such supportive functions as designing or building the study apparatus, suggesting or advising about the analysis, collecting or entering the data, modifying or structuring a computer program, recruiting participants, and obtaining animals. Conducting routine observations or diagnoses for use in studies does not constitute authorship. Combinations of these (and other) tasks, however, may justify authorship.

As early as practicable in a research project, the collaborators should decide which tasks are necessary for the project's completion, how the work will be divided, which tasks or combination of tasks merits authorship credit, and on what level credit will be given (first author, second author, etc.). Collaborators may need to reassess authorship credit and order if relative contributions change in the course of the project (and its publication). This is especially true in faculty–student collaborations when students need more intensive supervision than originally anticipated, when additional analyses are required beyond the scope of a student's current level of training, or when the level of the student's contribution exceeds what was originally anticipated.

When a manuscript is accepted for publication, each person listed in the byline must verify in writing that they (a) agree to serve as an author, (b) approve the order of authorship presented in the byline, and (c) accept the responsibilities of authorship.

1.22 Order of Authors

Professional Authors. Authors are responsible for determining authorship and for specifying the order in which two or more authors' names appear in the byline. Principal authorship and the order of authorship credit should accurately reflect the relative contributions of persons involved (APA Ethics Code Standard 8.12b, Publication Credit). Relative status (e.g., department chair, junior faculty member, student) should not determine the order of authorship. The general rule is that the name of the principal contributor appears first, with subsequent names appearing in order of decreasing contribution. In some cases, another principal contributor appears last. These conventions can vary from field to field and from journal to journal. Novice authors are advised to contact the editor of the journal to which they are submitting a manuscript for guidance. If authors played equal roles in the research and publication of their study, they may wish to note this in the author note (see Section 2.7).

Professional–Student Collaborations. Because doctoral work is expected to result in an independent and original contribution to the field by the student, except under rare circumstances, the student should be listed as the principal author of any papers with multiple authors that are substantially based on their dissertation (APA Ethics Code Standard 8.12c, Publication Credit). Unusual exceptions to doctoral student first authorship might occur when the dissertation is published as part of a collection of studies involving other researchers or when work on a final manuscript was performed substantially by a coauthor. Whether students merit principal authorship on papers based on master's-level or other predoctoral research will depend on their specific contributions to the research. When master's-level students make the primary contribution to a study, they should be listed as the first author. Students may also collaborate with a faculty member on a faculty-originated project as a way to acquire the skills to make a primary scientific contribution in their master's thesis. In such cases, authorship should be determined by the relative contributions of the student and faculty member to the project (Fisher, 2017).

Student Assignments. When students contribute equally to a group project that will be submitted to an instructor (not for publication), students may put their names in any order in the byline (e.g., alphabetical order, reverse alphabetical order).

1.23 Authors' Intellectual Property Rights During Manuscript Review

Editorial review of a manuscript requires that the editors and reviewers circulate and discuss the manuscript. During the review process, the manuscript is a confidential and privileged document. Editors and reviewers may not, without the authors' explicit permission, quote from a manuscript under review or circulate copies of it to others, including graduate or postdoctoral students, for any purpose other than editorial review (APA Ethics Code Standard 8.15, Reviewers; see Section 12.7 for a detailed discussion of the peer review process). If a reviewer wishes to consult with a colleague about some aspect of the manuscript, the reviewer must request permission from the editor prior to approaching the colleague. Publishers have different policies on how editorial review works, and reviewers should consult the editor for any questions. In addition, editors and reviewers may not use material from an unpublished manuscript to advance their own or others' work without the authors' consent.

1.24 Authors' Copyright on Unpublished Manuscripts

Authors are protected by federal statute against unauthorized use of their unpublished manuscripts. Under the Copyright Act of 1976 (Title 17 of the *United States Code*), an unpublished work is copyrighted "automatically from the moment the original work of authorship is fixed" (U.S. Copyright Office, 2017, p. 1), referring to the moment in which a work exists in any tangible form—for example, typed on a page. Until authors formally transfer copyright (see Section 12.20), they own the copyright on an unpublished manuscript; all exclusive rights due the copyright owner of a published work are also due the authors of an unpublished work. To ensure copyright protection, publishers include the copyright notice on all published works (e.g., Copyright [year] by [name of copyright holder]). The notice need not appear on unpublished works; nonetheless, it is recommended that authors include a copyright notice on all works, whether published or not. Registration of copyright (e.g., with the U.S. Copyright Office at https://www.copyright.gov/registration/) provides a public record and is usually a prerequisite for any legal action.

1.25 Ethical Compliance Checklist

The following checklist provides general guidance for ensuring compliance with ethics requirements.

Ethical Compliance Checklist

☐ Have you obtained written permission for use of unpublished instruments, procedures, or data that other researchers might consider theirs (proprietary)?

☐ Have you properly cited all published works, unpublished works, and ideas and creations of others presented in your manuscript? Have you secured needed permissions and written copyright attributions for items that require them?

☐ Have you reported institutional review of your study or studies in the Method section of your manuscript?

☐ Are you prepared to answer editorial questions about the informed consent, assent, and/or debriefing procedures you used?

☐ If your study involved nonhuman animal subjects, are you prepared to answer editorial questions about the humane care and treatment of such animals?

☐ Have all authors reviewed the manuscript and agreed on responsibility for its content?

☐ Have you adequately protected the confidentiality of research participants, clients/patients, organizations, third parties, or others who were a source of information presented in the manuscript?

☐ Have you released or shared participant data only in accordance with the agreement specified in the informed consent for your study?

☐ If your study was a clinical trial and has been registered, have you reported its registration in the author note and in the text?

2

PAPER ELEMENTS AND FORMAT

Contents

2

PAPER ELEMENTS AND FORMAT

Consistency in the order, structure, and format of paper elements allows readers to focus on a paper's content rather than its presentation. Following APA Style guidelines to achieve consistency in the presentation of paper elements is essential to crafting an effective scholarly work.

In this chapter, we provide an overview of the elements of a paper, including how to structure, format, and organize them. These guidelines apply broadly to any APA Style paper and may be especially useful to students or researchers who are not familiar with APA Style. For researchers preparing manuscripts for publication, more in-depth guidelines on journal article reporting standards (JARS) for quantitative, qualitative, and mixed methods research are discussed in Chapter 3. Students can find guidance on dissertations and theses in Sections 1.10 and 12.1. Sample APA Style papers are included at the end of this chapter; additional sample papers are available on the APA Style website (https://apastyle.apa.org).

Required Elements

2.1 Professional Paper Required Elements

Paper elements appear in various combinations depending on the nature of the work. Manuscripts submitted for publication (see Sections 1.1–1.9) should always include a title page (see Section 2.3), which contains the paper title (see Section 2.4), author names and affiliations (see Sections 2.5–2.6), and author note (see Section 2.7); page headers with a running head and page numbers (see Sections 2.8 and 2.18); an abstract (see Section 2.9); text (see Section 2.11); and a reference list (see Section 2.12). Papers may also include keywords (see Section 2.10), footnotes (see Section 2.13), tables (see Chapter 7), figures (see Chapter 7), appendices (see Section 2.14), and/or supplemental materials (see Section 2.15). Authors seeking publication should refer to the journal's instructions for authors or manuscript submission guidelines for any requirements that are different from or in addition to those specified by APA Style.

2.2 Student Paper Required Elements

Student papers (e.g., narrative essays, reaction or response papers, literature review papers; see Section 1.10) usually include, at minimum, a title page (see Sections 2.3–2.6), page numbers (see Section 2.18), text (see Section 2.11), and a reference list (see Section 2.12). They may also have tables (see Chapter 7), figures (see Chapter 7), and/or appendices (see Section 2.14). Student papers do not typically include a running head, an author note, or an abstract, unless specifically requested by the instructor or institution. Student papers have a student-specific version of the title page (see Section 2.3).

Paper Elements

2.3 Title Page

A title page is required for all APA Style papers. There are both professional and student versions of the title page.

Professional Title Page. The professional title page (see Figure 2.1) includes the following elements:

- title of the paper (see Section 2.4),
- name of each author of the paper (the byline; see Section 1.22 for determining the order of authorship and Section 2.5 for formatting the byline),
- affiliation for each author (see Section 2.6),
- author note (see Section 2.7),
- running head (also included on all pages; see Section 2.8), and
- page number (also included on all pages; see Section 2.18).

See the section indicated for each element for formatting instructions.

Student Title Page. Students should follow the guidelines of their instructor or institution when determining which title page format is most appropriate to use. If not instructed otherwise, students should include the following elements on the title page (see Figure 2.2):

- title of the paper (see Section 2.4);
- name of each author of the paper (the byline; see Section 1.22 for determining the order of authorship and Section 2.5 for formatting the byline);
- affiliation for each author, typically the university attended (including the name of any department or division; see Section 2.6);
- course number and name for which the paper is being submitted (use the format shown on institutional materials; e.g., PSY204, PSYC 4301, NURS 303);
- instructor name (check with the instructor for the preferred form; e.g., Dr. Hülya F. Akış; Professor Levin; Kwame Osei, PhD; Mariam Sherzai, RN);
- assignment due date, written in the month, date, and year format used in your country (usually November 4, 2020, or 4 November 2020; we recommend spelling out the month, although 2020-11-04 is the format in countries that use the international standard date); and
- page number (also included on all pages; see Section 2.18).

ELEMENTS & FORMAT

Figure 2.1 Sample Professional Title Page

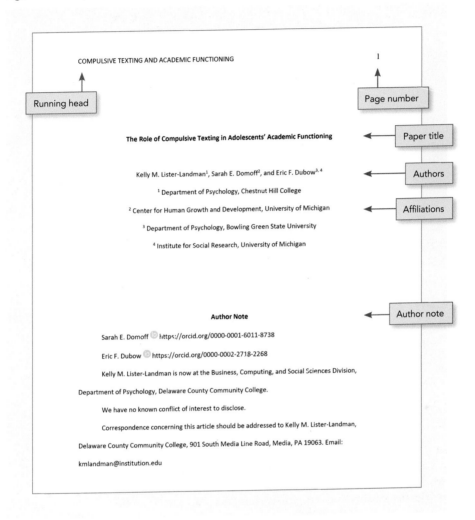

See the sections for the title, byline, affiliation, and page numbers for formatting instructions for these elements. Place the course number and name, instructor name, and assignment due date on separate lines, centered and in that order, below the affiliation (see Section 2.21 for more on line spacing).

2.4 Title

The *title* should summarize the main idea of the paper simply and, if possible, in a way that is engaging for readers. For research papers, it should be a concise statement of the main topic of the research and should identify the variables or theoretical issues under investigation and the relationship between them. Although there is no prescribed limit for title length in APA Style, authors are encouraged to keep their titles focused and succinct. Research has shown an association between simple, concise titles and higher numbers of article downloads and citations (Hallock & Dillner, 2016; Jamali & Nikzad, 2011).

Figure 2.2 Sample Student Title Page

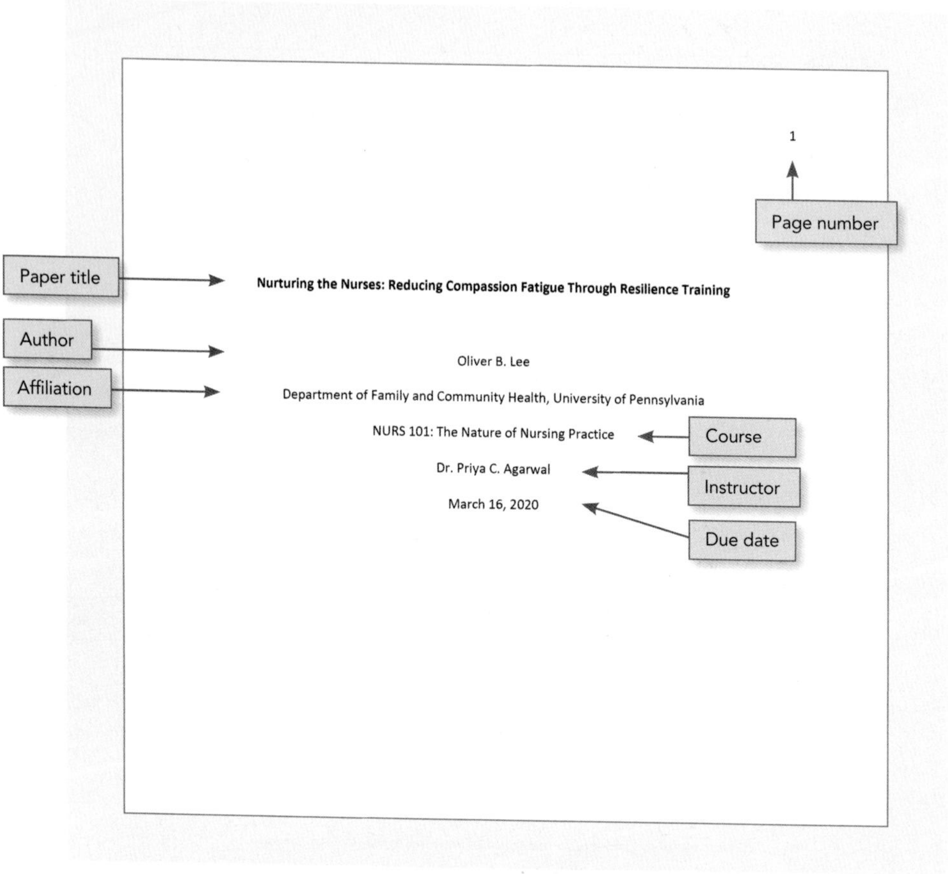

Include essential terms in the title to enhance readers' ability to find your work during a search and to aid abstracting and indexing in databases if the work is published. Avoid words that serve no purpose; they increase the title length and can mislead indexers. For example, the words "method" and "results" do not normally appear in a title, nor should such phrases as "a study of" or "an experimental investigation of." Occasionally terms such as "research synthesis," "meta-analysis," or "fMRI study" convey important information for potential readers and are included in the title. Avoid using abbreviations in a title; spelling out all terms helps ensure accurate, complete indexing of the article and allows readers to more readily comprehend its meaning. When an animal name—for example, "Rat"—is in the title, also include the scientific name in italics and parentheses—(*Rattus norvegicus*). See Table 2.1 for examples of effective versus ineffective paper titles.

Format. The paper title should be in title case (see Section 6.17), bold, centered, and positioned in the upper half of the title page (e.g., three or four lines down from the top margin of the page). Move the title up to accommodate a longer author note if necessary. If the title is longer than one line, the main title and the subtitle can be separated on double-spaced lines if desired. Note that the paper title also appears at the top of the first page of text (see Sections 2.11 and 2.28).

Table 2.1 Effective and Ineffective Paper Titles

Effective title	Ineffective title	Rationale
Effect of Depression on the Decision to Join a Clinical Trial	A Study of the Effect of Depression on the Decision to Join a Clinical Trial	More direct: Unnecessary words have been cut.
Why and When Hierarchy Impacts Team Effectiveness: A Meta-Analytic Integration	Hierarchy and Team Effectiveness	More precise: The relationship between variables has been clarified; the type of research (meta-analysis) has been specified.
Closing Your Eyes to Follow Your Heart: Avoiding Information to Protect a Strong Intuitive Preference	Closing Your Eyes to Follow Your Heart	More informative: A creative title has been balanced with a substantive subtitle.

2.5 Author Name (Byline)

Every paper includes the name of the author or authors—the *byline*. The preferred form of an author's name is first name, middle initial(s), and last name; this form reduces the likelihood of mistaken identity (e.g., that authors with the same first and last names are the same person). To assist researchers and librarians, use the same form of your name for publication throughout your career when possible; for example, do not use a middle initial on one paper and omit the initial on a different paper. Determining whether, for example, Marisol G. Rodríguez is the same person as M. G. Rodríguez can be difficult, particularly when citations span years and institutional affiliations change. If you change your name during your career, present your new name in a consistent form as well. Omit all professional titles (e.g., Dr., Professor) and academic degrees or licenses (e.g., PhD, EdD, MD, MA, RN, MSW, LCSW) from the byline.

Format. Write the byline on the title page after the paper title. Include one blank double-spaced line between the paper title and the byline. Follow these guidelines for byline formatting:

- If the paper has one author, write the author name centered and in standard (i.e., nonbold, nonitalic) font.
- If the paper has multiple authors, order the names of the authors according to their contributions. Write all names on the same line (flowing onto additional lines if needed), centered, and in standard font. For two authors, separate the names with the word "and"; for three or more authors, separate the names with commas and include "and" before the final author's name.
- For names with suffixes, separate the suffix from the rest of the name with a space, not a comma (e.g., Roland J. Thorpe Jr.).

See Table 2.2 for examples of how to set up author bylines and affiliations.

2.6 Author Affiliation

The *affiliation* identifies where the author(s) worked (or studied, in the case of student authors) when the work was conducted, which is usually a university or other institution. Include a dual affiliation only if two institutions contributed substantial support to the study. Include no more than two affiliations per author. If the affiliation has changed since the work was completed, give the

Table 2.2 Examples of Author Bylines and Affiliations

Variation	Example
One author, one affiliation	Maggie C. Leonard Department of Psychology, George Mason University
One author, two affiliations	Andrew K. Jones-Willoughby School of Psychology, University of Sydney Center for Behavioral Neuroscience, American University
One author, no institutional affiliation	Isabel de Vries Rochester, New York, United States
Two authors, shared affiliation	Mackenzie J. Clement and Talia R. Cummings College of Nursing, Michigan State University
Two authors, different affiliations	Wilhelm T. Weber[1] and Latasha P. Jackson[2] [1] Max Planck Institute for Human Development, Berlin, Germany [2] College of Education, University of Georgia
Three or more authors, shared affiliation	Madina Wahab, DeAndre L. Washington Jr., and Julian H. Lee School of Public Health, University of California, Berkeley
Three or more authors, different affiliations	Savannah C. St. John[1], Fen-Lei Chang[2,3], and Carlos O. Vásquez III[1] [1] Educational Testing Service, Princeton, New Jersey, United States [2] MRC Cognition and Brain Sciences Unit, Cambridge, England [3] Department of Psychology, University of Cambridge

current affiliation in the author note (see Section 2.7). Abide by these guidelines when presenting affiliations:

- Academic affiliations (e.g., universities, teaching hospitals affiliated with a university) should include the name of any department or division and the name of the institution, separated by a comma. It is not necessary to include the location of the institution unless the location is part of the institution's name.

- Nonacademic institutional affiliations (e.g., hospitals not affiliated with a university, independent laboratories, other organizations) should include the name of any department or division, the name of the institution, and the location of the institution, separated by commas.

- Authors who are in private practice or who have no institutional affiliation should include their location.

- When providing a location (as for nonacademic institutions and private practices), give the city; state, province, or territory as applicable; and country. Spell out state, province, and territory names rather than abbreviating them.

Format. The format of the affiliation depends on the number of authors and whether different authors have different affiliations, as follows. Begin the affiliation(s) on a new line after the byline. Place different affiliations on their own lines. Do not add blank lines between affiliations or between the byline and the first affiliation. See Table 2.2 for examples of how to set up author bylines and affiliations.

All Authors Share One Affiliation. If the paper has one author with one affiliation, or if all authors of a multiauthored paper share one affiliation, include the affiliation centered and in standard font on its own line, beginning one line below the byline. Do not include a superscript numeral.

All Authors Share Two Affiliations. If the paper has one author with two affiliations, or if all authors of a multiauthored paper share the same two affiliations, include each affiliation centered and in standard font on its own line, beginning one line below the byline. Do not include superscript numerals.

Multiple Authors With Different Affiliations. If the paper has two or more authors with different affiliations (even if only the department is different within the same university), use superscript Arabic numerals to connect author names to the appropriate affiliation(s). List authors' affiliations in the order the authors appear in the byline; for example, for a paper with two authors who have different affiliations, list the affiliation of the first author first, followed by the affiliation of the second author, with each affiliation centered and in standard font on its own line, beginning one line below the byline. Place a superscript numeral 1 after the first author's surname, without a space between the name and the numeral (when a paper has three or more authors and thus commas appear after author names, put the numeral after the surname and before the comma). Then put a corresponding superscript numeral 1 before the corresponding affiliation (with a space between the numeral and the start of the affiliation). Repeat this process for the second author using the numeral 2 (and so on when a paper has more authors).

If some, but not all, authors share an affiliation, list the affiliation once and reuse the superscript numeral in the byline. Identify authors with two affiliations in the byline by separating the appropriate superscript numerals with a superscript comma and space.

If the paper has only one author, or if there are multiple authors but all authors share the same one or two affiliations, then superscript numerals are not used.

Group Authors. For group authors (e.g., task forces, working groups, organizations), superscript numerals are not usually used because the group is essentially its own affiliation.

2.7 Author Note

An *author note* provides additional information about authors, study registration, data sharing, disclaimers or statements regarding conflicts of interest, and help or funding that supported the research. It also provides a point of contact for interested readers. Student papers do not typically include an author note.

Arrange the author note into separate paragraphs; if a paragraph is not applicable to your manuscript, omit it from the author note. Also, the following requirements apply for manuscripts submitted to APA journals; other publishers may have different requirements (e.g., some journals require authors to provide disclosures and acknowledgments on a separate page at the end of the manuscript rather than in the author note).

First Paragraph: ORCID iDs. Authors may include their ORCID identification number (iD), if they have one (see the ORCID website at https://orcid.org/ for more information). ORCID iDs help authors who have changed names or who share the same name ensure publications are correctly attributed to them. Provide the author's name, the ORCID iD symbol, and the full URL for the ORCID iD, listing each author on a separate, indented line. The iD symbol should be included in the link, per ORCID's recommendation.

Josiah S. Carberry ⓘ https://orcid.org/0000-0002-1825-0097
Sofia Maria Hernandez Garcia ⓘ https://orcid.org/0000-0001-5727-2427

Include only the names of authors who have ORCID iDs. If no authors have ORCID iDs, omit this paragraph.

Second Paragraph: Changes of Affiliation. Identify any changes in author affiliation subsequent to the time of the study. Use the following wording: "[Author's name] is now at [affiliation]." This paragraph may also be used to acknowledge the death of an author.

Third Paragraph: Disclosures and Acknowledgments. If the disclosures and acknowledgments are short, combine them into one paragraph; if they are long, separate them into multiple paragraphs.

Study Registration. If the study was registered, provide the registry name and document entry number in the author note. Clinical trials and meta-analyses are often registered. For example, write "This study was registered with ClinicalTrials.gov (Identifier NCT998877)." For more information on study registration information as it pertains to JARS, see Section 3.9.

Open Practices and Data Sharing. If the study data and/or materials are to be shared openly as part of the publication of the article (see also Section 1.14), acknowledge this in the author note. Cite the data set in the author note, and include the reference for the data set in the reference list (see Section 10.9).

Disclosure of Related Reports and Conflicts of Interest. If the article is based on data used in a previously published report (e.g., a longitudinal study), doctoral dissertation, or conference presentation, disclose this information, and include an in-text citation. For example, write "This article is based on data published in Pulaski (2017)" or "This article is based on the dissertation completed by Graham (2018)" and include an entry for Pulaski (2017) or Graham (2018) in the reference list. Also acknowledge the publication of related reports (e.g., reports on the same data). In addition, indicate in this paragraph whether any author has a possible or perceived conflict of interest (e.g., ownership of stock in a company that manufactures a drug used in the study); if not, state that no conflict of interest exists. If your employer or granting organization requires a disclaimer stating, for example, that the research reported does not reflect the views of that organization, include such a statement in this paragraph and follow the format or wording prescribed by that organization.

Acknowledgments of Financial Support and Other Assistance. Complete and accurate funding information for your article should be included in the author note. Report the names of all funding organizations; all grant, fellowship, or award numbers and/or names; the names of the funding recipients; and the names of principal investigators (if any) for the funded research. Do not precede grant numbers by "No." or "#" (e.g., write "We received funding from Grant A-123 from the National Science Foundation" or "National Science Foundation Grant A-123 funded this work," not "Grant No. A-123" or "Grant #A-123"). Next, acknowledge colleagues who assisted in conducting the study or critiquing the manuscript but who are not authors of the work. Study participants may be acknowledged for exceptional contributions if desired. Then provide any thanks for personal assistance, such as in manuscript preparation or copyediting. End this paragraph by explaining any special agreements concerning authorship, such as if authors contributed equally to the study. Do not acknowledge the people routinely involved in the review and acceptance of manuscripts in this paragraph, such as peer reviewers, editors, associate editors, and consulting editors of the journal to which you are submitting the manuscript. If you would like to acknowledge a specific idea raised by a reviewer or journal editor, do so in a footnote in the text where the idea is discussed.

Fourth Paragraph: Contact Information. The corresponding author answers queries regarding the work after it is published and ensures that any data are retained for the appropriate amount of time. Any author can serve as the corresponding author. Provide the full name and complete mailing address for the corresponding author, with the name and address separated by a comma and a period after the address. Then provide the corresponding author's email address, with no period after it. Use the following format:

> Correspondence concerning this article should be addressed to [author's name], [complete mailing address]. Email: author@institution.edu

Format. Place the author note in the bottom half of the title page, below the title, byline, and affiliation. Leave at least one blank line between the affiliation and the author note label. Center the label "Author Note" (in bold). Indent each paragraph of the author note and align paragraphs to the left. Although the paragraphs of the author note are labeled in this section to help explain them, do not label the paragraphs of the author note in your paper. See Figure 2.3 for a sample author note.

2.8 Running Head

The *running head* is an abbreviated version of the paper title that appears at the top of every page to identify it for readers, especially readers of a print copy of the published article. Running heads are required only for manuscripts being submitted for publication. Running heads are not required for student papers unless the instructor or institution requests them; thus, the header for a student paper includes only the page number.

Authors should supply the running head rather than leave this task to the publisher because authors are best able to select the most important words for an abbreviated title. The running head does not have to consist of the same words in the same order as the title; rather, the idea of the title should be conveyed in a shortened form. For example, an article titled "Restless Nights: Sleep Latency Increases and Sleep Quality Decreases With Caffeine Intake" can have a running head of "CAFFEINE-INDUCED REDUCTIONS IN SLEEP EFFICIENCY."

The running head should contain a maximum of 50 characters, counting letters, punctuation, and spaces between words as characters. If the title is already 50 characters or fewer, the full title can be used as the running head. Avoid using abbreviations in the running head; however, the ampersand symbol (&) may be used rather than "and" if desired.

Format. Write the running head in the page header, flush left, in all-capital letters, across from the right-aligned page number. Use the same running head on every page, including the title page; do not include the label "Running head" to identify the running head on any page (see the sample papers at the end of this chapter).

Figure 2.3 Sample Author Note

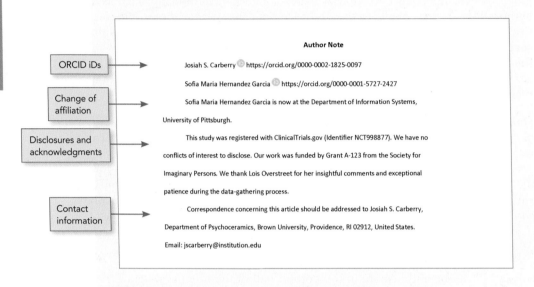

2.9 Abstract

An *abstract* is a brief, comprehensive summary of the contents of the paper. Authors writing for publication should follow the reporting standards for abstracts presented in Section 3.3. Most scholarly journals require an abstract. For any journal-specific instructions, consult the instructions for authors or the webpage of the journal to which you plan to submit your article. For example, some journals publish a public significance statement, which summarizes the significance of the study for a general audience, along with the abstract. An abstract is not usually required for student papers unless requested by the instructor or institution.

Format. Abstracts typically are limited to no more than 250 words. If you are submitting a work for publication, check the journal's instructions for authors for abstract length and formatting requirements, which may be different from those of APA journals. Place the abstract on its own page after the title page (i.e., page 2). Write the section label "Abstract" in bold title case, centered at the top of the page, and place the abstract below the label.

Abstracts may appear in paragraph or structured format. Abstracts in paragraph format are written as a single paragraph without indentation of the first line. Structured abstracts are also written as a single paragraph without indentation, and labels are inserted to identify various sections (e.g., Objective, Method, Results, Conclusions); use the labels and formatting prescribed by the journal to which you are submitting your manuscript (e.g., APA journals use bold italic for the labels).

2.10 Keywords

Keywords are words, phrases, or acronyms that describe the most important aspects of your paper. They are used for indexing in databases and help readers find your work during a search. For manuscripts being submitted to APA journals, provide three to five keywords describing the content. Keywords are not required for student papers unless requested by the instructor or institution.

Format. Write the label "*Keywords:*" (in italic) one line below the abstract, indented 0.5 in. like a regular paragraph, followed by the keywords in lowercase (but capitalize proper nouns; see Section 6.14), separated by commas. The keywords can be listed in any order. Do not use a period or other punctuation after the last keyword (see the sample professional paper at the end of this chapter). If the keywords run onto a second line, the second line is not indented.

2.11 Text (Body)

The *text,* or body of the paper, contains the authors' main contribution to the literature. Both professional and student authors should follow the content and formatting guidelines described in this chapter and the citation principles described in Chapters 8 and 9; researchers preparing manuscripts for publication should also review the reporting standards for quantitative, qualitative, or mixed methods research, as appropriate, described in Chapter 3. For guidance on the contents of various types of papers, see Sections 1.1 to 1.10.

The text can be organized in many ways, and the organization generally depends on the paper type (see also Sections 1.1–1.10). Most papers include an introduction that addresses the importance of the work, contextualizes the work within the existing literature, and states the aims of the work. Beyond the introduction, the paper should include paragraphs or sections explaining the main premises of the paper. There are many possible formats for the rest of the text; for example, a quantitative research paper typically includes sections called "Method," "Results," and "Discussion," whereas a qualitative research paper may include a section called "Findings" instead of "Results," or it may have different section headings altogether, depending on the nature of the inquiry. A brief student paper (e.g., a response paper) may not have section headings or may have sections with headings different from those described in this manual. See Section 2.26 for more on organization.

Format. The text should start on a new page after the title page and abstract (if the paper includes an abstract). On the first line of the first page of the text, write the title of the paper in title case, bold, and centered. The text should be left-aligned, double-spaced paragraphs, with the first line of each paragraph indented by one tab key (0.5 in.; see Sections 2.23–2.24). Use headings as needed and appropriate within the text to separate sections and to reflect the organizational structure of the content (see Sections 2.26–2.27). Do not start a new page or add extra line breaks when a new heading occurs; each section of the text should follow the next without a break.

2.12 Reference List

The *reference list* provides a reliable way for readers to locate the works authors cite to acknowledge previous scholarship. References are used to document and substantiate statements made about the literature, just as data in the paper are used to support interpretations and conclusions. The references cited in the paper do not need to be exhaustive but should be sufficient to support the need for your research and to enable readers to place it in the context of previous research and theorizing. For detailed guidance on citing sources in the text and preparing the reference list, consult Chapters 8 and 9, respectively.

Format. Start the reference list on a new page after the text and before any tables, figures, and/or appendices. Label the reference list "References," capitalized, in bold, and centered. Double-space all reference list entries (including between and within references). Use a hanging indent for all references, meaning that the first line of each reference is flush left and subsequent lines are indented by 0.5 in. Use the paragraph-formatting function of your word-processing program to automatically apply the hanging indent. For the order of works in the reference list, see Sections 9.44 to 9.49.

2.13 Footnotes

A *footnote* is a brief note that provides additional content or copyright attribution. Any type of paper may include footnotes.

Content Footnotes. Content footnotes supplement or enhance substantive information in the text; they should not include complicated, irrelevant, or nonessential information. Because they can be distracting to readers, content footnotes should be included only if they strengthen the discussion. A content footnote should convey just one idea; if you find yourself creating paragraphs or displaying equations as you are writing a footnote, then the main text or an appendix would likely be a more suitable place to present the information. Another alternative is to indicate in a short footnote that supplemental material is available online (see Section 2.15). In most cases, authors integrate an idea into an article best by presenting important information in the text, not in a footnote.

Copyright Attribution. When authors reproduce lengthy quotations and/or test or scale items in the text, a copyright attribution is usually required and should be presented in a footnote. A reproduced table or figure also requires a copyright attribution, but this attribution appears in the table or figure note. Further directions on seeking permission to reproduce material and appropriate wording for the copyright attribution appears in Sections 12.14 to 12.18.

Footnote Callout Numbering and Format. Number all footnotes consecutively in the order in which their callouts appear in the text with superscript Arabic numerals. Footnote callouts should be superscripted, like this,[1] following any punctuation mark except a dash. A footnote callout that appears with a dash—like this[2]—always precedes the dash. (The callout falls inside a closing parenthesis if it applies only to matter within the parentheses, like this.[3]) Do not put a space before the footnote callout in text. Do not place footnote callouts in headings. To refer to a footnote again after it has been called out, identify it in the text by the footnote number (e.g., write "see Footnote 3"); do not repeat the footnote callout or the whole footnote.

Place each footnote at the bottom of the page on which it is discussed using the footnote function of your word-processing program (see the sample professional paper at the end of this chapter for examples). Footnotes may alternatively be placed in consecutive order on a separate page after the references; in this case, put the section label "Footnotes" in bold, centered at the top of the page; then write the footnotes themselves as double-spaced indented paragraphs that begin with a superscript footnote number, and put a space between the footnote number and the text that follows. Be sure that the number of the footnote callout corresponds with the number that appears with the footnoted text.

2.14 Appendices

Sometimes authors wish to include material that supplements the paper's content but that would be distracting or inappropriate in the text of the paper. Such material can often be included in an *appendix,* which is included in the print and electronic versions of the article, or in *supplemental materials* (see Section 2.15), which are available in an online-only supplemental archive that the publisher maintains.

Include an appendix only if it helps readers understand, evaluate, or replicate the study or theoretical argument being made. Be sure that all relevant ethical standards have been followed for materials placed in the appendices, including copyright attribution, accurate representation of data, and protection of human participants (e.g., as the standards apply to images or videos of identifiable people; see Sections 1.18 and 12.17).

In general, an appendix is appropriate for materials that are relatively brief and easily presented in print format. Some examples of material suitable for an appendix are (a) lists of stimulus materials (e.g., those used in psycholinguistic research); (b) instructions to participants; (c) tests, scales, or inventories developed for the study being reported; (d) detailed descriptions of complex equipment; (e) detailed demographic descriptions of subpopulations in the study; and (f) other detailed or complex reporting items described in Chapter 3. Student papers may include appendices.

Format. Begin each appendix on a separate page after any references, footnotes, tables, and figures. Give each appendix a label and a title. If a paper has one appendix, label it "Appendix"; if a paper has more than one appendix, label each appendix with a capital letter (e.g., "Appendix A," "Appendix B") in the order in which it is mentioned in the text. Each appendix should be mentioned (called out) at least once in the text by its label (e.g., "see Appendix A"). The appendix title should describe its contents. Place the appendix label and title in bold and centered on separate lines at the top of the page on which the appendix begins. Use title case (see Section 6.17) for the appendix label and title.

The appendix may consist of text, tables, figures, or a combination of these. A text appendix may contain headings and displayed equations. If an appendix contains text, write the paragraphs as regular indented paragraphs the same as in the body of the paper. If a text appendix contains tables, figures, footnotes, and/or displayed equations, give each one a number preceded by the letter of the appendix in which it appears (e.g., Table A1 is the first table within Appendix A or of a sole appendix that is not labeled with a letter; Equation B1 is the first equation within Appendix B; Figure C2 is the second figure of Appendix C). In a sole text appendix, which is not labeled with a letter, precede all table, figure, footnote, and equation numbers with the letter "A" to distinguish them from those of the main text. All tables and figures within a text appendix must be mentioned in the appendix and numbered in order of mention. The tables and figures within a text appendix should be embedded within the text, as described in Section 7.6.

If an appendix consists of a table only or a figure only, then the appendix label takes the place of the table or figure number, and the appendix title takes the place of the table or figure title. Thus, if Appendix B is a table-only appendix, the table is referred to as Appendix B rather than as Table B1. Likewise, if Appendix C is a figure-only appendix, the figure is referred to as Appendix C rather than as Figure C1. If multiple tables and/or figures (but no text) are combined into one appendix, label and title the appendix and also number and title the tables and/or figures within the appendix (e.g., Tables D1 and D2 are two tables in Appendix D).

2.15 Supplemental Materials

Supplemental materials to a journal article are published online only. These materials enrich readers' experience and understanding of the content of the article. Online-only publication tends to be appropriate for materials that are more useful when available as downloadable files and for materials that are not easily presented in print. Student papers do not typically include supplemental materials.

Some examples of content provided as supplemental materials are

- video clips, audio clips, or animations
- lengthy computer code
- details of mathematical or computational models
- oversized tables
- detailed intervention protocols
- expanded methodology descriptions
- color figures or other images (see Section 7.26)
- printable templates and worksheets
- data files (e.g., generated using SPSS or other software)

Supplemental materials should include enough information to make their content interpretable when accompanied by the published text. Also keep in mind accessibility guidelines as they pertain to online or interactive materials to ensure that your files are not only openable but also accessible to all readers.[1] Complete data sets should be made available, as appropriate, in online repositories or archives (see Section 10.9 for the reference format) or in supplemental materials. See Sections 1.14 and 1.15 for more on data retention and sharing.

Because this content may be useful to the field, APA and many other publishers make it possible to provide supplemental materials to a wide audience by posting them online and placing a link with the published article. These files (like appendices) then become part of the primary journal record and cannot be augmented, altered, or deleted. As such, materials for inclusion in supplemental materials should be submitted in formats that are widely accessible. We recommend checking with the journal publisher for preferred file types and any limitations.

Less widely used file formats, including TeX, LaTeX, any client- or server-side scripting (e.g., Java, CGI), executable files, and software applications, might be acceptable but of less use to readers who do not have access to specialized programs. Because of the risk of downloading embedded viruses or malware, many uncommon file types or executable files may be blocked by firewalls and antivirus protection programs, system administrators, or users. Therefore, we do not

---

[1] The Web Content Accessibility Guidelines (WCAG) describe how to make online content accessible to people with disabilities (Web Accessibility Initiative, 2018).

recommend using such file types unless they are critical to understanding or using your material (e.g., syntax from a methodological paper such as an SPSS macro might be saved with an SPS extension so that it can be used directly by other researchers). Briefly describe any supplemental materials in the text or a footnote to the text as appropriate (see Section 2.13).

Most journals make supplemental materials subject to peer review and require that they be submitted with the initial manuscript. Once accepted, the supplemental materials are typically posted with no editing, formatting, or typesetting. For APA journals, a link to the supplemental materials appears in the published article and leads readers to a landing page that includes a bibliographic citation, a link to the published article, and a context statement and link for each supplemental file (see an example of a landing page at https://on.apa.org/2CmDGd6). Other journals may include links in the article that directly open the supplemental files. See Chapter 3 for more details on the role of supplemental materials in JARS. See the APA website (https://on.apa.org/2Qo7OhX) for additional information about supplemental materials.

Format

2.16 Importance of Format

Use the guidelines in this section to format all APA Style papers. The physical appearance of a paper can enhance or detract from it. A well-prepared paper encourages editors and reviewers, as well as instructors in the case of student work, to view authors' work as professional. In contrast, mechanical flaws can lead reviewers or instructors to misinterpret content or question the authors' expertise or attention to detail, and students may receive a lower grade because of formatting errors. For manuscripts being submitted for publication, publishers will use your word-processing file to produce the typeset version of your article, so it is important that you properly format your article.

2.17 Order of Pages

Arrange the pages of the paper in the following order:

- title page (page 1)
- abstract (start on a new page after the title page)
- text (start on a new page after the abstract, or after the title page if the paper does not have an abstract)
- references (start on a new page after the end of the text)
- footnotes (start on a new page after the references)
- tables (start each on a new page after the footnotes)
- figures (start each on a new page after the tables)
- appendices (start each on a new page after the tables and/or figures)

APA Style provides options for the display of footnotes, tables, and figures. Footnotes may appear either in the footer of the page where they are first mentioned (see Section 2.13) or on a separate page after the references. Tables and figures may be embedded within the text after they have been mentioned, or each table and figure can be displayed on a separate page after the footnotes (or after the references if there is no footnotes page; see Section 7.6).

2.18 Page Header

All papers should contain the page number, flush right, in the header of every page. Use the automatic page-numbering function of your word-processing program to insert page numbers in the top right corner; do not type page numbers manually. The title page is page number 1.

Manuscripts being submitted for publication should contain the running head (see Section 2.8) in the page header in addition to the page number. When both elements appear, the running head should be flush left and the page number should be flush right. Student papers need only the page number in the page header, unless the instructor or institution also requires a running head.

2.19 Font

APA Style papers should be written in a font that is accessible to all users. Historically, sans serif fonts have been preferred for online works and serif fonts for print works; however, modern screen resolutions can typically accommodate either type of font, and people who use assistive technologies can adjust font settings to their preferences. Thus, a variety of font choices are permitted in APA Style; also check with your publisher, instructor, or institution for any requirements regarding font.

Use the same font throughout the text of the paper. Options include

- a sans serif font such as 11-point Calibri, 11-point Arial, or 10-point Lucida Sans Unicode or
- a serif font such as 12-point Times New Roman, 11-point Georgia, or normal (10-point) Computer Modern (the latter is the default font for LaTeX).

We recommend these fonts because they are legible and widely available and because they include special characters such as math symbols and Greek letters.

An APA Style paper may contain other fonts or font sizes under the following circumstances:

- Within figure images, use a sans serif font with a type size between 8 and 14 points.
- When presenting computer code, use a monospace font, such as 10-point Lucida Console or 10-point Courier New.
- When presenting a footnote in a page footer, the default footnote settings of your word-processing program are acceptable (e.g., 10-point font with single line spacing).

Because different fonts take up different amounts of space on the page, we recommend using word count rather than page count to gauge paper length (see Section 2.25). See the APA Style website (https://apastyle.apa.org) for further discussion of font and accessible typography.

2.20 Special Characters

Special characters are accented letters and other diacritical marks, Greek letters, math signs, and symbols. Type special characters using the special character functions of your word-processing program or a plug-in such as MathType. Characters that are not available should be presented as images. For more information on Greek letters and mathematical symbols, see Sections 6.44 and 6.45.

2.21 Line Spacing

Double-space the entire paper, including the title page, abstract, text, headings, block quotations, reference list, table and figure notes, and appendices, with the following exceptions:

- **title page:** Elements of the title page are double-spaced, and an additional double-spaced blank line appears between the title and byline. At least one double-spaced blank line also appears between the final affiliation and any author note (see Figure 2.1).

- **table body and figure image:** The table body (cells) and words within the image part of a figure may be single-spaced, one-and-a-half-spaced, or double-spaced, depending on what format creates the most effective presentation of the data. If text appears on the same page as a table or figure, insert a double-spaced blank line between the text and the table or figure (for more information on placement of tables and figures, see Section 7.6).

- **footnotes:** Footnotes that appear at the bottom of the page on which they are called out should be single-spaced and formatted with the default settings of your word-processing program. Footnotes that appear on their own page after the references should be formatted like regular paragraphs of text—that is, indented and double-spaced.

- **displayed equations:** It is permissible to apply triple- or quadruple-spacing in special circumstances, such as before and after a displayed equation.

It is not necessary to add blank lines before or after headings, even if a heading falls at the end of a page. Do not add extra spacing between paragraphs.

2.22 Margins

Use 1-in. (2.54-cm) margins on all sides (top, bottom, left, and right) of the page. This is the default page margin in most word-processing programs. Dissertations and theses may have different requirements if they are to be bound (e.g., 1.5-in. left margins).

2.23 Paragraph Alignment

Align the text to the left and leave the right margin uneven ("ragged"). Do not use full justification, which adjusts the spacing between words to make all lines the same length (flush with the margins). Do not manually divide words at the end of a line, and do not use the hyphenation function to break words at the ends of lines. Do not manually insert line breaks into long DOIs or URLs; however, breaks in DOIs or URLs applied automatically by a word-processing program are permissible.

2.24 Paragraph Indentation

Indent the first line of every paragraph 0.5 in. For consistency, use the tab key or the automatic paragraph-formatting function of your word-processing program. The default settings in most word-processing programs are acceptable. The remaining lines of the paragraph should be left-aligned.

Exceptions to these paragraph indentation requirements are as follows:

- For professional papers, the title (in bold), byline, and affiliations on the title page should be centered (see Figure 2.1).
- For student papers, the title (in bold), byline, affiliations, course number and name, instructor, and assignment date should be centered (see Figure 2.2).
- Section labels should be centered (and bold; see Section 2.28).
- The first line of the abstract should be flush left (not indented; see Section 2.9).
- The entirety of a block quotation should be indented from the left margin 0.5 in. If the block quotation spans more than one paragraph, the first line of the second and any subsequent paragraphs of the block quotation should be indented another 0.5 in., such that those first lines are indented a total of 1 in. (see Section 8.27).
- Level 1 headings should be centered (and in bold), and Level 2 and 3 headings should be left-aligned (and in bold or bold italic, respectively; see Section 2.27).
- Table and figure numbers (Sections 7.10 and 7.24, respectively), titles (Sections 7.11 and 7.25), and notes (Sections 7.14 and 7.28) should be flush left.
- Reference list entries should have a hanging indent of 0.5 in. (see Section 2.12).
- Appendix labels and titles should be centered (and bold; see Section 2.14).

2.25 Paper Length

Journals differ in the average length of articles they publish; consult the journal's instructions for authors to determine the appropriate length for the type of article you are submitting. The length for student papers is determined by the assignment guidelines.

If a paper exceeds the target length, shorten it by stating points clearly and directly, confining discussion to the specific problem under investigation, deleting or combining data displays, eliminating repetition across sections, and writing in the active voice. For guidance on improving sentence and paragraph length, see Section 4.6. A professional paper that is still too long may need to be divided into two or more papers, each with a more specific focus (however, see Section 1.16 on piecemeal publication).

Paper length targets may be specified by either page count or word count; we recommend word count because different fonts are slightly different sizes and may produce variations in the number of pages. In general, to determine the page count, count every page, including the title page and reference list. Likewise, to determine word count, count every word from beginning to end, including all in-text citations, reference entries, tables, figures (other than words in a figure image, which may not be captured by word count), and appendices. The default settings of the word-count function of your word-processing program are acceptable for determining the word count. Do not count text in the page header (i.e., running head and/or page numbers) or manually add any words within figure images to the word count (these words are generally not included in the automatic word count in programs such as Microsoft Word, Academic Writer, or Google Docs). If the journal to which you are submitting has different specifications for determining the page count or word count, follow the instructions of the journal.

Organization

2.26 Principles of Organization

In scholarly writing, sound organizational structure is the key to clear, precise, and logical communication. Before beginning to write, consider the best paper length and structure for your findings. Ordering your thoughts logically at both sentence and paragraph levels will also strengthen the impact of your writing.

Headings in a document identify the topic or purpose of the content within each section. Headings help readers become familiar with how a paper's content is organized, allowing them to easily find the information they seek. Headings should be succinct yet long enough to describe the content; see the sample papers at the end of this chapter for examples of effective headings. Concise headings help readers anticipate key points and track the development of your argument. Headings that are well formatted and clearly worded aid both visual and nonvisual readers of all abilities. Headings must be clearly distinguishable from the text. For a deeper discussion of how to effectively create and use headings (and related text) for all users (including those using assistive technologies), visit the APA Style website (https://apastyle.apa.org).

There are five possible levels of heading in APA Style (see Section 2.27), and all topics of equal importance should have the same level of heading. For example, in a multiexperiment paper, the headings for the Method and Results sections for Experiment 1 should be the same level as the headings for the Method and Results sections for Experiment 2, with parallel wording. In a single-experiment paper, the Method, Results, and Discussion sections should all have the same heading level. Avoid having only one subsection heading within a section, just like in an outline; use at least two subsection headings within a section, or use none (e.g., in an outline, a section numbered with a Roman numeral would be divided into either a minimum of A and B subsections or no subsections; an A subsection could not stand alone).

2.27 Heading Levels

APA Style headings have five possible levels: Level 1 headings are used for top-level or main sections, Level 2 headings are subsections of Level 1, and so on. Regardless of the number of levels of subheading within a section, the heading structure for all sections follows the same top-down progression. Each section starts with the highest level of heading, even if one section has fewer levels of subheading than another section. For example, in a paper with Level 1 Method, Results, and Discussion headings, the Method and Results sections may each have two levels of subheading (Levels 2 and 3), and the Discussion section may have only one level of subheading (Level 2). Thus, there would be three levels of heading for the paper overall.

Headings in the Introduction. Because the first paragraphs of a paper are understood to be introductory, the heading "Introduction" is not needed. Do not begin a paper with an "Introduction" heading; the paper title at the top of the first page of text acts as a de facto Level 1 heading (see Figure 2.4). For subsections within the introduction, use Level 2 headings for the first level of subsection, Level 3 for subsections of any Level 2 headings, and so on. After the introduction (regardless of whether it includes headings), use a Level 1 heading for the next main section of the paper (e.g., Method).

Number of Headings in a Paper. The number of levels of heading needed for a paper depends on its length and complexity; three is average. If only one level of heading is needed, use Level 1; if two levels are needed, use Levels 1 and 2; if three levels are needed, use Levels 1, 2, and 3; and so forth. Use only the number of headings necessary to differentiate distinct sections in your paper; short student papers may not require any headings. Do not label headings with numbers or letters.[2]

Format. Table 2.3 shows how to format each level of heading, Figure 2.4 demonstrates the use of headings in the introduction, and Figure 2.5 lists all the headings used in a sample paper in correct format. The sample papers at the end of this chapter also show the use of headings in context.

Table 2.3 Format for the Five Levels of Heading in APA Style

Level	Format
1	<div align="center">**Centered, Bold, Title Case Heading**</div> Text begins as a new paragraph.
2	**Flush Left, Bold, Title Case Heading** Text begins as a new paragraph.
3	***Flush Left, Bold Italic, Title Case Heading*** Text begins as a new paragraph.
4	**Indented, Bold, Title Case Heading, Ending With a Period.** Text begins on the same line and continues as a regular paragraph.
5	***Indented, Bold Italic, Title Case Heading, Ending With a Period.*** Text begins on the same line and continues as a regular paragraph.

Note. In title case, most words are capitalized (see Section 6.17).

Figure 2.4 Use of Headings in a Sample Introduction

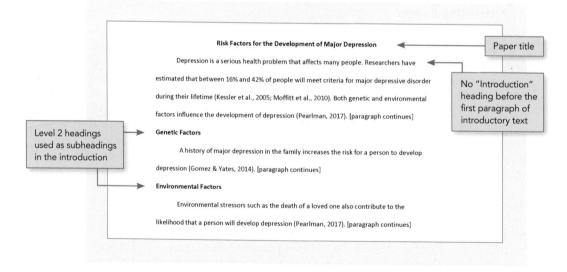

Figure 2.5 Format of Headings in a Sample Paper

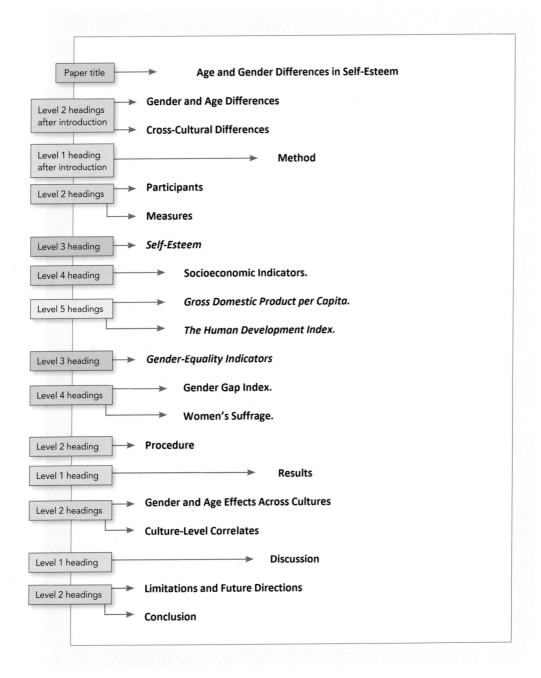

2.28 Section Labels

Section labels include "Author Note," "Abstract," the paper title at the top of the first page of text, "References," "Footnotes," and "Appendix A" (and other appendix labels). Place section labels on a separate line at the top of the page on which the section begins, in bold and centered.

ELEMENTS & FORMAT

Sample Papers

Sample Professional Paper

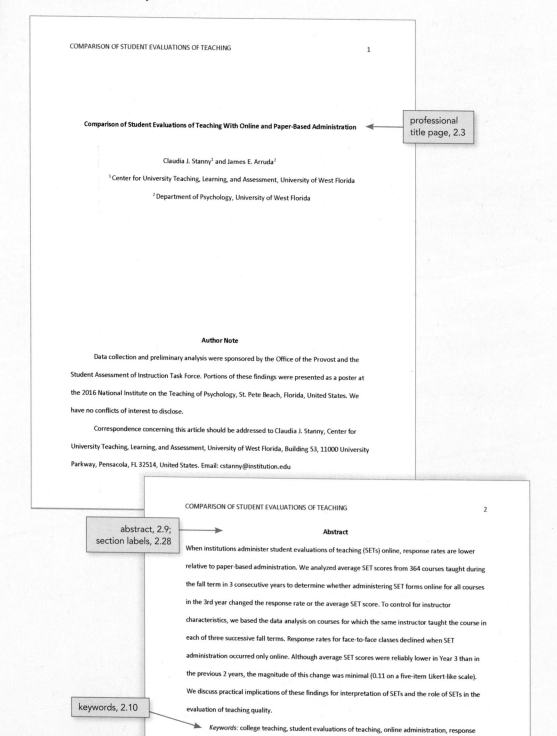

COMPARISON OF STUDENT EVALUATIONS OF TEACHING   1

Comparison of Student Evaluations of Teaching With Online and Paper-Based Administration

Claudia J. Stanny[1] and James E. Arruda[2]

[1] Center for University Teaching, Learning, and Assessment, University of West Florida

[2] Department of Psychology, University of West Florida

Author Note

Data collection and preliminary analysis were sponsored by the Office of the Provost and the Student Assessment of Instruction Task Force. Portions of these findings were presented as a poster at the 2016 National Institute on the Teaching of Psychology, St. Pete Beach, Florida, United States. We have no conflicts of interest to disclose.

Correspondence concerning this article should be addressed to Claudia J. Stanny, Center for University Teaching, Learning, and Assessment, University of West Florida, Building 53, 11000 University Parkway, Pensacola, FL 32514, United States. Email: cstanny@institution.edu

professional title page, 2.3

COMPARISON OF STUDENT EVALUATIONS OF TEACHING   2

abstract, 2.9; section labels, 2.28

Abstract

When institutions administer student evaluations of teaching (SETs) online, response rates are lower relative to paper-based administration. We analyzed average SET scores from 364 courses taught during the fall term in 3 consecutive years to determine whether administering SET forms online for all courses in the 3rd year changed the response rate or the average SET score. To control for instructor characteristics, we based the data analysis on courses for which the same instructor taught the course in each of three successive fall terms. Response rates for face-to-face classes declined when SET administration occurred only online. Although average SET scores were reliably lower in Year 3 than in the previous 2 years, the magnitude of this change was minimal (0.11 on a five-item Likert-like scale). We discuss practical implications of these findings for interpretation of SETs and the role of SETs in the evaluation of teaching quality.

keywords, 2.10

Keywords: college teaching, student evaluations of teaching, online administration, response rate, assessment

ELEMENTS & FORMAT

Sample Professional Paper *(continued)*

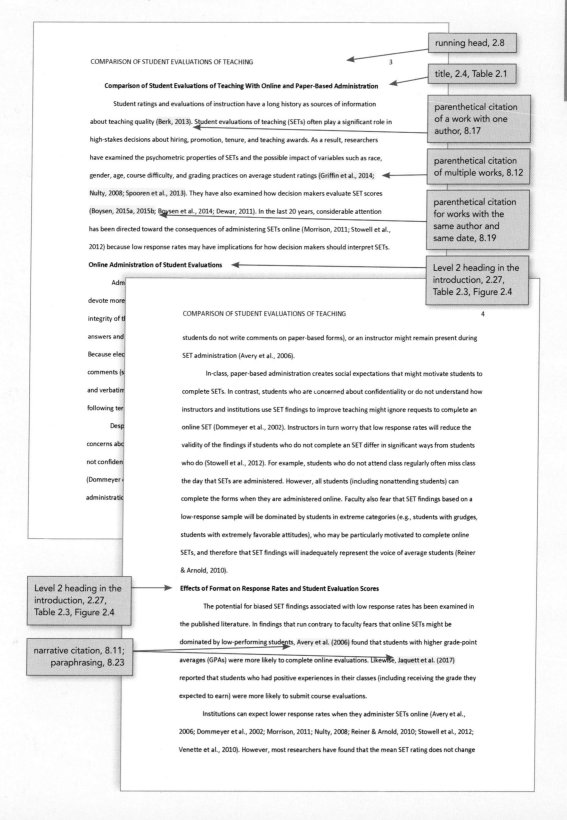

COMPARISON OF STUDENT EVALUATIONS OF TEACHING   3

running head, 2.8

Comparison of Student Evaluations of Teaching With Online and Paper-Based Administration

title, 2.4, Table 2.1

Student ratings and evaluations of instruction have a long history as sources of information about teaching quality (Berk, 2013). Student evaluations of teaching (SETs) often play a significant role in high-stakes decisions about hiring, promotion, tenure, and teaching awards. As a result, researchers have examined the psychometric properties of SETs and the possible impact of variables such as race, gender, age, course difficulty, and grading practices on average student ratings (Griffin et al., 2014; Nulty, 2008; Spooren et al., 2013). They have also examined how decision makers evaluate SET scores (Boysen, 2015a, 2015b; Boysen et al., 2014; Dewar, 2011). In the last 20 years, considerable attention has been directed toward the consequences of administering SETs online (Morrison, 2011; Stowell et al., 2012) because low response rates may have implications for how decision makers should interpret SETs.

parenthetical citation of a work with one author, 8.17

parenthetical citation of multiple works, 8.12

parenthetical citation for works with the same author and same date, 8.19

Online Administration of Student Evaluations

Level 2 heading in the introduction, 2.27, Table 2.3, Figure 2.4

Adm...
devote more...
integrity of t...
answers and...
Because elec...
comments (s...
and verbatim...
following ter...
Desp...
concerns abc...
not confiden...
(Dommeyer...
administratic...

COMPARISON OF STUDENT EVALUATIONS OF TEACHING   4

students do not write comments on paper-based forms), or an instructor might remain present during SET administration (Avery et al., 2006).

In-class, paper-based administration creates social expectations that might motivate students to complete SETs. In contrast, students who are concerned about confidentiality or do not understand how instructors and institutions use SET findings to improve teaching might ignore requests to complete an online SET (Dommeyer et al., 2002). Instructors in turn worry that low response rates will reduce the validity of the findings if students who do not complete an SET differ in significant ways from students who do (Stowell et al., 2012). For example, students who do not attend class regularly often miss class the day that SETs are administered. However, all students (including nonattending students) can complete the forms when they are administered online. Faculty also fear that SET findings based on a low-response sample will be dominated by students in extreme categories (e.g., students with grudges, students with extremely favorable attitudes), who may be particularly motivated to complete online SETs, and therefore that SET findings will inadequately represent the voice of average students (Reiner & Arnold, 2010).

Effects of Format on Response Rates and Student Evaluation Scores

Level 2 heading in the introduction, 2.27, Table 2.3, Figure 2.4

narrative citation, 8.11; paraphrasing, 8.23

The potential for biased SET findings associated with low response rates has been examined in the published literature. In findings that run contrary to faculty fears that online SETs might be dominated by low-performing students, Avery et al. (2006) found that students with higher grade-point averages (GPAs) were more likely to complete online evaluations. Likewise, Jaquett et al. (2017) reported that students who had positive experiences in their classes (including receiving the grade they expected to earn) were more likely to submit course evaluations.

Institutions can expect lower response rates when they administer SETs online (Avery et al., 2006; Dommeyer et al., 2002; Morrison, 2011; Nulty, 2008; Reiner & Arnold, 2010; Stowell et al., 2012; Venette et al., 2010). However, most researchers have found that the mean SET rating does not change

Sample Professional Paper *(continued)*

COMPARISON OF STUDENT EVALUATIONS OF TEACHING   5

significantly when they compare SETs administered on paper with those completed online. These

findings have been replicated in multiple settings using a variety of research methods (Avery et al., 2006;

Dommeyer et al., 2004; Morrison, 2011; Stowell et al., 2012; Venette et al., 2010).

Exceptions to this pattern of minimal or nonsignificant differences in average SET scores

appeared in Nowell et al. (2010) and Morrison (2011), who examined a sample of 29 business courses.

Both studies reported lower average scores when SETs were administered online. However, they also

found that SET scores for individual items varied more within an instructor when SETs were

administered online versus on paper. Students who completed SETs on paper tended to record the same

response for all questions, whereas students who completed the forms online tended to respond

differently to different questions. Both research groups argued that scores obtained online might not be

directly comparable to scores obtained through paper-based forms. They advised that institutions

administer SETs entirely online or entirely on paper to ensure consistent, comparable evaluations

across faculty.

Each university presents a unique environment and culture that could influence how seriously

students take SETs and how they respond to decisions to administer SETs online. Although a few large-

scale studies of the impact of online administration exist (Reiner & Arnold, 2010; Risquez et al., 2015), a

local replication answers questions about characteristics unique to that institution and generates

evidence about the generalizability of existing findings.

Purpose of the Present Study

In the present study we examined patterns of responses for online and paper-based SET scores

at a midsized, regional, comprehensive university in the United States. We posed two questions: First,

does the response rate or the average SET score change when an institution administers SET forms

online instead of on paper? Second, what is the minimal response rate required to produce stable

average SET scores for an instructor? Whereas much earlier research relied on small samples often

---

Annotations (callout boxes):

- parenthetical citation of multiple works, 8.12
- narrative citation used to paraphrase methods from two studies, 8.23
- long paraphrase, 8.24
- Level 2 heading in the introduction, 2.27, Table 2.3, Figure 2.4

Sample Professional Paper (continued)

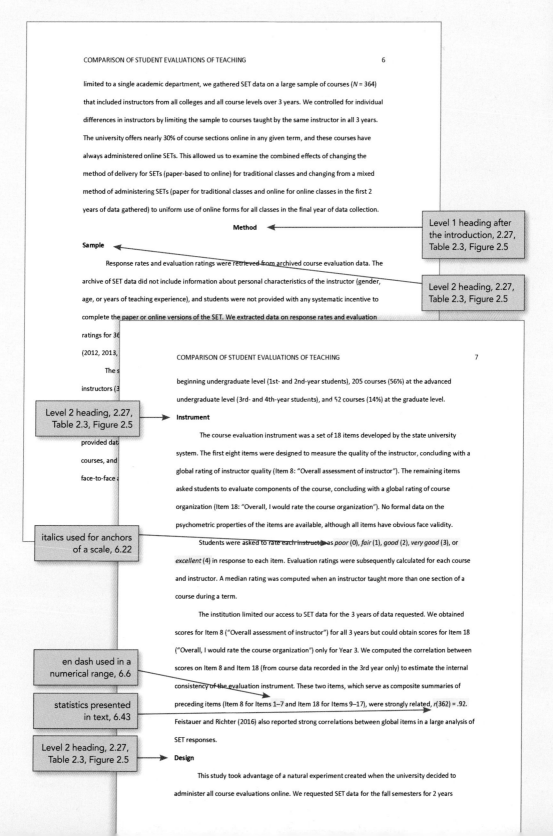

COMPARISON OF STUDENT EVALUATIONS OF TEACHING   6

limited to a single academic department, we gathered SET data on a large sample of courses (N = 364)

that included instructors from all colleges and all course levels over 3 years. We controlled for individual

differences in instructors by limiting the sample to courses taught by the same instructor in all 3 years.

The university offers nearly 30% of course sections online in any given term, and these courses have

always administered online SETs. This allowed us to examine the combined effects of changing the

method of delivery for SETs (paper-based to online) for traditional classes and changing from a mixed

method of administering SETs (paper for traditional classes and online for online classes in the first 2

years of data gathered) to uniform use of online forms for all classes in the final year of data collection.

Method ◄—

> Level 1 heading after the introduction, 2.27, Table 2.3, Figure 2.5

Sample ◄—

> Level 2 heading, 2.27, Table 2.3, Figure 2.5

Response rates and evaluation ratings were retrieved from archived course evaluation data. The

archive of SET data did not include information about personal characteristics of the instructor (gender,

age, or years of teaching experience), and students were not provided with any systematic incentive to

complete the paper or online versions of the SET. We extracted data on response rates and evaluation

ratings for 36

(2012, 2013,

The s

instructors (3

> Level 2 heading, 2.27, Table 2.3, Figure 2.5

provided dat

courses, and

face-to-face a

> italics used for anchors of a scale, 6.22

COMPARISON OF STUDENT EVALUATIONS OF TEACHING   7

beginning undergraduate level (1st- and 2nd-year students), 205 courses (56%) at the advanced

undergraduate level (3rd- and 4th-year students), and 52 courses (14%) at the graduate level.

Instrument

The course evaluation instrument was a set of 18 items developed by the state university

system. The first eight items were designed to measure the quality of the instructor, concluding with a

global rating of instructor quality (Item 8: "Overall assessment of instructor"). The remaining items

asked students to evaluate components of the course, concluding with a global rating of course

organization (Item 18: "Overall, I would rate the course organization"). No formal data on the

psychometric properties of the items are available, although all items have obvious face validity.

Students were asked to rate each instructor as *poor* (0), *fair* (1), *good* (2), *very good* (3), or

excellent (4) in response to each item. Evaluation ratings were subsequently calculated for each course

and instructor. A median rating was computed when an instructor taught more than one section of a

course during a term.

The institution limited our access to SET data for the 3 years of data requested. We obtained

scores for Item 8 ("Overall assessment of instructor") for all 3 years but could obtain scores for Item 18

("Overall, I would rate the course organization") only for Year 3. We computed the correlation between

> en dash used in a numerical range, 6.6

scores on Item 8 and Item 18 (from course data recorded in the 3rd year only) to estimate the internal

consistency of the evaluation instrument. These two items, which serve as composite summaries of

> statistics presented in text, 6.43

preceding items (Item 8 for Items 1–7 and Item 18 for Items 9–17), were strongly related, r(362) = .92.

Feistauer and Richter (2016) also reported strong correlations between global items in a large analysis of

SET responses.

> Level 2 heading, 2.27, Table 2.3, Figure 2.5

Design

This study took advantage of a natural experiment created when the university decided to

administer all course evaluations online. We requested SET data for the fall semesters for 2 years

Sample Professional Paper (continued)

COMPARISON OF STUDENT EVALUATIONS OF TEACHING   8

preceding the change, when students completed paper-based SET forms for face-to-face courses and

online SET forms for online courses, and data for the fall semester of the implementation year, when

students completed online SET forms for all courses. We used a 2 × 3 × 3 factorial design in which course

delivery method (face to face and online) and course level (beginning undergraduate, advanced

undergraduate, and graduate) were between-subjects factors and evaluation year (Year 1: 2012, Year 2:

2013, and Year 3: 2014) was a repeated-measures factor. The dependent measures were the response

rate (measured as a percentage of class enrollment) and the rating for Item 8 ("Overall assessment of

instructor").

   Data analysis was limited to scores on Item 8 because the institution agreed to release data on

this one item only. Data for scores on Item 18 were made available for SET forms administered in Year 3

to address questions about variation in responses across items. The strong correlation between scores

on Item 8 and scores on Item 18 suggested that Item 8 could be used as a surrogate for all the items.

These two items were of particular interest because faculty, department chairs, and review committees

frequently rely on these two items as stand-alone indicators of teaching quality for annual evaluations

and tenure and promotion reviews.

Results

Response Rates

   Response rates are presented in Table 1. The findings indicate that response rates for face-to-

face courses were much higher than for online courses, but only when face-to-face course evaluations

were administered in the classroom. In the Year 3 administration, when all course evaluations were

administered online, response rates for face-to-face courses declined (M = 47.18%, SD = 20.11), but

were still slightly higher than for online courses (M = 41.60%, SD = 18.23). These findings produced a

statistically significant interaction between course delivery method and evaluation year, $F(1.78, 716)$ =

Level 1 heading, 2.27, Table 2.3, Figure 2.5

Level 2 heading, 2.27, Table 2.3, Figure 2.5

table called out in text, 7.5; table numbers, 7.10

statistics presented in text, 6.43

Sample Professional Paper *(continued)*

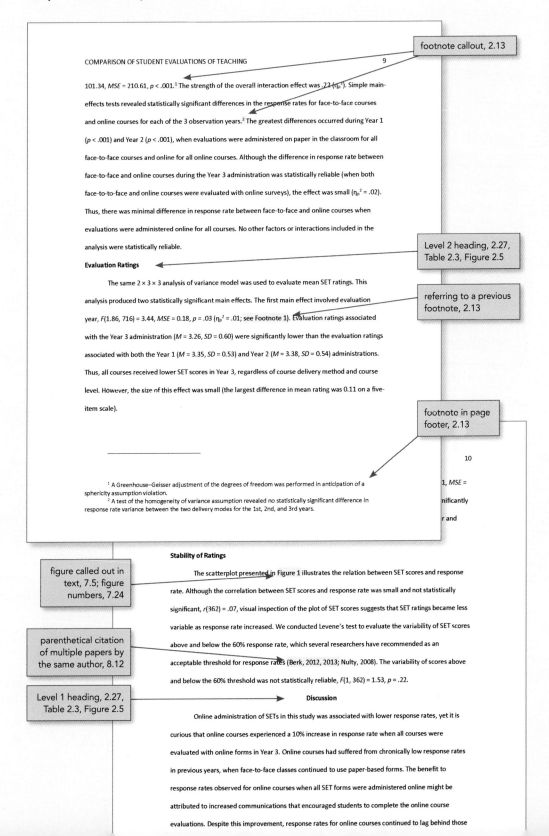

COMPARISON OF STUDENT EVALUATIONS OF TEACHING   9

101.34, MSE = 210.61, p < .001.[1] The strength of the overall interaction effect was .22 (η_p^2). Simple main-effects tests revealed statistically significant differences in the response rates for face-to-face courses and online courses for each of the 3 observation years.[2] The greatest differences occurred during Year 1 (p < .001) and Year 2 (p < .001), when evaluations were administered on paper in the classroom for all face-to-face courses and online for all online courses. Although the difference in response rate between face-to-face and online courses during the Year 3 administration was statistically reliable (when both face-to-to-face and online courses were evaluated with online surveys), the effect was small (η_p^2 = .02). Thus, there was minimal difference in response rate between face-to-face and online courses when evaluations were administered online for all courses. No other factors or interactions included in the analysis were statistically reliable.

Evaluation Ratings

The same 2 × 3 × 3 analysis of variance model was used to evaluate mean SET ratings. This analysis produced two statistically significant main effects. The first main effect involved evaluation year, $F(1.86, 716)$ = 3.44, MSE = 0.18, p = .03 (η_p^2 = .01; see Footnote 1). Evaluation ratings associated with the Year 3 administration (M = 3.26, SD = 0.60) were significantly lower than the evaluation ratings associated with both the Year 1 (M = 3.35, SD = 0.53) and Year 2 (M = 3.38, SD = 0.54) administrations. Thus, all courses received lower SET scores in Year 3, regardless of course delivery method and course level. However, the size of this effect was small (the largest difference in mean rating was 0.11 on a five-item scale).

_____

[1] A Greenhouse–Geisser adjustment of the degrees of freedom was performed in anticipation of a sphericity assumption violation.
[2] A test of the homogeneity of variance assumption revealed no statistically significant difference in response rate variance between the two delivery modes for the 1st, 2nd, and 3rd years.

10

1, MSE =

nificantly

r and

Stability of Ratings

The scatterplot presented in Figure 1 illustrates the relation between SET scores and response rate. Although the correlation between SET scores and response rate was small and not statistically significant, $r(362)$ = .07, visual inspection of the plot of SET scores suggests that SET ratings became less variable as response rate increased. We conducted Levene's test to evaluate the variability of SET scores above and below the 60% response rate, which several researchers have recommended as an acceptable threshold for response rates (Berk, 2012, 2013; Nulty, 2008). The variability of scores above and below the 60% threshold was not statistically reliable, $F(1, 362)$ = 1.53, p = .22.

Discussion

Online administration of SETs in this study was associated with lower response rates, yet it is curious that online courses experienced a 10% increase in response rate when all courses were evaluated with online forms in Year 3. Online courses had suffered from chronically low response rates in previous years, when face-to-face classes continued to use paper-based forms. The benefit to response rates observed for online courses when all SET forms were administered online might be attributed to increased communications that encouraged students to complete the online course evaluations. Despite this improvement, response rates for online courses continued to lag behind those

---

Annotation callouts:

footnote callout, 2.13

Level 2 heading, 2.27, Table 2.3, Figure 2.5

referring to a previous footnote, 2.13

footnote in page footer, 2.13

figure called out in text, 7.5; figure numbers, 7.24

parenthetical citation of multiple papers by the same author, 8.12

Level 1 heading, 2.27, Table 2.3, Figure 2.5

ELEMENTS & FORMAT

Sample Professional Paper *(continued)*

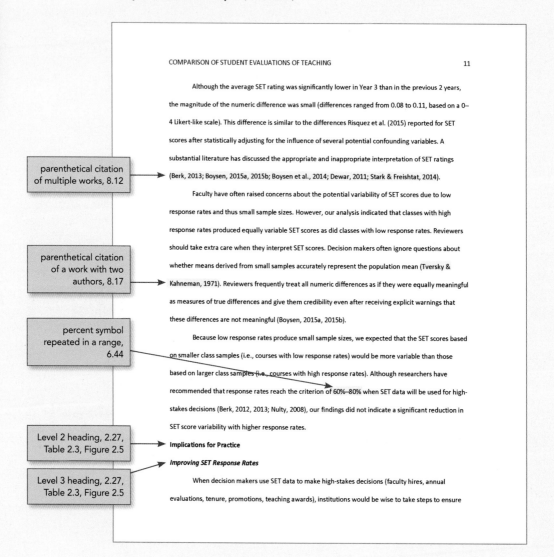

COMPARISON OF STUDENT EVALUATIONS OF TEACHING   11

Although the average SET rating was significantly lower in Year 3 than in the previous 2 years, the magnitude of the numeric difference was small (differences ranged from 0.08 to 0.11, based on a 0–4 Likert-like scale). This difference is similar to the differences Risquez et al. (2015) reported for SET scores after statistically adjusting for the influence of several potential confounding variables. A substantial literature has discussed the appropriate and inappropriate interpretation of SET ratings (Berk, 2013; Boysen, 2015a, 2015b; Boysen et al., 2014; Dewar, 2011; Stark & Freishtat, 2014).

Faculty have often raised concerns about the potential variability of SET scores due to low response rates and thus small sample sizes. However, our analysis indicated that classes with high response rates produced equally variable SET scores as did classes with low response rates. Reviewers should take extra care when they interpret SET scores. Decision makers often ignore questions about whether means derived from small samples accurately represent the population mean (Tversky & Kahneman, 1971). Reviewers frequently treat all numeric differences as if they were equally meaningful as measures of true differences and give them credibility even after receiving explicit warnings that these differences are not meaningful (Boysen, 2015a, 2015b).

Because low response rates produce small sample sizes, we expected that the SET scores based on smaller class samples (i.e., courses with low response rates) would be more variable than those based on larger class samples (i.e., courses with high response rates). Although researchers have recommended that response rates reach the criterion of 60%–80% when SET data will be used for high-stakes decisions (Berk, 2012, 2013; Nulty, 2008), our findings did not indicate a significant reduction in SET score variability with higher response rates.

Implications for Practice

Improving SET Response Rates

When decision makers use SET data to make high-stakes decisions (faculty hires, annual evaluations, tenure, promotions, teaching awards), institutions would be wise to take steps to ensure

Annotations (left margin):

parenthetical citation of multiple works, 8.12

parenthetical citation of a work with two authors, 8.17

percent symbol repeated in a range, 6.44

Level 2 heading, 2.27, Table 2.3, Figure 2.5

Level 3 heading, 2.27, Table 2.3, Figure 2.5

Sample Professional Paper (continued)

that SETs have acceptable response rates. Researchers have discussed effective strategies to improve

response rates for SETs (Nulty, 2008; see also Berk, 2013; Dommeyer et al., 2004; Jaquett et al., 2016).

These strategies include offering empirically validated incentives, creating high-quality technical systems

with good human factors characteristics, and promoting an institutional culture that clearly supports the

use of SET data and other information to improve the quality of teaching and learning. Programs and

instructors must discuss why information from SETs is important for decision-making and provide

students with tangible evidence of how SET information guides decisions about curriculum

improvement. The institution should provide students with compelling evidence that the administration

system protects the confidentiality of their responses.

Evaluating SET Scores

In addition to ensuring adequate response rates on SETs, decision makers should demand

multiple sources of evidence about teaching quality (Buller, 2012). High-stakes decisions should never

rely exclusively on numeric data from SETs. Reviewers often treat SET ratings as a surrogate for a

measure of the impact an instructor has on student learning. However, a recent meta-analysis (Uttl et

al., 2017) questioned whether SET scores have any relation to student learning. Reviewers need

evidence in addition to SET ratings to evaluate teaching, such as evidence of the instructor's disciplinary

content expertise, skill with classroom management, ability to engage learners with lectures or other

activities, impact on student learning, or success with efforts to modify and improve courses and

teaching strategies (Berk, 2013; Stark & Freishtat, 2014). As with other forms of assessment, any one

measure may be limited in terms of the quality of information it provides. Therefore, multiple measures

are more informative than any single measure.

A

include su

assignmer

Callout boxes (right margin):

"see also" citation, 8.12

Level 3 heading, 2.27, Table 2.3, Figure 2.5

parenthetical citation of a work with one author, 8.17

parenthetical citation of two works, 8.12

samples of student work. Course syllabi can identify intended learning outcomes; describe instructional

strategies that reflect the rigor of the course (required assignments and grading practices); and provide

other information about course content, design, instructional strategies, and instructor interactions with

students (Palmer et al., 2014; Stanny et al., 2015).

Conclusion

Psychology has a long history of devising creative strategies to measure the "unmeasurable,"

whether the targeted variable is a mental process, an attitude, or the quality of teaching (e.g., Webb et

al., 1966). In addition, psychologists have documented various heuristics and biases that contribute to

the misinterpretation of quantitative data (Gilovich et al., 2002), including SET scores (Boysen, 2015a,

2015b; Boysen et al., 2014). These skills enable psychologists to offer multiple solutions to the challenge

posed by the need to objectively evaluate the quality of teaching and the impact of teaching on student

learning.

Online administration of SET forms presents multiple desirable features, including rapid

feedback to instructors, economy, and support for environmental sustainability. However, institutions

should adopt implementation procedures that do not undermine the usefulness of the data gathered.

Moreover, institutions should be wary of emphasizing procedures that produce high response rates only

to lull faculty into believing that SET data can be the primary (or only) metric used for high-stakes

decisions about the quality of faculty teaching. Instead, decision makers should expect to use multiple

Callout boxes (left margin):

Level 2 heading, 2.27, Table 2.3, Figure 2.5

quotation marks used to indicate an ironic comment, 6.7

Sample Professional Paper *(continued)*

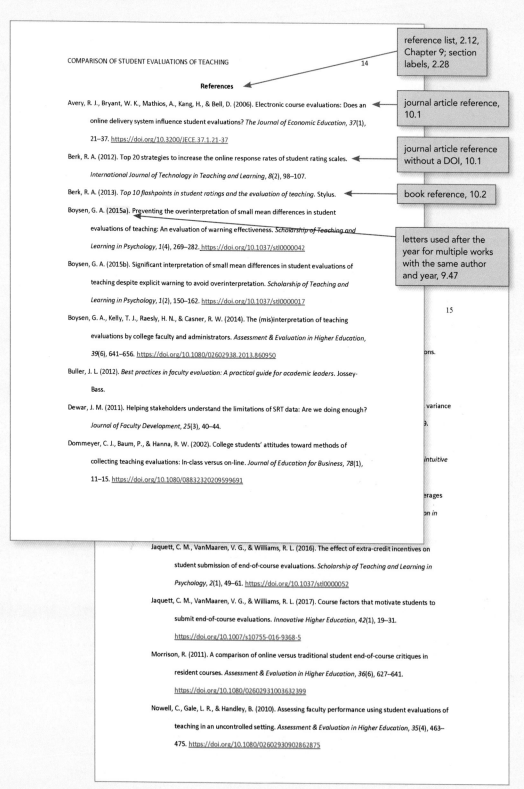

COMPARISON OF STUDENT EVALUATIONS OF TEACHING   14

reference list, 2.12, Chapter 9; section labels, 2.28

References

Avery, R. J., Bryant, W. K., Mathios, A., Kang, H., & Bell, D. (2006). Electronic course evaluations: Does an online delivery system influence student evaluations? *The Journal of Economic Education, 37*(1), 21–37. https://doi.org/10.3200/JECE.37.1.21-37

journal article reference, 10.1

Berk, R. A. (2012). Top 20 strategies to increase the online response rates of student rating scales. *International Journal of Technology in Teaching and Learning, 8*(2), 98–107.

journal article reference without a DOI, 10.1

Berk, R. A. (2013). *Top 10 flashpoints in student ratings and the evaluation of teaching.* Stylus.

book reference, 10.2

Boysen, G. A. (2015a). Preventing the overinterpretation of small mean differences in student evaluations of teaching: An evaluation of warning effectiveness. *Scholarship of Teaching and Learning in Psychology, 1*(4), 269–282. https://doi.org/10.1037/stl0000042

letters used after the year for multiple works with the same author and year, 9.47

Boysen, G. A. (2015b). Significant interpretation of small mean differences in student evaluations of teaching despite explicit warning to avoid overinterpretation. *Scholarship of Teaching and Learning in Psychology, 1*(2), 150–162. https://doi.org/10.1037/stl0000017

Boysen, G. A., Kelly, T. J., Raesly, H. N., & Casner, R. W. (2014). The (mis)interpretation of teaching evaluations by college faculty and administrators. *Assessment & Evaluation in Higher Education, 39*(6), 641–656. https://doi.org/10.1080/02602938.2013.860950

Buller, J. L. (2012). *Best practices in faculty evaluation: A practical guide for academic leaders.* Jossey-Bass.

Dewar, J. M. (2011). Helping stakeholders understand the limitations of SRT data: Are we doing enough? *Journal of Faculty Development, 25*(3), 40–44.

Dommeyer, C. J., Baum, P., & Hanna, R. W. (2002). College students' attitudes toward methods of collecting teaching evaluations: In-class versus on-line. *Journal of Education for Business, 78*(1), 11–15. https://doi.org/10.1080/08832320209599691

15

Jaquett, C. M., VanMaaren, V. G., & Williams, R. L. (2016). The effect of extra-credit incentives on student submission of end-of-course evaluations. *Scholarship of Teaching and Learning in Psychology, 2*(1), 49–61. https://doi.org/10.1037/stl0000052

Jaquett, C. M., VanMaaren, V. G., & Williams, R. L. (2017). Course factors that motivate students to submit end-of-course evaluations. *Innovative Higher Education, 42*(1), 19–31. https://doi.org/10.1007/s10755-016-9368-5

Morrison, R. (2011). A comparison of online versus traditional student end-of-course critiques in resident courses. *Assessment & Evaluation in Higher Education, 36*(6), 627–641. https://doi.org/10.1080/02602931003632399

Nowell, C., Gale, L. R., & Handley, B. (2010). Assessing faculty performance using student evaluations of teaching in an uncontrolled setting. *Assessment & Evaluation in Higher Education, 35*(4), 463–475. https://doi.org/10.1080/02602930902862875

Sample Professional Paper *(continued)*

COMPARISON OF STUDENT EVALUATIONS OF TEACHING   16

Nulty, D. D. (2008). The adequacy of response rates to online and paper surveys: What can be done?

Assessment & Evaluation in Higher Education, 33(3), 301–314.

https://doi.org/10.1080/02602930701293231

Palmer, M. S., Bach, D. J., & Streifer, A. C. (2014). Measuring the promise: A learning-focused syllabus

rubric. *To Improve the Academy: A Journal of Educational Development, 33*(1), 14–36.

https://doi.org/10.1002/tia2.20004

Reiner, C. M., & Arnold, K. E. (2010). Online course evaluation: Student and instructor perspectives and

assessment potential. *Assessment Update, 22*(2), 8–10. https://doi.org/10.1002/au.222

Risquez, A., Vaughan, E., & Murphy, M. (2015). Online student evaluations of teaching: What are we

sacrificing for the affordances of technology? *Assessment & Evaluation in Higher Education,*

40(1), 210–234. https://doi.org/10.1080/02602938.2014.890695

Spooren, P., Brockx, B., & Mortelmans, D. (2013). On the validity of student evaluation of teaching: The

state of the art. *Review of Educational Research, 83*(4), 598–642.

https://doi.org/10.3102/0034654313496870

Stanny, C. J., Gonzalez, M., & McGowan, B. (2015). Assessing the culture of teaching and learning

through a syllabus review. *Assessment & Evaluation in Higher Education, 40*(7), 898–913.

https://doi.org/10.1080/02602938.2014.956684

Stark, P. B., & Freishtat, R. (2014). An evaluation of course evaluations. *ScienceOpen Research.*

https://doi.org/10.14293/S2199-1006.1.SOR-EDU.AOFRQA.v1

Stowell, J. R

eva

http

Tversky, A.,

105

> title ending with a
> question mark, 9.19

> journal article
> reference with missing
> issue number, 9.26

COMPARISON OF STUDENT EVALUATIONS OF TEACHING   17

Uttl, B., White, C. A., & Gonzalez, D. W. (2017). Meta-analysis of faculty's teaching effectiveness: Student

evaluation of teaching ratings and student learning are not related. *Studies in Educational*

Evaluation, 54, 22–42. https://doi.org/10.1016/j.stueduc.2016.08.007

Venette, S., Sellnow, D., & McIntyre, K. (2010). Charting new territory: Assessing the online frontier of

student ratings of instruction. *Assessment & Evaluation in Higher Education, 35*(1), 101–115.

https://doi.org/10.1080/02602930802618336

Webb, E. J., Campbell, D. T., Schwartz, R. D., & Sechrest, L. (1966). *Unobtrusive measures: Nonreactive*

research in the social sciences. Rand McNally.

Sample Professional Paper (continued)

table number, 7.10

table title, 7.11

table note, 7.14

figure number, 7.24

figure title, 7.25

figure note, 7.28

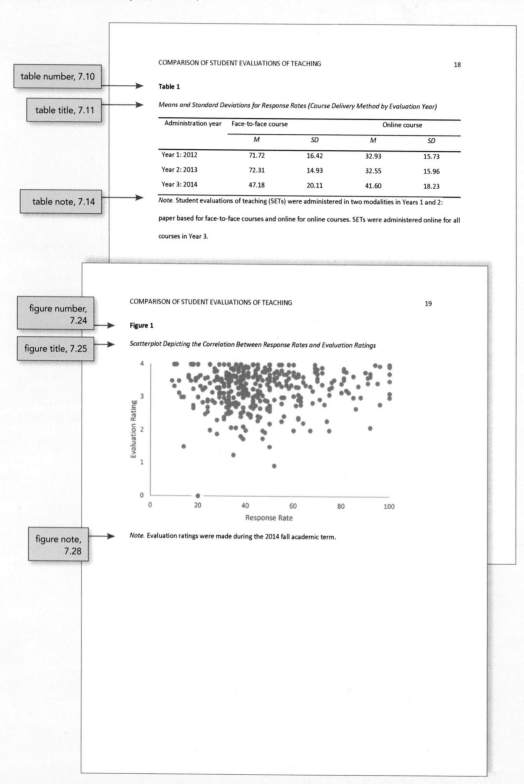

COMPARISON OF STUDENT EVALUATIONS OF TEACHING   18

Table 1

Means and Standard Deviations for Response Rates (Course Delivery Method by Evaluation Year)

Administration year	Face-to-face course		Online course	
	M	SD	M	SD
Year 1: 2012	71.72	16.42	32.93	15.73
Year 2: 2013	72.31	14.93	32.55	15.96
Year 3: 2014	47.18	20.11	41.60	18.23

Note. Student evaluations of teaching (SETs) were administered in two modalities in Years 1 and 2: paper based for face-to-face courses and online for online courses. SETs were administered online for all courses in Year 3.

COMPARISON OF STUDENT EVALUATIONS OF TEACHING   19

Figure 1

Scatterplot Depicting the Correlation Between Response Rates and Evaluation Ratings

Note. Evaluation ratings were made during the 2014 fall academic term.

Sample Student Paper

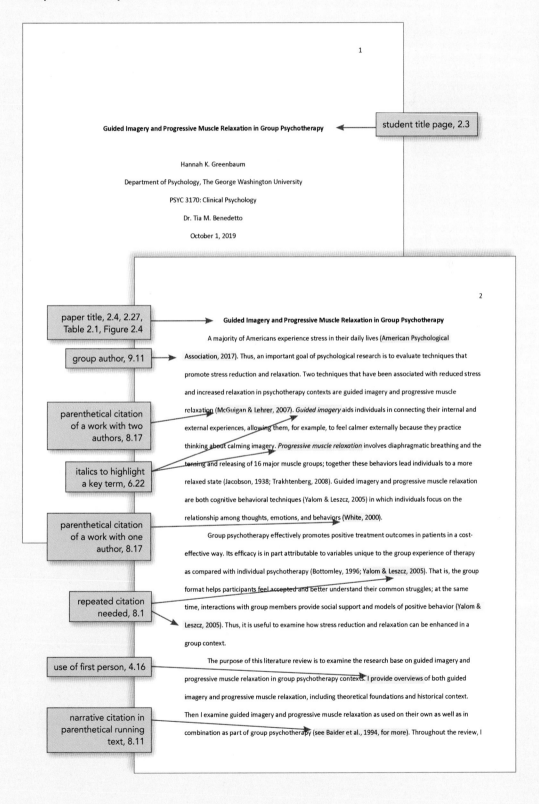

student title page, 2.3

Guided Imagery and Progressive Muscle Relaxation in Group Psychotherapy

Hannah K. Greenbaum

Department of Psychology, The George Washington University

PSYC 3170: Clinical Psychology

Dr. Tia M. Benedetto

October 1, 2019

paper title, 2.4, 2.27, Table 2.1, Figure 2.4

group author, 9.11

parenthetical citation of a work with two authors, 8.17

italics to highlight a key term, 6.22

parenthetical citation of a work with one author, 8.17

repeated citation needed, 8.1

use of first person, 4.16

narrative citation in parenthetical running text, 8.11

Guided Imagery and Progressive Muscle Relaxation in Group Psychotherapy

A majority of Americans experience stress in their daily lives (American Psychological Association, 2017). Thus, an important goal of psychological research is to evaluate techniques that promote stress reduction and relaxation. Two techniques that have been associated with reduced stress and increased relaxation in psychotherapy contexts are guided imagery and progressive muscle relaxation (McGuigan & Lehrer, 2007). *Guided imagery* aids individuals in connecting their internal and external experiences, allowing them, for example, to feel calmer externally because they practice thinking about calming imagery. *Progressive muscle relaxation* involves diaphragmatic breathing and the tensing and releasing of 16 major muscle groups; together these behaviors lead individuals to a more relaxed state (Jacobson, 1938; Trakhtenberg, 2008). Guided imagery and progressive muscle relaxation are both cognitive behavioral techniques (Yalom & Leszcz, 2005) in which individuals focus on the relationship among thoughts, emotions, and behaviors (White, 2000).

Group psychotherapy effectively promotes positive treatment outcomes in patients in a cost-effective way. Its efficacy is in part attributable to variables unique to the group experience of therapy as compared with individual psychotherapy (Bottomley, 1996; Yalom & Leszcz, 2005). That is, the group format helps participants feel accepted and better understand their common struggles; at the same time, interactions with group members provide social support and models of positive behavior (Yalom & Leszcz, 2005). Thus, it is useful to examine how stress reduction and relaxation can be enhanced in a group context.

The purpose of this literature review is to examine the research base on guided imagery and progressive muscle relaxation in group psychotherapy contexts. I provide overviews of both guided imagery and progressive muscle relaxation, including theoretical foundations and historical context. Then I examine guided imagery and progressive muscle relaxation as used on their own as well as in combination as part of group psychotherapy (see Baider et al., 1994, for more). Throughout the review, I

ELEMENTS & FORMAT

Sample Student Paper *(continued)*

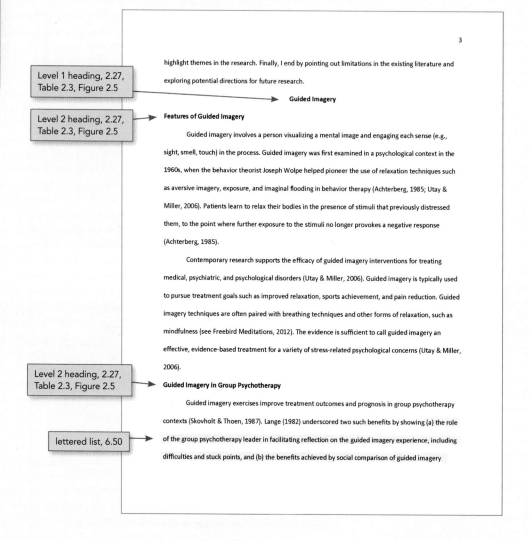

3

highlight themes in the research. Finally, I end by pointing out limitations in the existing literature and exploring potential directions for future research.

Level 1 heading, 2.27, Table 2.3, Figure 2.5

Guided Imagery

Level 2 heading, 2.27, Table 2.3, Figure 2.5

Features of Guided Imagery

Guided imagery involves a person visualizing a mental image and engaging each sense (e.g., sight, smell, touch) in the process. Guided imagery was first examined in a psychological context in the 1960s, when the behavior theorist Joseph Wolpe helped pioneer the use of relaxation techniques such as aversive imagery, exposure, and imaginal flooding in behavior therapy (Achterberg, 1985; Utay & Miller, 2006). Patients learn to relax their bodies in the presence of stimuli that previously distressed them, to the point where further exposure to the stimuli no longer provokes a negative response (Achterberg, 1985).

Contemporary research supports the efficacy of guided imagery interventions for treating medical, psychiatric, and psychological disorders (Utay & Miller, 2006). Guided imagery is typically used to pursue treatment goals such as improved relaxation, sports achievement, and pain reduction. Guided imagery techniques are often paired with breathing techniques and other forms of relaxation, such as mindfulness (see Freebird Meditations, 2012). The evidence is sufficient to call guided imagery an effective, evidence-based treatment for a variety of stress-related psychological concerns (Utay & Miller, 2006).

Level 2 heading, 2.27, Table 2.3, Figure 2.5

Guided Imagery in Group Psychotherapy

Guided imagery exercises improve treatment outcomes and prognosis in group psychotherapy contexts (Skovholt & Thoen, 1987). Lange (1982) underscored two such benefits by showing (a) the role

lettered list, 6.50

of the group psychotherapy leader in facilitating reflection on the guided imagery experience, including difficulties and stuck points, and (b) the benefits achieved by social comparison of guided imagery

Sample Student Paper *(continued)*

4

experiences between group members. Teaching techniques and reflecting on the group process are unique components of guided imagery received in a group context (Yalom & Leszcz, 2005).

Empirical research focused on guided imagery interventions supports the efficacy of the technique with a variety of populations within hospital settings, with positive outcomes for individuals diagnosed with depression, anxiety, and eating disorders (Utay & Miller, 2006). Guided imagery and relaxation techniques have even been found to "reduce distress and allow the immune system to function more effectively" (Trakhtenberg, 2008, p. 850). For example, Holden-Lund (1988) examined effects of a guided imagery intervention on surgical stress and wound healing in a group of 24 patients. Patients listened to guided imagery recordings and reported reduced state anxiety, lower cortisol levels following surgery, and less irritation in wound healing compared with a control group. Holden-Lund concluded that the guided imagery recordings contributed to improved surgical recovery. It would be interesting to see how the results might differ if guided imagery was practiced continually in a group context.

Guided imagery has also been shown to reduce stress, length of hospital stay, and symptoms related to medical and psychological conditions (Scherwitz et al., 2005). For example, Ball et al. (2003) conducted guided imagery in a group psychotherapy format with 11 children (ages 5–18) experiencing recurrent abdominal pai[n]

psychotherapy sessions

diaries and parent and ch[ild]

pain. Despite a small sam[ple]

that guided imagery in a

| short quotation, 8.25, 8.26 |

| repeated narrative citation with the year omitted, 8.16 |

| "et al." citations for works with three or more authors, 8.17 |

| Level 1 heading, 2.27, Table 2.3, Figure 2.5 |

| Level 2 heading, 2.27, Table 2.3, Figure 2.5 |

| secondary source citation, 8.6 |

| narrative citation with the year in the narrative, 8.11 |

| "for more" citation, 8.11 |

5

met once in a group to learn guided imagery and then practiced guided imagery individually on their own (see Menzies et al., 2014, for more). Thus, it is unknown whether guided imagery would have different effects if implemented on an ongoing basis in group psychotherapy.

Progressive Muscle Relaxation

Features of Progressive Muscle Relaxation

Progressive muscle relaxation involves diaphragmatic or deep breathing and the tensing and releasing of muscles in the body (Jacobson, 1938). Edmund Jacobson developed progressive muscle relaxation in 1929 (as cited in Peterson et al., 2011) and directed participants to practice progressive muscle relaxation several times a week for a year. After examining progressive muscle relaxation as an intervention for stress or anxiety, Joseph Wolpe (1960; as cited in Peterson et al., 2011) theorized that relaxation was a promising treatment. In 1973, Bernstein and Borkovec created a manual for helping professionals to teach their clients progressive muscle relaxation, thereby bringing progressive muscle relaxation into the fold of interventions used in cognitive behavior therapy. In its current state, progressive muscle relaxation is often paired with relaxation training and described within a relaxation framework (see Freebird Meditations, 2012, for more).

Research on the use of progressive muscle relaxation for stress reduction has demonstrated the efficacy of the method (McGuigan & Lehrer, 2007). As clients learn how to tense and release different muscle groups, the physical relaxation achieved then influences psychological processes (McCallie et al., 2006). For example, progressive muscle relaxation can help alleviate tension headaches, insomnia, pain, and irritable bowel syndrome. This research demonstrates that relaxing the body can also help relax the mind and lead to physical benefits.

Progressive Muscle Relaxation in Group Psychotherapy

Limited, but compelling, research has examined progressive muscle relaxation within group psychotherapy. Progressive muscle relaxation has been used in outpatient and inpatient hospital

Sample Student Paper (continued)

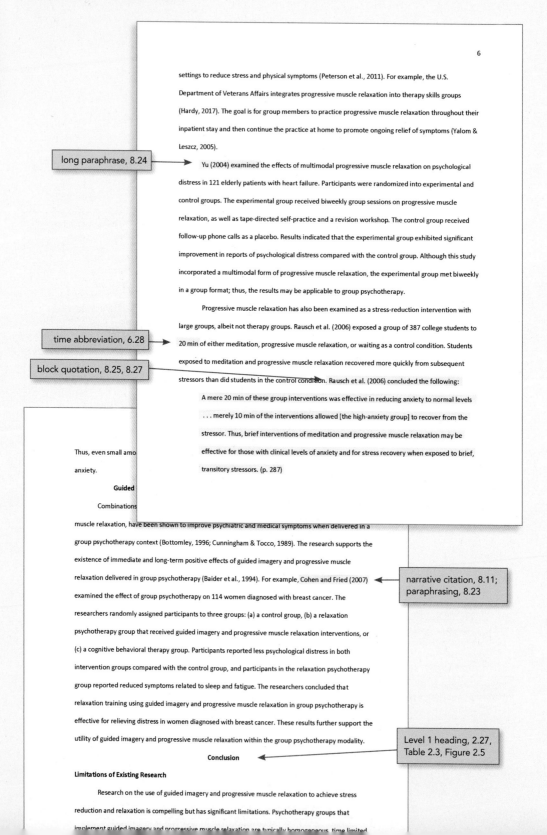

6

settings to reduce stress and physical symptoms (Peterson et al., 2011). For example, the U.S. Department of Veterans Affairs integrates progressive muscle relaxation into therapy skills groups (Hardy, 2017). The goal is for group members to practice progressive muscle relaxation throughout their inpatient stay and then continue the practice at home to promote ongoing relief of symptoms (Yalom & Leszcz, 2005).

long paraphrase, 8.24

Yu (2004) examined the effects of multimodal progressive muscle relaxation on psychological distress in 121 elderly patients with heart failure. Participants were randomized into experimental and control groups. The experimental group received biweekly group sessions on progressive muscle relaxation, as well as tape-directed self-practice and a revision workshop. The control group received follow-up phone calls as a placebo. Results indicated that the experimental group exhibited significant improvement in reports of psychological distress compared with the control group. Although this study incorporated a multimodal form of progressive muscle relaxation, the experimental group met biweekly in a group format; thus, the results may be applicable to group psychotherapy.

Progressive muscle relaxation has also been examined as a stress-reduction intervention with large groups, albeit not therapy groups. Rausch et al. (2006) exposed a group of 387 college students to

time abbreviation, 6.28

20 min of either meditation, progressive muscle relaxation, or waiting as a control condition. Students exposed to meditation and progressive muscle relaxation recovered more quickly from subsequent stressors than did students in the control condition. Rausch et al. (2006) concluded the following:

block quotation, 8.25, 8.27

> A mere 20 min of these group interventions was effective in reducing anxiety to normal levels . . . merely 10 min of the interventions allowed [the high-anxiety group] to recover from the stressor. Thus, brief interventions of meditation and progressive muscle relaxation may be effective for those with clinical levels of anxiety and for stress recovery when exposed to brief, transitory stressors. (p. 287)

Thus, even small amo[unt]

anxiety.

Guided

Combinations

muscle relaxation, have been shown to improve psychiatric and medical symptoms when delivered in a group psychotherapy context (Bottomley, 1996; Cunningham & Tocco, 1989). The research supports the existence of immediate and long-term positive effects of guided imagery and progressive muscle relaxation delivered in group psychotherapy (Baider et al., 1994). For example, Cohen and Fried (2007) examined the effect of group psychotherapy on 114 women diagnosed with breast cancer. The researchers randomly assigned participants to three groups: (a) a control group, (b) a relaxation psychotherapy group that received guided imagery and progressive muscle relaxation interventions, or (c) a cognitive behavioral therapy group. Participants reported less psychological distress in both intervention groups compared with the control group, and participants in the relaxation psychotherapy group reported reduced symptoms related to sleep and fatigue. The researchers concluded that relaxation training using guided imagery and progressive muscle relaxation in group psychotherapy is effective for relieving distress in women diagnosed with breast cancer. These results further support the utility of guided imagery and progressive muscle relaxation within the group psychotherapy modality.

narrative citation, 8.11; paraphrasing, 8.23

Conclusion

Level 1 heading, 2.27, Table 2.3, Figure 2.5

Limitations of Existing Research

Research on the use of guided imagery and progressive muscle relaxation to achieve stress reduction and relaxation is compelling but has significant limitations. Psychotherapy groups that implement guided imagery and progressive muscle relaxation are typically homogeneous, time-limited

Sample Student Paper *(continued)*

8

usually expected to practice the techniques by themselves (see Menzies et al., 2014). Future research should address how these relaxation techniques can assist people in diverse groups and how the impact of relaxation techniques may be amplified if treatments are delivered in the group setting over time.

Future research should also examine differences in inpatient versus outpatient psychotherapy groups as well as structured versus unstructured groups. The majority of research on the use of guided imagery and progressive muscle relaxation with psychotherapy groups has used unstructured inpatient groups (e.g., groups in a hospital setting). However, inpatient and outpatient groups are distinct, as are structured versus unstructured groups, and each format offers potential advantages and limitations (Yalom & Leszcz, 2005). For example, an advantage of an unstructured group is that the group leader can reflect the group process and focus on the "here and now," which may improve the efficacy of the relaxation techniques (Yalom & Leszcz, 2005). However, research also has supported the efficacy of structured psychotherapy groups for patients with a variety of medical, psychiatric, and psychological disorders (Hashim & Zainol, 2015; see also Baider et al., 1994; Cohen & Fried, 2007). Empirical research `← "see also" citation, 8.12` assessing these interventions is limited, and further research is recommended.

Directions for Future Research `← Level 2 heading, 2.27, Table 2.3, Figure 2.5`

There are additional considerations when interpreting the results of previous studies and planning for future studies of these techniques. For example, a lack of control groups and small sample sizes have contributed to low statistical power and limited the generalizability of findings. Although the current data support the efficacy of psychotherapy groups that integrate guided imagery and progressive muscle relaxation, further research with control groups and larger samples would bolster confidence in the effica[...] participants over time, r[...] attrition. These factors a[...] rates and changes in me[...]

`personal communication, 8.9`

9

participation (L. Plum, personal communication, March 17, 2019). Despite these challenges, continued research examining guided imagery and progressive muscle relaxation interventions within group psychotherapy is warranted (Scherwitz et al., 2005). The results thus far are promising, and further investigation has the potential to make relaxation techniques that can improve people's lives more effective and widely available.

ELEMENTS & FORMAT

Sample Student Paper *(continued)*

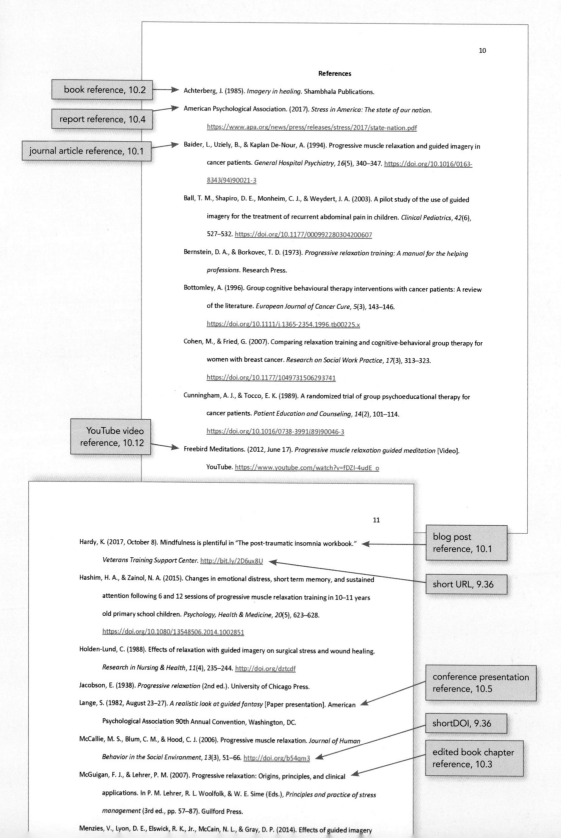

10

References

book reference, 10.2 →

Achterberg, J. (1985). *Imagery in healing.* Shambhala Publications.

report reference, 10.4 →

American Psychological Association. (2017). *Stress in America: The state of our nation.*

https://www.apa.org/news/press/releases/stress/2017/state-nation.pdf

journal article reference, 10.1 →

Baider, L., Uziely, B., & Kaplan De-Nour, A. (1994). Progressive muscle relaxation and guided imagery in

cancer patients. *General Hospital Psychiatry, 16*(5), 340–347. https://doi.org/10.1016/0163-

8343(94)90021-3

Ball, T. M., Shapiro, D. E., Monheim, C. J., & Weydert, J. A. (2003). A pilot study of the use of guided

imagery for the treatment of recurrent abdominal pain in children. *Clinical Pediatrics, 42*(6),

527–532. https://doi.org/10.1177/000992280304200607

Bernstein, D. A., & Borkovec, T. D. (1973). *Progressive relaxation training: A manual for the helping*

professions. Research Press.

Bottomley, A. (1996). Group cognitive behavioural therapy interventions with cancer patients: A review

of the literature. *European Journal of Cancer Cure, 5*(3), 143–146.

https://doi.org/10.1111/j.1365-2354.1996.tb00225.x

Cohen, M., & Fried, G. (2007). Comparing relaxation training and cognitive-behavioral group therapy for

women with breast cancer. *Research on Social Work Practice, 17*(3), 313–323.

https://doi.org/10.1177/1049731506293741

Cunningham, A. J., & Tocco, E. K. (1989). A randomized trial of group psychoeducational therapy for

cancer patients. *Patient Education and Counseling, 14*(2), 101–114.

https://doi.org/10.1016/0738-3991(89)90046-3

YouTube video reference, 10.12 →

Freebird Meditations. (2012, June 17). *Progressive muscle relaxation guided meditation* [Video].

YouTube. https://www.youtube.com/watch?v=fDZI-4udE_o

11

Hardy, K. (2017, October 8). Mindfulness is plentiful in "The post-traumatic insomnia workbook."

Veterans Training Support Center. http://bit.ly/2D6ux8U

blog post reference, 10.1

short URL, 9.36

Hashim, H. A., & Zainol, N. A. (2015). Changes in emotional distress, short term memory, and sustained

attention following 6 and 12 sessions of progressive muscle relaxation training in 10–11 years

old primary school children. *Psychology, Health & Medicine, 20*(5), 623–628.

https://doi.org/10.1080/13548506.2014.1002851

Holden-Lund, C. (1988). Effects of relaxation with guided imagery on surgical stress and wound healing.

Research in Nursing & Health, 11(4), 235–244. http://doi.org/dztcdf

Jacobson, E. (1938). *Progressive relaxation* (2nd ed.). University of Chicago Press.

Lange, S. (1982, August 23–27). *A realistic look at guided fantasy* [Paper presentation]. American

Psychological Association 90th Annual Convention, Washington, DC.

conference presentation reference, 10.5

shortDOI, 9.36

McCallie, M. S., Blum, C. M., & Hood, C. J. (2006). Progressive muscle relaxation. *Journal of Human*

Behavior in the Social Environment, 13(3), 51–66. http://doi.org/b54qm3

edited book chapter reference, 10.3

McGuigan, F. J., & Lehrer, P. M. (2007). Progressive relaxation: Origins, principles, and clinical

applications. In P. M. Lehrer, R. L. Woolfolk, & W. E. Sime (Eds.), *Principles and practice of stress*

management (3rd ed., pp. 57–87). Guilford Press.

Menzies, V., Lyon, D. E., Elswick, R. K., Jr., McCain, N. L., & Gray, D. P. (2014). Effects of guided imagery recovery. *International Journal of Stress Management, 13*(3), 273–290.

https://doi.org/10.1037/1072-5245.13.3.273

Scherwitz, L. W., McHenry, P., & Herrero, R. (2005). Interactive guided imagery therapy with medical

patients: Predictors of health outcomes. *The Journal of Alternative and Complementary*

Medicine, 11(1), 69–83. https://doi.org/10.1089/acm.2005.11.69

Skovholt, T. M., & Thoen, G. A. (1987). Mental imagery and parenthood decision making. *Journal of*

Counseling & Development, 65(6), 315–316. http://doi.org/fzmtjd

Trakhtenberg, E. C. (2008). The effects of guided imagery on the immune system: A critical review.

International Journal of Neuroscience, 118(6), 839–855. http://doi.org/fxfsbq

Utay, J., & Miller, M. (2006). Guided imagery as an effective therapeutic technique: A brief review of its

history and efficacy research. *Journal of Instructional Psychology, 33*(1), 40–43.

White, J. R. (2000). Introduction. In J. R. White & A. S. Freeman (Eds.), *Cognitive-behavioral group*

therapy: For specific problems and populations (pp. 3–25). American Psychological Association.

https://doi.org/10.1037/10352-001

Yalom, I. D., & Leszcz, M. (2005). *The theory and practice of group psychotherapy* (5th ed.). Basic Books.

Yu, S. F. (2004). *Effects of progressive muscle relaxation training on psychological and health-related*

quality of life outcomes in elderly patients with heart failure (Publication No. 3182156) [Doctoral

dissertation, The Chinese University of Hong Kong]. ProQuest Dissertations and Theses Global.

12

shortDOI, 9.36

doctoral dissertation reference, 10.6

ELEMENTS & FORMAT

3

JOURNAL ARTICLE REPORTING STANDARDS

Contents

3

JOURNAL ARTICLE
REPORTING STANDARDS

This chapter orients readers to a specialized set of guidelines developed by APA referred to as *journal article reporting standards*, or JARS. These standards provide guidelines for authors on what information should be included, at minimum, in journal articles. By using JARS, authors can make their research clearer, more accurate, and more transparent for readers. Writing clearly and reporting research in a way that is easier to comprehend helps ensure scientific rigor and methodological integrity and improves the quality of published research. Reporting standards are closely related to the way studies are designed and conducted, but they do not prescribe how to design or execute studies, and they are not dependent on the topic of the study or the particular journal in which the study might be published. Comprehensive, uniform reporting standards make it easier to compare research, to understand the implications of individual studies, and to allow techniques of meta-analysis to proceed more efficiently. Decision makers in policy and practice have also emphasized the importance of understanding how research was conducted and what was found.

This chapter contains practical guidance for authors who will use JARS when reporting their research—primarily, authors seeking professional publication as well as undergraduate or graduate students conducting advanced research projects. Undergraduate students who are writing less complicated research papers may also find the standards on the abstract and introduction helpful (see Sections 3.3–3.4). Note that the information available regarding JARS is substantial and detailed; this chapter is only an introduction. The APA Style JARS website (https://apastyle.apa.org/jars) contains a wealth of resources (links to many appear throughout this chapter). JARS may also be revised and expanded in the future as new standards are developed; any such changes will be reflected on the website. The sections that follow discuss the application of the principles of JARS, including why the standards exist and how they have evolved; terminology used to discuss JARS, with a link to a glossary on the JARS website; reporting standards for abstracts and introductions that pertain to all types of research articles; and specific standards for quantitative, qualitative, and mixed methods research.

Overview of Reporting Standards

3.1 Application of the Principles of JARS

By adopting and following JARS in their articles, researchers

- help readers fully understand the research being reported and draw valid conclusions from the work,
- allow reviewers and editors to properly evaluate manuscripts submitted for publication for their scientific value,
- enable future researchers to replicate the research reported,
- foster transparency (for more on the ethic of transparency in JARS, see the JARS website at https://apastyle.apa.org/jars/transparency), and
- improve the quality of published research.

Within these guidelines for reporting standards, however, is flexibility in how the standards are applied across different types of research studies. Guidelines on where to include information recommended in JARS within an article are flexible in most cases (exceptions are information that must appear in the title page, abstract, or author note; see Tables 3.1–3.3 later in this chapter). In general, any information that is necessary to comprehend and interpret the study should be in the text of the journal article, and information that might be needed for replication can be included in supplemental materials available online with few barriers to readers. Authors should consult with journal editors to resolve questions regarding what information to include and where, keeping readability of the article as a prime consideration. Reviewers and editors are encouraged to learn to recognize whether reporting standards have been met regardless of the rhetorical style of the research presentation.

Reporting standards are evolving to reflect the needs of the research community. The original JARS, published in *American Psychologist* (APA Publications and Communications Board Working Group on Journal Article Reporting Standards, 2008) as well as in the sixth edition of the *Publication Manual* (APA, 2010), addressed only quantitative research. The updated JARS, published in 2018 (see Appelbaum et al., 2018; Levitt et al., 2018), expands on the types of quantitative research (JARS–Quant) addressed and now includes standards for reporting qualitative (JARS–Qual) and mixed methods (JARS–Mixed) research. As research approaches continue to evolve, authors should use these standards to support the publication of research; they should not allow these standards to restrict the development of new methods.

3.2 Terminology Used in JARS

Researchers use many methods and strategies to meet their research goals, and the guidelines in JARS were developed to facilitate the reporting of research across a range of research traditions (Appelbaum et al., 2018; Levitt et al., 2018). These methods fall into either quantitative (Sections 1.1 and 3.5–3.8), qualitative (Sections 1.2 and 3.13–3.16), or mixed methods (Sections 1.3 and 3.18) traditions; separate reporting standards exist for each tradition. There are also specialized standards for particular quantitative (see Sections 3.9–3.12) and qualitative methodologies (see Section 3.17), such as meta-analysis.

Given this diversity, the terms used in this chapter may be unfamiliar to some readers. See the JARS website (https://apastyle.apa.org/jars/glossary) for a glossary of related terms, including "approaches to inquiry," "data-analytic strategies," "data-collection strategies," "methodological integrity," "research design," and "trustworthiness." Because researchers do not always agree on terminology, we encourage authors to translate these terms to reflect their own preferred approaches, taking care to define terms for readers. We recognize that our language inevitably carries philosophical implications (e.g., do researchers "discover," "understand," or "co-construct" findings?). We also encourage reviewers and editors to view our terms as placeholders that may be usefully varied by authors to reflect the values of their research traditions.

Common Reporting Standards Across Research Designs

Many aspects of the scientific process are common across quantitative, qualitative, and mixed methods approaches. This section reviews reporting standards that have considerable overlap for the two initial elements of journal articles—the abstract and the introduction. We present the common reporting standards for the abstract and introduction as well as some distinctive features for each approach. For descriptions of and formatting guidelines for the title, byline and institutional affiliation, author note, running head, abstract, keywords, text (the body of a paper), reference list, footnotes, appendices, and supplemental materials, see Chapter 2 (Sections 2.4–2.15).

3.3 Abstract Standards

An *abstract* is a brief, comprehensive summary of the contents of the paper. A well-prepared abstract can be the most important paragraph in an article. Many people have their first contact with an article by reading the title and abstract, usually in comparison with several others, as they conduct a literature search. Readers frequently decide on the basis of the abstract whether to read the entire article. The abstract needs to be dense with information. By embedding essential terms in your abstract, you enhance readers' ability to find the article. This section addresses the qualities of a good abstract and standards for what to include in abstracts for different paper types (see Sections 1.1–1.10). Requirements for abstract length and instructions on formatting the abstract are presented in Section 2.9.

Qualities of a Good Abstract. A good abstract is

- **accurate:** Ensure that the abstract correctly reflects the purpose and content of the paper. Do not include information that does not appear in the paper body. If the study extends or replicates previous research, cite the relevant work with an author–date citation.

- **nonevaluative:** Report rather than evaluate; do not add to or comment on what is in the body of the paper.

- **coherent and readable:** Write in clear and deliberate language. Use verbs rather than their noun equivalents and the active rather than the passive voice (e.g., "investigated" instead of "an investigation of"; "we present results" instead of "results are presented"; see Section 4.13). Use the present tense to describe conclusions drawn or results with continuing applicability; use the past tense to describe specific variables manipulated or outcomes measured. If presenting statistical or mathematical information, see Sections 6.40 to 6.48 for the appropriate formats.

- **concise:** Be brief, and make each sentence maximally informative, especially the lead sentence. Begin the abstract with the most important points. Do not waste space by repeating the title. Include only the four or five most important concepts, findings, or implications. Use the specific words in your abstract that you think your audience will use in their searches.

Empirical Articles. The abstract for an empirical article (quantitative, qualitative, or mixed methods; see Sections 1.1–1.3) should describe the following:

- the problem under investigation, in one sentence, if possible; when presenting quantitative analyses, include the main hypotheses, questions, or theories under investigation
- participants or data sources, specifying pertinent characteristics (e.g., for nonhuman animal research, include the genus and species); participants will be described in greater detail in the body of the paper
- essential features of the study method, including
  - research design (e.g., experimental, observational, qualitative, mixed methods)
  - analytic strategy (e.g., ethnography, factor analysis)
  - data-gathering procedures
  - sample size (typically for quantitative analyses) or description of the volume of observations or number of participants (typically for qualitative analyses)
  - materials or central measures used
  - a statement about whether the study is a secondary data analysis
- basic findings, including
  - for quantitative analyses, effect sizes and confidence intervals in addition to statistical significance levels when possible
  - for qualitative methods, main findings in relation to central contextual features
- conclusions and implications or applications of the research findings

Replication Articles. The abstract for a replication article (see Section 1.4) should describe the following:

- type of replication being reported (e.g., direct [exact, literal], approximate, conceptual [construct])
- scope of the replication in detail
- original study or studies that are being replicated
- general conclusions reached in the replication

Quantitative or Qualitative Meta-Analyses. The abstract for a quantitative or qualitative meta-analysis (see Section 1.5) should describe the following:

- research problems, questions, or hypotheses under investigation

- characteristics for the inclusion of studies, including
  - for quantitative meta-analyses, independent variables, dependent variables, and eligible study designs
  - for qualitative meta-analyses, criteria for eligibility in terms of study topic and research design
- methods of synthesis, including statistical or qualitative metamethods used to summarize or compare studies and specific methods used to integrate studies
- main results, including
  - for all studies, the number of studies; the number of participants, observations, or data sources; and their important characteristics
  - for quantitative analyses, the most important effect sizes and any important moderators of these effect sizes
  - for qualitative analyses, the most important findings in their context
- conclusions (including limitations)
- implications for theory, policy, and/or practice

Literature Review Articles. The abstract for a literature review article (also called a *narrative literature review article*; see Section 1.6) should describe the substantive content being reviewed, including the following:

- scope of the literature examined in the review (e.g., journals, books, unpublished abstracts) and the number of items included in the review
- period of time covered in the review (e.g., range of years)
- general conclusions reached in the review

Theoretical Articles. The abstract for a theoretical article (see Section 1.7) should describe the following:

- how the theory or model works and/or the principles on which it is based
- what phenomena the theory or model accounts for and linkages to empirical results

Methodological Articles. The abstract for a methodological article (see Section 1.8) should describe the following:

- general class, essential features, and range of applications of the methods, methodologies, or epistemological beliefs being discussed
- essential features of the approaches being reported, such as robustness or power efficiency in the case of statistical procedures or methodological integrity and trustworthiness in the case of qualitative methods

3.4 Introduction Standards

The body of a paper always opens with an introduction. The *introduction* contains a succinct description of the issues being reported, their historical antecedents, and the study objectives.

Frame the Importance of the Problem. The introduction of an article frames the issues being studied. Consider the various concerns on which your issue touches and its effects on other outcomes (e.g., the effects of shared storybook reading on word learning in children). This framing may be in terms of fundamental psychological theory, potential application including therapeutic uses, input for public policy, and so forth. Proper framing helps set readers' expectations for what the report will and will not include.

Historical Antecedents. Review the literature succinctly to convey to readers the scope of the problem, its context, and its theoretical or practical implications. Clarify which elements of your paper have been subject to prior investigation and how your work differs from earlier reports. In this process, describe any key issues, debates, and theoretical frameworks and clarify barriers, knowledge gaps, or practical needs. Including these descriptions will show how your work builds usefully on what has already been accomplished in the field.

Articulate Study Goals. Clearly state and delimit the aims, objectives, and/or goals of your study. Make explicit the rationale for the fit of your design in relation to your aims and goals. Describe the goals in a way that clarifies the appropriateness of the methods you used.

Quantitative Goals. In a quantitative article, the introduction should identify the primary and secondary hypotheses as well as any exploratory hypotheses, specifying how the hypotheses derive from ideas discussed in previous research and whether exploratory hypotheses were derived as a result of planned or unplanned analyses.

Qualitative Goals. In a qualitative article, the introduction may contain case examples, personal narratives, vignettes, or other illustrative materials. It should describe your research goal(s) and approach to inquiry. Examples of qualitative research goals include developing theory, hypotheses, and deep understandings (e.g., Hill, 2012; Stiles, 1993); examining the development of a social construct (e.g., Neimeyer et al., 2008); addressing societal injustices (e.g., Fine, 2013); and illuminating social discursive practices—that is, the way interpersonal and public communications are enacted (e.g., Parker, 2015). The term *approaches to inquiry* refers to the philosophical assumptions that underlie research traditions or strategies—for example, the researchers' epistemological beliefs, worldview, paradigm, strategies, or research traditions (Creswell & Poth, 2018; Morrow, 2005; Ponterotto, 2005). For instance, you might indicate that your approach or approaches to inquiry are constructivist, critical, descriptive, feminist, interpretive, postmodern, postpositivist, pragmatic, or psychoanalytic. Note that researchers may define these philosophies differently, and some qualitative research is more question driven and pragmatic than theoretical. You might also address your approach to inquiry in the Method section (see Section 3.14).

Mixed Methods Goals. In a mixed methods or multimethod article, the introduction should describe the objectives for all study components presented, the rationale for their being presented in one study, and the rationale for the order in which they are presented within the paper (see Section 3.18). In all cases, clarify how the questions or hypotheses under examination led to the research design to meet the study aims.

Goals for Other Types of Papers. Introductions for other types of papers follow similar principles and articulate the specific motivation for the study. For instance, a replication study conducted as a quantitative study would have an introduction that follows the principles for the introduction of a quantitative study but that emphasizes the need to replicate a certain study or set of studies as well as the methods used to accomplish the desired replication.

Reporting Standards for Quantitative Research

3.5 Basic Expectations for Quantitative Research Reporting

Whereas standards for reporting information in the abstract and introduction of a paper are common to all kinds of research (see Sections 3.3–3.4), there are specific reporting standards for quantitative research articles, including the Method, Results, and Discussion sections (see Sections 3.6–3.8). Note that this is a conceptual separation, but in practice, the information specified in these three sets of reporting standards may be intermixed in several sections of the paper to optimize readability. Standards specific to qualitative and mixed methods research are presented in Sections 3.13 to 3.17 and 3.18, respectively.

The basic expectations for reporting quantitative research are presented in Table 3.1.[1] This table describes minimal reporting standards that apply to all quantitative-based inquires. Additional tables describe other reporting features that are added because of particular design features or empirical claims. Consult Figure 3.1 to determine which tables to use for your quantitative research and for links to all tables on the JARS website (because this chapter is an orientation to JARS, only the main quantitative table is presented here). Every empirical study must include features from Table 3.1 plus features from at least one additional table. The content of Table 3.1 by itself is not sufficient as a description of reporting standards for quantitative studies. See Sections 3.9 to 3.12 for descriptions of each additional table.

Table 3.1 Quantitative Design Reporting Standards (JARS–Quant)

Title and Title Page
Title
• Identify main variables and theoretical issues under investigation and the relationships between them.   • Identify the populations studied.
Author Note

• Provide acknowledgment and explanation of any special circumstances, including
   – registration information if the study has been registered
   – use of data also appearing in previous publications
   – prior reporting of the fundamental data in dissertations or conference papers
   – sources of funding or other support
   – relationships or affiliations that may be perceived as conflicts of interest
   – previous (or current) affiliation of authors if different from the location where the study was conducted
   – contact information for the corresponding author
   – additional information of importance to the reader that may not be appropriately included in other sections of the paper

Abstract
Objectives
• State the problem under investigation, including main hypotheses.

---

[1] The tables and figure in this chapter can also be found on the JARS website (https://apastyle.apa.org/jars) in the guidelines for quantitative, qualitative, and mixed methods research designs, with different numbering. The JARS website has additional tables for other research designs, including experimental (e.g., clinical trials), nonexperimental (e.g., observational), and special (e.g., longitudinal) designs for authors to use in their research.

Table 3.1 Quantitative Design Reporting Standards (JARS–Quant) *(continued)*

Abstract *(continued)*

Participants

- Describe subjects (nonhuman animal research) or participants (human research), specifying their pertinent characteristics for the study; in animal research, include genus and species. Participants are described in greater detail in the body of the paper.

Study Method

- Describe the study method, including
  - research design (e.g., experiment, observational study)
  - sample size
  - materials used (e.g., instruments, apparatus)
  - outcome measures
  - data-gathering procedures, including a brief description of the source of any secondary data. If the study is a secondary data analysis, so indicate.

Findings

- Report findings, including effect sizes and confidence intervals or statistical significance levels.

Conclusions

- State conclusions, beyond just results, and report the implications or applications.

Introduction

Problem

- State the importance of the problem, including theoretical or practical implications.

Review of Relevant Scholarship

- Provide a succinct review of relevant scholarship, including
  - relation to previous work
  - differences between the current report and earlier reports if some aspects of this study have been reported on previously

Hypothesis, Aims, and Objectives

- State specific hypotheses, aims, and objectives, including
  - theories or other means used to derive hypotheses
  - primary and secondary hypotheses
  - other planned analyses
- State how hypotheses and research design relate to one another.

Method

Inclusion and Exclusion

- Report inclusion and exclusion criteria, including any restrictions based on demographic characteristics.

Participant Characteristics

- Report major demographic characteristics (e.g., age, sex, ethnicity, socioeconomic status) and important topic-specific characteristics (e.g., achievement level in studies of educational interventions).
- In the case of animal research, report the genus, species, and strain number or other specific identification, such as the name and location of the supplier and the stock designation. Give the number of animals and the animals' sex, age, weight, physiological condition, genetic modification status, genotype, health–immune status, drug or test naïveté, and previous procedures to which the animal may have been subjected.

Table 3.1 Quantitative Design Reporting Standards (JARS–Quant) (continued)

Method (continued)

Sampling Procedures

- Describe procedures for selecting participants, including
  - sampling method if a systematic sampling plan was implemented
  - percentage of the sample approached that actually participated
  - whether self-selection into the study occurred (either by individuals or by units, such as schools or clinics)
- Describe settings and locations where data were collected as well as dates of data collection.
- Describe agreements and payments made to participants.
- Describe institutional review board agreements, ethical standards met, and safety monitoring.

Sample Size, Power, and Precision

- Describe the sample size, power, and precision, including
  - intended sample size
  - achieved sample size, if different from the intended sample size
  - determination of sample size, including
    - ▷ power analysis, or methods used to determine precision of parameter estimates
    - ▷ explanation of any interim analyses and stopping rules employed

Measures and Covariates

- Define all primary and secondary measures and covariates, including measures collected but not included in the report.

Data Collection

- Describe methods used to collect data.

Quality of Measurements

- Describe methods used to enhance the quality of measurements, including
  - training and reliability of data collectors
  - use of multiple observations

Instrumentation

- Provide information on validated or ad hoc instruments created for individual studies (e.g., psychometric and biometric properties).

Masking

- Report whether participants, those administering the experimental manipulations, and those assessing the outcomes were aware of condition assignments.
- If masking took place, provide a statement regarding how it was accomplished and whether and how the success of masking was evaluated.

Psychometrics

- Estimate and report reliability coefficients for the scores analyzed (i.e., the researcher's sample), if possible. Provide estimates of convergent and discriminant validity where relevant.
- Report estimates related to the reliability of measures, including
  - interrater reliability for subjectively scored measures and ratings
  - test–retest coefficients in longitudinal studies in which the retest interval corresponds to the measurement schedule used in the study
  - internal consistency coefficients for composite scales in which these indices are appropriate for understanding the nature of the instruments being used in the study
- Report the basic demographic characteristics of other samples if reporting reliability or validity coefficients from those samples, such as those described in test manuals or in norming information for the instrument.

Table 3.1 Quantitative Design Reporting Standards (JARS–Quant) *(continued)*

Method *(continued)*

Conditions and Design

- State whether conditions were manipulated or naturally observed. Report the type of design as per the JARS–Quant tables:
  - experimental manipulation with participants randomized
    - ▷ Table 2 and Module A
  - experimental manipulation without randomization
    - ▷ Table 2 and Module B
  - clinical trial with randomization
    - ▷ Table 2 and Modules A and C
  - clinical trial without randomization
    - ▷ Table 2 and Modules B and C
  - nonexperimental design (i.e., no experimental manipulation): observational design, epidemiological design, natural history, and so forth (single-group designs or multiple-group comparisons)
    - ▷ Table 3
  - longitudinal design
    - ▷ Table 4
  - *N*-of-1 studies
    - ▷ Table 5
  - replications
    - ▷ Table 6
- Report the common name given to designs not currently covered in JARS–Quant.

Data Diagnostics

- Describe planned data diagnostics, including
  - criteria for post-data-collection exclusion of participants, if any
  - criteria for deciding when to infer missing data and methods used for imputation of missing data
  - definition and processing of statistical outliers
  - analyses of data distributions
  - data transformations to be used, if any

Analytic Strategy

- Describe the analytic strategy for inferential statistics and protection against experiment-wise error for
  - primary hypotheses
  - secondary hypotheses
  - exploratory hypotheses

Results

Participant Flow

- Report the flow of participants, including
  - total number of participants in each group at each stage of the study
  - flow of participants through each stage of the study (include figure depicting flow, when possible; see Figure 7.5)

Recruitment

- Provide dates defining the periods of recruitment and repeated measures or follow-up.

Statistics and Data Analysis

- Provide information detailing the statistical and data-analytic methods used, including
  - missing data
    - ▷ frequency or percentages of missing data
    - ▷ empirical evidence and/or theoretical arguments for the causes of data that are missing—for example, missing completely at random (MCAR), missing at random (MAR), or missing not at random (MNAR)
    - ▷ methods actually used for addressing missing data, if any

Table 3.1 Quantitative Design Reporting Standards (JARS–Quant) *(continued)*

Results *(continued)*

- descriptions of each primary and secondary outcome, including the total sample and each subgroup, that includes the number of cases, cell means, standard deviations, and other measures that characterize the data used
- inferential statistics, including
  ▷ results of all inferential tests conducted, including exact *p* values if null hypothesis significance testing (NHST) methods were used, and reporting the minimally sufficient set of statistics (e.g., *df*s, mean square [*MS*] effect, *MS* error) needed to construct the tests
  ▷ effect-size estimates and confidence intervals on estimates that correspond to each inferential test conducted, when possible
  ▷ clear differentiation between primary hypotheses and their tests–estimates, secondary hypotheses and their tests–estimates, and exploratory hypotheses and their test–estimates
- complex data analyses—for example, structural equation modeling analyses (see Table 7 on the JARS website), hierarchical linear models, factor analysis, multivariate analyses, and so forth, including
  ▷ details of the models estimated
  ▷ associated variance–covariance (or correlation) matrix or matrices
  ▷ identification of the statistical software used to run the analyses (e.g., SAS PROC GLM or the particular R package)
- estimation problems (e.g., failure to converge, bad solution spaces), regression diagnostics, or analytic anomalies that were detected and solutions to those problems
- other data analyses performed, including adjusted analyses, if performed, indicating those that were planned and those that were not planned (though not necessarily in the level of detail of primary analyses)
- Report any problems with statistical assumptions and/or data distributions that could affect the validity of findings.

Discussion

Support of Original Hypotheses

- Provide a statement of support or nonsupport for all hypotheses, whether primary or secondary, including
  - distinction by primary and secondary hypotheses
  - discussion of the implications of exploratory analyses in terms of both substantive findings and error rates that may be uncontrolled

Similarity of Results

- Discuss similarities and differences between reported results and work of others.

Interpretation

- Provide an interpretation of the results, taking into account
  - sources of potential bias and threats to internal and statistical validity
  - imprecision of measurement protocols
  - overall number of tests or overlap among tests
  - adequacy of sample sizes and sampling validity

Generalizability

- Discuss generalizability (external validity) of the findings, taking into account
  - target population (sampling validity)
  - other contextual issues (setting, measurement, time; ecological validity)

Implications

- Discuss implications for future research, programs, or policy.

3.6 Quantitative Method Standards

The Method section of a paper provides most of the information that readers need to fully comprehend what was done in the execution of an empirical study. This section provides information that allows readers to understand the research being reported and that is essential for replication of the study, although the concept of replication may depend on the nature of the study. The basic information needed to understand the results should (as a rule) appear in the main article, whereas other methodological information (e.g., detailed descriptions of procedures) may appear in supplemental materials. Readability of the resulting paper must be part of the decision about where material is ultimately located. Details of what content needs to be presented in the Method section of a quantitative article are presented in Table 3.1 and must be used in conjunction with JARS–Quant Tables 2 to 9 on the JARS website (https://apastyle.apa.org/jars/quantitative).

Participant (Subject) Characteristics. Appropriate identification of research participants is critical to the science and practice of psychology, particularly for generalizing the findings, making comparisons across replications, and using the evidence in research syntheses and secondary data analyses.

Figure 3.1 Flowchart of Quantitative Reporting Standards to Follow Depending on Research Design

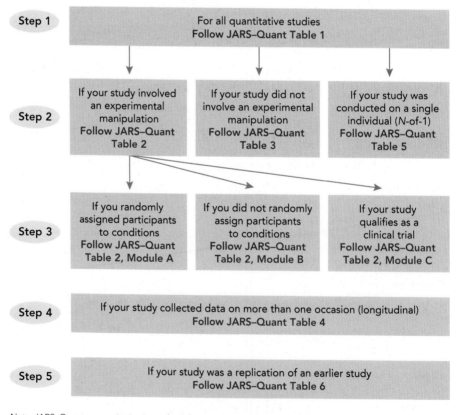

Note. JARS–Quant = quantitative journal article reporting standards. For more information, see the APA Style JARS website (https://apastyle.apa.org/jars).

Detail the major demographic characteristics of the sample, such as age; sex; ethnic and/or racial group; level of education; socioeconomic, generational, or immigrant status; disability status; sexual orientation; gender identity; and language preference, as well as important topic-specific characteristics (e.g., achievement level in studies of educational interventions). As a rule, describe the groups as specifically as possible, emphasizing characteristics that may have bearing on the interpretation of results. Participant characteristics can be important for understanding the nature of the sample and the degree to which results can be generalized. For example, the following is a useful characterization of a sample:

> The second group included 40 cisgender women between the ages of 20 and 30 years ($M = 24.2$, $SD = 2.1$, $Mdn = 25.1$), all of whom had emigrated from El Salvador; had at least 12 years of education; had been permanent residents of the United States for at least 10 years; and lived in Washington, DC.

To help readers determine how far the data can be generalized, you may find it useful to identify subgroups.

> The Asian participants included 30 Chinese and 45 Vietnamese persons.

> Among the Latino and Hispanic American men, 20 were Mexican American and 20 were Puerto Rican.

Even when a characteristic is not used in analysis of the data, reporting it may give readers a more complete understanding of the sample and the generalizability of results and may prove useful in meta-analytic studies that incorporate the article's results. The descriptions of participant characteristics should be sensitive to the ways the participants understand and express their identities, statuses, histories, and so forth. Chapter 5 contains further guidance on writing without bias.

When nonhuman animal subjects are used, report the genus, species, and strain number or other specific identifier, such as the name and location of the supplier and the stock designation. Give the number of nonhuman animal subjects and their sex, age, weight, and physiological condition.

Sampling Procedures. Describe the procedures for selecting participants, including (a) the sampling method, if a systematic plan was implemented; (b) the percentage of the sample approached that participated; and (c) whether self-selection into the study occurred (either by individuals or by units such as schools or clinics) and the number of participants who selected themselves into the sample. Report inclusion and exclusion criteria, including any restriction based on demographic characteristics.

Describe the settings and locations in which the data were collected and provide the dates of data collection as a general range of dates, including dates for repeated measurements and follow-ups. Describe any agreements with and payments made to participants. Note institutional review board approvals, data safety board arrangements, and other indications of compliance with ethical standards.

Sample Size, Power, and Precision. Provide the intended size of the sample and number of individuals meant to be in each condition if separate conditions were used. State whether the achieved sample differed in known ways from the intended sample. Conclusions and interpretations should not go beyond what the achieved sample warrants. State how the intended sample size was determined (e.g., analysis of power or precision). If interim analysis and stopping rules were used to modify the desired sample size, describe the methodology and results of applying that methodology.

Measures and Covariates. Include in the Method section definitions of all primary and secondary outcome measures and covariates, including measures collected but not included in the current report. Provide information on instruments used, including their psychometric and biometric properties and evidence of cultural validity (Section 10.10 for how to cite hardware and apparatuses; see Section 10.11 for how to cite tests, scales, and inventories).

Data Collection. Describe the methods used to collect data (e.g., written questionnaires, interviews, observations). Provide information on any masking of participants in the research (i.e., whether participants, those administering the manipulations, and/or those assessing the outcomes were unaware of participants' assignment to conditions), how masking was accomplished, and how the masking was assessed. Describe the instrumentation used in the study, including standardized assessments, physical equipment, and imaging protocols, in sufficient detail to allow exact replication of the study.

Quality of Measurements. Describe methods used to enhance the quality of measurements, including training and reliability of data collectors, use of multiple observers, translation of research materials, and pretesting of materials on populations who were not included in the initial development of the instrumentation. Pay attention to the psychometric properties of the measurement in the context of contemporary testing standards and the sample being investigated; report the psychometric characteristics of the instruments used following the principles articulated in the *Standards for Educational and Psychological Testing* (American Educational Research Association et al., 2014). In addition to psychometric characteristics for paper-and-pencil measures, provide interrater reliabilities for subjectively scored measures and ratings. Internal consistency coefficients can be useful for understanding composite scales.

Research Design. Specify the research design in the Method section. For example, were participants placed into conditions that were manipulated, or were they observed in their natural setting? If multiple conditions were created, how were participants assigned to conditions—through random assignment or some other selection mechanism? Was the study conducted as a between-subjects or a within-subjects design? Reporting standards vary on the basis of the research design (e.g., experimental manipulation with randomization, clinical trial without randomization, longitudinal design). Consult Figure 3.1 to determine which tables on the JARS website to use for your research design. See Sections 3.9 and 3.10 for a summary of design-specific reporting standards. See Section 3.11 for standards for particular analytic methods and Section 3.12 for quantitative meta-analysis standards.

Studies can be mixtures of various types; for instance, a study may involve an experimental manipulation with randomization with some factors repeated in a longitudinal fashion. For studies not currently covered by JARS, provide the commonly used name for that design. For more on mixed methods designs, see Section 3.18.

Experimental Manipulations or Interventions. If experimental manipulations or interventions were used in the study, describe their specific content. Include details of the interventions or manipulations intended for each study condition, including control groups (if any), and describe how and when interventions or experimental manipulations were administered. Describe the essential features of "treatment as usual" if that is included as a study or control condition.

Carefully describe the content of the specific interventions or experimental manipulations used. Often, this involves presenting a brief summary of instructions given to participants. If the instructions are unusual, or if the instructions themselves constitute the experimental manipulation, present them verbatim in an appendix or supplemental materials. If the text is brief, present it in the body of the paper if it does not interfere with the readability of the report.

Describe the methods of manipulation and data acquisition. If a mechanical apparatus was used to present stimulus materials or to collect data, include in the description of procedures the apparatus model number and manufacturer (when important, as in neuroimaging studies), its key settings or parameters (e.g., pulse settings), and its resolution (e.g., stimulus delivery, recording precision). As with the description of the experimental manipulation or intervention, this material may be presented in the body of the paper, in an appendix, or in supplemental materials, as appropriate.

When relevant—such as in the delivery of clinical and educational interventions—the procedures should also contain a description of who delivered the intervention, including their level of professional training and their level of training in the specific intervention. Present the number of deliverers along with the mean, standard deviation, and range of number of individuals or units treated by each deliverer.

Provide information about (a) the setting in which the manipulation or intervention was delivered, (b) the intended quantity and duration of exposure to the manipulation or intervention (i.e., how many sessions, episodes, or events were intended to be delivered and how long they were intended to last), (c) the time span for the delivery of the manipulation or intervention of each unit (e.g., whether the manipulation delivery was completed in one session, or, if participants returned for multiple sessions, how much time passed between the first and last session), and (d) activities or incentives used to increase compliance.

When an instrument is translated into a language other than the language in which it was developed, describe the specific method of translation (e.g., *back-translation*, in which a text is translated into another language and then back into the first language to ensure that it is equivalent enough that results can be compared).

Describe how participants were grouped during data acquisition (i.e., was the manipulation or intervention administered individual by individual, in small groups, or in intact groupings such as classrooms?). Indentify the smallest unit (e.g., individuals, work groups, classes) that was analyzed to assess effects. If the unit used for statistical analysis differed from the unit used to deliver the intervention or manipulation (i.e., from the unit of randomization), describe the analytic method used to account for this (e.g., adjusting the standard error estimates, using multilevel analysis).

Data Diagnosis. Describe how data were inspected after collection and, if relevant, any modifications of those data. These procedures may include outlier detection and processing, data transformations based on empirical data distributions, and treatment of missing data or imputation of missing values.

Analytic Strategies. Describe the quantitative analytic strategies (usually statistical) used in analysis of the data, being careful to describe error-rate considerations (e.g., experiment-wise, false discovery rate). The analytic strategies should be described for primary, secondary, and exploratory hypotheses. Exploratory hypotheses are ones that were suggested by the data collected in the study being reported, as opposed to ones generated by theoretical considerations or previously reported empirical studies.

When applying inferential statistics, take seriously the statistical power considerations associated with the tests of hypotheses. Such considerations relate to the likelihood of correctly rejecting the tested hypotheses given a particular alpha level, effect size, and sample size. In that regard, provide evidence that the study has sufficient power to detect effects of substantive interest. Be careful in discussing the role played by sample size in cases in which not rejecting the null hypothesis is desirable (i.e., when one wishes to argue that there are no differences), when testing various assumptions underlying the statistical model adopted (e.g., normality, homogeneity of variance, homogeneity of regression), and in model fitting. Alternatively, use calculations based on a chosen target precision (confidence interval width) to determine sample sizes. Use the resulting confidence intervals to justify conclusions reached concerning effect sizes.

3.7 Quantitative Results Standards

In the Results section of a quantitative paper, summarize the collected data and the results of any analyses performed on those data relevant to the discourse that is to follow. Report the data in sufficient detail to justify your conclusions. Mention all relevant results, regardless of whether your hypotheses were supported, including results that run counter to expectation; include small effect sizes (or statistically nonsignificant findings) when theory predicts large (or statistically significant) ones. Do not hide uncomfortable results by omission. In the spirit of data sharing (encouraged by APA and other professional associations and sometimes required by funding agencies; see Section 1.14), raw data, including study characteristics and individual effect sizes used in a meta-analysis, can be made available as supplemental materials (see Section 2.15) or archived online (see Section 10.9). However, raw data (and individual scores) generally are not presented in the body of the article because of length considerations. The implications of the results should be discussed in the Discussion section.

Participant Flow. For experimental and quasi-experimental designs, provide a description of the flow of participants (humans, nonhuman animals, or units such as classrooms or hospital wards) through the study. Present the total number of participants recruited into the study and the number of participants assigned to each group. Provide the number of participants who did not complete the experiment or who crossed over to other conditions and explain why. Note the number of participants used in the primary analyses. (This number might differ from the number who completed the study because participants might not show up for or complete the final measurement.) See Figure 7.5 in Section 7.36 for an example flowchart that displays the flow of participants through each stage of a study.

Recruitment. Provide dates defining the periods of recruitment and follow-up and the primary sources of participants, when appropriate. If recruitment and follow-up dates differ by group, provide the dates for each group.

Statistics and Data Analysis. Analyses of the data and reporting of the results of those analyses are fundamental aspects of the conduct of research. Accurate, unbiased, complete, and insightful reporting of the analytic treatment of data (be it quantitative or qualitative) must be a component of all research reports. Researchers in the field of psychology use numerous approaches to the analysis of data, and no one approach is uniformly preferred as long as the method is appropriate to the research questions being asked and the nature of the data collected. The methods used must support their analytic burdens, including robustness to violations of the assumptions that underlie them, and must provide clear, unequivocal insights into the data. In reporting your statistical and data analyses, adhere to the organizational structure suggested in the Method section (see Section 3.6): primary hypotheses, secondary hypotheses, and exploratory hypotheses. Ensure that you have reported the results of data diagnoses (see Section 3.6) in the Method section before you report the results linked to hypothesis confirmation or disconfirmation. Discuss any exclusions, transformations, or imputation decisions that resulted from the data diagnosis.

Historically, researchers in psychology have relied heavily on null hypothesis significance testing (NHST) as a starting point for many of their analytic approaches. Different fields and publishers have different policies; APA, for example, stresses that NHST is but a starting point and that additional reporting elements such as effect sizes, confidence intervals, and extensive description are needed to convey the most complete meaning of the results (Wilkinson & the Task Force on Statistical Inference, 1999; see also APA, n.d.-b). The degree to which any journal emphasizes NHST is a decision of the individual editor. However, complete reporting of all tested hypotheses and estimates of appropriate effect sizes and confidence intervals are the minimum expectations for all APA journals. Researchers are always responsible for the accurate and responsible reporting of the results of their research study.

Assume that readers have a professional knowledge of statistical methods. Do not review basic concepts and procedures or provide citations for the most commonly used statistical procedures. If, however, there is any question about the appropriateness of a particular statistical procedure, justify its use by clearly stating the evidence that exists for the robustness of the procedure as applied.

Missing Data. Missing data can have a detrimental effect on the legitimacy of the inferences drawn by statistical tests. It is critical that the frequency or percentages of missing data be reported along with any empirical evidence and/or theoretical arguments for the causes of data that are missing. Data might be described as *missing completely at random* (as when values of the missing variable are not related to the probability that they are missing or to the value of any other variable in the data set), *missing at random* (as when the probability of missing a value on a variable is not related to the missing value itself but may be related to other completely observed variables in the data set), or *not missing at random* (as when the probability of observing a given value for a variable is related to the missing value itself). It is also important to describe the methods for addressing missing data, if any were used (e.g., multiple imputation).

Reporting Results of Inferential Statistical Tests. When reporting the results of inferential statistical tests or when providing estimates of parameters or effect sizes, include sufficient information to help readers fully understand the analyses conducted and possible alternative explanations for the outcomes of those analyses. Because each analytic technique depends on different aspects of the data and assumptions, it is impossible to specify what constitutes a "sufficient set of statistics" in general terms. However, such a set usually includes at least the following: per-cell sample sizes, observed cell means (or frequencies of cases in each category for a categorical variable), and cell standard deviations or pooled within-cell variance. In the case of multivariable analytic systems, such as multivariate analyses of variance, regression analyses, structural equation modeling, and hierarchical linear modeling, the associated means, sample sizes, and variance–covariance (or correlation) matrix or matrices often represent a sufficient set of statistics. At times, the amount of information that constitutes a sufficient set of statistics is extensive; when this is the case, the information could be supplied in a supplementary data set or an appendix (see Sections 2.14–2.15). For analyses based on small samples (including *N*-of-1 investigations; see Section 3.10), consider providing the complete set of raw data in a table or figure, provided that confidentiality can be maintained. Your work will more easily become a part of the cumulative knowledge of the field if you include enough statistical information to allow its inclusion in future meta-analyses.

For inferential statistical tests (e.g., *t*, *F*, and chi-square tests), include the obtained magnitude or value of the test statistic, the degrees of freedom, the probability of obtaining a value as extreme as or more extreme than the one obtained (exact *p* value), and the size and direction of the effect. When point estimates (e.g., sample means, regression coefficients) are provided, always include an associated measure of variability (precision), with an indication of the specific measure used (e.g., standard error).

Inclusion of Confidence Intervals. It can be extremely effective to include confidence intervals (for estimates of parameters; functions of parameters, such as differences in means; and effect sizes) when reporting results. Because confidence intervals combine information on location and precision and can be directly used to infer significance levels, they are generally the best reporting strategy. As a rule, it is best to use a single confidence level, specified on an a priori basis (e.g., a 95% or 99% confidence interval), throughout the article. Wherever possible, base discussion and interpretation of results on point and interval estimates.

When using complex data-analytic techniques—such as structural equation modeling, Bayesian techniques, hierarchical linear modeling, factor analysis, multivariate analysis, and similar approaches—provide details of the models estimated (see Section 3.11). Also provide (usually in supplemental materials) the associated variance–covariance (or correlation) matrices. Identify the software used to run the analysis (e.g., SAS PROC GLM or a particular R package) and any parametric settings used in running the analyses (references are not necessary for these software programs). Report any estimation problems (e.g., failure to converge), regression diagnosis issues, or analytic anomalies. Report any problems with statistical assumptions or data issues that might affect the validity of the findings.

Effect Sizes. For readers to appreciate the magnitude or importance of a study's findings, it is recommended to include some measure of effect size in the Results section. Effect sizes are statistical estimates; therefore, whenever possible, provide a confidence interval for each effect size reported to indicate the precision of estimation of the effect size. Effect sizes may be expressed in the original units (e.g., mean number of questions answered correctly, kilograms per month for a regression slope) and are most easily understood when reported as such. It is valuable to also report an effect size in some standardized or units-free or scale-free unit (e.g., Cohen's *d* value) or a standardized regression weight. Multiple degree-of-freedom effect-size indicators are less useful than effect-size indicators that decompose multiple degree-of-freedom tests into meaningful one degree-of-freedom effects, particularly when the latter are the results that inform the discussion. The general principle to follow is to provide readers with enough information to assess the magnitude of the observed effect.

Studies With Experimental Manipulations or Interventions. In studies reporting the results of experimental manipulations or interventions, clarify whether the analysis was by intent to treat. That is, were all participants assigned to conditions included in the data analysis regardless of whether they actually received the intervention, or were only participants who completed the intervention satisfactorily included? Give a rationale for the choice.

Ancillary Analyses. Report any other analyses performed, including subgroup analyses and adjusted analyses, indicating those that were prespecified and those that were exploratory (although not necessarily in the level of detail of primary analyses). Consider putting the detailed results of ancillary analyses in supplemental materials. Discuss the implications, if any, of the ancillary analyses for statistical error rates.

Baseline Data. Be sure to provide baseline demographic and/or clinical characteristics of each group.

Adverse Events. If interventions were studied, detail all important adverse events (i.e., events with serious consequences) and/or side effects in each intervention group. If none occurred, note this as well.

3.8 Quantitative Discussion Standards

After presenting the results, you are in a position to evaluate and interpret their implications, especially with respect to your original hypotheses. In the Discussion section of a quantitative paper, examine, interpret, and qualify the results of your research and draw inferences and conclusions from them. In the case of empirical studies, there should be a tight relationship between the results that are reported and their discussion. Emphasize any theoretical or practical consequences of the results. When the discussion is relatively brief and straightforward, you can combine it with the Results section, creating a section called "Results and Discussion." If a manuscript presents multiple studies, discuss the findings in the order that the studies were presented within the article.

Open the Discussion section with a clear statement of support or nonsupport for all hypotheses, distinguished by primary and secondary hypotheses. In the case of ambiguous outcomes, explain why the results are judged as such.

Discuss the implications of exploratory analyses in terms of both substantive findings and error rates that may be uncontrolled.

Similarities and differences between your results and the work of others (where they exist) should be used to contextualize, confirm, and clarify your conclusions. Do not simply reformulate and repeat points already made; each new statement should contribute to your interpretation and to readers' understanding of the problem.

Limitations and Strengths. Your interpretation of the results should take into account (a) sources of potential bias and other threats to internal validity, (b) the imprecision of measures, (c) the overall number of tests and/or overlap among tests, (d) the adequacy of sample sizes and sampling validity, and (e) other limitations or weaknesses of the study. If an intervention or manipulation is involved, discuss whether it was successfully implemented, and note the mechanism by which it was intended to work (i.e., its causal pathways and/or alternative mechanisms). Discuss the fidelity with which the intervention or manipulation was implemented, and describe the barriers that were responsible for any lack of fidelity. Acknowledge the limitations of your research, and address alternative explanations of the results. Discuss the generalizability, or external validity, of the findings. This critical analysis should take into account differences between the target population and the accessed sample. For interventions, discuss characteristics that make them more or less applicable to circumstances not included in the study, what outcomes were measured and how (relative to other measures that might have been used), the length of time to measurement (between the end of the intervention and the measurement of outcomes), incentives, compliance rates, and specific settings involved in the study as well as other contextual issues.

Study Implications. End the Discussion section with a reasoned and justifiable commentary on the importance of your findings. This concluding section may be brief, or it may be extensive if it is tightly reasoned, self-contained, and not overstated. In the conclusion, consider returning to a discussion of why the problem is important (as stated in the introduction); what larger issues, meaning those that transcend the particulars of the subfield, might hinge on the findings; and what propositions are confirmed or disconfirmed by the extrapolation of these findings to such overarching issues.

Also consider the following issues:

- What is the theoretical, clinical, or practical significance of the outcomes, and what is the basis for these interpretations?
- If the findings are valid and replicable, what real-life psychological phenomena might be explained or modeled by the results?
- Are applications warranted on the basis of this research?
- What problems remain unresolved or arise anew because of these findings?

The responses to these questions are the core of the contribution of your study and justify why readers both inside and outside your specialty should attend to the findings. Readers should receive clear, unambiguous, and direct answers.

3.9 Additional Reporting Standards for Typical Experimental and Nonexperimental Studies

As mentioned in Section 3.5, the reporting standards in Table 3.1 apply to all quantitative studies. Additional standards apply because of particular design features or empirical claims made. Studies with experimental (e.g., studies using random assignment, studies using nonrandom assignment, clinical trials) and nonexperimental designs have these additional specific reporting standards. See Figure 3.1 for a flowchart of what standards to use for your research and links to the associated standards on the JARS website.

Studies Using Random Assignment. Describe the unit of randomization and the procedures used to generate assignments. Be careful to note when units such as classrooms are the unit of randomization, even though data collection may be from individual students within the classroom. Indicate the unit of randomization in the analysis of such study outcomes as well. Describe masking provisions used to ensure the quality of the randomization process.

Studies Using Nonrandom Assignment. Describe the unit of assignment and the method (rules) used to assign the unit to the condition, including details of any assignment restrictions such as blocking, stratification, and so forth. Describe any procedures used to minimize selection bias such as matching or propensity score matching.

Clinical Trials. Within the JARS context, a *clinical trial* or a *randomized clinical trial* is a research investigation that evaluates the effects of one or more health-related interventions (e.g., psychotherapy, medication) on health outcomes by prospectively assigning people to experimental conditions. As used here, a clinical trial is a subset of a class of studies called "randomized control studies," and the reporting standards for clinical trials apply to randomized control studies as well. Most clinical trials are experimental studies with random assignment, so all reporting standards for those types of studies also apply. Report information about the clinical trial aspect of the study. If the trial has been registered (e.g., on ClinicalTrials.gov), report its registration on the title page in the author note (see Section 2.7) and in the text. In the Method section, provide details of any site-specific considerations if the trial is a multisite trial. Provide access to the study protocol; if the study is a comparison to a current "standard" treatment, describe that standard treatment in sufficient detail that it can be accurately replicated in any follow-up or replication study. Describe the data safety and monitoring board and any stopping rules if used. If there was a follow-up, provide the rationale for the length of the follow-up period.

Nonexperimental Designs. Nonexperimental studies (in which no variable is manipulated) are sometimes called, among other things, "observational," "correlational," or "natural history" studies. Their purpose is to observe, describe, classify, or analyze naturally occurring relationships between variables of interest. In general, describe the design of the study, methods of participant selection and sampling (e.g., prospective, retrospective, case-control, cohort, cohort-sequential), and data sources. Define all variables and describe the comparability of assessment across natural groups. Indicate how predictors, confounders, and effect modifiers were included in the analysis. Discuss the potential limitations of the study as relevant (e.g., the possibility of unmeasured confounding).

3.10 Reporting Standards for Special Designs

Studies with some special designs (e.g., longitudinal, N-of-1, replication) have specific reporting standards. See Figure 3.1 for a flowchart of what standards to use for your research, including studies with special designs, and links to the associated standards on the JARS website.

Longitudinal Studies. A *longitudinal study* involves the observation of the same individuals using the same set of measurements (or attributes) at multiple times or occasions. This multiple observational structure may be combined with other research designs, including those with and without experimental manipulations, randomized clinical trials, or any other study type. Reporting standards for longitudinal studies must combine those for the basic underlying study structure with those specific to a longitudinal study.

Thus, in addition to the information dictated by the underlying structure of the study, report information about the longitudinal aspects of the study. For example, describe sample recruitment and retention methods, including attrition at each wave of data collection and how any missing data were handled. Describe any contextual changes that occurred during the progress of the study (e.g., a major economic recession). Report any changes in instrumentation that occurred over the course of the study, such as a change in level of a measure of school achievement. Because longitudinal studies are often reported in a segmental fashion, report where any portions of the data have been previously published and the degree of overlap with the current report (see Section 1.16).

N-of-1 Studies. Studies with N-of-1 designs occur in several different forms; however, the essential feature of all these designs is that the unit of study is a single entity (usually a person). In some N-of-1 studies, several individual results are described, and consistency of results may be a central point of the discussion. No N-of-1 study, however, combines the results from several cases (e.g., by computing averages).

Describe the design type (e.g., withdrawal–reversal, multiple baseline, alternating–simultaneous treatments, changing criterion) and its phases and phase sequence when one or more manipulations have been used. Indicate whether and how randomization was used. For each participant, report the sequence actually completed and the participant's results, including raw data for target behaviors and other outcomes.

Replication Articles. For a replication article (see Section 1.4), indicate the type of replication (e.g., direct [exact, literal], approximate, conceptual [construct]). Provide comparisons between the original study and the replication being reported so readers can evaluate the degree to which there may be factors present that would contribute to any differences between the findings of the original study and the findings of the replication being reported. Compare recruitment procedures; demographic characteristics of participants; and instrumentation, including hardware and "soft" measures (e.g., questionnaires, interviews, psychological tests), modifications made to measures (e.g., translation or back-translation), psychometric characteristics of scores analyzed, and informants and methods of administration (e.g., paper-and-pencil vs. online). Report results of the same analytic methods (statistical or other quantitative manipulations) used in the original study, as well as any results from additional or different analyses. Report in detail the rules (e.g., comparison of effect sizes) that were used in deciding the degree to which the original results were replicated in the new study being reported.

3.11 Standards for Analytic Approaches

Although reporting standards are generally associated with entire research designs, some quantitative procedures (e.g., structural equation modeling, Bayesian techniques) are of sufficient complexity and open to such internal variation that additional information (beyond just the name of the technique and a few parameters) must be reported for readers to be able to fully comprehend the analysis. Other researchers may need additional information to evaluate the conclusions the authors have drawn or to replicate the analysis with their own data. Standards for structural equation modeling and Bayesian techniques are on the JARS website (https://apastyle.apa.org/jars/quantitative).

Structural Equation Modeling. *Structural equation modeling* is a family of statistical techniques that involve the specification of a structural or measurement model. The analysis involves steps that estimate the effects represented in the model (parameters) and evaluate the extent of correspondence between the model and the data. These standards are complex and call for a comprehensive description of data preparation, specification of the initial model(s), estimation, model fit assessment, respecification of the model(s), and reporting of results.

Bayesian Techniques. *Bayesian techniques* are inferential statistical procedures in which researchers estimate parameters of an underlying distribution on the basis of the observed distribution. These standards are complex and address the needs of this analytic approach, including how to specify the model, describe and plot the distributions, describe the computation of the model, report any Bayes factors, and report Bayesian model averaging.

3.12 Quantitative Meta-Analysis Standards

Quantitative meta-analyses (see Section 1.5) have specific reporting standards that are available in full on the JARS website (https://apastyle.apa.org/jars/quant-table-9.pdf). These standards are specific to meta-analyses but can easily generalize to other quantitative research synthesis approaches. One feature of meta-analyses that makes them different (in reporting demands) from other study types is that the units of analysis are research reports—usually articles that have been published or archived. The primary features of the included studies are numerical estimates of the effect sizes of the phenomena of interest. The reporting standards for quantitative meta-analyses are complex and include how to describe study selection, study inclusion and exclusion criteria, and data collection, as well as how to summarize the selected studies and their characteristics (e.g., through tables and figures; see Table 7.4 in Section 7.21 for a sample summary meta-analysis table).

Reporting Standards for Qualitative Research

3.13 Basic Expectations for Qualitative Research Reporting

Whereas standards for reporting information in the abstract and introduction of a paper are common to all kinds of research (see Sections 3.3–3.4), there are specific reporting standards for qualitative research articles, including the Method (Section 3.14), Findings or Results (Section 3.15), and Discussion (Section 3.16) sections. Standards specific to quantitative and mixed methods research are presented in Sections 3.5 to 3.12 and 3.18, respectively.

The basic expectations for reporting qualitative research are presented in Table 3.2. An additional table on the JARS website describes the reporting standards for qualitative meta-analyses (see Section 3.17). There are many qualitative procedures and methods as well as many designs and approaches to inquiry in which they can be embedded; because of this variation, all the elements described in Table 3.2 and the guidelines in Sections 3.14 to 3.16 may not be appropriate for all qualitative studies.

Authors must decide how sections should be organized within the context of their specific study. For example, qualitative researchers may combine the Results and Discussion sections because they may not find it possible to separate a given finding from its interpreted meaning within a broader context. Qualitative researchers may also use headings that reflect the values in their tradition (such as "Findings" instead of "Results") and omit ones that do not. As long as the necessary information is present, the paper does not need to be segmented into the same sections and subsections as a quantitative paper.

Qualitative papers may appear different from quantitative papers because they tend to be longer. This added length is due to the following central features of qualitative reporting: (a) In place of referencing statistical analyses, researchers must include detailed rationales and procedural descriptions to explain how an analytic method was selected, applied, and adapted to fit each specific question or context; (b) researchers must include a discussion of their own backgrounds and beliefs and how they managed them throughout the study; and (c) researchers must show how they moved from their raw data to develop findings by adding quoted materials or other demonstrative evidence into their presentation of results. Because qualitative articles need to be lengthier to provide the information necessary to support an adequate review, limitations on length should be more flexible than they are for quantitative articles, which may not need to include this information. When journal page limits conflict with the length of a qualitative paper, qualitative researchers should work with journal editors to reach a solution that enables an adequate review of the paper in question.

3.14 Qualitative Method Standards

The Method section of a qualitative article includes the following types of information (see also Table 3.2).

Research Design Overview. The Method section of a qualitative article begins with a paragraph that summarizes the research design. It might mention the data-collection strategies, data-analytic strategies, and approaches to inquiry and provide a brief rationale for the design selected if this was not described in the objectives section of the introduction (see Section 3.4).

Researcher Description. To situate the investigation within the expectations, identities, and positions of the researchers (e.g., interviewers, analysts, research team), describe the researchers' backgrounds in approaching the study, emphasizing their prior understandings of the phenomena under study. Descriptions of researchers relevant to the analysis could include (but are not limited to) their

Table 3.2 Qualitative Design Reporting Standards (JARS–Qual)

Title Page

Title

- Identify key issues/topic under consideration.

Author Note

- Acknowledge funding sources or contributors.
- Acknowledge conflicts of interest, if any.

Abstract

- State the problem/question/objectives under investigation.
- Indicate the study design, including types of participants or data sources, analytic strategy, main results/ findings, and main implications/significance.
- Identify five keywords.

    Guidance for Authors
    - Consider including at least one keyword that describes the method and one that describes the types of participants or phenomena under investigation.
    - Consider describing your approach to inquiry when it will facilitate the review process and intelligibility of your paper. If your work is not grounded in a specific approach to inquiry or your approach would be too complicated to explain in the allotted word count, however, it would not be advisable to provide explication on this point in the abstract.

Introduction

Description of Research Problem or Question

- Frame the problem or question and its context.
- Review, critique, and synthesize the applicable literature to identify key issues/debates/theoretical frameworks in the relevant literature to clarify barriers, knowledge gaps, or practical needs.

    Guidance for Reviewers
    - The introduction may include case examples, personal narratives, vignettes, or other illustrative material.

Study Objectives/Aims/Research Goals

- State the purpose(s)/goal(s)/aim(s) of the study.
- State the target audience, if specific.
- Provide the rationale for fit of design used to investigate this purpose/goal (e.g., theory building, explanatory, developing understanding, social action, description, highlighting social practices).
- Describe the approach to inquiry, if it illuminates the objectives and research rationale (e.g., descriptive, interpretive, feminist, psychoanalytic, postpositivist, critical, postmodern, constructivist, or pragmatic approaches).

    Guidance for Authors
    - If relevant to objectives, explain the relation of the current analysis to prior articles/publications.
    Guidance for Reviewers
    - Qualitative studies often legitimately need to be divided into multiple manuscripts because of journal article page limitations, but each manuscript should have a separate focus.
    - Qualitative studies tend not to identify hypotheses, but rather research questions and goals.

Method

Research Design Overview

- Summarize the research design, including data-collection strategies, data-analytic strategies, and, if illuminating, approaches to inquiry (e.g., descriptive, interpretive, feminist, psychoanalytic, postpositivist, critical, postmodern, constructivist, or pragmatic approaches).
- Provide the rationale for the design selected.

    Guidance for Reviewers
    - Method sections can be written in a chronological or narrative format.
    - Although authors provide a method description that other investigators should be able to follow, it is not required that other investigators arrive at the same conclusions but rather that the method description leads other investigators to conclusions with a similar degree of methodological integrity.

Table 3.2 Qualitative Design Reporting Standards (JARS–Qual) *(continued)*

Method *(continued)*

- At times, elements may be relevant to multiple sections and authors need to organize what belongs in each subsection in order to describe the method coherently and reduce redundancy. For instance, the overview and the objectives statement may be presented in one section.
- Processes of qualitative research are often iterative versus linear, may evolve through the inquiry process, and may move between data collection and analysis in multiple formats. As a result, data collection and analysis sections might be combined.
- For the reasons stated previously and because qualitative methods often are adapted and combined creatively, requiring detailed description and rationale, an average qualitative Method section typically is longer than an average quantitative Method section.

Study Participants or Data Sources

RESEARCHER DESCRIPTION

- Describe the researchers' backgrounds in approaching the study, emphasizing their prior understandings of the phenomena under study (e.g., interviewers, analysts, or research team).
- Describe how prior understandings of the phenomena under study were managed and/or influenced the research (e.g., enhancing, limiting, or structuring data collection and analysis).

  Guidance for Authors
  - Prior understandings relevant to the analysis could include, but are not limited to, descriptions of researchers' demographic/cultural characteristics, credentials, experience with phenomena, training, values, and/or decisions in selecting archives or material to analyze.

  Guidance for Reviewers
  - Researchers differ in the extensiveness of reflexive self-description in reports. It may not be possible for authors to estimate the depth of description desired by reviewers without guidance.

PARTICIPANTS OR OTHER DATA SOURCES

- Provide the numbers of participants/documents/events analyzed.
- Describe the demographics/cultural information, perspectives of participants, or characteristics of data sources that might influence the data collected.
- Describe existing data sources, if relevant (e.g., newspapers, internet, archive).
- Provide data repository information for openly shared data, if applicable.
- Describe archival searches or process of locating data for analyses, if applicable.

RESEARCHER–PARTICIPANT RELATIONSHIP

- Describe the relationships and interactions between researchers and participants relevant to the research process and any impact on the research process (e.g., was there a relationship prior to research, are there any ethical considerations relevant to prior relationships).

Participant Recruitment

RECRUITMENT PROCESS

- Describe the recruitment process (e.g., face-to-face, telephone, mail, email) and any recruitment protocols.
- Describe any incentives or compensation, and provide assurance of relevant ethical processes of data collection and consent process as relevant (may include institutional review board approval, particular adaptations for vulnerable populations, safety monitoring).
- Describe the process by which the number of participants was determined in relation to the study design.
- Provide any changes in numbers through attrition and final number of participants/sources (if relevant, refusal rates or reasons for dropout).
- Describe the rationale for decision to halt data collection (e.g., saturation).
- Convey the study purpose as portrayed to participants, if different from the purpose stated.

  Guidance for Authors/Reviewers
  - The order of the recruitment process and the selection process and their contents may be determined in relation to the authors' methodological approach. Some authors will determine a selection process and then develop a recruitment method based on those criteria. Other authors will develop a recruitment process and then select participants responsively in relation to evolving findings.

  Guidance for Reviewers
  - There is no agreed-upon minimum number of participants for a qualitative study. Rather, the author should provide a rationale for the number of participants chosen.

Table 3.2 Qualitative Design Reporting Standards (JARS–Qual) *(continued)*

Method *(continued)*

PARTICIPANT SELECTION
- Describe the participant/data source selection process (e.g., purposive sampling methods, such as maximum variation; convenience sampling methods, such as snowball selection; theoretical sampling; diversity sampling) and inclusion/exclusion criteria.
- Provide the general context for the study (when data were collected, sites of data collection).
- If your participant selection is from an archived data set, describe the recruitment and selection process from that data set as well as any decisions in selecting sets of participants from that data set.
    Guidance for Authors
    - A statement can clarify how the number of participants fits with practices in the design at hand, recognizing that transferability of findings in qualitative research to other contexts is based in developing deep and contextualized understandings that can be applied by readers rather than quantitative estimates of error and generalizations to populations.
    Guidance for Authors/Reviewers
    - The order of the recruitment process and the selection process and their contents may be determined in relation to the authors' methodological approach. Some authors will determine a selection process and then develop a recruitment method based on those criteria. Other authors will develop a recruitment process and then select participants responsively in relation to evolving findings.

Data Collection

DATA–COLLECTION OR IDENTIFICATION PROCEDURES
- State the form of data collected (e.g., interviews, questionnaires, media, observation).
- Describe the origins or evolution of the data-collection protocol.
- Describe any alterations of data-collection strategy in response to the evolving findings or the study rationale.
- Describe the data-selection or data-collection process (e.g., were others present when data were collected, number of times data were collected, duration of collection, context).
- Convey the extensiveness of engagement (e.g., depth of engagement, time intensiveness of data collection).
- For interview and written studies, indicate the mean and range of the time duration in the data-collection process (e.g., interviews were held for 75 to 110 min, with an average interview time of 90 min).
- Describe the management or use of reflexivity in the data-collection process, as it illuminates the study.
- Describe questions asked in data collection: content of central questions, form of questions (e.g., open vs. closed).
    Guidance for Reviewers
    - Researchers may use terms for data collection that are coherent within their research approach and process, such as "data identification," "data collection," or "data selection." Descriptions should be provided, however, in accessible terms in relation to the readership.
    - It may not be useful for researchers to reproduce all of the questions they asked in an interview, especially in the case of unstructured or semistructured interviews as questions are adapted to the content of each interview.

RECORDING AND DATA TRANSFORMATION
- Identify data audio/visual recording methods, field notes, or transcription processes used.

Analysis

DATA–ANALYTIC STRATEGIES
- Describe the methods and procedures used and for what purpose/goal.
- Explicate in detail the process of analysis, including some discussion of the procedures (e.g., coding, thematic analysis) following a principle of transparency.
- Describe coders or analysts and their training, if not already described in the researcher description section (e.g., coder selection, collaboration groups).
- Identify whether coding categories emerged from the analyses or were developed a priori.
- Identify units of analysis (e.g., entire transcript, unit, text) and how units were formed, if applicable.

Table 3.2 Qualitative Design Reporting Standards (JARS–Qual) *(continued)*

Method *(continued)*

- Describe the process of arriving at an analytic scheme, if applicable (e.g., if one was developed before or during the analysis or was emergent throughout).
- Provide illustrations and descriptions of the analytic scheme development, if relevant.
- Indicate software, if used.
  Guidance for Authors
  – Provide rationales to illuminate analytic choices in relation to the study goals.
  Guidance for Reviewers
  – Researchers may use terms for data analysis that are coherent within their research approach and process (e.g., "interpretation," "unitization," "eidetic analysis," "coding"). Descriptions should be provided, however, in accessible terms in relation to the readership.

METHODOLOGICAL INTEGRITY

- Demonstrate that the claims made from the analysis are warranted and have produced findings with methodological integrity. The procedures that support methodological integrity (i.e., fidelity and utility) typically are described across the relevant sections of a paper, but they could be addressed in a separate section when elaboration or emphasis would be helpful. Issues of methodological integrity include the following:
  – Assess the *adequacy* of the data in terms of the ability to capture forms of diversity most relevant to the question, research goals, and inquiry approach.
  – Describe how the *researchers' perspectives* were managed in both the data collection and analysis (e.g., to limit their effect on the data collection, to structure the analysis).
  – Demonstrate that findings are *grounded* in the evidence (e.g., using quotes, excerpts, or descriptions of researchers' engagement in data collection).
  – Demonstrate that the contributions are *insightful* and *meaningful* (e.g., in relation to the current literature and the study goal).
  – Provide relevant *contextual* information for findings (e.g., setting of study, information about participants, interview question asked is presented before excerpt as needed).
  – Present findings in a *coherent* manner that makes sense of contradictions or disconfirming evidence in the data (e.g., reconcile discrepancies, describe why a conflict might exist in the findings).
- Demonstrate *consistency* with regard to the analytic processes (e.g., analysts may use demonstrations of analyses to support consistency, describe their development of a stable perspective, interrater reliability, consensus) or describe responses to inconsistencies, as relevant (e.g., coders switching midway through analysis, an interruption in the analytic process). If alterations in methodological integrity were made for ethical reasons, explicate those reasons and the adjustments made.
- Describe how support for claims was supplemented by any checks added to the qualitative analysis. Examples of supplemental checks that can strengthen the research may include
  – transcripts/data collected returned to participants for feedback
  – triangulation across multiple sources of information, findings, or investigators
  – checks on the interview thoroughness or interviewer demands
  – consensus or auditing process
  – member checks or participant feedback on findings
  – data displays/matrices
  – in-depth thick description, case examples, or illustrations
  – structured methods of researcher reflexivity (e.g., sending memos, field notes, diary, logbooks, journals, bracketing)
  – checks on the utility of findings in responding to the study problem (e.g., an evaluation of whether a solution worked)

  Guidance for Reviewers
  – Research does not need to use all or any of the checks (as rigor is centrally based in the iterative process of qualitative analyses, which inherently includes checks within the evolving, self-correcting iterative analyses), but their use can augment a study's methodological integrity. Approaches to inquiry have different traditions in terms of using checks and which checks are most valued.
- Describe research findings (e.g., themes, categories, narratives) and the meaning and understandings that the researcher has derived from the data analysis.
- Demonstrate the analytic process of reaching findings (e.g., quotes, excerpts of data).

Table 3.2 Qualitative Design Reporting Standards (JARS–Qual) *(continued)*

Findings/Results

Findings/Results Subsections

- Present research findings in a way that is compatible with the study design.
- Present synthesizing illustrations (e.g., diagrams, tables, models), if useful in organizing and conveying findings. Photographs or links to videos can be used.

  Guidance for Authors
  - Findings presented in an artistic manner (e.g., a link to a dramatic presentation of findings) should also include information in the reporting standards to support the research presentation.
  - Use quotes or excerpts to augment data description (e.g., thick, evocative description, field notes, text excerpts), but these should not replace the description of the findings of the analysis.

  Guidance for Reviewers
  - The Findings section tends to be longer than in quantitative papers because of the demonstrative rhetoric needed to permit the evaluation of the analytic procedure.
  - Depending on the approach to inquiry, findings and discussion may be combined or a personalized discursive style might be used to portray the researchers' involvement in the analysis.
  - Findings may or may not include quantified information, depending upon the study's goals, approach to inquiry, and study characteristics.

Discussion

Discussion Subsections

- Describe the central contributions and their significance in advancing disciplinary understandings.
- Describe the types of contributions made by findings (e.g., challenging, elaborating on, and supporting prior research or theory in the literature describing the relevance) and how findings can be best utilized.
- Identify similarities and differences from prior theories and research findings.
- Reflect on any alternative explanations of the findings.
- Identify the study's strengths and limitations (e.g., consider how the quality, source, or types of the data or the analytic processes might support or weaken its methodological integrity).
- Describe the limits of the scope of transferability (e.g., what readers should bear in mind when using findings across contexts).
- Revisit any ethical dilemmas or challenges that were encountered, and provide related suggestions for future researchers.
- Consider the implications for future research, policy, or practice.

  Guidance for Reviewers
  - Accounts could lead to multiple solutions rather than a single one. Many qualitative approaches hold that there may be more than one valid and useful set of findings from a given data set.

demographic, cultural, and/or identity characteristics; credentials; experience with the phenomena under study; training; values; or decisions in selecting archives or material to analyze. Describe how prior understandings of the phenomena under study were managed and/or how they influenced the research (e.g., by enhancing, limiting, or structuring data collection and analysis).

Participants or Other Data Sources. When describing participants or data sources, the following information should be reported: number of participants, documents, or events that were analyzed; demographic or cultural information relevant to the research topic; and perspectives of participants and characteristics of data sources relevant to the research topic. As applicable, data sources should be described (e.g., newspapers, internet, archive). Information about data repositories used for openly shared data should be reported if used. The processes entailed in performing archival searches or locating data for analysis should be described as well.

Qualitative researchers should report participant characteristics (listed in Section 3.6) and personal history factors (e.g., age, trauma exposure, abuse history, substance abuse history, family history, geographic history) that are relevant to the specific contexts and topics of their research (see Morse, 2008). Certain characteristics hold influence across many spheres of participants' lives within a given context and would be expected in most research reports; in the United States, these typically include age, gender, race, ethnicity, and socioeconomic status, but other features may be highly relevant as well to a given research question and context (e.g., sexual orientation, immigration status, disability). The descriptions of participant characteristics should be sensitive to the participants and the ways in which they understand and express their identities, statuses, histories, and so forth. Chapter 5 contains further guidance on writing about participant characteristics without bias.

In addition to participant characteristics and personal history factors, other features within a study may influence the experience of a given phenomenon (e.g., psychotherapy orientation in research on psychotherapists, political party membership in a study on economic beliefs) and therefore are important to report. The decision of which participant characteristics and features to report can be driven by a review of prior research, the researchers' experience with a phenomenon, pilot interviews, study goals, contextual dynamics, and empirical data that are analyzed as the data collection proceeds. In this way, reporting considerations may be experientially, theoretically, and empirically driven.

Researcher–Participant Relationships. To increase transparency, describe the relationships and interactions between researchers and participants that are relevant to the research process and any impact on the research process (e.g., any relationships prior to the study, any ethical considerations relevant to prior relationships). Existing relationships may be helpful (e.g., by increasing trust and facilitating disclosure) or harmful (e.g., by decreasing trust and inhibiting disclosure), so the specific dynamics of the relationships should be considered and reported.

Participant Recruitment. There is no minimum number of participants for a qualitative study (see Levitt et al., 2017, for a discussion on adequacy of data in qualitative research). Authors should provide a rationale for the number of participants chosen, often in light of the method or approach to inquiry that is used. Some studies begin with researchers recruiting participants to the study and then selecting participants from the pool that responds. Other studies begin with researchers selecting a type of participant pool and then recruiting from within that pool. The content of Method sections should be ordered to reflect the study's process. Specifically, participant selection might follow participant recruitment or vice versa; thus, discussion of the number of participants is likely to be placed in reference to whichever process came second.

Recruitment Process. Report the method of recruitment (e.g., face-to-face, telephone, mail, email) and any recruitment protocols, and describe how you conveyed the study purpose to participants, especially if it was different from the purpose stated in the study objectives (see Section 3.4). For instance, researchers might describe a broader study aim to participants (e.g., to explore participants' experience of being on parole) but then focus their analysis in a specific manuscript on one aspect of that aim (e.g., the relationships between participants and parole officers). Provide details on any incentives or compensation given to participants, and state relevant ethical processes of data collection and consent, potentially describing institutional review board approval, any adaptations for vulnerable populations, or safety monitoring practices. Present the process for determining the number of participants in relation to the study design (e.g., approaches to inquiry, data-collection strategies, data-analytic strategies). Any changes in this number through attrition (e.g., refusal rates, reasons for dropout) and the final number of participants or sources should be conveyed, as should the rationale for decisions to halt data collection (e.g., saturation).

Participant Selection. To describe how participants were selected from within an identified group, explain any inclusion and/or exclusion criteria as well as the participant and/or data source selection process that was used. This selection process can consist of purposive sampling methods, such as maximum variation; convenience sampling methods, such as snowball selection; theoretical sampling; or diversity sampling. Provide the general context for your study (e.g., when data were collected, sites of data collection). If you selected participants from an archived data set, describe the recruitment and selection process for that data set and any decisions affecting the selection of participants from that data set.

Data Collection. Researchers may use terms for data collection that are coherent with their research approach and process, such as "data identification," "collection," or "selection." Descriptions should be provided, however, in terms that are accessible to readers.

Data-Collection or Identification Procedures. In addition to describing the form of data collected (e.g., interviews, questionnaires, media, observation), convey any alterations to the data-collection strategy (e.g., in response to evolving findings or the study rationale). It may not be useful to reproduce all of the questions asked in an interview, especially in the case of unstructured or semistructured interviews in which questions are adapted to the content of each interview. The content of central or guiding questions should be communicated, however, and the format of the questions can be described (e.g., open questions, nonleading paraphrases, written prompts). Describe the process of data selection or data collection (e.g., whether others were present when data were collected, number of times data were collected, duration of collection, context). Convey the extensiveness of the researchers' engagement (e.g., depth of engagement, time intensiveness of data collection). Describe the management or use of reflexivity in the data-collection process when it illuminates the study.

Recording and Data Transformation. Identify how data were recorded for analysis and explain whether and how data were transformed. This might include a statement regarding audio or visual recording methods, field notes, or transcription.

Analysis. The two primary topics to report in the description of qualitative analyses are the data analysis and the establishment of methodological integrity. Researchers may use terms for data analysis that are coherent within their research approach and process (e.g., "interpretation," "unitization," "eidetic analysis," "coding"). Descriptions should be provided, however, in terms that are accessible to readers.

Data-Analytic Strategies. Describe the methods and procedures of data analysis and the purpose or goal for which they were used. Explain in detail the process of analysis. Describe the process of arriving at an analytic approach (e.g., whether a set of categories of coding was developed before or during the analysis, whether findings emerged from an inductively driven process of analysis; see the glossary on the JARS website at https://apastyle.apa.org/jars/glossary). Also include a discussion of analytic procedures (e.g., coding, thematic analysis) and a description of coders or analysts and their training if not already described in the researcher description section. In this description, identify units of analysis (e.g., entire transcript, unit, text) and how units were formed, if applicable. Indicate whether any categories or codes emerged from the analyses or were developed a priori, and outline the process used in each case. Provide illustrations and descriptions of their development, if relevant. Indicate software, if used.

Methodological Integrity. Highlight procedures that support methodological integrity throughout the paper or summarize central points in a separate section of the Method section when elaboration or emphasis would be helpful (for more on methodological integrity, see Levitt et al., 2017, and the glossary on the JARS website at https://apastyle.apa.org/jars/glossary). Demonstrate that the claims made from the analysis are warranted. Highlight key features of methodological integrity, as follows:

- **adequacy:** Assess the adequacy of the data in terms of their ability to capture forms of diversity most relevant to the research questions, research goals, and inquiry approach.
- **researchers' perspectives:** Describe how the researchers' perspectives were managed in both the data collection and the analysis (e.g., to limit their effect on the data collection, to structure the analysis).
- **groundedness:** Demonstrate that findings are grounded in the evidence (e.g., using quotes, excerpts, or descriptions of researchers' engagement in data collection).
- **meaningfulness:** Demonstrate that the contributions are insightful and meaningful (e.g., in relation to the current literature and the study goals).
- **context:** Provide relevant contextual information for findings (e.g., setting of the study, information about participants; present the interview question asked before an excerpt as needed).
- **coherence:** Present findings in a coherent manner that makes sense of contradictions or disconfirming evidence in the data (e.g., reconcile discrepancies, describe why a conflict might exist in the findings).
- **consistency:** As relevant, comment on consistency with regard to the analytic processes, especially in the face of changing conditions or contexts (e.g., use demonstrations of analyses to support consistency or to describe the development of a stable perspective, such as through the use of interrater reliability or consensus), or describe responses to inconsistencies (e.g., coders switching in the middle of analysis, an interruption in the analytic process).

Support for claims of methodological integrity may be supplemented by any checks added to the qualitative analysis. Approaches to inquiry have different traditions in terms of using checks, and researchers do not need to use all or any of the checks, but their use can augment a study's methodological integrity. The following are examples of supplemental checks that can strengthen the research:

- transcripts or data returned to participants for feedback;
- triangulation across multiple sources of information, findings, or investigators;
- checks on interview thoroughness or interviewer demands;
- consensus or auditing processes;
- member checks or participant feedback on findings;
- data displays or matrices;
- in-depth thick description, case examples, and illustrations;
- structured methods of researcher reflexivity (e.g., memos, field notes, logbooks, diaries, journals, bracketing); and
- checks on the utility of findings in responding to the study problem (e.g., evaluation of whether a solution worked).

3.15 Qualitative Findings or Results Standards

In qualitative research papers, findings may or may not include quantified information, depending on the study's goals, approach to inquiry, and study characteristics. Note that the heading "Findings" may be used rather than "Results."

Descriptions of Both the Development of Findings and the Findings Themselves. Describe research findings (e.g., themes, categories, narratives) and the meaning and understandings that the researchers derived from the data analysis in relation to the purpose of the study. Descriptions of results often include quotes, evidence, or excerpts that demonstrate the process of data analysis and of reaching findings (e.g., thick, evocative description; field notes; text excerpts). These should not replace the description of the findings of the analysis, however. Instead, balance these illustrations with text descriptions that make clear the meanings drawn from individual quotes or excerpts and how they answer the study question.

Compatibility With Study Design. Findings should be presented in a manner that is compatible with the study design. For instance, findings of a grounded theory study might be described using categories organized in a hierarchical form and marked by discrete divisions, whereas findings of an ethnographic study might be written in a chronological narrative format. Also, findings should be written in a style that is coherent with the approach to inquiry used.

Depictions of Findings. Qualitative findings can be presented in various ways. Illustrations (e.g., diagrams, tables, models; see Chapter 7) may be used to organize and convey findings. Photographs or links to videos can be used as well (see Sections 2.15 and 7.30). Findings presented in an artistic manner (e.g., link to a dramatic presentation), however, should also include the information called for in the reporting standards to support the research presentation and a description that clarifies the analytic process and meanings drawn from the findings.

3.16 Qualitative Discussion Standards

The purpose of a qualitative Discussion section is to communicate the contributions of the study in relation to the prior literature and the study goals. In this process, the interpretations of the findings are described in a way that takes into account the limitations of the study as well as plausible alternative explanations. The Discussion section conveys applications of your findings and provides directions for future investigators. If you present multiple studies, discuss the findings in the order in which they are presented within the paper.

Interpreting the Meaning of Your Findings. Instead of simply restating results, a good Discussion section develops readers' understanding of the issues at hand. To do this, describe the central contributions of your research and their significance in advancing disciplinary understandings. Identifying similarities and differences from prior theories and research findings will help in this process. Describe the contributions the findings make (e.g., elaborating on, challenging, or supporting prior research or theory) and how findings can be best utilized. Reflect on any alternative explanations of the findings to clarify the strengths and weaknesses of the explanation that you selected. More than one valid or useful set of findings may emerge from a given data set. It is not considered a drawback for there to be more than one possible interpretation because researchers may centralize different processes or perspectives; however, findings should remain grounded in the empirical analysis of the data.

Limitations and Strengths. Include a subsection to identify the strengths and limitations of the study (e.g., consider how the quality, source, or types of data or the analytic processes might support or weaken the study's methodological integrity, reliability, or validity). Within this subsection, describe the limits of the scope of generalizability or transferability (e.g., issues readers should consider when using findings across contexts).

Study Implications. Convey to readers how your findings might be used and their implications. In this process, you might outline emerging research questions, theoretical insights, new understandings, or methodological designs that advantage the conceptualization, implementation, review, or reporting of future studies. In addition, implications for policy, clinical practice, and advocacy can be communicated to assist readers in implementing your findings.

3.17 Qualitative Meta-Analysis Standards

Qualitative meta-analyses (see Section 1.5) have unique reporting standards that are available in full on the JARS website (https://apastyle.apa.org/jars/qual-table-2.pdf). Two features of qualitative meta-analysis reporting highlighted in this section are reporting on the aggregative process and reporting situatedness.

Reporting on the Aggregative Process. The methodological integrity of the results of meta-analyses rests largely on the extent to which those carrying out the analysis can detail and defend the choices they made of studies to review and the process they undertook to weigh and integrate the findings of the studies. Authors of meta-analyses often aggregate qualitative studies from multiple methodological or theoretical approaches, and they must communicate the approaches of the studies they reviewed as well as their own approach to secondary data analysis. Qualitative meta-analysis involves the interpretive aggregation of thematic findings rather than reanalysis of primary data. Forms of qualitative meta-analysis range on a continuum from assessing the ways findings do or do not replicate each other to arranging interpreted findings into narrative accounts that relate the studies to one another. Authors of meta-analyses enhance their fidelity to the findings by considering the contradictions and ambiguities within and across studies.

Reporting Situatedness. Another factor that distinguishes qualitative meta-analyses from primary qualitative analyses is that they often include an examination of the situatedness of the authors of the primary studies reviewed (e.g., the perspectives of the primary researchers as well as their social positions and contexts and their studies' reflection of these perspectives). Situatedness can be considered in the Findings/Results or Discussion section and may be presented narratively or in tables when simplifying the presentation of trends. See the online table for complete information on reporting qualitative meta-analyses.

Reporting Standards for Mixed Methods Research

3.18 Basic Expectations for Mixed Methods Research Reporting

Whereas standards for reporting information in the abstract and introduction of a paper are common to all kinds of research (see Sections 3.3–3.4), there are specific reporting standards for mixed methods research articles. The basic expectations for reporting mixed methods research are presented in Table 3.3. Standards specific to quantitative and qualitative research are presented in Sections 3.5 to 3.12 and 3.13 to 3.17, respectively.

The inherent assumption of mixed methods research is that the combined qualitative findings and quantitative results lead to additional insights not gleaned from the qualitative or quantitative findings alone (Creswell, 2015; Greene, 2007; Tashakkori & Teddlie, 2010). In mixed methods research, the thoughtful integration of qualitative findings and quantitative results leads to a deeper understanding of the data and enhanced insights. In addition, authors can publish multiple papers from a single mixed methods study, such as a qualitative study paper, a quantitative study paper, and a mixed methods overview paper.

Incorporating Both Quantitative and Qualitative Standards. The thoughtful and robust use of mixed methods requires researchers to meet the standards of both quantitative and qualitative research methodology in the design, implementation, and reporting stages. To this end, various mixed methods designs have emerged in the literature (Creswell & Plano Clark, 2017), and they help inform the procedures used in reporting studies (e.g., convergent design, exploratory sequential design, explanatory sequential design). Typically, additional mixed methods standards also need to be met along with quantitative and qualitative standards. Authors may use their discretion in presenting the sequence of studies but are encouraged to present them in a way that shows a logical progression of narrative as well as an audit trail (Merriam & Tisdell, 2016).

Reflecting on the Gains From Integration. The standards for mixed methods designs emphasize the need to not only present both qualitative and quantitative aspects of the research but also describe their integration throughout the sections of the paper. The mixed methods guidelines assist authors in describing the combination of qualitative and quantitative methods. Authors should convey not only how the qualitative and quantitative methods contribute to the study goals but also how they enhance one another to provide a greater depth of understanding or further the research aims.

Table 3.3 Mixed Methods Design Reporting Standards (JARS–Mixed)

Title Page

Title

- See the JARS–Quant and JARS–Qual Standards (Tables 3.1–3.2).

  Guidance for Authors
  - Refrain from using words that are either qualitative (e.g., "explore," "understand") or quantitative (e.g., "determinants," "correlates") because mixed methods stands in the middle between qualitative and quantitative research.
  - Reference the mixed methods, qualitative methods, and quantitative methods used.

Author Note

- See the JARS–Quant and JARS–Qual Standards (Tables 3.1–3.2).

Abstract

- See the JARS–Quant and JARS–Qual Standards (Tables 3.1–3.2).
- Indicate the mixed methods design, including types of participants or data sources, analytic strategy, main results/findings, and major implications/significance.

  Guidance for Authors
  - Specify the type of mixed methods design used. See the note on types of designs in the Research Design Overview section of this table.
  - Consider using one keyword that describes the type of mixed methods design and one that describes the problem addressed.
  - Describe your approach(es) to inquiry and, if relevant, how intersecting approaches to inquiry are combined when this description will facilitate the review process and intelligibility of your paper. If your work is not grounded in a specific approach(es) to inquiry or your approach would be too complicated to explain in the allotted word count, however, it would not be advisable to provide explication on this point in the abstract.

Introduction

Description of Research Problems/Questions

- See the JARS–Quant and JARS–Qual Standards (Tables 3.1–3.2).

  Guidance for Authors
  - This section may convey barriers in the literature that suggest a need for both qualitative and quantitative data.

  Guidance for Reviewers
  - Theory or conceptual framework use in mixed methods varies depending on the specific mixed methods design or procedures used. Theory may be used inductively or deductively (or both) in mixed methods research.

Study Objectives/Aims/Research Goals

- See the JARS–Quant and JARS–Qual Standards (Tables 3.1–3.2).
- State three types of research objectives/aims/goals: qualitative, quantitative, and mixed methods. Order these goals to reflect the type of mixed methods design used.
- Describe the ways approaches to inquiry were combined, as it illuminates the objectives and mixed methods rationale (e.g., descriptive, interpretive, feminist, psychoanalytic, postpositivist, critical, postmodern, constructivist, or pragmatic approaches).

  Guidance for Reviewers
  - A mixed methods objective, aim, or goal may not be familiar to reviewers. It describes the results to be obtained from using the mixed methods design type where "mixing" or integration occurs (e.g., the aim is to explain quantitative survey results with qualitative interviews in an explanatory sequential design). For instance, the goal of a qualitative phase could be the development of a conceptual model, the goal of a quantitative phase could be hypothesis testing based upon that model, and the goal of the mixed methods phase could be to generate integrated support for a theory based upon quantitative and qualitative evidence.

Table 3.3 **Mixed Methods Design Reporting Standards (JARS–Mixed)** *(continued)*

Method

Research Design Overview

- See the JARS–Quant and JARS–Qual Standards (Tables 3.1–3.2).
- Explain why mixed methods research is appropriate as a methodology given the paper's goals.
- Identify the type of mixed methods design used and define it.
- Indicate the qualitative approach to inquiry and the quantitative design used within the mixed methods design type (e.g., ethnography, randomized experiment).
- If multiple approaches to inquiry were combined, describe how this was done and provide a rationale (e.g., descriptive, interpretive, feminist, psychoanalytic, postpositivist, critical, postmodern, constructivist, or pragmatic approaches), as it illuminates the mixed method in use.
- Provide a rationale or justification for the need to collect both qualitative and quantitative data and the added value of integrating the results (findings) from the two data sets.

Guidance for Reviewers
- Because mixed methods research is a relatively new methodology, it is helpful to provide a definition of it from a major reference in the field.
- Mixed methods research involves rigorous methods, both qualitative and quantitative. Refer to the qualitative and quantitative standards for details of rigor.
- One of the most widely discussed topics in the mixed methods literature would be research designs. There is not a generic mixed methods design but rather multiple types of designs. Basic, core designs include convergent design, explanatory sequential design, and exploratory sequential design. Although the names and types of designs may differ among mixed methods writers, a common understanding is that the procedures for conducting a mixed methods study may differ from one project to another. Further, these basic procedures can be expanded by linking mixed methods to other designs (e.g., an intervention or experimental trial mixed methods study), to theories or standpoints (e.g., a feminist mixed methods study), or to other methodologies (e.g., a participatory action research mixed methods study).

PARTICIPANTS OR OTHER DATA SOURCES
- See the JARS–Quant and JARS–Qual Standards (Tables 3.1–3.2).
- When data are collected from multiple sources, clearly identify the sources of qualitative and quantitative data (e.g., participants, text), their characteristics, and the relationship between the data sets, if there is one (e.g., an embedded design).
- State the data sources in the order of procedures used in the design type (e.g., qualitative sources first in an exploratory sequential design followed by quantitative sources), if a sequenced design is used in the mixed methods study.

Guidance for Authors
- Because multiple sources of data are collected, separate descriptions of samples are needed when they differ. A table of qualitative sources and quantitative sources is helpful. This table could include type of data, when data were collected, and from whom. This table might also include study aims/research questions for each data source and anticipated outcomes of the study. In mixed methods research, this table is often called an "implementation matrix."
- Rather than describe data as represented in numbers versus words, it is better to describe sources of data as open-ended information (e.g., qualitative interviews) and closed-ended information (e.g., quantitative instruments).

RESEARCHER DESCRIPTION
- See the JARS–Qual Standards (Table 3.2).

Guidance for Authors
- Because mixed methods research includes qualitative research, and reflexivity is often included in qualitative research, we recommend statements as to how the researchers' backgrounds influence the research.

Guidance for Reviewers
- It is helpful to establish in a publication the researchers' experiences (or research teams' experiences) with both qualitative and quantitative research as a prerequisite for conducting mixed methods research.

Table 3.3 Mixed Methods Design Reporting Standards (JARS–Mixed) *(continued)*

Method *(continued)*

Participant Recruitment

PARTICIPANT SAMPLING OR SELECTION
- See the JARS–Quant and JARS–Qual Standards (Tables 3.1–3.2).
- Describe the qualitative and the quantitative sampling in separate sections.
- Relate the order of the sections to the procedures used in the mixed methods design type.

PARTICIPANT RECRUITMENT
- See the JARS–Quant and JARS–Qual Standards (Tables 3.1–3.2).
- Discuss the recruitment strategy for qualitative and quantitative research separately.

Data Collection

DATA-COLLECTION/IDENTIFICATION PROCEDURES
- See the JARS–Quant and JARS–Qual Standards (Tables 3.1–3.2).

RECORDING AND TRANSFORMING THE DATA
- See the JARS–Qual Standards (Table 3.2).

Data Analysis

- See the JARS–Quant and JARS–Qual Standards (Tables 3.1–3.2).
- Devote separate sections to the qualitative data analysis, the quantitative data analysis, and the mixed methods analysis. This mixed methods analysis consists of ways that the quantitative and qualitative results were "mixed" or integrated according to the type of mixed methods design used (e.g., merged in a convergent design, connected in explanatory sequential designs and in exploratory sequential designs).

Validity, Reliability, and Methodological Integrity

- See the JARS–Quant and JARS–Qual Standards (Tables 3.1–3.2).
- Indicate methodological integrity, quantitative validity and reliability, and mixed methods validity or legitimacy. Further assessments of mixed methods integrity are also indicated to show the quality of the research process and the inferences drawn from the intersection of the quantitative and qualitative data.

Findings/Results

Findings/Results Subsections

- See the JARS–Quant and JARS–Qual Standards (Tables 3.1–3.2).
- Indicate how the qualitative and quantitative results were "mixed" or integrated (e.g., discussion; tables of joint displays; graphs; data transformation in which one form of data is transformed to the other, such as qualitative text, codes, or themes transformed into quantitative counts or variables).
  Guidance for Authors
  – In mixed methods research, the Findings section typically includes sections on qualitative findings, quantitative results, and mixed methods results. This section should mirror the type of mixed methods design in terms of sequence (i.e., whether quantitative strand or qualitative strand comes first; if both are gathered at the same time, either qualitative findings or quantitative results could be presented first).
  Guidance for Reviewers
  – In mixed methods Results sections (or in the Discussion section to follow), authors are conveying their mixed methods analysis through "joint display" tables or graphs that array qualitative results (e.g., themes) against the quantitative results (e.g., categorical or continuous data). This enables researchers to directly compare results or to see how results differ between the quantitative and qualitative strands.

Discussion

Discussion Subsections

- See the JARS–Quant and JARS–Qual Standards (Tables 3.1–3.2).
  Guidance for Authors
  – Typically, the Discussion section, like the Method and Findings/Results, mirrors in sequence the procedures used in the type of mixed methods design. It also reflects on the implications of the integrated findings from across the two methods.

Note. JARS–Qual = qualitative journal article reporting standards; JARS–Quant = quantitative journal article reporting standards.

4

WRITING STYLE AND
GRAMMAR

Contents

4

WRITING STYLE AND GRAMMAR

The main objective of scholarly writing is clear communication, which can be achieved by presenting ideas in an orderly and concise manner. Establishing a tone that conveys the essential points of your work in an interesting way will engage readers and communicate your ideas effectively. Precise, clear word choice and sentence structure also contribute to the creation of a substantive, impactful work.

In this chapter, we provide guidance on achieving the four qualities of effective scholarly writing: continuity, flow, conciseness, and clarity. This is followed by general rules for grammar and usage and suggested strategies for improving your writing.

Effective Scholarly Writing

Being able to communicate ideas clearly and succinctly is a recipe for success for all writers, be they students submitting assignments to their instructor or professionals submitting manuscripts to a journal. Effective scholarly writing balances continuity and flow with conciseness and clarity. By implementing the techniques and principles described in Sections 4.1 to 4.11, writers will improve these aspects of their communication and become more effective communicators.

Continuity and Flow

4.1 Importance of Continuity and Flow

Effective writing is characterized by *continuity*, the logical consistency of expression throughout a written work, and by *flow*, the smooth cadence of words and sentences. Inconsistencies, contradictions, omissions, and irrelevancies in your writing style and presentation of ideas can make your arguments seem less credible. A work that lacks continuity and flow may seem disorganized or confusing, and details may seem incomplete or inconsistent. Readers will better understand your ideas if you aim for continuity in words, concepts, and thematic development from the opening statement to the conclusion. Explain relationships between ideas clearly, and present ideas in a logical order to improve the readability of your paper.

4.2 Transitions

To improve continuity and flow in your writing, check transitions between sentences, paragraphs, and ideas to ensure that the text is smooth and clear rather than abrupt or disjointed. When editing your writing, use additional transitional devices to make it less choppy. Text that sounds choppy or disjointed may indicate that you have abandoned an argument or theme prematurely—instead consider amplifying its discussion.

Punctuation marks contribute to continuity and flow by signaling transitions and demonstrating relationships between ideas. They also reflect the pauses, inflections, subordination, and pacing normally heard in speech. Use the full range of punctuation. Neither overuse nor underuse one type of punctuation, such as commas or dashes: Overuse may annoy readers, whereas underuse may cause confusion. Instead, use punctuation to support meaning.

Likewise, transitional words and phrases help maintain the flow of ideas, especially when the material is complex or abstract. For example, using a pronoun that refers to a noun in the preceding sentence not only serves as a transition but also avoids repetition. Be sure the referent is obvious. Other transitional words and phrases include the following:

- time links (e.g., "then," "next," "after," "while," "since")
- cause–effect links (e.g., "therefore," "consequently," "as a result")
- addition links (e.g., "in addition," "moreover," "furthermore," "similarly")
- contrast links (e.g., "but," "conversely," "nevertheless," "however," "although")

Use adverbs judiciously as introductory or transitional words (e.g., adverbs such as "certainly," "consequently," "conversely," "fortunately," "importantly," "interestingly," "more importantly," "regrettably," and "similarly"). Writers often overuse adverbs, so ask yourself whether the introduction or transition is needed. For example, both "importantly" and "interestingly" can often be recast to enhance the message of a sentence or simply omitted without a loss of meaning.

4.3 Noun Strings

Noun strings, meaning several nouns placed one after another to modify a final noun, can confuse readers and force them to question how the words relate to one another. Although skillful hyphenation can clarify the relationships between words, often the best option is to untangle the string. One approach to untangling is to move the final noun earlier in the string and show relationships between the other nouns by using verbs and prepositions. For example, "culturally sensitive qualitative interview techniques" can be rearranged to "culturally sensitive techniques for qualitative interviews." Consider the following, nearly uninterpretable noun strings and how each could be better structured:

Noun string	Better sentence structure
skinfold test body fat percentage examination	• a caliper examination to determine body fat percentage • a skinfold test to determine body fat percentage • determination of body fat percentage using calipers to measure skinfold thickness
preliminary online collegiate instructional methods survey results	• preliminary results of an online survey of collegiate instructional methods • preliminary results of an online survey to assess college students' preferred instructional methods

Conciseness and Clarity

4.4 Importance of Conciseness and Clarity

Say only what needs to be said in your writing: The author who is more concise—that is, more frugal with words—writes a more readable paper. Authors seeking publication and students completing assignments increase their chances of success when they write concisely. Likewise, writing that is clear and precise is more accurate and transparent. In combination, conciseness and clarity in your writing ensure that readers understand your meaning.

Some writers may fear that writing concisely will make their papers too short. However, adding extraneous material or "fluff" to make your paper longer will dilute its focus and meaning and will not improve your chances of publication or of getting a favorable grade. If your paper is too short when written concisely, your ideas and themes may need to be further developed to add substance.

Where possible, tighten language to eliminate wordiness, redundancy (see Section 4.5), evasiveness, overuse of the passive voice, circumlocution, and clumsy prose. Shorten or eliminate overly detailed descriptions of equipment or apparatus, participants, or procedures (beyond those called for in journal article reporting standards; see Chapter 3); elaborations of the obvious; and irrelevant observations or asides. Information that would cause the paper to be too long and is not essential to understanding the research—but would nonetheless be helpful to a subset of readers—may be placed, when appropriate, in supplemental materials (see Section 2.15).

Short words and short sentences are easier to comprehend than long ones (see Section 4.6). A long technical term, however, may be more precise than several short words, and technical terms are inseparable from scientific reporting. However, a paper with too much jargon or terminology familiar to only a few specialists does not sufficiently contribute to the literature because its meaning is obfuscated (see Section 4.9). Rather, the technical terms in a paper should be either readily understood by readers across disciplines or defined for readers who may be unfamiliar with them.

Concise writing must also be clear. Be deliberate in your word choices, making certain that every word means exactly what you intend. For example, in informal style, "feel" broadly substitutes for "think" or "believe," but in academic style, such latitude in word choice is not acceptable. Likewise, using a word with multiple meanings can cause confusion. For example, some writers use the word "significant" to mean "important," whereas others use "significant" only in the context of statistical significance testing; ensure that your intended meaning is clear. Choose words and phrases carefully, and specify the intended meaning if there is potential for ambiguity.

If you use a word or phrase multiple times, do so consistently (e.g., do not switch between "participants in the music condition" and "participants who heard the music while completing the task"—choose one presentation and use it consistently). Some writers deliberately use synonyms or near-synonyms to avoid repeating a word or phrase. The intention is commendable, but in practice the use of synonyms can lead to imprecision: By using synonyms, you may unintentionally suggest a subtle difference. Therefore, use synonyms with care.

Word choice is especially important when talking about people who are members of specific groups, such as in a Method section. Carefully consider the descriptors you use, making sure they are accurate, consistent with current preferred terminology, and in line with how the individuals you are writing about describe themselves. In no case should you use biased, pejorative, or demeaning language (see Chapter 5 for guidelines on using bias-free language).

Strive for a professional tone and professional language (see Sections 4.7–4.9). Avoid heavy alliteration, rhyming, poetic expressions, and clichés. Use metaphors sparingly; although they can help simplify complicated ideas, metaphors can also be distracting or unclear. Avoid mixed metaphors (e.g., "a theory representing one branch of a growing body of evidence") and words with surplus or unintended meanings (e.g., "outstanding" for "remaining"), which may distract or mislead readers. Use figurative expressions with restraint and colorful expressions with care; because these expressions can be open to interpretation and even cultural differences, they generally do not add to understanding for all possible readers. Instead, make direct, logical comparisons (see Section 4.10) and clearly attribute actions (see Section 4.11).

4.5 Wordiness and Redundancy

Wordiness can impede readers' understanding by forcing them to sort through unnecessary words to decipher your ideas. Unconstrained wordiness lapses into embellishment and flowery writing, which are inappropriate in academic style. Consider the following examples of wordy and concise language:

Wordy	Concise
at the present time	now
for the purpose of	for, to
there were several students who completed	several students completed

Whereas *wordiness* refers to using more words than are necessary, *redundancy* means using multiple words with the same meaning. Writers often use redundant language to be emphatic. Instead, use sentence structure to convey emphasis, for example, by placing the words to be emphasized at the beginning or end of a sentence. When possible and appropriate for the context, use the active voice (see Section 4.13) to reduce wordiness and redundancy. In the following examples, the highlighted words are redundant and should be omitted:

they were both alike	one and the same
a sum total	in close proximity to
four different groups saw	completely unanimous
were exactly the same as	positioned very close
absolutely essential	period of time
has been previously found	summarize briefly
small in size	the reason is because

4.6 Sentence and Paragraph Length

There is no minimum or maximum sentence length in APA Style. Overuse of short, simple sentences produces choppy prose, however, and overuse of long, involved sentences results in difficult, sometimes incomprehensible, language. Varied sentence length helps readers maintain interest and comprehension. When involved concepts require long sentences, the components should proceed logically. Avoid including multiple ideas in a single sentence; instead, break the sentence into shorter ones. Direct, declarative sentences with simple, common words are usually best.

Similar cautions apply to paragraph length. Single-sentence paragraphs are abrupt and should be used infrequently. Paragraphs that are too long (i.e., longer than one double-spaced manuscript page) risk losing readers' attention. A new paragraph signals a shift to a new idea and provides a pause for readers—a chance to assimilate one step in the conceptual development before beginning another. Look for a logical place (or places) to break up a long paragraph or reorganize the material.

4.7 Tone

Although scientific writing differs in form and content from creative or literary writing, it need not lack style or be dull. When writing a scholarly paper, keep in mind that scientific prose and creative or literary writing serve different purposes. Devices that are often used in creative writing—for example, setting up ambiguity; inserting the unexpected; omitting the expected; and suddenly shifting the topic, tense, or person—do not support the objective of clear communication in scientific writing. Similarly, devices or embellishments that attract attention to words and sounds instead of to ideas are inappropriate in scientific writing.

Thus, when describing your research, present the ideas and findings in a direct, straightforward manner, while also aiming for an interesting and compelling style—for example, by fully elaborating on an idea or concept (see Section 4.2), making word choices that reflect your involvement with the problem (see Section 4.4), and varying sentence and paragraph lengths (see Section 4.6). Use language that conveys professionalism and formality (see Section 4.8). For example, scientific writing often contrasts the positions of different researchers, and these differences should be presented in a professional, noncombative manner: Stating "Gerard (2019) did not address" is acceptable, whereas "Gerard (2019) completely overlooked" is not.

One way to achieve the right tone is to imagine a specific reader you intend to reach and write in a way that will inform and persuade that individual. For example, your reader might be a researcher in a related field who is trying to keep abreast of the literature but is not familiar with the jargon or insider perspectives of your field. What would facilitate this reader's understanding of and appreciation for the importance of your work?

4.8 Contractions and Colloquialisms

Avoid using contractions and colloquialisms, which detract from a professional tone in scholarly writing. *Contractions*—shortened forms of one or two words in which an apostrophe is used in place of missing letters—generally do not appear in scholarly writing because they convey an informal tone. To avoid contractions and improve your writing, evaluate words with apostrophes carefully. Except for cases noted, rewrite a word like "can't" into "cannot." Use apostrophes to indicate possession (e.g., "the student's work"), but remember that possessive pronouns do not include apostrophes (e.g., write "its purpose was" not "it's purpose was"). However, contractions can be appropriately used in some circumstances, such as in reproducing a direct quotation that contains a contraction (e.g., when quoting a research participant, do not change a participant's use of "let's go" to "let us go"), referring to a contraction as a linguistic example (e.g., when discussing confusion of "who's" with "whose"), or referring to an idiom or common saying that contains a contraction (e.g., "you can't take it with you").

Likewise, avoid *colloquialisms*, which are informal expressions used in everyday speech and writing (e.g., "to write up" instead of "to report," "gonna" instead of "going to"). These expressions often diffuse meaning, as in the case of approximations of quantity; "quite a large part," "practically all," and "very few" are interpreted differently by different readers or in different contexts. Approximations weaken statements, especially those describing empirical observations. Instead, use precise, scholarly language.

4.9 Jargon

Jargon is specialized terminology that is unfamiliar to those outside a specific group. Overuse of jargon, even in papers in which that vocabulary is relevant, hinders comprehension. Jargon also may be euphemistic if substituted for a familiar term (e.g., "period of economic adjustment" instead of "recession"), and you should avoid using jargon in this way. Bureaucratic jargon has had the greatest publicity, but academic or scientific jargon may also grate on readers, encumber communication, and waste space. Ensure that the language you use allows readers to understand your writing even if they are not experts in your field, and define on first use any specialized terms that are key to your topic.

4.10 Logical Comparisons

Ensure that the comparisons you make are expressed clearly and logically. Ambiguous or illogical comparisons result from the omission of key words or from nonparallel structure (see Section 4.24). Consider, for example, "Twelve-year-olds were more likely to play with age peers than 6-year-olds." Does this sentence mean that 12-year-olds were more likely than 6-year-olds to play with age peers? Or does it mean that 12-year-olds were more likely to play with age peers and less likely to play with 6-year-olds? Ambiguity occurs when parallelism is overlooked for the sake of brevity, as in "The responses of transgender participants were more positive than cisgender participants." One correct way to write this sentence would be "The responses of transgender participants were more positive than those of cisgender participants." Thoughtful attention to good sentence structure and word choice reduces the chance of this kind of ambiguity.

4.11 Anthropomorphism

Do not attribute human characteristics to animals or to inanimate sources—doing so is called *anthropomorphism*.

Correct	Incorrect	Rationale
Pairs of rats (cage mates) were allowed to forage together.	Rat couples (cage mates) were allowed to forage together.	"Rat couples" implies a misleading parallel between human romantic couples and pairs of rats.
The theory addresses	The theory concludes	A theory might address, indicate, or present, but it is the researchers (not the theory itself) who conclude.

Pair active verbs with human actors (e.g., write "we extrapolated the rate of change" rather than "the study extrapolated the rate of change"). However, many acceptable constructions in widespread use do not constitute anthropomorphism because they do not impede understanding or mislead readers. When describing the content of different sections of a paper, you may write, for example, "this section addresses" or "the chapter focuses on" as well as "in this section we address" or "in this chapter, we focus on" (see Section 6.3 for comma use with introductory phrases). Similarly, when describing the results of a study, you may write "the results suggest," "the data provide," "the research contributes," "the study found," and so forth.

Determining what constitutes anthropomorphism can be challenging, and even distinguished scholars may disagree. In ambiguous cases, we recommend that authors keep the principle of clear communication at the forefront of their word choice and sentence structure.

Grammar and Usage

Incorrect grammar and careless construction of sentences distract readers, introduce ambiguity, and impede clear communication. The examples in this section represent common grammar and usage errors that often appear in papers submitted to journal editors and academic instructors.

Verbs

4.12 Verb Tense

Verbs are vigorous, direct communicators. The past tense is appropriate when expressing an action or a condition that occurred at a specific, definite time in the past, such as when discussing another researcher's work. The present perfect tense is appropriate to express a past action or condition that did not occur at a specific, definite time or to describe an action beginning in the past and continuing to the present.

Use verb tenses consistently, and stay within the chosen tense to ensure smooth expression. Sudden, unnecessary shifts in verb tense in the same paragraph or in adjacent paragraphs may confuse readers. Use the verb tenses shown in Table 4.1 to report information in various parts of the paper.

4.13 Active and Passive Voice

Voice describes the relationship between a verb and the subject and object associated with it. In the *active voice*, the subject of a sentence is presented first, followed by the verb and then the object of the verb (e.g., "students completed surveys"). In the *passive voice*, the object of the verb is presented first, followed by the verb (usually a form of "to be" + past participle + the word "by") and then the subject last (e.g., "surveys were completed by students"); sometimes, the subject is omitted altogether, resulting in confusion about who is performing the action.

Choose voice carefully. Both the active and passive voices are permitted in APA Style, but many writers overuse the passive voice. Use the active voice as much as possible to create direct, clear, and concise sentences. For example, use the active voice to describe the actions of participants and others involved in your study (see Section 5.6), as in "the patients took the medication orally," not "the medication was taken orally by the patients."

The passive voice is acceptable in expository writing when focusing on the object or recipient of the action rather than on the actor. For example, a description of the experimental setup in the Method section might read, "the speakers were attached to either side of the chair," which appropriately emphasizes the placement of the speakers, not who placed them. Similarly, "the tests were gathered promptly" emphasizes the importance of the tests and their timely collection. When it is important to know who performed the action, use the active voice.

Table 4.1 Recommended Verb Tenses in APA Style Papers

Paper section	Recommended tense	Example
Literature review (or whenever discussing other researchers' work)	Past	Quinn (2020) presented
	Present perfect	Since then, many investigators have used
Method Description of procedure	Past	Participants completed a survey
	Present perfect	Others have used similar approaches
Reporting of results	Past	Results were nonsignificant Scores increased Hypotheses were supported
Discussion of implications of results	Present	The results indicate
Presentation of conclusions, limitations, future directions, and so forth	Present	We conclude Limitations of the study are

4.14 Mood

Mood refers to the form of a verb authors use to express their attitude toward what they are saying (e.g., whether they believe what they are saying or just wish it were true). Use the indicative mood to make factual statements (e.g., "we addressed," "the findings demonstrate"). Use the subjunctive mood only to describe conditions that are contrary to fact or improbable; do not use the subjunctive to describe simple conditions or contingencies.

Correct	Incorrect	Rationale
If the campus were larger, we would have had access to more participants.	If the campus was larger, we would have had access to more participants.	The campus is not in fact larger; the writer is only wishing that this were so.

Use the word "would" with care. "Would" can be used in the indicative mood to mean "habitually," as in "The child would walk about the classroom," or in the conditional mood to express a condition of action, as in "We would sign the letter if we could." Do not use "would" to hedge; for example, change "it would appear that" to "it appears that."

4.15 Subject and Verb Agreement

A verb must agree in number (i.e., singular or plural; see Section 6.11) with its subject, regardless of intervening phrases such as "together with," "including," "plus," and "as well as."

> *Correct:* The percentage of correct responses, as well as the speed of the responses, increases with practice.

> *Incorrect:* The percentage of correct responses, as well as the speed of the responses, increase with practice.

Collective Nouns. Collective nouns (e.g., "series," "set," "faculty," "pair," "social media") can refer to several individuals or to a single unit. If the action of the verb applies to the group as a whole, treat the noun as singular and use a singular verb. If the action of the verb applies to members of the group as individuals, treat the noun as plural and use a plural verb. The context (i.e., your emphasis) determines whether the action applies to the group or to individuals.

> *Singular in context:* The number of people in the state is growing.
> A pair of animals was in each cage.

> *Plural in context:* A number of people are watching.
> A pair of animals were then yoked.

Use of "None." The subject pronoun "none" can be singular or plural. When the noun that follows it is singular, use a singular verb; when the noun is plural, use a plural verb.

> *Singular in context:* None of the information was correct.
> *Plural in context:* None of the children were finished in the time allotted.

Compound Subjects Joined by "Or" or "Nor." When a compound subject is composed of a singular and a plural noun joined by "or" or "nor," the verb agrees with the noun that is closer to the verb.

Correct: Neither the participants nor the confederate was in the room.

Neither the confederate nor the participants were in the room.

Incorrect: Neither the participants nor the confederate were in the room.

Pronouns

4.16 First- Versus Third-Person Pronouns

Pronouns replace nouns, and each pronoun should refer clearly to its antecedent. To avoid ambiguity in attribution, use the first person rather than the third person when describing the work you did as part of your research and when expressing your own views. If you are writing a paper by yourself, use the pronoun "I"; do not use the pronoun "we" to refer to yourself if you do not have coauthors (see also Section 4.17). If you are writing a paper with coauthors, use the pronoun "we." Do not refer to yourself or your coauthors in the third person as "the author(s)" or "the researcher(s)."

However, use the third person to refer to the specific contribution of a particular coauthor within a paper with multiple authors. In the following example, Sonia J. Cousteau is one of the authors of the paper:

We assessed children's language abilities. Sonia J. Cousteau, who is a speech-language pathologist, trained all testers.

Keep in mind that if you refer to coauthors by name in the text of your manuscript, you may need to mark out their names each time they appear if your paper is to undergo masked review (see Section 12.7).

4.17 Editorial "We"

Do not use "we" to refer to people in general, as in "We live on the same planet, but we rarely truly understand each other"; this use is called the *editorial "we."* It is especially important to avoid the editorial "we" in multiauthored papers because readers may wonder whether you are referring to all people, members of your professional group(s), or yourself and your coauthors. Substitute a more specific noun or clarify your usage.

Correct: Psychological researchers typically study decision making in a laboratory setting.

Incorrect: We typically study decision making in a laboratory setting.

Some alternatives to "we" are "people," "humans," "researchers," "psychologists," "nurses," and so on. However, "we" is an appropriate and useful referent once a specific subject has been established.

Correct: As nurses, we tend to rely on . . .

Incorrect: We tend to rely on . . .

4.18 Singular "They"

Writers should always use the singular "they" to refer to a person who uses "they" as their pronoun (see Section 5.5 for more on gender and pronoun usage). Also use "they" as a generic third-person singular pronoun to refer to a person whose gender is unknown or irrelevant to the context of the usage. Although usage of the singular "they" was once discouraged in academic writing, many advocacy groups and publishers have accepted and endorsed it, including *Merriam-Webster's*

Dictionary (Merriam-Webster, n.d.-b). The use of the singular "they" is inclusive of all people, helps writers avoid making assumptions about gender, and is part of APA Style.

When using the singular "they," use the forms "they," "them," "their," "theirs," and "themselves." The variant "themself" is also acceptable because the referent is clearly singular, although "themselves" is currently the more common usage. The following are examples of correct usage of the singular "they."

> Each participant turned in their questionnaire.
>
> Jamie shared their experiences as a genderqueer person.
>
> A child should learn to play by themselves [or themself] as well as with friends.
>
> Rowan, a transgender person, helped themselves [or themself] to the free coffee.

Do not use "he" or "she" alone as a generic third-person pronoun. Use "he or she" and "she or he" sparingly, and ensure that these pronouns match the pronouns of the people being described; if you do not know the pronouns used by the people being described, use "they" instead or rewrite the sentence. Do not use the combination forms "(s)he" and "s/he" or alternate "he" and "she" (unless you know that a person uses these forms); these choices may have unintentional implications. For further discussion of gender and pronoun usage, see Section 5.5.

Keep in mind that there are typically many possible ways to write a sentence. If the singular "they" as a generic third-person pronoun seems awkward or distracting, try one of the following strategies to rewrite the sentence.

Strategy	Gender neutral	Gender biased
Rephrasing	When an individual attends psychotherapy, that person can improve emotional regulation. Therapy can help an individual improve emotional regulation.	When an individual attends psychotherapy, she can improve emotional regulation.
Using plural nouns or plural pronouns	Therapists who are too much like their clients can lose their objectivity.	A therapist who is too much like his client can lose his objectivity.
Replacing the pronoun with an article	A researcher must apply for the grant by September 1.	A researcher must apply for his grant by September 1.
Dropping the pronoun	The researcher must avoid letting biases and expectations influence the interpretation of the results.	The researcher must avoid letting her own biases and expectations influence the interpretation of the results.

4.19 Pronouns for People and Animals ("Who" vs. "That")

Relative pronouns introduce subordinate clauses linked to nouns. Use the relative pronoun "who" for human beings; use the relative pronoun "that" or "which" for nonhuman animals (e.g., rats, chimpanzees) and for inanimate objects.

> *Correct:* The students who completed the task
>
> *Correct:* The instructions that were included
>
> *Incorrect:* The students that completed the task

Use neuter pronouns to refer to animals (e.g., "the dog . . . it"). However, it is acceptable to use gendered pronouns if the animal has been named and its sex is known, as in the following example:

WRITING & GRAMMAR

The chimps were tested daily. Sheba was tested unrestrained in an open testing area, which was her usual context for training and testing.

4.20 Pronouns as Subjects and Objects ("Who" vs. "Whom")

Relative pronouns can be subjects or objects of verbs or prepositions. Use "who" as the subject of a verb and "whom" as the object of a verb or a preposition. You can determine whether a pronoun is the subject or object of a verb by turning the subordinate clause around and substituting a personal pronoun. If you can substitute "he," "she," or "they," then "who" is correct. In the following examples, "who" and its replacement personal pronoun are highlighted to show the substitutions. The sentence with the substitution is a way to verify whether the original sentence is correct.

Use of "who"	Original sentence	Substitution sentence
Correct	The participants who passed the exam were given course credit.	They passed the exam and were given course credit.
Incorrect	Eligible participants were mothers, each of who had a child under the age of 21 with cancer.	Eligible participants were mothers; each of they had a child under the age of 21 with cancer.

Likewise, if you can substitute "him," "her," or "them," then "whom" is correct.

Use of "whom"	Original sentence	Substitution sentence
Correct	Eligible participants were mothers, each of whom had a child under the age of 21 with cancer.	Eligible participants were mothers; each of them had a child under the age of 21 with cancer.
Incorrect	The participants whom passed the exam were given course credit.	Them passed the exam and were given course credit.

4.21 Pronouns in Restrictive and Nonrestrictive Clauses ("That" vs. "Which")

Relative pronouns (e.g., "who," "whom," "that," "which") introduce an element that is subordinate to the main clause of the sentence, and that subordinate clause may be either restrictive or nonrestrictive.

Restrictive clauses—also called "that" clauses—are essential to the meaning of the sentence. Restrictive clauses are not set off with commas.

Therapist self-disclosure that conflicts with the patient's story might hinder the therapeutic process.

In the example, only self-disclosure that conflicts with the patient's story, not all self-disclosure, might hinder the therapeutic process.

Nonrestrictive clauses—also called "which" clauses—add further information to the sentence but are not essential to its meaning. Nonrestrictive clauses are set off with commas.

All interviews were conducted at participants' offices, which provided suitable privacy to secure participants' anonymity.

In the example, all interviews were conducted at the offices, and all offices provided suitable privacy.

Although some writers use "which" for both restrictive and nonrestrictive clauses, APA Style reserves "which" for nonrestrictive clauses and "that" for restrictive clauses. Consistent use of "that" for restrictive clauses and "which" for nonrestrictive clauses will help make your writing clear and precise.

Sentence Construction

4.22 Subordinate Conjunctions

Subordinate conjunctions (e.g., "since," "while," "although," "because," "whereas"), like relative pronouns (see Sections 4.19–4.21), introduce subordinate clauses. Select these conjunctions with care; interchanging conjunctions with more than one meaning may reduce the precision of your writing. Although some writers use "while" and "since" when they do not refer strictly to time, restricting your use of "while" and "since" to their temporal meanings can be helpful to readers.

"While" Versus "Although," "Despite," "And," or "But." Use "while" to link events occurring simultaneously.

> Individual goal striving in late adulthood may enrich life while reducing stagnation and boredom.

Otherwise, use "although," "despite," "and," or "but" in place of "while."

> *Precise:* Although goal progress predicted well-being for all genders, the associations tended to be stronger for women.
>
> Goal progress predicted well-being for all genders, but the associations tended to be stronger for women.
>
> *Imprecise:* While goal progress predicted well-being for all genders, the associations tended to be stronger for women.

"Since" Versus "Because." In cases where the meaning of "since" is ambiguous (it could be either "from a time in the past" or "because"), replace "since" with "because." If the meaning is not ambiguous, it is acceptable to use either "since" or "because" to mean "because."

> *Precise:* Participants were leaving because the light turned green.
>
> *Imprecise:* Participants were leaving since the light turned green.

4.23 Misplaced and Dangling Modifiers

An adjective or an adverb, whether a single word or a phrase, must clearly refer to the word that it modifies. Having modifiers without clear referents can make it hard for readers to follow the logic of your sentence.

Misplaced Modifiers. Because of their placement in a sentence, misplaced modifiers ambiguously or illogically modify a word. Eliminate misplaced modifiers by placing an adjective or an adverb as close as possible to the word it modifies.

Correct	Incorrect	Rationale
Using this procedure, the investigator tested the participants. The investigator tested the participants who were using the procedure.	The investigator tested the participants using this procedure.	The incorrect sentence is unclear about whether the investigator or the participants used this procedure.
On the basis of this assumption, we developed a model. Based on this assumption, the model . . .	Based on this assumption, we developed a model.	The incorrect construction says, "we are based on this assumption."

Many writers misplace the word "only." Place "only" next to the word or phrase it modifies.

Correct	Incorrect	Rationale
These data provide only a partial answer.	These data only provide a partial answer.	The answer is partial, not the providing of it.

Squinting modifiers are a type of misplaced modifier. Because of their ambiguous placement, they make it difficult to tell whether the modifier refers to the phrase before or after the modifier.

Correct	Incorrect	Rationale
My comprehension is improved when I read slowly.	Reading books slowly improves my comprehension.	It is unclear whether the reading or the improvement is slow.

Dangling Modifiers. Dangling modifiers have no referent in the sentence. Many of these result from the use of the passive voice (see Section 4.13). You can avoid many dangling modifiers by writing in the active voice.

Correct	Incorrect	Rationale
Using this procedure, I tested the participants.	The participants were tested using this procedure.	I, not the participants, used the procedure.
Armitage and Martinez (2017) found that the treatment group performed better, a result congruent with those of other studies.	Congruent with other studies, Armitage and Martinez (2017) found that the treatment group performed better.	The result, not Armitage and Martinez, is congruent.

4.24 Parallel Construction

To enhance readers' understanding, present parallel ideas in parallel or coordinate form. Use parallel structure in compound sentences, series and lists (see Sections 6.49–6.52), and table stubs (see Section 7.12).

Repetition of Parallel Elements. Ensure that all elements of the parallelism are present before and after the coordinating conjunction (e.g., "and," "but," "or," "nor"). For example, if the first part of the clause is introduced by "that," the second part of the clause should be as well. When a clause has two parts (and not three or more), do not use a comma or semicolon before the conjunction.

Correct: Ford (2020) found that homework is positively related to achievement and that the association is stronger in middle and high school than in elementary school.

Incorrect: Ford (2020) found that homework is positively related to achievement, and that the association is stronger in middle and high school than in elementary school.

Coordinating Conjunctions Used in Pairs. With coordinating conjunctions used in pairs ("between . . . and," "both . . . and," "neither . . . nor," "either . . . or," "not only . . . but also"), place the first conjunction immediately before the first part of the parallelism.

"Between" and "And."

Correct: We recorded the difference between the performance of participants who completed the first task and the performance of those who completed the second task.

Incorrect: We recorded the difference between the performance of participants who completed the first task and the second task.

Correct: between 2.5 and 4.0 years old

Incorrect: between 2.5–4.0 years old

"Both" and "And."

Correct: The names were difficult both to pronounce and to spell.

Incorrect: The names were difficult both to pronounce as well as to spell.

Never use "both" with "as well as": The resulting construction is redundant.

"Neither" and "Nor"; "Either" and "Or."

Correct: Neither the responses to the auditory stimuli nor the responses to the tactile stimuli were repeated.

Incorrect: Neither the responses to the auditory stimuli nor to the tactile stimuli were repeated.

Correct: The respondents either gave the worst answer or gave the best answer.

Correct: The respondents gave either the worst answer or the best answer.

Incorrect: The respondents either gave the worst answer or the best answer.

"Not Only" and "But Also."

Correct: It is surprising not only that pencil-and-paper scores predicted this result but also that all other predictors were less accurate.

Incorrect: It is not only surprising that pencil-and-paper scores predicted this result but also that all other predictors were less accurate.

Elements in a Series. Elements in a series should also be parallel in form.

Correct: The participants were told to make themselves comfortable, to read the instructions, and to ask about anything they did not understand.

Incorrect: The participants were told to make themselves comfortable, to read the instructions, and that they should ask about anything they did not understand.

Strategies to Improve Your Writing

Good writing is a skill learned through practice. In this section, we recommend strategies to improve your writing. These strategies can aid both professionals preparing manuscripts for journal submission and students preparing papers for course submission.

4.25 Reading to Learn Through Example

Reading is one of the most effective practices for authors to improve their writing because it enables them to learn through example. For instance, a student tasked with writing a literature review would benefit from reading other literature reviews (including the literature review sections of longer works) to see the various ways in which information can be organized and discussed. Likewise, an author who needs to present complex statistical information in a table would benefit from seeing how other authors have organized similar information in their tables. Careful reading in your chosen area of study will help you learn about not only new developments in the field but also ways to effectively convey information on the page.

4.26 Writing From an Outline

Writing from an outline ensures that the flow of your paper reflects the logic of your research or ideas. Creating and using an outline helps you identify main ideas, define subordinate ideas, focus your writing, avoid tangential excursions, and find omissions. In the outline, you can also designate headings and subheadings you will use in your paper (see Sections 2.26–2.27 for more on principles of organization and levels of heading). Outlines can take many forms, including the traditional format with Roman numeral headings or a concept map.

4.27 Rereading the Draft

Rereading your own work after setting it aside for a few hours or days allows you to look at it from a fresh perspective. Taking the further step of reading your paper aloud may reveal faults that you previously overlooked and may help strengthen the tone and style of your writing. You can also try reading the sections of your paper in reverse order—from the conclusion back to the introduction—to ensure that you have set up arguments appropriately. Budget ample time when writing to allow yourself to take advantage of these strategies.

4.28 Seeking Help From Colleagues

After you have reread your draft, give a revised copy to a colleague—preferably a person who has published in or studied a related field but who is not familiar with your own work—for a critical review. Even better, get critiques from two colleagues, and you will have a trial run of a journal's review process. Students are also encouraged to solicit feedback from their instructor and peers.

4.29 Working With Copyeditors and Writing Centers

Some writers, particularly new writers and those writing in a nonnative language, may benefit from extra help with their writing. They might hire a copyeditor to review and proofread their paper or visit a tutor at a university writing center. A copyeditor or writing center tutor can assist with idiomatic language use, organization, and other areas. We highly recommend use of these services for authors who consistently face obstacles in getting their work published or students who would like to attain more success in the classroom. Students should check the academic integrity policies of their institution to determine what kinds of assistance are acceptable.

4.30 Revising a Paper

Revising a draft into a polished paper takes time and effort. Writers should develop a revision plan. It is best to start with the big picture and work down to the details. Consider the following broad questions when reviewing your paper:

- Is the central point or thesis of your paper clear? Do the arguments follow logically from the thesis?

- Is the information well organized?

- For students, does the draft meet the parameters of the assignment? If there is a rubric for the assignment, does the paper address each element of the rubric?

- For authors seeking publication, does the draft fit the journal style and formatting requirements (see Sections 12.2–12.4)?

At the detail level, check sentences for correct grammar and usage (see Sections 4.12–4.24). Also check for spelling and grammar errors using the automatic spell-check and grammar-check functions of your word-processing program. Although an electronic spell-check cannot take the place of careful proofreading (because words spelled correctly may be used incorrectly), it will lessen the chances that typographical errors make their way into the published article or the submitted assignment. APA uses *Merriam-Webster's Dictionary* and the *APA Dictionary of Psychology* as its authorities on spelling (for additional information on spelling, see Sections 6.11–6.12). Grammar-check functions are useful for identifying problematic sentence structure. Keep in mind, however, that grammar is complex and therefore grammar-checkers are not infallible.

Although the *Publication Manual* addresses many aspects of grammar and usage, it focuses on the areas that are the most problematic for writers of scholarly work. For grammatical questions not addressed in the *Publication Manual*, consult a trusted grammar reference.

WRITING & GRAMMAR

5

BIAS-FREE LANGUAGE
GUIDELINES

Contents

5

BIAS-FREE LANGUAGE GUIDELINES

Authors must strive to use language that is free of *bias*, meaning the implied or irrelevant evaluation of the group or groups they are writing about. As an organization, APA is committed to both the advancement of science and the fair treatment of individuals and groups. These principles require that authors and students who use APA Style avoid perpetuating demeaning attitudes in their writing. It is unacceptable to use constructions that might imply prejudicial beliefs or perpetuate biased assumptions against persons on the basis of age, disability, gender, participation in research, racial or ethnic identity, sexual orientation, socioeconomic status, or some combination of these or other personal factors (e.g., marital status, immigration status, religion). Instead, authors should use affirming and inclusive language.

Long-standing cultural practice can exert a powerful influence over even the most conscientious writer. Just as you have learned to check what you write for spelling, grammar, and wordiness, practice rereading your work for preconceptions about groups of people. Ask people from the groups about which you are writing to read and comment on your material or consult self-advocacy groups to determine appropriate terminology. If you work directly with participants, ask them what terms they use to describe themselves. Language changes over time, and it is important to use the terms that individuals and/or communities use to describe themselves, their experiences, and their practices.

Some attempts to follow the guidelines in this chapter may result in wordiness or clumsy prose. As always, good judgment is required—these are not rigid rules. If your writing reflects respect for your participants and your readers, and if you write with appropriate specificity and precision, you contribute to the goal of accurate, unbiased communication. This chapter contains general guidelines for writing without bias that apply across a range of issues and additional guidelines that address specific topics, including age, disability, gender, participation in research, race and ethnicity, sexual orientation, socioeconomic status, and intersectionality. Additional examples of bias-free language can be found on the APA Style website (https://apastyle.apa.org).

General Guidelines for Reducing Bias

5.1 Describe at the Appropriate Level of Specificity

Precision is essential in scholarly writing; when you refer to a person or persons, choose words that are accurate, clear, and free from bias or prejudicial connotations. Bias, like inaccurate or unclear language, can be a form of imprecision. For example, using "man" to refer to all human beings is not as accurate or inclusive as using the terms "individuals," "people," or "persons."

Focus on Relevant Characteristics. Be mindful to describe only relevant characteristics. Although it is possible to describe a person's age, disability, gender identity, participation in research, racial and ethnic identity, sexual orientation, socioeconomic status, or other characteristic without bias, it is not always necessary to include all of this information in your report (for a more detailed discussion of participant characteristics to report in quantitative and qualitative studies, refer to Sections 3.6 and 3.14, respectively). For example, you would be unlikely to mention participants' sexual orientation in a study of cognition because sexual orientation is not relevant to cognition; however, you would likely mention participants' gender in a study of stereotype threat because gender is relevant to the examination of stereotype threat. Furthermore, there may be multiple relevant characteristics to discuss; when this is the case, address the ways in which the characteristics intersect, as appropriate (see Section 5.10).

Acknowledge Relevant Differences That Do Exist. Part of writing without bias is not only recognizing that differences should be mentioned only when relevant but also acknowledging relevant differences when they do exist. Evaluate the meaning of the word "difference" carefully in relation to the target population, not the dominant group. For example, a researcher who wants to generalize the study results to people overall, or students overall, and so forth, should assess and report whether the sample studied is different from the target population and, if so, describe how it is different.

Be Appropriately Specific. Once you have determined which characteristics to describe, choose terms that are appropriately specific, which will depend on the research question and the present state of knowledge in the field. Do not mention characteristics gratuitously; however, when in doubt, be more specific rather than less because it is easier to aggregate data than to disaggregate them. Consider the appropriate level of specificity early in the research process—such as when designing the study—because it may not be possible to gather more data once the study is underway or finished. Using specific terms improves readers' ability to understand the generalizability of your findings and other researchers' ability to use your data in a meta-analysis or replication.

Examples of Specificity by Topic. Next, we present examples of specific language for the topics covered in these bias-free language guidelines; again, the proper choice will depend on the situation, and these examples represent just some of the possible options.

- When writing about age, exact ages or age ranges (e.g., 15–18 years old, 65–80 years old) are more specific than broad categories (e.g., under 18 years old, over 65 years old; see Section 5.3). Also include the age mean and median in addition to the range of ages to increase the specificity of the reporting.

- When writing about disability, names of conditions (e.g., Alzheimer's disease) are more specific than categories of conditions (e.g., types of dementia) or general references such as "people with disabilities" (see Section 5.4).

- When writing about gender identity, descriptors with modifiers (e.g., cisgender women, transgender women) are more specific than descriptors without modifiers (e.g., women) or general nongendered terms (e.g., people, individuals; see Section 5.5 for how to differentiate between gender and sex).

- When writing about people who took part in research, terms that indicate the context of the research (e.g., patients, participants, clients) are more specific than general terms (e.g., people, children, women; see Section 5.6).

- When writing about racial or ethnic groups, the nation or region of origin (e.g., Chinese Americans, Mexican Americans) is more specific than a generalized origin (e.g., Asian Americans, Latin Americans; see Section 5.7).

- When writing about sexual orientation, the names of people's orientations (e.g., lesbians, gay men, bisexual people, straight people) are more specific than broad group labels (e.g., gay; see Section 5.8).

- When writing about socioeconomic status, income ranges or specific designations (e.g., below the federal poverty threshold for a family of four) are more specific than general labels (e.g., low income; see Section 5.9).

5.2 Be Sensitive to Labels

Respect the language people use to describe themselves; that is, call people what they call themselves. Accept that language changes with time and that individuals within groups sometimes disagree about the designations they use. Make an effort to determine what is appropriate for your study or paper, particularly when these designations are debated within groups. You may need to ask your participants which designations they use and/or consult self-advocacy groups that represent these communities to research the issue if you are not working directly with participants. However, note that some individuals may use slurs or stigmatizing language to refer to themselves; researchers should use extreme caution before repeating this language because doing so can propagate that stigma (see Sections 5.3–5.4 for more on the use of stigmatizing language with regard to age and disability, respectively).

Acknowledge People's Humanity. Choose labels with sensitivity, ensuring that the individuality and humanity of people are respected. Avoid using adjectives as nouns to label people (e.g., "the gays," "the poor") or labels that equate people with their condition (e.g., "amnesiacs," "schizophrenics," "the learning disabled," "drug users"). Instead, use adjectival forms (e.g., gay men, older adults) or nouns with descriptive phrases (e.g., people living in poverty, people with learning disabilities, people who use drugs). Some groups (e.g., the Deaf) have chosen to use a capitalized label to identify and promote a sense of unity and community (Solomon, 2012); use the label that the community uses, even when that label is adjectival (note, however, that not everyone who has hearing loss identifies as Deaf). In particular, the use of labels where disability is concerned is evolving, and people may disagree about the preferred approach. When writing about disability, person-first language (e.g., "a person with paraplegia" rather than "a paraplegic"), identity-first language (e.g., "an autistic person" rather than "a person with autism"), or both may be acceptable depending on the group you are writing about (see Section 5.4).

Provide Operational Definitions and Labels. If you provide operational definitions of groups early in your paper (e.g., "participants scoring a minimum of X on the Y scale constituted the high verbal group, and those scoring below X constituted the low verbal group"), the best practice is to describe participants thereafter in terms of the measures used to classify them (e.g., "the contrast for the high verbal group was statistically significant"), provided the terms are not inappropriate. A pejorative label should not be used in any form. Abbreviations or series labels for groups usually sacrifice clarity and may be problematic: "LDs" or "LD group" to describe people with specific learning difficulties is problematic; "HVAs" for "high verbal ability group" is difficult to decipher. "Group A" is not problematic, but it is also not descriptive. Instead, ensure that operational group labels are clear and appropriate (e.g., "group with dysgraphia").

Avoid False Hierarchies. Compare groups with care. Bias occurs when authors use one group (often their own group) as the standard against which others are judged (e.g., using citizens of the United States as the standard without specifying why that group was chosen). For example, usage of "normal" may prompt readers to make the comparison with "abnormal," thus stigmatizing individuals with differences. Likewise, contrasting lesbians with "the general public" or "normal women" portrays lesbians as marginal to society. More appropriate comparison groups for lesbians might be straight individuals, straight women, or gay men. Use parallel designations for groups, especially when presenting racial and ethnic information (see Section 5.7).

Be aware that the order of social group presentation may imply that the first-mentioned group is the norm or standard and that later-mentioned groups are abnormal or deviant. Thus, the phrases "men and women" and "White Americans and racial minorities" subtly reflect the perceived dominance of men and White people over other groups (furthermore, listing specific racial minority groups is preferable to writing about racial minorities in general; see Section 5.7). Similarly, when presenting group data, placing socially dominant groups such as men and White people on the left side of a graph or at the top of a table may also imply that these groups are the universal standard (Hegarty & Buechel, 2006). When referring to multiple groups, thoughtfully consider the order in which to present them. Do not put groups in order of social dominance by default; instead, consider options such as alphabetical order or sample size order. For ease of comprehension, list groups in the same order consistently throughout a paper.

Reducing Bias by Topic

5.3 Age

Age should be reported as part of the description of participants in the Method section. Be specific in providing age ranges, means, and medians (see also Section 5.1). Avoid open-ended definitions such as "under 18 years" or "over 65 years," unless referring, for instance, to broad research study eligibility criteria.

Terms for Different Age Groups. Different terms are used for individuals of different ages, and these terms are often gendered (see Section 5.5). Use the terms individuals use to self-describe, whether these are binary gender categories of boy–girl or man–woman or descriptive and possibly nonbinary categories of transgender, genderqueer, agender, or gender-fluid.

- For an individual of any age, appropriate terms are "person," "individual," and so on. In general, avoid using "males" and "females" as nouns; instead use "men" and "women" or other age-appropriate words (see Section 5.5). "Males" and "females" are appropriate when groups include individuals with a broad age range (e.g., "males" to describe a group that includes both boys and men).

- For an individual aged 12 years and younger, appropriate terms are "infant" (for a very young child), "child," "girl," "boy," "transgender girl," "transgender boy," "gender-fluid child," and so on.

- For an individual aged 13 to 17 years, appropriate terms are "adolescent," "young person," "youth," "young woman," "young man," "female adolescent," "male adolescent," "agender adolescent," and so on.

- For an individual aged 18 years and older, appropriate terms are "adult," "woman," "man," "transgender man," "trans man," "transgender woman," "trans woman," "genderqueer adult," "cisgender adult," and so on.

Terms for Older Adults. Older adults are a subgroup of adults, and the age groups of older adults may be described with adjectives. On first reference to a group of older people, be as specific as possible by including the age range, average age, and median age, when available. Terms such as "older persons," "older people," "older adults," "older patients," "older individuals," "persons 65 years and older," and "the older population" are preferred. Avoid using terms such as "seniors," "elderly," "the aged," "aging dependents," and similar "othering" terms because they connote a stereotype and suggest that members of the group are not part of society but rather a group apart (see Lundebjerg et al., 2017; Sweetland et al., 2017). Do not use these stigmatizing terms in your research even if your participants use them to refer to themselves (see Section 5.4 for similar guidance regarding disability). Likewise, avoid negativistic and fatalistic attitudes toward aging, such as age as being an obstacle to overcome (Lindland et al., 2015). Do not use "senile"; it is an outdated term with no agreed-upon meaning. Use "dementia" instead of "senility"; specify the type of dementia when known (e.g., dementia due to Alzheimer's disease). Be sure your language conveys that aging is a normal part of the human experience and is separate from disease and disorder.

Gerontologists may use combination terms for older age groups (e.g., "young-old," "old-old," "oldest old"); provide the specific ages of these groups when introducing them in your paper, and use the group names only as adjectives, not as nouns (i.e., refer to "young-old individuals," not to "the young-old"). When contrasting older adults with adults of other ages, describe that other age group specifically (e.g., young adults vs. older adults, middle-aged adults vs. older adults). You can use decade-specific descriptors if desired (e.g., octogenarian, centenarian). Generational descriptors such as "baby boomers," "Gen X," "millennials," "centennials," "Gen Z," and so on should be used only when discussing studies related to the topic of generations. For more information on writing about age, see "Guidelines for the Evaluation of Dementia and Age-Related Cognitive Change" (APA, 2012c) and "Guidelines for Psychological Practice With Older Adults" (APA, 2014).

5.4 Disability

Disability is a broad term that is defined in both legal and scientific ways and encompasses physical, psychological, intellectual, and socioemotional impairments (World Health Organization, 2001, 2011). The members of some groups of people with disabilities—effectively subcultures within the larger culture of disability—have particular ways of referring to themselves that they would prefer others to adopt. When you use the disability language choices made by groups of disabled individuals, you honor their preferences. For example, some Deaf individuals culturally prefer to be called "Deaf" (capitalized) rather than "people with hearing loss" or "people who are deaf" (Dunn & Andrews, 2015). Likewise, use the term "hard of hearing" rather than "hearing-impaired." Honoring the preference of the group is not only a sign of professional awareness and respect for any disability group but also a way to offer solidarity.

The language to use where disability is concerned is evolving. The overall principle for using disability language is to maintain the integrity (worth and dignity) of all individuals as human beings. Authors who write about disability are encouraged to use terms and descriptions that both honor and explain person-first and identity-first perspectives. Language should be selected with the understanding that the expressed preference of people with disabilities regarding identification supersedes matters of style.

Person-First Language. In person-first language, the person is emphasized, not the individual's disabling or chronic condition (e.g., use "a person with paraplegia" and "a youth with epilepsy" rather than "a paraplegic" or "an epileptic"). This principle applies to groups of people as well (e.g., use "people with substance use disorders" or "people with intellectual disabilities" rather than "substance abusers" or "the mentally retarded"; University of Kansas, Research and Training Center on Independent Living, 2013).

Identity-First Language. In identity-first language, the disability becomes the focus, which allows the individual to claim the disability and choose their identity rather than permitting others (e.g., authors, educators, researchers) to name it or to select terms with negative implications (Brown, 2011/n.d.; Brueggemann, 2013; Dunn & Andrews, 2015). Identity-first language is often used as an expression of cultural pride and a reclamation of a disability that once conferred a negative identity. This type of language allows for constructions such as "blind person," "autistic person," and "amputee," whereas in person-first language, the constructions would be "person who is blind," "person with autism," and "person with an amputation," respectively.

Choosing Between Person-First and Identity-First Language. Both person-first and identity-first approaches to language are designed to respect disabled persons; both are fine choices overall. It is permissible to use either approach or to mix person-first and identity-first language unless or until you know that a group clearly prefers one approach, in which case, you should use the preferred approach (Dunn & Andrews, n.d.). Mixing this language may help you avoid cumbersome repetition of "person with . . ." and is also a means to change how authors and readers regard disability and people within particular disability communities. Indeed, the level of disability identity integration can be an effective way to decipher the language that is preferred by the persons about whom you are writing. Those who embrace their disability as part of their cultural and/or personal identity are more likely to prefer identity-first language (Dunn & Andrews, 2015). If you are unsure of which approach to use, seek guidance from self-advocacy groups or other stakeholders specific to a group of people (see, e.g., Brown, 2011/n.d.). If you are working with participants directly, use the language they use to describe themselves.

Relevance of Mentioning a Disability. The nature of a disability should be indicated when it is relevant. For example, if a sample included people with spinal cord injuries and people with autism—two different groups with disabilities—then it makes sense to mention the presence of the particular disabilities. Within each group, there may be additional heterogeneity that should, under some circumstances, be articulated (e.g., different levels of spinal cord injury, different symptom severities of autism spectrum disorder).

Negative and Condescending Terminology. Avoid language that uses pictorial metaphors or negativistic terms that imply restriction (e.g., "wheelchair bound" or "confined to a wheelchair"; use the term "wheelchair user" instead) and that uses excessive and negative labels (e.g., "AIDS victim," "brain damaged"; use the terms "person with AIDS" or "person with a traumatic brain injury" instead). Avoid terms that can be regarded as slurs (e.g., "cripple," "invalid," "nuts," "alcoholic," "meth addict"); use terms like "person with a physical disability," "person with a mental illness," "person with alcohol use disorder," or "person with substance use disorder" instead, or be more specific (e.g., "person with schizophrenia"). Labels such as "high functioning" or "low functioning" are both problematic and ineffective in describing the nuances of an individual's experience with a developmental and/or intellectual disability; instead, specify the individual's strengths and weaknesses. As with other diverse groups, insiders in disability culture may use negative and condescending terms with one another; it is not appropriate for an outsider (nondisabled person) to use these terms.

Avoid euphemisms that are condescending when describing individuals with disabilities (e.g., "special needs," "physically challenged," "handi-capable"). Many people with disabilities consider these terms patronizing and inappropriate. When writing about populations or participants with disabilities, emphasize both capabilities and concerns to avoid reducing them to a "bundle of deficiencies" (Rappaport, 1977). Refer to individuals with disabilities as "patients" (or "clients") within the context of a health care setting (see Section 5.6).

5.5 Gender

Gender offers an added layer of specificity when interpreting patterns or phenomena of human behavior. However, the terms related to gender and sex are often conflated, making precision essential to writing about gender and/or sex without bias. The language related to gender identity and sexual orientation has also evolved rapidly, and it is important to use the terms people use to describe themselves (Singh, 2017; for how to determine appropriate terms, see Section 5.2; for a list of terms and definitions, see APA, n.d.-a).

Gender Versus Sex. *Gender* refers to the attitudes, feelings, and behaviors that a given culture associates with a person's biological sex (APA, 2012b). Gender is a social construct and a social identity. Use the term "gender" when referring to people as social groups. For example, when reporting the genders of participants in the Method section, write something like this: "Approximately 60% of participants identified as cisgender women, 35% as cisgender men, 3% as transgender women, 1% as transgender men, and 1% as nonbinary." *Sex* refers to biological sex assignment; use the term "sex" when the biological distinction of sex assignment (e.g., sex assigned at birth) is predominant. Using "gender" instead of "sex" also avoids ambiguity over whether "sex" means "sexual behavior." In some cases, there may not be a clear distinction between biological and acculturative factors, so a discussion of both sex and gender would be appropriate. For example, in the study of sexual orientation (see Section 5.8), researchers continue to examine the extent to which sexuality or sexual orientation—attraction to sex, gender, or some combination of both—is a biological and/or acculturative phenomenon.

Gender Identity. *Gender identity* is a component of gender that describes a person's psychological sense of their gender. Many people describe gender identity as a deeply felt, inherent sense of being a boy, a man, or male; a girl, a woman, or female; or a nonbinary gender (e.g., genderqueer, gender-nonconforming, gender-neutral, agender, gender-fluid) that may or may not correspond to a person's sex assigned at birth, presumed gender based on sex assignment, or primary or secondary sex characteristics (APA, 2015a). Gender identity applies to all individuals and is not a characteristic only of transgender or gender-nonconforming individuals. Gender identity is distinct from sexual orientation (see Section 5.8); thus, the two must not be conflated (e.g., a gay transgender man has a masculine gender identity and a gay sexual orientation, a straight cisgender woman has a feminine gender identity and a straight sexual orientation).

Reporting of Gender. Authors are strongly encouraged to explicitly designate information about the gender identities of the participants making up their samples (e.g., whether participants are transgender, cisgender, or other gender identities) rather than assuming cisgender identities. *Cisgender* refers to individuals whose sex assigned at birth aligns with their gender identity (APA, 2015a). *Cisgenderism* or *cissexism* refers to the belief that being cisgender is normative, as indicated by the assumption that individuals are cisgender unless otherwise specified (both terms are in use). *Genderism* refers to the belief that there are only two genders and that gender is automatically linked to an individual's sex assigned at birth (American Psychological Association of Graduate Students, 2015).

Transgender and Gender-Nonconforming People. *Transgender* is used as an adjective to refer to persons whose gender identity, expression, and/or role does not conform to what is culturally associated with their sex assigned at birth. Some transgender people hold a binary gender, such as man or woman, but others have a gender outside of this binary, such as gender-fluid or nonbinary. Individuals whose gender varies from presumptions based on their sex assigned at birth may use terms other than "transgender" to describe their gender, including "gender-nonconforming," "genderqueer," "gender-nonbinary," "gender-creative," "agender," or "two-spirit," to name a few. (Note that "two-spirit" is a term specific to Indigenous and Native American communities.) *Transprejudice* and *transnegativity* denote discriminatory attitudes toward individuals who are transgender. Diverse identity terms are used by transgender and gender-nonconforming (TGNC) people, and "TGNC" is a generally agreed-upon umbrella term. These terms are generally used in an identity-first way (e.g., "transgender people," "TGNC people"). However, there is some variation in the field; for example, clinicians often refer to individuals according to identity (self-identified) or describe *gender variance*, *gender expansiveness*, or *gender diversity* rather than *gender nonconformity* or *nonbinary gender*. Be sure to use identity labels that are in accordance with the stated identities of the people you are describing, and clearly define how you are using such identity labels within your writing.

Sex Assignment. The terms "birth sex," "natal sex," "tranny," and "transvestite" are considered disparaging by scholars in TGNC psychological research; by many individuals identifying as transgender, gender-nonconforming, or nonbinary; and by people exhibiting gender diversity. Thus, these disparaging terms should be avoided. Additionally, "birth sex" and "natal sex" imply that sex is an immutable characteristic without sociocultural influence. It is more appropriate to use "assigned sex" or "sex assigned at birth," as this functionally describes the assignment of a sex term (frequently binary male or female; however, intersex is an accurate assignment for some) predicated on observation of genitalia and/or determination of chromosomes and anatomical structures of the body at birth, which necessarily is interpreted within a sociocultural context. The term "transsexual" is largely outdated, but some people identify with it; this term should be used only for an individual who specifically claims it.

Gender and Noun Usage. Refer to all people, including transgender people, by the name they use to refer to themselves, which may be different from their legal name or the name on their birth certificate, keeping in mind provisions for respecting confidentiality (see Sections 1.18–1.19; see also Section 1.15 for confidentiality in qualitative research). Likewise, to reduce the possibility of stereotypic bias and avoid ambiguity, use specific nouns to identify people or groups of people (e.g., women, men, transgender men, trans men, transgender women, trans women, cisgender women, cisgender men, gender-fluid people). Use "male" and "female" as adjectives (e.g., a male participant, a female experimenter) when appropriate and relevant. Use "male" and "female" as nouns only when the age range is broad or ambiguous or to identify a transgender person's sex assignment at birth (e.g., "person assigned female at birth" is correct, not "person assigned girl at birth"). Otherwise, avoid using "male" and "female" as nouns and instead use the specific nouns for people of different ages (e.g., women) as described in Section 5.3.

To refer to all human beings, use terms like "individuals," "people," or "persons" rather than "man" or "mankind" to be accurate and inclusive. Avoid gendered endings such as "man" in occupational titles (e.g., use "police officer" instead of "policeman"), as these can be ambiguous and may imply incorrectly that all persons in the group self-identify as one gender. Instead, use a non-gendered term if possible (e.g., "homemaker" instead of "housewife"). If you use sources that include the generic "man," generic "he," or dated occupational titles, clarify the historical context in which these terms were used (for more details, see the APA Style website at https://apastyle.apa.org).

Gender and Pronoun Usage. Pronoun usage requires specificity and care on the author's part. Do not refer to the pronouns that transgender and gender-nonconforming people use as "preferred pronouns" because this implies a choice about one's gender. Use the terms "identified pronouns," "self-identified pronouns," or "pronouns" instead. When writing about a known individual, use that person's identified pronouns. Some individuals use "they" as a singular pronoun; some use alternative pronouns such as "ze," "xe," "hir," "per," "ve," "ey," and "hen" (Swedish gender-neutral pronoun), among others. Some individuals may alternate between "he" and "she" or between "he and/or she" and "they," whereas others use no pronouns at all and use their name in place of pronouns. Refer to a transgender person using language appropriate to the person's gender, regardless of sex assigned at birth—for example, use the pronouns "he," "him," and "his" in reference to a transgender man who indicates use of these pronouns.

When referring to individuals whose identified pronouns are not known or when the gender of a generic or hypothetical person is irrelevant within the context, use the singular "they" to avoid making assumptions about an individual's gender. Use the forms "they," "them," "theirs," and so forth. Sexist bias can occur when pronouns are used carelessly, as when the pronoun "he" is used to refer to all people, when a gendered pronoun is used exclusively to define roles by sex (e.g., "the nurse . . . she"), or when "he" and "she" are alternated as though these terms are generic. Pronouns associated with a specific gender have been found to induce readers to think of individuals of that gender even when the pronoun use is intended to be generic (Gastil, 1990; Moulton et al., 1978). In addition, exposure to gender-specific language in a professional context has been linked with a lower sense of belonging, reduced motivation, and professional disidentification for individuals who do not identify with that gender (Stout & Dasgupta, 2011). When writers use the singular "they," it reduces bias in the way that readers perceive the individuals referred to in the text and thereby helps ensure that readers do not feel ostracized by that text.

Avoid using combinations such as "he or she," "she or he," "he/she," and "(s)he" as alternatives to the singular "they" because such constructions imply an exclusively binary nature of gender and exclude individuals who do not use these pronouns. These forms can also appear awkward and distracting, especially with repetition. However, the combinations "he or she" or "she or he" (but not the combinations with slashes or parentheses) can be used sparingly if all people being referred to by the pronouns use these terms. For further guidance on and examples of how to use the singular "they," see Section 4.18.

Terms That Imply Binaries. Avoid referring to one sex or gender as the "opposite sex" or "opposite gender"; appropriate wording may be "another sex" or "another gender." The word "opposite" implies strong differences between two sexes or genders; however, there are more similarities than differences among people of different genders or sexes (see, e.g., Zell et al., 2015). As noted previously, some individuals do not identify with either binary gender, and these phrases ignore the existence of individuals who have disorders or differences of sex development or who are intersex (for more information, see Accord Alliance, n.d.; APA, 2015a; Blackless et al., 2000; Intersex Society of North America, n.d.). To describe members of a relationship (e.g., romantic couples, people in polyamorous relationships), use the phrases "mixed gender" or "mixed sex" when the partners have different genders or sexes, rather than "opposite gender" or "opposite sex"; use the phrases "same gender" or "same sex" when the partners have the same gender or sex.

5.6 Participation in Research

People participate in research in a variety of settings, including laboratories, homes, schools, businesses, clinics, and hospitals. Specific terms are used in certain contexts. When writing about people who participate in research, descriptive terms such as "college students," "children," or "respondents" as well as the more general terms "participants" and "subjects" are acceptable. "Subjects" and "sample" are also customary when discussing established statistical terms and experimental designs (e.g., "within-subjects design," "between-subjects design," "sample-size-adjusted Bayesian information criterion," "between-samples estimate of the variance").

Use the term "patient" to describe an individual diagnosed with a mental health, behavioral health, and/or medical disease, disorder, or problem who is receiving services from a health care provider (e.g., psychologist, physician, nurse, or other provider). This language is consistent with the language used in the health care system and promotes psychologists as being perceived a part of, and consistently integrated into, the culture of interprofessional, integrated health care. However, in academic, business, school, or other settings, the term "client" (or some other term) might be preferred instead of "patient." Within all contexts, respect the individual and/or cultural preferences expressed by recipients of psychological services and their families when you choose language to describe those individuals, families, or populations. (For further information, see *Resolution for the Use of the Term* Patient; APA, 2018).

It is also important to recognize the difference between a *case*, which is an occurrence of a disorder or illness, and a *person* who is affected by the disorder or illness and is receiving care from a health care professional. For instance, "manic–depressive cases were treated" is problematic; revising the sentence to read "the people with bipolar disorder were treated" differentiates the people from the disorder. Likewise, in the medical context, avoid the terms "patient management" and "patient placement"; in most cases, the treatment, not the patient, is managed; some alternatives are "coordination of care," "supportive services," and "assistance."

Broad clinical terms such as "borderline" and "at risk" should be properly explained when used. Avoid using these terms in a broad sense (e.g., "the diagnosis was borderline," "at-risk students") because such usage obscures the specific clinical or psychometric meaning of the terms. For example, "the diagnosis was borderline" in a neuropsychology and psychometric testing context may be clarified to specify a score on a specific test or instrument (e.g., "standard scores between 70 and 80 are considered psychometrically borderline, or between the low average and mildly impaired ranges, indicating a risk for a diagnosis of X"), whereas in a diagnostic context, "the diagnosis was borderline" may be clarified to specify a diagnosis (e.g., borderline personality disorder). When using the term "at risk," specify who is at risk and the nature of that risk (e.g., "adolescents who use substances are at risk for early school dropout").

Across contexts, write about the people who participated in your work in a way that acknowledges their contributions and agency. Sentence structure plays a key role in this acknowledgment, as does using professional language (see Section 4.7). Use the active voice to describe your actions and the actions of participants (see Section 4.13); the passive voice suggests individuals are acted upon instead of being actors (e.g., "the subjects completed the trial" and "we collected data from the participants" are preferable to "the trial was completed by the subjects" and "the participants were run"). Avoid the term "failed," as in "eight participants failed to complete the Rorschach test," because it can imply a personal shortcoming instead of a research result; "did not complete" is a more neutral choice (Knatterud, 1991). These choices will help ensure that you convey respect for the people about whom you are writing.

5.7 Racial and Ethnic Identity

Terms used to refer to racial and ethnic groups continue to change over time. One reason for this is simply personal preference; preferred designations are as varied as the people they name. Another reason is that designations can become dated over time and may hold negative connotations. When describing racial and ethnic groups, be appropriately specific and sensitive to issues of labeling (see Sections 5.1–5.2).

Race refers to physical differences that groups and cultures consider socially significant. For example, people might identify their race as Aboriginal, African American or Black, Asian, European American or White, Native American, Native Hawaiian or Pacific Islander, Māori, or some other race. *Ethnicity* refers to shared cultural characteristics such as language, ancestry, practices, and beliefs. For example, people might identify as Latino or another ethnicity. Be clear about whether you are referring to a racial group or to an ethnic group. Race is a social construct that is not universal, so one must be careful not to impose racial labels on ethnic groups. Whenever possible, use the racial and/or ethnic terms that your participants themselves use. Be sure that the racial and ethnic categories you use are as clear and specific as possible. For example, instead of categorizing participants as Asian American or Hispanic American, you could use more specific labels that identify their nation or region of origin, such as Japanese American or Cuban American. Use commonly accepted designations (e.g., census categories) while being sensitive to participants' preferred designation.

Spelling and Capitalization of Racial and Ethnic Terms. Racial and ethnic groups are designated by proper nouns and are capitalized. Therefore, use "Black" and "White" instead of "black" and "white" (do not use colors to refer to other human groups; doing so is considered pejorative). Likewise, capitalize terms such as "Native American," "Hispanic," and so on. Capitalize "Indigenous" and "Aboriginal" whenever they are used. Capitalize "Indigenous People" or "Aboriginal People" when referring to a specific group (e.g., the Indigenous Peoples of Canada), but use lowercase for "people" when describing persons who are Indigenous or Aboriginal (e.g., "the authors were all Indigenous people but belonged to different nations").

Do not use hyphens in multiword names, even if the names act as unit modifiers (e.g., write "Asian American participants," not "Asian-American participants"). If people belong to multiple racial or ethnic groups, the names of the specific groups are capitalized, but the terms "multiracial," "biracial," "multiethnic," and so on are lowercase.

Terms for Specific Groups. Designations for specific ethnic and racial groups are described next. These groups frequently are included in studies published in APA journals; the examples provided are far from exhaustive but illustrate some of the complexities of labeling.

People of African Origin. When writing about people of African ancestry, several factors inform the appropriate terms to use. People of African descent have widely varied cultural backgrounds, family histories, and family experiences. Some will be from Caribbean islands, Latin America, various regions in the United States, countries in Africa, or elsewhere. Some American people of African ancestry prefer "Black," and others prefer "African American"; both terms are acceptable. However, "African American" should not be used as an umbrella term for people of African ancestry worldwide because it obscures other ethnicities or national origins, such as Nigerian, Kenyan, Jamaican, or Bahamian; in these cases use "Black." The terms "Negro" and "Afro-American" are outdated; therefore, their use is generally inappropriate.

People of Asian Origin. When writing about people of Asian ancestry from Asia, the term "Asian" is appropriate; for people of Asian descent from the United States or Canada, the appropriate term is "Asian American" or "Asian Canadian," respectively. It is problematic to group "Asian" and "Asian American" as if they are synonymous. This usage reinforces the idea that Asian Americans are perpetual foreigners. "Asian" refers to Asians in Asia, not in the United States, and should not be used to refer to Asian Americans. The older term "Oriental" is primarily used to refer to cultural objects such as carpets and is pejorative when used to refer to people. To provide more specificity, "Asian origin" may be divided regionally, for example, into South Asia (including most of India and countries such as Afghanistan, Pakistan, Bangladesh, and Nepal), Southeast Asia (including the eastern parts of India and countries such as Vietnam, Cambodia, Thailand, Indonesia, and the Philippines), and East Asia (including countries such as China, Vietnam, Japan, South Korea and North Korea, and Taiwan). The corresponding terms (e.g., East Asian) can be used; however, refer to the specific nation or region of origin when possible.

People of European Origin. When writing about people of European ancestry, the terms "White" and "European American" are acceptable. Adjust the latter term as needed for location, for example, "European," "European American," and "European Australian" for people of European descent living in Europe, the United States, and Australia, respectively. The use of the term "Caucasian" as an alternative to "White" or "European" is discouraged because it originated as a way of classifying White people as a race to be favorably compared with other races. As with all discussions of race and ethnicity, it is preferable to be more specific about regional (e.g., Southern European, Scandinavian) or national (e.g., Italian, Irish, Swedish, French, Polish) origin when possible.

Indigenous Peoples Around the World. When writing about Indigenous Peoples, use the names that they call themselves. In general, refer to an Indigenous group as a "people" or "nation" rather than as a "tribe."

- In North America, the collective terms "Native American" and "Native North American" are acceptable (and may be preferred to "American Indian"). "Indian" usually refers to people from India. Specify the nation or people if possible (e.g., Cherokee, Navajo, Sioux).

- Hawaiian Natives may identify as "Native American," "Hawaiian Native," "Indigenous Peoples of the Hawaiian Islands," and/or "Pacific Islander."

- In Canada, refer to the Indigenous Peoples collectively as "Indigenous Peoples" or "Aboriginal Peoples" (*International Journal of Indigenous Health*, n.d.); specify the nation or people if possible (e.g., People of the First Nations of Canada, People of the First Nations, or First Nations People; Métis; Inuit).

- In Alaska, the Indigenous People may identify as "Alaska Natives." The Indigenous Peoples in Alaska, Canada, Siberia, and Greenland may identify as a specific nation (e.g., Inuit, Iñupiat). Avoid the term "Eskimo" because it may be considered pejorative.

- In Latin America and the Caribbean, refer to the Indigenous Peoples collectively as "Indigenous Peoples" and by name if possible (e.g., Quechua, Aymara, Taíno, Nahuatl).

- In Australia, the Indigenous Peoples may identify as "Aboriginal People" or "Aboriginal Australians" and "Torres Strait Islander People" or "Torres Strait Island Australians." Refer to specific groups when people use these terms to refer to themselves (e.g., Anangu Pitjantjatjara, Arrernte).

- In New Zealand, the Indigenous People may identify as "Māori" or the "Māori people" (the proper spelling includes the diacritical macron over the "a").

For information on citing the Traditional Knowledge or Oral Traditions of Indigenous Peoples as well as the capitalization of terms related to Indigenous Peoples, see Section 8.9.

People of Middle Eastern Origin. When writing about people of Middle Eastern and North African (MENA) descent, state the nation of origin (e.g., Iran, Iraq, Egypt, Lebanon, Israel) when possible. In some cases, people of MENA descent who claim Arab ancestry and reside in the United States may be referred to as "Arab Americans." In all cases, it is best to allow individuals to self-identify.

People of Hispanic or Latinx Ethnicity. When writing about people who identify as Hispanic, Latino (or Latinx, etc.), Chicano, or another related designation, authors should consult with their participants to determine the appropriate choice. Note that "Hispanic" is not necessarily an all-encompassing term, and the labels "Hispanic" and "Latino" have different connotations. The term "Latino" (and its related forms) might be preferred by those originating from Latin America, including Brazil. Some use the word "Hispanic" to refer to those who speak Spanish; however, not every group in Latin America speaks Spanish (e.g., in Brazil, the official language is Portuguese). The word "Latino" is gendered (i.e., "Latino" is masculine and "Latina" is feminine); the use of the word "Latin@" to mean both Latino and Latina is now widely accepted. "Latinx" can also be used as a gender-neutral or nonbinary term inclusive of all genders. There are compelling reasons to use any of the terms "Latino," "Latina," "Latino/a," "Latin@," and/or "Latinx" (see de Onís, 2017), and various groups advocate for the use of different forms.

Use the term(s) your participants or population uses; if you are not working directly with this population but it is a focus of your research, it may be helpful to explain why you chose the term you used or to choose a more inclusive term like "Latinx." In general, naming a nation or region of origin is preferred (e.g., Bolivian, Salvadoran, or Costa Rican is more specific than Latino, Latinx, Latin American, or Hispanic).

Parallel Comparisons Among Groups. Nonparallel designations (e.g., "African Americans and Whites," "Asian Americans and Black Americans") should be avoided because one group is described by color, whereas the other group is not. Instead, use "Blacks and Whites" or "African Americans and European Americans" for the former example and "Asian Americans and African Americans" for the latter example. Do not use the phrase "White Americans and racial minorities"; the rich diversity within racial minorities is minimized when it is compared with the term "White Americans."

Avoiding Essentialism. Language that essentializes or reifies race is strongly discouraged and is generally considered inappropriate. For example, phrases such as "the Black race" and "the White race" are essentialist in nature, portray human groups monolithically, and often perpetuate stereotypes.

Writing About "Minorities." To refer to non-White racial and ethnic groups collectively, use terms such as "people of color" or "underrepresented groups" rather than "minorities." The use of "minority" may be viewed pejoratively because it is usually equated with being less than, oppressed, or deficient in comparison with the majority (i.e., White people). Rather, a *minority group* is a population subgroup with ethnic, racial, social, religious, or other characteristics different from those of the majority of the population, though the relevance of this term is changing as the demographics of the population change (APA, 2015a). If a distinction is needed between the dominant racial group and nondominant racial groups, use a modifier (e.g., "ethnic," "racial") when using the word "minority" (e.g., ethnic minority, racial minority, racial-ethnic minority). When possible, use the specific name of the group or groups to which you are referring.

Do not assume that members of minority groups are underprivileged; *underprivileged* means having less money, education, resources, and so forth than the other people in a society and may refer to individuals or subgroups in any racial or ethnic group. Terms such as "economically marginalized" and "economically exploited" may also be used rather than "underprivileged." Whenever possible, use more specific terms (e.g., schools with majority Black populations that are underfunded) or refer to discrimination or systematic oppression as a whole.

5.8 Sexual Orientation

Sexual orientation is a part of individual identity that includes "a person's sexual and emotional attraction to another person and the behavior and/or social affiliation that may result from this attraction" (APA, 2015a, p. 862). Use the term "sexual orientation" rather than "sexual preference," "sexual identity," or "sexual orientation identity." All people choose their partners regardless of their sexual orientation; however, the orientation itself is not a choice.

Sexual orientation can be conceptualized first by the degree to which a person feels sexual and emotional attraction; some parallel terms are "sexual," "demisexual" (or "gray-asexual" or "gray-A"), and "asexual" (see The Asexual Visibility & Education Network, n.d.). A person who identifies as sexual feels sexual and emotional attraction toward some or all types of people, a person who identifies as demisexual feels sexually attracted only within the context of a strong emotional connection with another person, and a person who identifies as asexual does not experience sexual attraction or has little interest in sexual behavior (see APA, 2015b).

Second, sexual orientation can be conceptualized as having a direction. For people who identify as sexual or demisexual, their attraction then may be directed toward people who are similarly gendered, differently gendered, and so on. That is, sexual orientation indicates the gendered directionality of attraction, even if that directionality is very inclusive (e.g., nonbinary). Thus, a person might be attracted to men, women, both, neither, masculinity, femininity, and/ or to people who have other gender identities such as genderqueer or androgynous, or a person may have an attraction that is not predicated on a perceived or known gender identity.

Terms for Sexual Orientation. Some examples of sexual orientation are lesbian, gay, heterosexual, straight, asexual, bisexual, queer, polysexual, and pansexual (also called multisexual and omnisexual). For example, a person who identifies as lesbian might describe herself as a woman (gender identity) who is attracted to women (sexual orientation)—the sexual orientation label of "lesbian" is predicated on a perceived or known gender identity of the other person. However, someone who identifies as pansexual might describe their attraction to people as being inclusive of gender identity but not determined or delineated by gender identity. Note that these definitions are evolving and that self-identification is best when possible.

Use the umbrella term "sexual and gender minorities" to refer to multiple sexual and/or gender minority groups, or write about "sexual orientation and gender diversity" (these terms are used by the Office on Sexual Orientation and Gender Diversity at APA and the Sexual & Gender Minority Research Office at the National Institutes of Health). Abbreviations such as LGBTQ, LGBTQ+, LGBTQIA, and LGBTQIA+ may also be used to refer to multiple groups. The form "LGBT" is considered outdated, but there is not consensus about which abbreviation including or beyond LGBTQ to use. If you use the abbreviation LGBTQ (or a related one), define it (see Section 6.25) and ensure that it is representative of the groups about which you are writing. Be specific about the groups to which you refer (e.g., do not use LGBTQ and related abbreviations to write about legislation that primarily affects transgender people; instead, specify the impacted group). However, if in doubt, use one of the umbrella terms rather than a potentially inaccurate abbreviation.

When using specific terms for orientations, define them if there is ambiguity. For example, the adjective "gay" can be interpreted broadly, to include all genders, or more narrowly, to include only men, so define "gay" when you use it in your paper, or use the phrase "gay men" to clarify the usage. By convention, the term "lesbians" is appropriate to use interchangeably with "lesbian women," but "gay men" or "gay people" should be used, not "gays."

Inaccurate or Pejorative Terms. Avoid the terms "homosexual" and "homosexuality." Instead, use specific, identity-first terms to describe people's sexual orientation (e.g., bisexual people, queer people). These specific terms refer primarily to identities and to the culture and communities that have developed among people who share those identities. It is inaccurate to collapse these communities into the term "homosexual." Furthermore, the term "homosexuality" has been and continues to be associated with negative stereotypes, pathology, and the reduction of people's identities to their sexual behavior. *Homoprejudice*, *biprejudice*, *homonegativity*, and so forth are terms used to denote prejudicial and discriminatory attitudes toward lesbians, gay men, bisexual individuals, or other sexual minorities. *Heterosexism* refers to the belief that heterosexuality is normative, as indicated in the assumption that individuals are heterosexual unless otherwise specified (American Psychological Association of Graduate Students, 2015). The terms "straight" and "heterosexual" are both acceptable to use when referring to people who are attracted to individuals of another gender; the term "straight" may help move the lexicon away from a dichotomy of heterosexual and homosexual. For more information regarding sexual orientation, see "Guidelines for Psychological Practice With Transgender and Gender Nonconforming People" (APA, 2015a).

5.9 Socioeconomic Status

Socioeconomic status (SES) encompasses not only income but also educational attainment, occupational prestige, and subjective perceptions of social status and social class. SES encompasses quality of life attributes and opportunities afforded to people within society and is a consistent predictor of a vast array of psychological outcomes. Thus, SES should be reported as part of the description of participants in the Method section. Because SES is complex, it is not indexed similarly in all studies; therefore, precise terminology that appropriately describes a level of specificity and sensitivity is essential to minimize bias in language around SES (for a discussion, see Diemer et al., 2013).

Reporting SES. When reporting SES, provide as much detailed information as possible about people's income, education, and occupations or employment circumstances. For example, when referring to "low-income participants" or "high-income participants," classify whether reported incomes take into account household size, or provide information about the relation between household incomes and federal poverty guidelines. Additionally, SES can be described by providing information related to specific contextual and environmental conditions such as participants' housing arrangement (e.g., renting a home, owning a home, residing in subsidized housing) and neighborhood characteristics such as median household income, percentage of unemployed people, or proportion of students who qualify for free or reduced-price lunch in local schools.

Pejorative or Stereotyping Terms. Avoid using broad, pejorative, and generalizing terms to discuss SES. Specifically, negative connotations are associated with terms such as "the homeless," "inner-city," "ghetto," "the projects," "poverty stricken," and "welfare reliant." Instead, use specific, person-first language such as "mothers who receive TANF benefits" rather than "welfare mothers" ("TANF" stands for "Temporary Assistance for Needy Families" and is the proper term for the current welfare program in the United States). When discussing people without a fixed, regular, or adequate nighttime residence, use specific language that addresses the quality or lack of housing or length of time without housing, not whether the people consider their residence a home. That is, use language like "people experiencing homelessness," "people who are homeless," "people in emergency shelter," or "people in transitional housing," rather than calling people "the homeless."

It is important to note that SES terms such as "low-income" and "poor" have historically served as implicit descriptors for racial and/or ethnic minority people. Thus, it is critical that authors include racial and/or ethnic descriptors within SES categories—for example, "This sample includes low-income and middle-income Puerto Rican fathers." Implicit biases around economic and occupational status can result in deficit-based language that blames individuals for their occupational, educational, or economic situation (e.g., "attendant economic deficits") rather than recognizing a broader societal context that influences individual circumstances. Deficit-based language also focuses on what people lack rather than on what they possess. Instead of labeling people as "high school dropouts," "being poorly educated," or "having little education," provide more sensitive and specific descriptors such as "people who do not have a high school diploma or equivalent." Alternatively, by adopting a strengths-based perspective, authors can write about "people who have a grade school education." Likewise, instead of writing about an "achievement gap," write about an "opportunity gap" to emphasize how the context in which people live affects their outcomes or opportunities.

5.10 Intersectionality

When authors write about personal characteristics, they should be sensitive to *intersectionality*—that is, to the way in which individuals are shaped by and identify with a vast array of cultural, structural, sociobiological, economic, and social contexts (Howard & Renfrow, 2014). Intersectionality is a paradigm that addresses the multiple dimensions of identity and social systems as they intersect with one another and relate to inequality, such as racism, genderism, heterosexism, ageism, and classism, among other variables (APA, 2017b). Thus, individuals are located within a range of social groups whose structural inequalities can result in marginalized identities.

Because people are unique, many identities are possible. As one example of a group with an intersectional identity, Black lesbian women may have similarities to and differences from other oppressed groups in the meanings that are assigned to their multiple positionalities. Black women may identify with the oppressive and discriminatory experiences of White women as well as with those of Black men. At the same time, Black lesbian women's experiences may not be equivalent to those of these other groups. They may experience discrimination as a response to their race, gender, and/or sexual orientation. Thus, their experience does not necessarily reflect the sum of oppressions of racism, sexism, and heteronormativity (i.e., race + sex + heterosexism) but rather their unique identities and social locations as Black lesbian women that are not based in or driven by the perspectives of White women or of Black men (Bowleg, 2008; Crenshaw, 1989). That is, for example, even though Black women and White women are both women, and Black women and Black men are both Black, this does not mean that the perspectives and experiences of the latter groups are the same as or related to those of Black lesbian women.

Intersectional identities also include experiences of privileged contexts that intersect with those of oppression. For example, a Laotian immigrant woman with a disability may experience a sense of safety and privilege because of her legal immigration status in the United States, but she may experience discrimination and a lack of access to appropriate resources within and outside of her family and ethnic community on the basis of her disability status. A Jewish American adolescent may experience privilege as a result of being perceived as White but may be the target of anti-Semitic slurs at school and in social media because of their religious beliefs. These examples illustrate how perspectives are shaped by the multiplicity of identities and contexts to which an individual belongs, some oppressed and some privileged. Aspects of identity such as race, gender, and class can be oppressed or privileged, in ways that may differ across contexts, and can result in differing experiences that interact dynamically to shape an individual's experiences, advantages, and disadvantages across time and space. The intersections of multiple identities transform the oppressed and privileged aspects of each person's layered, interlocking identities.

To address intersectionality in a paper, identify individuals' relevant characteristics and group memberships (e.g., ability and/or disability status, age, gender, gender identity, generation, historical as well as ongoing experiences of marginalization, immigrant status, language, national origin, race and/or ethnicity, religion or spirituality, sexual orientation, social class, and socioeconomic status, among other variables), and describe how their characteristics and group memberships intersect in ways that are relevant to the study. Report participant data for each group using specific terms as described in Sections 5.3 to 5.9. For example, when describing participants in terms of their race and gender, write "20 participants were African American women, 15 participants were European American women, 23 participants were African American men, and 18 participants were European American men (all participants were cisgender)" rather than "35 participants were women and 41 were men; 43 were African American and 33 were European American." Reporting participant characteristics in this way helps readers understand how many groups there are that are composed of individuals with the same characteristics. Likewise, when reporting and interpreting the results, note the impact of any intersections on the findings rather than assuming that one characteristic is responsible for what you found. For more discussion of intersectionality, see the *Multicultural Guidelines: An Ecological Approach to Context, Identity, and Intersectionality* (APA, 2017b).

6

MECHANICS OF STYLE

Contents

6

MECHANICS OF STYLE

Style refers to guidelines for ensuring clear, consistent communication and presentation in written works. APA Style, as described in this *Publication Manual*, provides guidelines for writing scholarly papers. Publishers and instructors often require authors writing for publication and students writing for a course or degree requirement to follow specific style guidelines to avoid inconsistencies among and within journal articles, book chapters, and academic papers. For example, without style guidelines, authors might use the spellings "health care," "health-care," and "healthcare" interchangeably in one work. Although their meaning is the same and the choice of one style over another may seem arbitrary (in this case, "health care," with a space and no hyphen, is APA Style), such variations in style can distract or confuse readers.

In this chapter, we provide essential style guidelines for scholarly writing, including punctuation, spelling, capitalization, italics, abbreviations, numbers, statistical and mathematical copy, and lists. These guidelines often overlap with those for general good writing practices. However, we omit general grammar rules explained in widely available writing manuals and examples of grammar or usage with little relevance to manuscripts submitted to journals that use APA Style. Style manuals agree more often than they disagree; when they disagree, the *Publication Manual* takes precedence for APA Style papers or publications.

Punctuation

Punctuation establishes the cadence of a sentence, telling readers where to pause (comma, semicolon, and colon), stop (period and question mark), or take a detour (dash, parentheses, and square brackets). Punctuation of a sentence usually denotes a pause in thought; different kinds of punctuation indicate different kinds and lengths of pauses.

6.1 Spacing After Punctuation Marks

Insert one space after the following:

- periods or other punctuation marks at the end of a sentence
- commas, colons, and semicolons
- periods that separate parts of a reference list entry (see Section 9.5)
- periods following initials in names (M. P. Clark)

Do not insert a space in the following cases:

- after internal periods in abbreviations (e.g., a.m., i.e., U.S.)
- after periods in identity-concealing labels for study participants (F.I.M.)
- around colons in ratios (1:4)

> *Note:* We recommend using one space after the period or other punctuation mark at the end of a sentence; however, follow the guidelines of your publisher or instructor if they have different requirements.

6.2 Period

Use a period or periods in the following cases:

- to end a complete sentence
- with initials in names (Bazerman, M. H.)
- in the abbreviations for "United States" and "United Kingdom" when they are used as adjectives (U.S. Navy; it is not required to abbreviate these terms)
- in identity-concealing labels for study participants (F.I.M.)
- in Latin abbreviations (a.m., cf., e.g., i.e., p.m., vs.)
- in reference abbreviations (Vol. 1, 2nd ed., p. 6, paras. 11–12, F. Supp.)
- in era designations (B.C.E., C.E., B.C., A.D.; see Section 9.42)
- to end each element within a reference (except DOIs and URLs; see Section 9.5)

Do not use periods in the following cases:

- in abbreviations of state, province, or territory names (NY; CA; Washington, DC; BC; ON; NSW)
- in capital letter abbreviations and acronyms (APA, NDA, NIMH, IQ)
- in abbreviations for academic degrees (PhD, PsyD, EdD, MD, MA, RN, MSW, LCSW, etc.; see Section 2.5)
- in abbreviations for routes of administration (icv, im, ip, iv, sc)
- in metric and nonmetric measurement abbreviations (cm, hr, kg, min, ml, s)

> *Note:* Use a period with the abbreviation for "inch" or "inches" (in.) because otherwise it could be misread.

- after URLs in the text (see Section 8.22); instead, place URLs in the middle of the sentence or in parentheses to avoid ending a sentence with a URL
- after DOIs or URLs in the reference list (see Section 9.35)

6.3 Comma

Use a comma in the following cases:

- between elements in a series of three or more items, including before the final item (see also Section 6.49); this last comma is called a *serial comma* or *Oxford comma*

  Correct: height, width, and depth
  Incorrect: height, width and depth

- after an introductory phrase (if the introductory phrase is short, the comma after it is optional)

  After the nurses administered the medication, patients rated their pain.

  in this section, we discuss

  > *or*

  in this section we discuss

- to set off a nonessential or nonrestrictive clause (see Section 4.21)—that is, a clause that embellishes a sentence but if removed would leave the grammatical structure and meaning of the sentence intact

  Strong fearful faces, which are rarely seen in everyday life, convey intense expression of negative emotions.

- to set off statistics in the text that already contain parentheses, to avoid nested parentheses

  Sleep amount was not significantly different between the three groups (nap: $M = 7.48$ hr, $SD = 1.99$; wake: $M = 8.13$ hr, $SD = 1.22$; nap + wake: $M = 7.25$ hr, $SD = 0.76$), $F(2, 71) = 2.32$, $p = .11$.

  There was a main effect of group on corrected recognition, $F(2, 71) = 3.38$, $p < .04$, $\eta_p^2 = .087$.

- to separate two independent clauses joined by a conjunction

  Facial expressions were presented, and different photo models were chosen randomly.

- to set off the year in exact dates in the text or in a retrieval date (see Section 9.16); however, when only a month and year appear in the text, do not use a comma

  Retrieved April 24, 2020, from
  in April 2020

- to set off the year in parenthetical in-text citations

  (Bergen-Abramoff, 2018)
  (Horowitz, 2019, discovered . . .)

- to separate groups of three digits in most numbers of 1,000 or more (see Section 6.38 for exceptions)

Do not use a comma in the following cases:

- before an essential or restrictive clause (see Section 4.21) because removing such a clause from the sentence would alter the intended meaning

  Adolescents who spent a small amount of time on electronic communication activities were happier than those who spent no time on such activities.

- between the two parts of a compound predicate

  Correct: Participants rated the items and completed a demographic questionnaire.
  Incorrect: Participants rated the items, and completed a demographic questionnaire.

- to separate parts of measurement

  7 years 4 months
  2 min 35 s
  5 ft 10 in.

6.4 Semicolon

Use a semicolon in the following cases:

- to separate two independent clauses that are not joined by a conjunction

  Students received course credit for participation; community members received $10.

- to separate two independent clauses joined by a conjunctive adverb such as "however," "therefore," or "nevertheless"

  The children studied the vocabulary words; however, they had difficulties with recall.

- to separate items in a list that already contain commas (see Section 6.49)

  The color groups were red, yellow, and blue; orange, green, and purple; or black, gray, and brown.

- to separate multiple parenthetical citations (see Section 8.12)

  (Gaddis, 2018; Lai et al., 2016; Williams & Peng, 2019)

- to separate different types of information in the same set of parentheses, to avoid back-to-back parentheses

  ($n = 33$; Fu & Ginsburg, 2020)

- to separate sets of statistics that already contain commas

  (age, $M = 34.5$ years, 95% CI [29.4, 39.6]; years of education, $M = 10.4$ [8.7, 12.1]; and weekly income, $M = \$612$ [522, 702]).

6.5 Colon

Use a colon in the following cases:

- between a grammatically complete introductory clause (one that could stand alone as a sentence, including an imperative statement) and a final phrase or clause that illustrates, extends, or amplifies the preceding thought (if the clause following the colon is a complete sentence, begin it with a capital letter; see Section 6.13)

  There are three main patterns of mother–infant attachment: secure, avoidant, and resistant/ambivalent (Ainsworth et al., 1978).

  Yang et al. (2019) confirmed the finding: Test performance depended on preparation.

- in ratios and proportions

  The proportion of salt to water was 1:8.

Do not use a colon in the following case:

- after an introduction that is not an independent clause or complete sentence

  The formula is $r_i = a_i + e$.

  Target behaviors included eating, sleeping, and socializing.

  The participants were asked to
  - rank the 15 items,
  - explain their choices, and
  - close their notebooks when finished.

6.6 Dash

Two kinds of dash are used in APA Style: the *em dash* (long dash) and the *en dash* (midsized dash). These dashes are different from hyphens (see Section 6.12) and minus signs (see Section 6.45).

Em Dash. Use an em dash to set off an element added to amplify or digress from the main clause. Overuse of the em dash weakens the flow of material, so use it judiciously. Do not use a space before or after an em dash. Word-processing programs can be set to automatically convert two back-to-back hyphens to an em dash. (See Section 6.17 for capitalization following em dashes in titles.)

  Social adjustment—but not academic adjustment—was associated with extraversion.

En Dash. An en dash is longer and thinner than a hyphen but shorter than an em dash. Use an en dash between words of equal weight in a compound adjective and to indicate a numerical range, such as a page or date range. Do not insert a space before or after an en dash. Word-processing programs have options for inserting an en dash.

  author–date citation
  Sydney–Los Angeles flight
  pp. 4–7
  50%–60%

A hyphen rather than an en dash is generally used in an abbreviation that contains dashes, such as the abbreviation for a test or scale (e.g., MMPI-2) or a diagnostic manual (*DSM-5, ICD-11*; see Section 6.25).

6.7 Quotation Marks

This section addresses how to use quotation marks other than with direct quotations (see Sections 8.25–8.36). Quotation marks often appear with other punctuation marks. Place commas and periods inside closing quotation marks. Place other punctuation marks (e.g., colons, semicolons, ellipses) outside closing quotation marks.

Use double quotation marks in the following cases:

- to refer to a letter, word, phrase, or sentence as a linguistic example or as itself

  the letter "m"
  the singular "they"
  answered "yes" or "no"

Instead of referring to someone as a "defective child," talk about a "child with a congenital disability" or a "child with a birth impairment."

Students wrote "I promise to uphold the honor code" at the top of the test page.

- to present stimuli in the text (long lists of stimuli may be better presented in a table, where quotation marks are not needed)

The stimulus words were "garden," "laundry," "briefcase," and "salary."

> *Note:* Some publishers prefer italics for the presentation of stimuli and so forth; consult the manuscript preparation guidelines or journal editor for the preferred format.

- to reproduce material from a test item or verbatim instructions to participants (if instructions are long, present them in an appendix or set them off from text in block quote format without quotation marks; see Sections 2.14 and 8.27)

The first item was "How tired do you feel after a long day at work?"

Participants read, "You can write as much as you like when answering the questions."

- to introduce a word or phrase used as an ironic comment, as slang, or as an invented or coined expression; use quotation marks only for the first occurrence of the word or phrase, not for subsequent occurrences

First occurrence:
considered "normal" behavior
called a "friendly link"

Subsequent occurrence:
normal behavior
a friendly link

- to introduce a label; after the label has been used once, do not use quotation marks for subsequent occurrences

The image label changed from "spiderweb" to "dartboard." The spiderweb and dartboard labels . . .

- to set off the title of a periodical article or book chapter when the title is used in the text or in a copyright attribution (do not use quotation marks around the article or book chapter title in the reference list entry)

In text:
Oerlemans and Bakker's (2018) article, "Motivating Job Characteristics and Happiness at Work: A Multilevel Perspective," described . . .

In the reference list:
Oerlemans, W. G. M., & Bakker, A. B. (2018). Motivating job characteristics and happiness at work: A multilevel perspective. *Journal of Applied Psychology, 103*(11), 1230–1241. https://doi.org/10.1037/apl0000318

In a copyright attribution:
Adapted from "Motivating Job Characteristics and Happiness at Work: A Multilevel Perspective," by W. G. M. Oerlemans and A. B. Bakker, 2018, *Journal of Applied Psychology, 103*(11), p. 1236 (https://doi.org/10.1037/apl0000318). Copyright 2018 by the American Psychological Association.

Do not use double quotation marks in the following cases:

- to highlight a key term or phrase (e.g., around a term for which you are going to provide a definition); instead, use italics (see Section 6.22)

- to identify the anchors of a scale; instead, use italics (see Section 6.22)

- to refer to a numeral as itself because the meaning is sufficiently clear without quotation marks

  The numeral 2 was displayed onscreen.

- to hedge or downplay meaning (do not use any punctuation with these expressions)

  Correct: The teacher rewarded the class with tokens.
  Incorrect: The teacher "rewarded" the class with tokens.

6.8 Parentheses

Use parentheses in the following cases:

- to set off structurally independent elements

  The patterns were statistically significant (see Figure 5).

- to set off in-text citations (see Section 8.11)

  Barnes and Spreitzer (2019) described
  (Proctor & Hoffmann, 2016)

- to introduce an abbreviation in the text (see also Section 6.25)

  galvanic skin response (GSR)
  Child Report of Parental Behavior Inventory (CRPBI; Schaefer, 1965)

- to set off letters that identify items in a list within a sentence or paragraph (see also Section 6.50)

  The subject areas included (a) synonyms associated with cultural interactions, (b) descriptors for ethnic group membership, and (c) psychological symptoms and outcomes associated with bicultural adaptation.

- to group mathematical expressions (see also Sections 6.9 and 6.46)

  $(k - 1)/(g - 2)$

- to enclose numbers that identify displayed formulas and equations

  $$M_j = \alpha M_{j-1} + f_j + g_j * g_j' \tag{1}$$

- to enclose statistical values that do not already contain parentheses

  was statistically significant ($p = .031$)

- to enclose degrees of freedom

  $t(75) = 2.19$
  $F(2, 116) = 3.71$

> *Note:* (When a complete sentence is enclosed in parentheses, like this, place the end punctuation inside the parentheses.) If only part of a sentence is enclosed in parentheses, place punctuation outside the parentheses (like this).

Do not use parentheses in the following cases:

- to enclose text within other parentheses; instead, use square brackets to avoid nested parentheses

  (Beck Depression Inventory [BDI]; Beck et al., 1996)

MECHANICS OF STYLE

- to enclose statistics that already contain parentheses; instead, use a comma before the statistics to avoid nested parentheses

were significantly different, $F(4, 132) = 13.62$, $p < .001$.

- to enclose back-to-back parenthetical information; instead, place the information in one set of parentheses, separated with a semicolon

Correct: (e.g., flow; Csikszentmihalyi, 2014)
Incorrect: (e.g., flow) (Csikszentmihalyi, 2014)

6.9 Square Brackets

Use square brackets in the following cases:

- to enclose parenthetical material that is already in parentheses

(The results for the control group [$n = 8$] are also presented in Figure 2.)

- to enclose abbreviations when the abbreviated term appears in parentheses

(Minnesota Multiphasic Personality Inventory–2 [MMPI-2]; Butcher et al., 2001)

- to enclose values that are the limits of a confidence interval

95% CIs [–7.2, 4.3], [9.2, 12.4], and [–1.2, –0.5]

- to enclose material inserted in a quotation by someone other than the original author (see also Section 8.31)

Schofield et al. (2016) found that "these types of [warm and accepting] parenting behaviors are positively associated with healthy child and adolescent adjustment" (p. 615).

- to enclose a description of form for some works (e.g., those outside the typical peer-reviewed academic literature; see Section 9.21) in a reference list entry

Do not use square brackets in the following cases:

- to set off statistics that already include parentheses

Correct: in the first study, $F(1, 32) = 4.37$, $p = .045$.
Incorrect: in the first study ($F[1, 32] = 4.37$, $p = .045$).
Incorrect: in the first study [$F(1, 32) = 4.37$, $p = .045$].

> *Note:* In mathematical material, the placement of brackets and parentheses is reversed; that is, parentheses appear within brackets (see Section 6.46).

- around the year in a narrative citation when the sentence containing the narrative citation appears in parentheses; instead, use commas (see Section 8.11)

Correct: (as Gregory, 2020, concluded . . .)
Incorrect: (as Gregory [2020] concluded . . .)

6.10 Slash

Use a slash (also called a "virgule," "solidus," or "shill") in the following cases:

- to clarify a comparison in a compound adjective, especially when one of the elements is a hyphenated compound (alternatively, use an en dash; see Section 6.6) the classification/similarity-judgment condition

hits/false-alarms comparison

test/retest reliability, test–retest reliability

- to specify either of two possibilities

  and/or (use sparingly)

  Latino/a

- to separate a numerator from a denominator

  X/Y

- to separate units of measurement accompanied by a numeric value (see Section 6.27); if no numeric value appears with the unit of measurement, spell out the word "per."

  0.5 deg/s

  7.4 mg/kg

  cost per square meter

- to set off phonemes

  /o/

- in citations of translated, reprinted, reissued, or republished works in the text (see Section 9.41)

  Freud (1923/1961)

Do not use a slash in the following cases:

- more than once to express compound units; use centered dots and parentheses as needed to prevent ambiguity

  Correct: nmol • hr^{-1} • mg^{-1}

  Incorrect: nmol/hr/mg

- when a phrase would be clearer

  Correct: Each child handed the toy to their parent or guardian.

  Incorrect: Each child handed the toy to their parent/guardian.

Spelling

6.11 Preferred Spelling

Spelling in APA Style papers should conform to the *Merriam-Webster.com Dictionary* (https://www.merriam-webster.com). The spellings of psychological terms should conform to the *APA Dictionary of Psychology* (https://dictionary.apa.org). If a word appears differently in these two dictionaries, follow the spelling in the *APA Dictionary of Psychology*. If a word is not in either of these dictionaries, consult an unabridged edition of *Webster's* dictionary (see https://unabridged.merriam-webster.com). If the dictionary offers a choice of spellings, select one and use it consistently throughout your paper.

The plural forms of some words of Latin or Greek origin can be troublesome (particularly those that end in the letter "a"). A list of preferred spellings of some of the more common ones follows.

| **Singular:** | appendix | criterion | curriculum | datum | phenomenon |
| **Plural:** | appendices | criteria | curricula | data | phenomena |

Remember that plural nouns take plural verbs.

Correct: The data indicate

Incorrect: The data indicates

In general, form the possessive of a singular name by adding an apostrophe and an "s" (e.g., "Milner's theory"). This guideline also applies when a name ends in "s" (e.g., "Descartes's philosophy," "James's work").

The spellings of terms related to technology evolve over time. Use the following spellings for some common technology words in APA Style papers:

email	ebook	ereader	database
data set	smartphone	internet	intranet
Wi-Fi	website	webpage	the web
home page	username	login page (but "log in" when used as a verb)	emoji (for the plural, either "emoji" or "emojis")

6.12 Hyphenation

Compound words—words composed of two or more words—take many forms; they may be written as (a) two separate words (open), (b) one hyphenated word, or (c) one solid word. Compound words are often introduced into the language as separate or hyphenated words; as they become more commonplace, they tend to fuse into a solid word. For example, "data base" has become "database," and "e-mail" has become "email." The dictionary is an excellent guide for choosing the proper form: When a compound appears in the dictionary, its usage is established, and it is considered a permanent compound (e.g., "health care," "self-esteem," "caregiver"). In general, follow the hyphenation shown in the dictionary for permanent compounds (e.g., write "health care" without a hyphen, even in a phrase like "health care setting"); adjust hyphenation only to prevent misreading. Dictionaries do not always agree on the way a compound should be written (open, hyphenated, or solid); Section 6.11 specifies the dictionaries to use for APA Style papers.

Another form of compound—the temporary compound—is made up of two or more words that occur together, perhaps only in a particular paper, to express a thought. Temporary compounds are not usually listed in the dictionary. To determine how to hyphenate temporary compounds, follow these guidelines:

- If a temporary compound can be misread or expresses a single thought, use a hyphen, especially when the temporary compound appears as an adjective before the noun. When in doubt, use a hyphen for clarity. For example, "Adolescents resided in two parent homes" may mean that two homes served as residences or that each adolescent lived with two parents; a hyphen in "two-parent homes" specifies the latter meaning.

- If the compound appears after the noun it modifies, do not use a hyphen because, in almost all cases, the phrase is sufficiently clear without one. See Table 6.1 for further examples of hyphen use in temporary compounds.

t-test results	*but*	results of *t* tests
same-sex children	*but*	children of the same sex

Table 6.1 Guide to Hyphenating Temporary Compound Terms

Grammar guideline	Example
Hyphenate	
A compound with a participle when it precedes the term it modifies	decision-making behavior water-deprived animals Canadian-born actor
A phrase used as an adjective when it precedes the term it modifies	trial-by-trial analysis to-be-recalled items one-on-one interviews
An adjective-and-noun compound when it precedes the term it modifies	high-anxiety group middle-class families low-frequency words
A compound with a number as the first element when the compound precedes the term it modifies	six-trial problem 12th-grade students 16-min interval
A fraction used as an adjective	two-thirds majority
Do not hyphenate	
A compound that follows the term it modifies	behavior related to decision making students in the 12th grade a majority of two thirds
A compound including an adverb ending in "-ly"	widely used test relatively homogeneous sample randomly assigned participants
A compound including a comparative or superlative adjective	better written paper less informed interviewers higher order learning highest scoring students
Chemical terms	sodium chloride solution amino acid compound
Latin phrases used as adjectives or adverbs	a posteriori test post hoc comparisons were fed ad lib (but hyphenate the adjectival form: ad-lib feeding)
A modifier including a letter or numeral as the second element	Group B participants Type II error Trial 1 performance
Fractions used as nouns	one third of the participants

- Write most words formed with prefixes and suffixes as one word without a hyphen. See Table 6.2 for examples of prefixes and suffixes that do not require hyphens; see Table 6.3 for examples of prefixed and suffixed words that do require hyphens. The same suffix may be hyphenated in some cases and not in others (e.g., "nationwide" and "worldwide" vs. "industry-wide").

- When two or more compound modifiers have a common base, that base is sometimes omitted in all except the last modifier, but the hyphens are retained. Leave a space after the hyphen when the base has been omitted, unless punctuation follows the hyphen.

  long- and short-term memory
  2-, 3-, and 10-min trials

Table 6.2 Prefixes and Suffixes That Do Not Require Hyphens

Prefix or suffix	Example	Prefix or suffix	Example
able	retrievable	mid	midterm
after	aftercare	mini	minisession
anti	antisocial	multi	multimethod
bi	bilingual	non	nonsignificant
cede/sede/ceed	intercede	over	oversampling
co	covariate	phobia	agoraphobia
cyber	cyberwarfare	post	posttest
equi	equimax	pre	preexperimental
extra	extracurricular	pseudo	pseudoscience
gram	cardiogram	quasi	quasiperiodic
infra	infrared	re	reevaluate
inter	intersex	semi	semidarkness
like	wavelike	socio	socioeconomic
macro	macrocosm	sub	subtest
mega	megawatt	super	superordinate
meta	metaethnography	supra	supraliminal
meter	nanometer	un	unbiased
micro	microcosm	under	underdeveloped

Note. However, use a hyphen in "meta-analysis" and "quasi-experimental."

Table 6.3 Compound Words That Require Hyphens

Occurrence	Example
Compounds in which the base word is • capitalized	pro-Freudian Likert-type Stroop-like
• a number	post-1977
• an abbreviation	pre-UCS trial
• more than one word	non-achievement-oriented students
All "self-" compounds, whether adjectives or nouns [a]	self-report technique the test was self-paced self-esteem
Words that could be misunderstood	re-pair (pair again) re-form (form again) un-ionized (not ionized)
Words in which the prefix ends and the base word begins with "a," "i," or "o" [b]	meta-analysis anti-intellectual co-occur

[a] *But* "self psychology."
[b] "Pre" and "re" compounds are not hyphenated with base words beginning with "e" (e.g., "preexisting," "reexamine").

Capitalization

APA Style is a "down" style, meaning that words are lowercase unless there is specific guidance to capitalize them, as described in the following sections.

6.13 Words Beginning a Sentence

Capitalize the following:

- the first word in a complete sentence

- the first word after a colon if what follows the colon is a complete sentence

  The statement was emphatic: Further research is needed.

Do not capitalize the following:

- a personal name that begins with a lowercase letter when the name begins a sentence; alternatively, reword the sentence

  . . . after the test. van de Vijver et al. (2019) concluded

- a proper noun (other than a personal name) that begins with a lowercase letter (e.g., iPad, eBay) or a lowercase statistical term (e.g., t test, p value) when it begins a sentence (see Section 6.26); instead, reword the sentence to avoid beginning with a lowercase letter

6.14 Proper Nouns and Trade Names

Capitalize the following:

- proper nouns and proper adjectives

- names of racial and ethnic groups (see also Section 5.7)

  We interviewed 25 Black women living in rural Louisiana.

- names of specific university departments, academic institutions, and academic courses

Capitalize	Do not capitalize
Department of Psychology, San Francisco State University	a psychology department, a university
Psychology 101	a psychology course
Science of Nursing Practice	a nursing course

- trade and brand names (in general, do not include the copyright or trademark symbol after a trade or brand name used in an academic paper; however, such symbols may be included in business and marketing materials)

Capitalize	Do not capitalize
APA Style	a writing style
Zoloft	sertraline (generic name for Zoloft)
iPhone, Android phone	smartphone
Wi-Fi	wireless, hotspot

Do not capitalize the following:

- proper adjectives that have a common meaning (consult a dictionary for guidance; see Section 6.11), except for personal names within these terms

  eustachian tube
  cesarean section

  but

  Freudian slip
  Wilks's lambda
  Euclidean geometry

6.15 Job Titles and Positions

Capitalize a job title or position when the title precedes a name (titles are not used in bylines; see Section 2.5):

  President Lincoln was elected in 1860.

  Executive Director of Marketing Carolina Espinoza led the meeting.

  Dr. Aisha Singh, Dr. Singh

  Registered Nurse Paul T. Lo, Nurse Lo

Do not capitalize a job title or position when the title follows the name or refers to a position in general:

  Abraham Lincoln was president of the United States.

  Carolina Espinoza, executive director of marketing, led the meeting.

  president, vice president, chief executive officer, executive director, manager

  professor, instructor, faculty, dean

  psychologist, psychiatrist, counselor, social worker

  physician, doctor, physician assistant

  nurse, registered nurse, advanced practice nurse, nurse practitioner

6.16 Diseases, Disorders, Therapies, Theories, and Related Terms

Do not capitalize the names of the following:

- diseases or disorders

autism spectrum disorder	diabetes
major depression	leukemia

- therapies and treatments

cognitive behavior therapy	immunotherapy
applied behavior analysis	cataract surgery

- theories, concepts, hypotheses, principles, models, and statistical procedures

object permanence	theory of mind
associative learning model	law of effect
psychoanalytic theory	two-group t test

However, capitalize personal names that appear within the names of diseases, disorders, therapies, treatments, theories, concepts, hypotheses, principles, models, and statistical procedures.

Alzheimer's disease	Down syndrome
non-Hodgkin's lymphoma	Maslow's hierarchy of needs
Freudian theory	Pavlovian conditioning

6.17 Titles of Works and Headings Within Works

APA Style uses two types of capitalization for titles of works and headings within works: title case and sentence case. In *title case*, major words are capitalized. In *sentence case*, most words are lowercased. Nouns, verbs (including linking verbs), adjectives, adverbs, pronouns, and all words of four letters or more are considered major words. Short (i.e., three letters or fewer) conjunctions, short prepositions, and all articles are considered minor words.

Title Case. In title case, capitalize the following words in a title or heading:

- the first word, even a minor word such as "The"
- the first word of a subtitle, even if it is a minor word
- the first word after a colon, em dash, or end punctuation in a heading, even if it is a minor word
- major words, including the second part of hyphenated major words (e.g., "Self-Report," not "Self-report")
- words of four letters or more (e.g., "With," "Between," "From")

Lowercase only minor words that are three letters or fewer in a title or heading (except the first word in a title or subtitle or the first word after a colon, em dash, or end punctuation in a heading):

- short conjunctions (e.g., "and," "as," "but," "for," "if," "nor," "or," "so," "yet")
- articles ("a," "an," "the")
- short prepositions (e.g., "as," "at," "by," "for," "in," "of," "off," "on," "per," "to," "up," "via")

When to Use Title Case. Use title case for the following:

- titles of articles, books, reports, and other works appearing in text
  In the book *Bilingualism Across the Lifespan: Factors Moderating Language Proficiency*
  In the article "Media Influences on Self-Stigma of Seeking Psychological Services: The Importance of Media Portrayals and Person Perception"
- titles of tests or measures, including subscales (see Section 6.18)
  Wechsler Adult Intelligence Scale
  WAIS-IV Verbal Comprehension Index
- all headings within a work (Levels 1–5; see Section 2.27)
- the title of your own paper and of named sections and subsections within it
  the Data Analyses section
- titles of periodicals (these are also italicized)
  Journal of Experimental Psychology: Learning, Memory, and Cognition
  The Washington Post
- table titles (these are also italicized; see Section 7.11)
- figure titles (these are also italicized), axis labels, and legends (see Sections 7.25–7.27)

Sentence Case. In sentence case, lowercase most words in the title or heading. Capitalize only the following words:

- the first word of the title or heading
- the first word of a subtitle
- the first word after a colon, em dash, or end punctuation in a heading
- nouns followed by numerals or letters
- proper nouns

When to Use Sentence Case. Use sentence case for the following:

- titles of articles, books, reports, webpages, and other works in reference list entries, even if title case was used in the original work (see also Section 9.19)

> Golden, A. R., Griffin, C. B., Metzger, I. W., & Cooper, S. M. (2018). School racial climate and academic outcomes in African American adolescents: The protective role of peers. *Journal of Black Psychology, 44*(1), 47–73. https://doi.org/10.1177/0095798417736685

> Mena, J. A., & Quina, K. (Eds.). (2019). *Integrating multiculturalism and intersectionality into the psychology curriculum: Strategies for instructors.* American Psychological Association. https://doi.org/10.1037/0000137-000

- table column headings, entries, and notes (see Sections 7.12–7.14)
- figure notes (see Section 7.28)

> *Note*: Words in the image of a figure (see Section 7.26) may be in either title case or sentence case. Follow the same guidelines for capitalization in a figure image as used in the text.

6.18 Titles of Tests and Measures

Capitalize titles of published and unpublished tests and measures and their subscales. Do not capitalize words such as "test" and "scale" unless they are part of the test or subscale title. See Section 10.11 for more on use of italics with the titles of test and measures.

> Thematic Apperception Test
> Minnesota Multiphasic Personality Inventory–2
> MMPI-2 Depression scale
> Stroop Color–Word Interference Test
> the authors' Mood Adjective Checklist
> SF–36 Physical Functioning scale

Do not capitalize shortened, inexact, or generic titles of tests or measures.

> a vocabulary test   Stroop-like color test

6.19 Nouns Followed by Numerals or Letters

Capitalize nouns followed by numerals or letters that denote a specific place in a series.

> Figure 3   Table 1, Row 2, Column 6
> Appendix B   Research Question 3
> Footnote 2   Days 7–9
> Trials 5 and 6   Part 4
> Grant AG11214   Chapter 8

Exception: Do not capitalize the words "page" or "paragraph" before a numeral, in accordance with long-standing practice.

    page 2
    paragraph 4

Do not capitalize the following:

- the words "numeral" or "letter" when referring to a numeral or letter as itself because the numeral or letter does not denote a place in a series beyond integers or the alphabet

    the numeral 7
    the letter "a"

- nouns that precede a variable

    trial *n* and item *x*

        but

    Trial 3 and Item b (The number and letter are not variables.)

- names of genes and proteins that include numerals or letters

    nuclear receptor subfamily 3, group C, member 1

6.20 Names of Conditions or Groups in an Experiment

Do not capitalize names of conditions or groups in an experiment.

    the experimental and control groups

    participants were assigned to information and no-information conditions

        but

    Conditions A and B (see Section 6.19)

6.21 Names of Factors, Variables, and Effects

Capitalize names of derived variables within a factor or principal components analysis. The words "factor" and "component" are not capitalized unless followed by a numeral (see Section 6.19).

    Big Five personality factors of Extraversion, Agreeableness, Openness to Experience, Conscientiousness, and Neuroticism

    Mealtime Behavior (Factor 4)

Do not capitalize effects or variables unless they appear with multiplication signs. (Be careful not to use the term "factor" when you mean "effect" or "variable," e.g., in an interaction or analysis of variance.)

    small age effect
    sex, age, and weight variables

        but

    Sex × Age × Weight interaction
    3 × 3 × 2 (Groups × Trials × Responses) design
    2 (methods) × 2 (item types)

Italics

6.22 Use of Italics

Use italics for the following:

- key terms or phrases, often accompanied by a definition

  Mindfulness is defined as "the act of noticing new things, a process that promotes flexible responding to the demands of the environment" (Pagnini et al., 2016, p. 91).

  > *Note:* Use italics for a term or phrase only once, when it is most appropriate to draw readers' attention to the term or phrase; elsewhere, the term should be in standard (nonitalic) type. For example, if a word is used in a heading and then defined in the text that follows, italicize the term as part of the definition rather than in the heading.

- titles of books, reports, webpages, and other stand-alone works (see Section 9.19)

  Concise Guide to APA Style

- titles of periodicals (see Section 9.25)

  Cultural Diversity & Ethnic Minority Psychology

- genera, species, and varieties

  Cebus apella

- letters used as statistical symbols or algebraic variables

  Cohen's $d = 0.084$
  $a/b = c/d$
  MSE

- some test scores and scales

  Rorschach scores: $F+\%$, Z
  MMPI-2 scales: Hs, Pd

- periodical volume numbers in reference lists

  Neuropsychology, 30(5), 525–531.

- anchors of a scale (but not the associated number)

  ranged from 1 (*poor*) to 5 (*excellent*)
  rated using a Likert scale (1 = *strongly disagree* to 5 = *strongly agree*)

- the first use of a word, phrase, or abbreviation from another language when readers may not be familiar with it; however, if the term appears in a dictionary for the language in which you are writing (see Section 6.11), do not use italics

- gene symbols (see Section 6.31)

  NR3C1

Do not use italics for the following:

- titles of book series (e.g., the Harry Potter series)

- the punctuation mark after an italicized word or phrase

  What is *plurality*?

> *Note:* Italicize a punctuation mark that is part of an italic element, such as a colon, comma, or question mark within a book title, periodical title, or heading.
>
> Miles and Sweet's (2017) book *Chicken or Egg: Who Comes First?* addressed . . .

- punctuation between elements of a reference list entry (e.g., the comma after a volume and issue number, the period after a book title)

- words, phrases, and abbreviations of foreign origin that appear in a dictionary for the language in which you are writing (see Section 6.11)

a posteriori	et al.	a priori	per se
ad lib	vis-à-vis	fait accompli	mens rea
force majeure	zeitgeist		

- chemical terms

  NaCl, LSD

- trigonometric terms

  sin, tan, log

- nonstatistical subscripts to statistical symbols or mathematical expressions

  F_{max}

  $S_A + S_B$

- Greek letters

  β, α, χ^2

- letters used as abbreviations

  reaction time (RT)

- gene names and gene proteins (see Section 6.31)

  glucocorticoid receptor gene, GR protein

- mere emphasis

  Incorrect: It is important to bear in mind that *this* process is *not* proposed as a *stage* theory of development.

> *Note:* Italics for emphasis are acceptable if emphasis might otherwise be lost or the material misread; in general, however, use syntax to provide emphasis. See Section 8.31 for how to add emphasis in quoted material. Italics and bold may be used for emphasis in tables, depending on the requirements of the journal (e.g., to show factor loadings of a particular size; see Table 7.14 in Section 7.21).

6.23 Reverse Italics

When words that would normally be italicized appear within text that is already italicized, those words should be set in standard (nonitalic) type, referred to as *reverse italicization*. For example, when the title of a book contains the title of another book, use standard type for the title within the title. In the text, use title case for both titles; in the reference list entry, use sentence case for both titles. In the following example, Marinelli and Mayer wrote a book about Freud's book

The Interpretation of Dreams; Marinelli and Mayer's book title is italicized, and Freud's book title within it is written in standard type.

In text:

In *Dreaming by the Book: Freud's* The Interpretation of Dreams *and the History of the Psychoanalytic Movement*, Marinelli and Mayer (2003) explored . . .

In the reference list:

Marinelli, L., & Mayer, A. (2003). *Dreaming by the book: Freud's* The interpretation of dreams *and the history of the psychoanalytic movement*. Other Press.

Abbreviations

An *abbreviation* is a shortened form of a word or phrase; abbreviations of phrases are often composed of the first letter of each word of the phrase (i.e., acronym). To maximize clarity, use abbreviations sparingly and consider readers' familiarity with the abbreviation.

6.24 Use of Abbreviations

Although abbreviations can be useful for long, technical terms in scholarly writing, communication is often garbled rather than clarified if an abbreviation is unfamiliar to readers. In general, use an abbreviation if (a) it is conventional and readers are likely to be more familiar with the abbreviation than with the complete form and (b) considerable space can be saved and cumbersome repetition avoided. For example, the abbreviations "L" for large and "S" for small in a paper describing different sequences of reward (LLSS or LSLS) would be effective and readily understood shortcuts. In another paper, however, writing about the "L reward" and the "S reward" might be both unnecessary and confusing. In most instances, abbreviating experimental group names is ineffective because the abbreviations are not adequately informative or easily recognizable; some are more cumbersome than the full name. For the same reason, do not use the abbreviations "S," "E," and "O" for subject, experimenter, and observer in the text.

Overuse. Sometimes the space saved by using abbreviations is not justified by the time necessary for readers to master the meaning, as in the following example:

The advantage of the LH was clear from the RT data, which reflected high FP and FN rates for the RH.

Without abbreviations, the previous passage reads as follows:

The advantage of the left hand was clear from the reaction time data, which reflected high false-positive and false-negative rates for the right hand.

Although there is no absolute limit for the use of abbreviations, writing is generally easier to understand when most words are written out rather than when overflowing with abbreviations.

Underuse. In general, if you abbreviate a term, use the abbreviation at least three times in a paper. If you use the abbreviation only one or two times, readers may have difficulty remembering what it means, so writing the term out each time aids comprehension. However, a standard abbreviation for a long, familiar term is clearer and more concise even if it is used fewer than three times.

6.25 Definition of Abbreviations

In APA Style papers, do not define abbreviations that are listed as terms in the dictionary (e.g., AIDS, IQ). Also do not define measurement abbreviations (see Section 6.27), time abbreviations (see Section 6.28), Latin abbreviations (see Section 6.29), or many statistical abbreviations (see Section 6.44). Define all other abbreviations, even those that may be familiar to your readers (e.g., "RT" for reaction time or "ANOVA" for analysis of variance; see also Section 6.24). After you define an abbreviation, use only the abbreviation; do not alternate between spelling out the term and abbreviating it.

Definition in the Text. When you first use a term that you want to abbreviate in the text, present both the full version of the term and the abbreviation.

- When the full version of a term appears for the first time in a heading, do not define the abbreviation in the heading; instead define the abbreviation when the full version next appears. Use abbreviations in headings only if the abbreviations have been previously defined in the text or if they are listed as terms in the dictionary.

- When the full version of a term first appears in a sentence in the text, place the abbreviation in parentheses after it.

  attention-deficit/hyperactivity disorder (ADHD)

- When the full version of a term first appears in parenthetical text, place the abbreviation in square brackets after it. Do not use nested parentheses.

  (i.e., attention-deficit/hyperactivity disorder [ADHD])

- If a citation accompanies an abbreviation, include the citation after the abbreviation, separated with a semicolon. Do not use nested or back-to-back parentheses.

  Beck Depression Inventory–II (BDI-II; Beck et al., 1996)
  (Beck Depression Inventory–II [BDI-II]; Beck et al., 1996)

Definition in Tables and Figures. Define abbreviations used in tables and figures within each table and figure, even if the abbreviations have already been defined in the text. The abbreviation can appear in parentheses after first use of the term within the table or figure, including in the table or figure title, or the definition can appear in a table or figure general note or a figure legend. If an abbreviation is used in multiple tables and figures, define it in each table or figure. Do not define abbreviations that do not appear in a table or figure. Do not define or write out standard abbreviations for units of measurement and statistics in a table or figure (see Sections 6.44 and 7.15).

6.26 Format of Abbreviations

Plural Forms. To form the plural of most abbreviations and statistical symbols, add a lowercase "s" alone, without an apostrophe.

  IQs   DOIs   URLs   Eds.   vols.   *M*s   *p*s   *n*s   ESs

---

Note: To form the plural of the reference abbreviation for "page" (p.), write "pp." Do not add an "s" to make abbreviations for units of measurement plural.

  3 cm (not 3 cms)   24 hr (not 24 hrs)

Abbreviations Beginning a Sentence. Never begin a sentence with a lowercase abbreviation (e.g., lb) or with a stand-alone symbol (e.g., α). Begin a sentence with a symbol connected to a word (e.g., β-Endorphins) only when necessary to avoid indirect or awkward phrasing. When a chemical compound begins a sentence, capitalize the first letter of the word to which the symbol is connected; keep the locant, descriptor, or positional prefix (i.e., Greek, small capital, and italic letters and numerals) intact.

In running text:	*At beginning of sentence:*
L-methionine	L-Methionine
N, N'-dimethylurea	*N, N'*-Dimethylurea
γ-hydroxy-β-aminobutyric acid	γ-Hydroxy-β-aminobutyric acid

6.27 Unit of Measurement Abbreviations

Metrication. APA uses the metric system in its journals. If you used instruments that record measurements in nonmetric units, report the nonmetric units followed by the established metric equivalents in parentheses.

Measurement in metric units:
The rods were spaced 19 mm apart.

Measurement in nonmetric units with the rounded metric equivalent:
The rod was 3 ft (0.91 m) long.

Presentation. Write out the full names of units of measurement that are not accompanied by numeric values.

several kilograms   age in years   duration of hours   centimeters

Use abbreviations and symbols for units of measurement that are accompanied by numeric values; do not make symbols or abbreviations of units plural.

4 cm   30 kg   12 min   18 hr   22 °C

Also use the abbreviation or symbol in column and row (stub) headings of tables to conserve space, even when the term appears without a numeric value.

lag in ms

Do not define or spell out unit of measurement abbreviations, even the first time they are used. See Table 6.4 for a list of abbreviations for common units of measurement (for statistical symbols and abbreviations, including percentages and money symbols, see Section 6.44).

Capitalization and Spelling. In most cases, use lowercase letters for symbols (e.g., kg), even in capitalized material. However, the following are exceptions:

- Symbols derived from the name of a person usually include uppercase letters (e.g., Gy).

- Symbols for prefixes that represent powers of 10 are usually written in uppercase letters: exa (E), peta (P), tera (T), giga (G), and mega (M).

- Use the symbol "L" for liter when it stands alone (e.g., 5 L, 0.3 mg/L) because a lowercase "l" may be misread as the numeral 1 (use lowercase "l" for fractions of a liter: 5 ml, 9 ng/dl).

Table 6.4 Abbreviations for Common Units of Measurement

Abbreviation	Unit of measurement	Abbreviation	Unit of measurement
A	ampere	m	meter
Å	angstrom	µg	microgram
AC	alternating current	µm	micrometer
Bq	becquerel	mA	milliampere
°C	degrees Celsius	mEq	milliequivalent
cc	cubic centimeter	meV	million electron volts
cd	candela	mg	milligram
Ci	curie	mi	mile [a]
cm	centimeter	ml	milliliter
cps	cycles per second	mm	millimeter
dB	decibel (specify scale)	mM	millimolar
DC	direct current	mmHg	millimeters of mercury
deg/s	degrees per second	mmol	millimole
dl	deciliter	mol	mole
F	farad	mol wt	molecular weight
°F	degrees Fahrenheit [a]	mph	miles per hour [a]
ft	foot [a]	MΩ	megohm
g	gram	N	newton
g	gravity	ng	nanogram
Gy	gray	nmol	nanomole
H	henry	Ω	ohm
Hz	hertz	oz	ounce [a]
in.	inch [a]	Pa	pascal
IU	international unit	ppm	parts per million
J	joule	psi	pounds per square inch [a]
K	kelvin	rpm	revolutions per minute
kg	kilogram	S	siemens
km	kilometer	Sv	sievert
km/h	kilometers per hour	T	tesla
kW	kilowatt	V	volt
L	liter	W	watt
lb	pound [a]	Wb	weber
lm	lumen	yd	yard [a]
lx	lux		

Note. These abbreviations do not need to be defined when they are used in a paper.
[a] Include the metric unit equivalent in parentheses when using nonmetric units.

Do not use a period after a symbol, except at the end of a sentence. An exception is to include a period after the abbreviation for "inch" (in.), which could be misread without the period.

    Use a space between a symbol and the number to which it refers (e.g., degrees, minutes, and seconds). An exception is the measure of angles, in which case the symbol is written without a space after the measurement.

    4.5 m   6 hr   12 °C   *but*   45° angle

Repeated Units of Measurement. Do not repeat abbreviated units of measurement when expressing multiple amounts.

16–30 kHz   0.3, 1.5, and 3.0 mg/dl

When reporting related statistics, such as means and standard deviations, report the unit with the main statistic but do not repeat it for the related statistic(s) when the unit remains the same.

Correct: (M = 8.7 years, SD = 2.3)
Incorrect: (M = 8.7 years, SD = 2.3 years)

Compound Units. Use a centered dot between the symbols of a compound term formed by the multiplication of units.

Pa • s

Use a space between the full names of units of a compound unit formed by the multiplication of units; do not use a centered dot.

pascal second

6.28 Time Abbreviations

To prevent misreading, do not abbreviate the words "day," "week," "month," and "year," even when they are accompanied by numeric values. Do abbreviate the words "hour," "minute," "second," "millisecond," "nanosecond," and any other division of the second when they are accompanied by numeric values.

Term	Abbreviation	Example
hour	hr	6 hr
minute	min	30 min
second	s	5 s
millisecond	ms	2.65 ms
nanosecond	ns	90 ns

6.29 Latin Abbreviations

Use the following standard Latin abbreviations only in parenthetical material; in the narrative, use the translation of the Latin term. In both cases, punctuate as if the abbreviation were spelled out in the language in which you are writing.

Latin abbreviation	Translation
cf.	compare
e.g.,	for example,
, etc.	, and so forth
i.e.,	that is,
viz.,	namely,
vs.	versus or against

Exceptions: Use the abbreviation "v." (for "versus") in the title or name of a court case in the reference list and in all in-text citations (see Section 11.4). Use the Latin abbreviation "et al." (which means "and others") in both narrative and parenthetical citations (see Section 8.17). (The abbreviation "ibid." is not used in APA Style.)

6.30 Chemical Compound Abbreviations

Chemical compounds may be expressed by the common name or the chemical name. If you prefer to use the common name, provide the chemical name in parentheses on first mention. Avoid expressing compounds with chemical formulas because these are usually less informative to readers and have a high likelihood of being typed or typeset incorrectly (e.g., "aspirin" or "salicylic acid," not "$C_9H_8O_4$"). If names of compounds include Greek letters, retain the letters as symbols and do not write them out (e.g., "β carotene," not "beta carotene"). If a compound name containing a Greek letter appears at the beginning of a sentence, capitalize the first letter of the word to which the symbol is connected (see Section 6.26).

Long names of organic compounds are often abbreviated. If the abbreviation is listed as a term in a dictionary (see Section 6.25; e.g., "NADP" for "nicotinamide adenine dinucleotide phosphate"), you do not need to write it out in full on first use.

Concentrations. If you express a solution as a percentage concentration instead of as a molar concentration, specify the percentage as a weight-per-volume ratio (wt/vol), a volume ratio (vol/vol), or a weight ratio (wt/wt) of solute to solvent. The higher the concentration, the more ambiguous the expression is as a percentage. Specifying the ratio is especially necessary for concentrations of alcohol, glucose, and sucrose. Specifying the salt form is also essential for precise reporting of d-amphetamine HCl or d-amphetamine SO_4 (expression of a chemical name in combination with a formula is acceptable in this case).

> 12% (vol/vol) ethyl alcohol solution
> 1% (wt/vol) saccharin solution

Routes of Administration. Abbreviate a route of administration when it is paired with a number-and-unit combination. Do not use periods with abbreviations for routes of administration: icv = intracerebral ventricular, im = intramuscular, ip = intraperitoneal, iv = intravenous, sc = subcutaneous, and so forth.

> anesthetized with sodium pentobarbital (90 mg/kg ip)
> two subcutaneous injections (*not* sc injections)

6.31 Gene and Protein Name Abbreviations

Writing about genes can be challenging. Each gene has an official full name and symbol, designated by the HUGO Gene Nomenclature Committee, that describe the gene's function or location and often the protein it produces. Use standard gene names found in gene databases such as those from the National Center for Biotechnology Information (https://www.ncbi.nlm.nih.gov/gene) and the HUGO Gene Nomenclature Committee (https://www.genenames.org/). Gene names are organism specific (e.g., human, mouse), so use an appropriate database. Additionally, the same gene may be known by an "alias" (or alternate scientific, informal, and/or historical) name and symbol. For example, the glucocorticoid receptor gene, which is highly implicated in the response to stress, has the official name "nuclear receptor subfamily 3, group C, member 1"; has the official symbol *NR3C1*; and produces GR proteins; it is also commonly known as the "glucocorticoid receptor," abbreviated "GR." If a gene is known by more than one name or symbol, select one presentation and use it consistently;

the first time you mention a gene in your paper, you may also note the other name and/or symbol by which it is known to alert readers who may not be familiar with the designation you chose. Also state whether you are referring to the gene or to its protein, and use appropriate terminology (e.g., use "expression" when discussing genes and "levels" when discussing proteins).

Do not italicize gene names written out in full (e.g., corticotropin-releasing hormone) and gene proteins (e.g., CRH). However, do italicize gene symbols (e.g., *CRH*). It is not required to abbreviate the full name of a gene and to use its symbol; follow the guidelines in Section 6.24 if you are considering using an abbreviation for a gene. For further discussion of gene names and formatting, see Wain et al. (2002) and the International Committee on Standardized Genetic Nomenclature for Mice and Rat Genome and Nomenclature Committee (2018).

Numbers

In general, use numerals to express numbers 10 and above and words to express numbers below 10. Consider on a case-by-case basis whether to follow the general guideline or if an exception applies.

6.32 Numbers Expressed in Numerals

Use numerals to express the following:

- numbers 10 and above throughout the paper, including the abstract (for exceptions, see Sections 6.33–6.34) and both cardinal and ordinal numbers (see Section 6.35)

15th trial	200 participants
13 lists	10th-grade students
12 models	105 stimulus words

- numbers that immediately precede a unit of measurement

a 5-mg dose	with 10.5 cm of

- numbers that represent statistical or mathematical functions, fractional or decimal quantities, percentages, ratios, and percentiles and quartiles

multiplied by 5	3 times as many
0.33 of the sample	more than 5%
a ratio of 16:1	the 5th percentile

- numbers that represent time, dates, ages, scores and points on a scale, exact sums of money, and numerals as numerals

5 days	about 8 months
4 decades	was 2 years old
12:30 a.m.	scored 4 on a 7-point scale
1 hr 34 min	the numeral 6 on the keyboard
2-year-olds	approximately 3 years ago
ages 65–70 years	received $5 in compensation

- numbers that denote a specific place in a numbered series and parts of books and tables (the noun before the number is also capitalized when it denotes a specific place in a series; see Section 6.19); however, when the number precedes the noun, the usual guidelines for number use apply

Number after a noun	Number before a noun
Year 1	the 1st year
Grade 4, Grade 10	the fourth grade, the 10th grade
Items 3 and 5	the third and fifth items
Question 2	the second question
Table 2, Figure 5	the second table, the fifth figure
Column 8, Row 7	the eighth column, the seventh row
Chapter 1, Chapter 12	the first chapter, the 12th chapter

Exceptions: Do not capitalize the abbreviations for page(s) or paragraph(s), even when they are followed by a numeral (e.g., p. 3, pp. 2–5, para. 9, paras. 1–4).

6.33 Numbers Expressed in Words

Use words to express the following:

- numbers zero through nine (except as described in Sections 6.32 and 6.34) in the text, including the abstract

- any number that begins a sentence, title, or heading (when possible, reword the sentence to avoid beginning with a number)

  Forty-eight percent of the sample showed an increase; 2% showed no change.
  Twelve students improved, and 12 students did not improve.

- common fractions

  one fifth of the class   two-thirds majority

- universally accepted usage

  Twelve Apostles   Five Pillars of Islam

6.34 Combining Numerals and Words to Express Numbers

Use a combination of numerals and words to express back-to-back numerical modifiers.

  2 two-way interactions   ten 7-point scales

However, if this makes the text more difficult for readers, consider rewording the sentence.

6.35 Ordinal Numbers

Treat ordinal numbers as you would cardinal numbers.

Ordinal	Cardinal base
second-order factor	two orders
fourth grade, 10th grade	four grades, 10 grades
first item of the 75th trial	one item, 75 trials
first and third groups	one group, three groups
3rd year	3 years

The suffixes of ordinal numbers can be presented with or without a superscript (e.g., either 4th or 4th), but be consistent in presentation throughout your paper.

6.36 Decimal Fractions

Use a zero before the decimal point in numbers that are less than 1 when the statistic can exceed 1.

$t(20) = 0.86$ $F(1, 27) = 0.57$
Cohen's $d = 0.70$ 0.48 cm

Do not use a zero before a decimal fraction when the statistic cannot be greater than 1 (e.g., correlations, proportions, levels of statistical significance).

$r(24) = -.43, p = .028$

The number of decimal places to use in reporting the results of experiments and data-analytic manipulations should be governed by the following principle: Round as much as possible while considering prospective use and statistical precision. As a general rule, fewer decimal digits are easier to comprehend than are more digits; therefore, it is usually better to round to two decimal places or to rescale the measurement (in which case effect sizes should be presented in the same metric). For instance, a difference in distances that must be carried to four decimals to be seen when scaled in meters can be more effectively illustrated in millimeters, which would require only a few decimal digits to illustrate the same difference.

When properly scaled, most data can be effectively presented with two decimal digits of accuracy. Report correlations, proportions, and inferential statistics such as t, F, and chi-square to two decimals. When reporting data measured on integer scales (as with many questionnaires), report means and standard deviations to one decimal place (as group measures, they are more stable than individual scores). Report exact p values (e.g., $p = .031$) to two or three decimal places. However, report p values less than .001 as $p < .001$. The tradition of reporting p values in the form of $p < .10$, $p < .05$, $p < .01$, and so forth was appropriate in a time when only limited tables of critical values were available. However, in tables the "$p <$" notation may be necessary for clarity (see Section 7.14). For guidance on the types of statistics to report in your paper, see the reporting standards for quantitative methods and results (Sections 3.6–3.7).

6.37 Roman Numerals

If Roman numerals are part of an established terminology, do not change them to Arabic numerals. For example, use "Type II error," not "Type 2 error." Use Arabic numerals for routine seriation (e.g., Step 1, Experiment 2, Study 3).

6.38 Commas in Numbers

Use commas between groups of three digits in most figures of 1,000 or more. Some exceptions are as follows:

Category	Example of exception
page numbers	page 1029
binary digits	00110010
serial numbers	290466960
degrees of temperature	3414 °C
acoustic frequency designations	2000 Hz
degrees of freedom	$F(24, 1000)$

6.39 Plurals of Numbers

To form the plurals of numbers, whether expressed as numerals or as words, add "s" or "es" alone, without an apostrophe.

twos and sixes   the 1960s   30s and 40s

Statistical and Mathematical Copy

APA Style for presenting statistical and mathematical copy reflects (a) the standards of content and form agreed on in the field and (b) the requirements of clear communication. The *Publication Manual* addresses standards for presentation only; it does not provide guidance on how to choose statistics, conduct analyses, or interpret results. Consult a statistics reference work or a statistician for help if needed.

6.40 Selecting Effective Presentation

Statistical and mathematical copy can be presented in text, in tables, and/or in figures. In deciding which approach to take, follow these general guidelines:

- If you need to present three or fewer numbers, first try using a sentence.
- If you need to present four to 20 numbers, first try using a table.
- If you need to present more than 20 numbers, first try using a figure.

Select the mode of presentation that optimizes readers' understanding of the data. Detailed displays that allow fine-grained understanding of a data set may be more appropriate to include in supplemental materials (see Section 2.15) than in the print version of an article. However, editors publish tables and figures at their discretion; they may also request new tables and figures.

6.41 References for Statistics

Do not provide a reference for a statistic in common use (e.g., Cohen's *d*); this convention applies to most statistics used in journal articles. Provide a reference when (a) less common statistics are used, (b) a statistic is used in an unconventional or controversial way, or (c) the statistic itself is the focus of the paper.

6.42 Formulas

Do not provide a formula for a statistic in common use; however, provide a formula when the statistic or mathematical expression is new, rare, or essential to the paper. The presentation of equations is described in Sections 6.46 and 6.47.

6.43 Statistics in Text

When reporting inferential statistics (e.g., *t* tests, *F* tests, chi-square tests, and associated effect sizes and confidence intervals), include sufficient information to allow readers to fully understand the analyses conducted. The data supplied, preferably in the text but possibly in supplemental materials depending on the magnitude of the data arrays, should allow readers to confirm the basic reported analyses (e.g., cell means, standard deviations, sample sizes, correlations) and should enable interested readers to construct some effect-size estimates and confidence intervals beyond those supplied in the paper per se. In the case of multilevel data, present summary statistics for each level of aggregation. What constitutes sufficient information depends on the analytic approach reported.

F *ratios:*

For immediate recognition, the omnibus test of the main effect of sentence format was significant, $F(2, 177) = 6.30$, $p = .002$, est $\omega^2 = .07$.

t *values:*

The one-degree-of-freedom contrast of primary interest was significant at the specified $p < .05$ level, $t(177) = 3.51$, $p < .001$, $d = 0.65$, 95% CI [0.35, 0.95].

Hierarchical and other sequential regression statistics:

High school GPA predicted college mathematics performance, $R^2 = .12$, $F(1, 148) = 20.18$, $p < .001$, 95% CI [.02, .22].

If you present descriptive statistics in a table or figure, do not repeat them in the text, although you should (a) mention the table in which the statistics can be found in the text and (b) emphasize particular data in the text when they aid in the interpretation of the findings.

When enumerating a series of similar statistics, be certain that the relation between the statistics and their referents is clear. Words such as "respectively" and "in order" can clarify this relationship.

Means (with standard deviations in parentheses) for Trials 1–4 were 2.43 (0.50), 2.59 (1.21), 2.68 (0.39), and 2.86 (0.12), respectively.

When reporting confidence intervals, use the format 95% CI [*LL*, *UL*], where *LL* is the lower limit of the confidence interval and *UL* is the upper limit. Every report of a confidence interval must clearly state the level of confidence. However, when confidence intervals are repeated in a series or within the same paragraph, the level of confidence (e.g., 95%) has remained unchanged, and the meaning is clear, do not repeat "95% CI."

95% CIs [5.62, 8.31], [–2.43, 4.31], and [–4.29, –3.11], respectively

When a confidence interval follows the report of a point estimate, do not repeat the units of measurement.

$M = 30.5$ cm, 99% CI [18.0, 43.0]

6.44 Statistical Symbols and Abbreviations

Symbols and abbreviations are often used for statistics (e.g., "mean" is abbreviated "*M*"). Table 6.5 contains common statistical abbreviations and symbols.

- Do not define symbols or abbreviations that represent statistics (e.g., *M*, *SD*, *F*, *t*, *df*, *p*, *N*, *n*, *OR*, *r*) or any abbreviations or symbols composed of Greek letters (e.g., α, β, χ^2) in Table 6.5.

- However, define the other abbreviations in Table 6.5 (e.g., AIC, ANOVA, BIC, CFA, CI, NFI, RMSEA, SEM) when they are used anywhere in your paper (see Sections 6.25 and 7.14–7.15).

Some terms are used as both abbreviations and symbols. Use the abbreviation when referring to the concept and the symbol when specifying a numeric value. The symbol form will usually be either a non-English letter or an italicized

Table 6.5 Statistical Abbreviations and Symbols

Abbreviation or symbol	Definition
English character set	
a	in item response theory, the slope parameter
AIC	Akaike information criterion
ANCOVA	analysis of covariance
ANOVA	analysis of variance
AVE	average value explained
b, b_i	in regression and multiple regression analyses, estimated values of raw (unstandardized) regression coefficients; in item response theory, the difficulty-severity parameter
$b*, b_i^*$	estimated values of standardized regression coefficients in regression and multiple regression analyses
BIC, aBIC	Bayesian information criterion, sample-size-adjusted Bayesian information criterion
CAT	computerized adaptive testing
CDF	cumulative distribution function
CFA	confirmatory factor analysis
CFI	comparative fit index
CI	confidence interval
d	Cohen's measure of sample effect size for comparing two sample means
d'	discriminability, a measure of sensitivity in signal detection theory
df	degrees of freedom
DIF	differential item functioning
EFA	exploratory factor analysis
EM	expectation maximization
ES	effect size
f	frequency
f_e	expected frequency
f_o	observed frequency
F	F distribution; Fisher's F ratio
$F(\nu_1, \nu_2)$	F with ν_1 and ν_2 degrees of freedom
F_{crit}	critical value for statistical significance in an F test
F_{max}	Hartley's test of homogeneity of variance
FDR	false discovery rate
FIML	full information maximum likelihood
g	Hedges's measure of effect size
GFI	goodness-of-fit index
GLM	generalized linear model
GLS	generalized least squares
H_0	null hypothesis, hypothesis under test
H_1 (or H_a)	alternative hypothesis
HLM	hierarchical linear model(ing)
HSD	Tukey's honestly significant difference
IRT	item response theory

MECHANICS OF STYLE

Table 6.5 Statistical Abbreviations and Symbols *(continued)*

Abbreviation or symbol	Definition
k	coefficient of alienation; number of studies in a meta-analysis; number of levels in an experimental design or individual study
k^2	coefficient of nondetermination
$KR20$	Kuder–Richardson reliability index
LGC	latent growth curve
LL	lower limit (as of a CI)
LR	likelihood ratio
LSD	least significant difference
M (or $\bar{X}$)	sample mean; arithmetic average
MANOVA	multivariate analysis of variance
MANCOVA	multivariate analysis of covariance
MCMC	Markov chain Monte Carlo
Mdn	median
MLE	maximum likelihood estimator; maximum likelihood estimate
MLM	multilevel model(ing)
MS	mean square
MSE	mean square error
n	number of cases (generally in a subsample)
N	total number of cases
NFI, NNFI	normed fit index, nonnormed fit index
ns	not statistically significant
OLS	ordinary least squares
OR	odds ratio
p	probability; probability of a success in a binary trial
p_{rep}	probability a replication would give a result with the same sign as the original result
PDF	probability density function
q	probability of a failure in a binary trial; $1 - p$
Q	test of homogeneity of effect sizes
r	estimate of the Pearson product–moment correlation coefficient
$r_{ab.c}$	partial correlation of a and b with the effect of c removed
$r_{a(b.c)}$	partial (or semipartial) correlation of a and b with the effect of c removed from b
r^2	coefficient of determination; measure of strength of relationship; estimate of the Pearson product–moment correlation squared
r_b	biserial correlation
r_{pb}	point biserial correlation
r_s	Spearman rank-order correlation
R	multiple correlation
R^2	multiple correlation squared; measure of strength of association
RMSEA	root-mean-square error of approximation
s	sample standard deviation (denominator $\sqrt{n-1}$)
$\mathbf{S}$	sample variance–covariance matrix

Table 6.5 Statistical Abbreviations and Symbols *(continued)*

Abbreviation or symbol	Definition
s^2	sample variance (unbiased estimator) – denominator $n-1$
S^2	sample variance (biased estimator) – denominator n
SD	standard deviation
SE	standard error
SEM	standard error of measurement; standard error of the mean
SEM	structural equation model(ing)
SRMR	standardized root-mean-square residual
SS	sum of squares
t	Student's *t* distribution; a statistical test based on the Student *t* distribution; the sample value of the *t*-test statistic
T^2	Hotelling's multivariate test for the equality of the mean vector in two multivariate populations
T_k	generic effect-size estimate
TLI	Tucker–Lewis index
U	Mann–Whitney test statistic
UL	upper limit (as of a CI)
V	Pillai–Bartlett multivariate trace criterion; Cramér's measure of association in contingency tables
w_k	fixed-effects weights
w_{k*}	random-effects weights
W	Kendall's coefficient of concordance and its estimate
WLS	weighted least squares
z	a standardized score; the value of a statistic divided by its standard error
Greek character set	
α (alpha)	in statistical hypothesis testing, the probability of making a Type I error; Cronbach's index of internal consistency (a form of reliability)
β (beta)	in statistical hypothesis testing, the probability of making a Type II error ($1-\beta$ denotes statistical power); population values of regression coefficients (with appropriate subscripts as needed)
B (capital beta)	in SEM, matrix of regression coefficients among dependent constructs
Γ (capital gamma)	Goodman–Kruskal's index of relationship; Γ, matrix of regression coefficients between independent and dependent constructs in SEM
δ (delta)	population value of Cohen's effect size; noncentrality parameter in hypothesis testing and noncentral distributions
Δ (capital delta)	increment of change
ε^2 (epsilon-squared)	measure of strength of relationship in analysis of variance
η^2 (eta-squared)	measure of strength of relationship
θ_k (theta k)	generic effect size in meta-analysis
Θ (capital theta)	Roy's multivariate test criterion; Θ, matrix of covariances among measurement errors in SEM
κ (kappa)	Cohen's measure of agreement corrected for chance agreement
λ (lambda)	element of a factor loading matrix; Goodman–Kruskal measure of predictability

Table 6.5 **Statistical Abbreviations and Symbols** (continued)

Abbreviation or symbol	Definition
Λ (capital lambda)	Wilks's multivariate test criterion; $\boldsymbol{\Lambda}$, matrix of factor loadings in SEM
μ (mu)	population mean; expected value
ν (nu)	degrees of freedom
ρ (rho)	population product–moment correlation
ρ_I (rho I)	population intraclass correlation
σ (sigma)	population standard deviation
σ^2 (sigma-squared)	population variance
Σ (capital sigma)	population variance–covariance matrix
τ (tau)	Kendall's rank-order correlation coefficient; Hotelling's multivariate trace criterion
ϕ (phi)	standard normal probability density function
Φ (capital phi)	measure of association in contingency tables; standard normal cumulative distribution function; $\boldsymbol{\Phi}$, matrix of covariances among independent constructs in SEM
χ^2 (chi-squared)	the chi-square distribution; a statistical test based on the chi-square distribution; the sample value of the chi-square test statistic
Ψ (capital psi)	in statistical hypothesis testing, a statistical contrast; $\boldsymbol{\Psi}$, matrix of covariances among prediction errors in SEM
ω^2 (omega-squared)	strength of a statistical relationship
	Mathematical symbols
$\lvert a \rvert$	absolute value of a
Σ (capital sigma)	summation

Note. It is acceptable to use the form est(θ) or $\hat{\theta}$ to indicate an estimator or estimate of the parameter θ.

English letter. Most abbreviations can be turned into symbols (for use when reporting numerical estimates) by simply italicizing the abbreviation.

> *Note:* Some quantitative approaches (e.g., structural equation modeling) use multiple notation systems; any notation system is acceptable as long as it is used consistently. If you use a notation system other than the one shown in Table 6.5, identify it for readers. Do not mix notation systems within a paper.

As with all aspects of paper preparation, ensure that there are no ambiguities that could lead to errors in final production, particularly with mathematical and statistical symbols, unusual characters, and complex alignments (e.g., subscripts, superscripts). Avoid misunderstandings and corrections by preparing mathematical copy carefully.

Symbols Versus Words. When using a statistical term in narrative text, use the term, not the symbol. For example, state "the means were" not "the *M*s were." When using a statistical term in conjunction with a mathematical operator, use the symbol or abbreviation. For example, write "($M = 7.74$)," not "(*mean* = 7.74)."

Symbols for Population Versus Sample Statistics. Population parameters are usually represented by Greek letters. Most estimators are represented by italicized Latin letters. For example, the population correlation would be represented as ρ, and the estimator would be represented as r; est(ρ) and $\hat{\rho}$ are also acceptable. Some test statistics are represented by italicized Latin letters (e.g., t and F), and a few are represented by Greek letters (e.g., Γ).

Symbols for Number of Subjects. Use an uppercase, italicized N to designate the number of members in the total sample (e.g., $N = 135$). Use a lowercase, italicized n to designate the number of members in a limited portion or subsample of the total sample (e.g., $n = 80$ in the treatment group).

Symbols for Percentage and Currency. Use the percent symbol and currency symbols only when they are accompanied by a numeral; also use them in table headings and in figure labels and legends to conserve space. Use the word "percentage" or the name of the currency when a number is not given. Repeat the symbol for a range of percentages or quantities of currency.

> 18%–20%
> determined the percentage
> $10.50, £10, €9.95, ¥100–¥500
> in Australian dollars, in U.S. dollars

Standard, Bold, and Italic Type. Statistical symbols and mathematical information in papers are prepared with three different type styles: standard (roman), **bold**, and *italic*. The same type style is used in text, tables, and figures.

- Use standard type for Greek letters, subscripts and superscripts that function as identifiers (i.e., are not variables, as in the subscript "girls" in the example that follows), and for abbreviations that are not variables (e.g., log, GLM, WLS).

  μ_{girls}, α, β_i

- Use bold type for symbols for vectors and matrices.

  V, **Σ**

- Use italic type for all other statistical symbols.

  N, M_x, df, SSE, MSE, t, F

On occasion, an element may serve as both an abbreviation and a symbol (e.g., SD); in this case, use the type style that reflects the function of the element (see Table 6.5).

6.45 Spacing, Alignment, and Punctuation for Statistics

Space mathematical copy as you would space words: $a+b=c$ is as difficult to read as *wordswithoutspacing*. Instead, type $a + b = c$. For a minus sign indicating subtraction, use a space on each side of the sign (e.g., $z - y = x$); for a minus sign indicating a negative value, use a space before but not after the sign (e.g., -8.25).

> *Note:* A minus sign is a different typographical character than a hyphen (it is longer and slightly higher); your word-processing program has options for inserting a minus sign in your paper.

Align signs and symbols carefully. Use the subscript and superscript functions of your word-processing program. In most cases, type subscripts first and then superscripts ($x_a{}^2$). However, place a subscript or superscript such as the symbol for prime right next to its letter or symbol (x'_a). Because APA prefers to align subscripts and superscripts one under the other ("stacking") for ease of reading instead of setting one to the right of the other ("staggering"), if you are publishing an article that includes statistics in an APA journal, your subscripts and superscripts will be stacked when they are typeset. If subscripts and superscripts should not be stacked, indicate this in a cover letter or in the manuscript.

Presentation of Equations

Punctuate all equations, whether they are in the line of text or displayed (i.e., typed on a separate line), to conform to their place in the syntax of the sentence (see the period following Equation 3 in Section 6.47). If your paper will be typeset and you have an equation that exceeds the column width of a typeset page, indicate in the accepted manuscript where breaks would be acceptable.

6.46 Equations in Text

Place short and simple equations, such as $a = [(1 + b)/x]^{1/2}$, in the line of text. To present fractions in the line of text, use a slash (/). To make the order of operations in an equation visually unambiguous, use parentheses, square brackets, and braces (together referred to as "fences"). Use parentheses first to enclose material; use square brackets to enclose material already in parentheses; and use braces (curly brackets) to enclose material already in square brackets and parentheses: first ( ), then [( )], and finally {[( )]}.

Equations in the line of text should not project above or below the line; for example, the equation at the beginning of this section would be difficult to set in the line of text if it were in this form:

$$a = \sqrt{\frac{1 + b}{x}}.$$

Instead, such equations are displayed on their own line (see Section 6.47).

6.47 Displayed Equations

Display simple equations if they must be numbered for later reference. Display all complex equations. Number all displayed equations consecutively, with the number in parentheses near the right margin of the page.

$$w_j \pm z_{1 - \alpha/2} \hat{\sigma}_{wj}. \tag{3}$$

When referring to numbered equations, include the full word "equation" (e.g., "Equation 3" or "the third equation," not "Eq. 3").

6.48 Preparing Statistical and Mathematical Copy for Publication

Display all mathematical signs and symbols in typed form, when possible. If a character cannot be produced by your word-processing program, insert it as an image. Type fences (i.e., parentheses, brackets, and braces), uppercase and lowercase letters, punctuation, subscripts and superscripts, and all other elements exactly as you want them to appear in the published article.

Lists

6.49 List Guidelines

Just as heading structure alerts readers to the order of ideas in a paper, *seriation*—that is, lists—helps readers understand a related set of key points within a sentence or paragraph. In a series, all items should be syntactically and conceptually parallel (see Section 4.24 for a more detailed discussion of parallelism).

When a list within a sentence contains three or more items, use a serial comma before the final item (see also Section 6.3).

> Participants were similar with respect to age, gender, and ethnicity.

However, if any item in a list of three or more items already contains commas, use semicolons instead of commas between the items (see Section 6.4).

> We were interested in how students describe their gender identities and expressions; their perceptions of emotional and physical safety on campus, including whether and how such perceptions impact their gender expression; and their perceptions of trans-affirming versus trans-negative reactions among fellow students and faculty.

6.50 Lettered Lists

Within a sentence or paragraph narrative, identify elements in a series with lowercase letters in parentheses when doing so will help readers understand the separate, parallel items in a complex list. Lettered lists may also be used to draw attention to the items—but not as much attention as a numbered or bulleted list. Use commas or semicolons between items as described in Section 6.49.

> Our sample organization used a waterfall model that featured the following sequential stages: (a) requirements analysis, (b) specification, (c) architecture, (d) design, and (e) deployment.

> We tested three groups: (a) low scorers, who scored fewer than 20 points; (b) moderate scorers, who scored between 20 and 50 points; and (c) high scorers, who scored more than 50 points.

6.51 Numbered Lists

Use a numbered list to display complete sentences or paragraphs in a series (e.g., itemized conclusions, steps in a procedure). Use a lettered or bulleted list rather than a numbered list if the items are phrases. Use the numbered list function of your word-processing program to create the numbered list;

this will automatically indent the list as well. Select the option for an Arabic numeral followed by a period but not enclosed in or followed by parentheses. Capitalize the first word after the number (and the first word in any subsequent sentence), and end each sentence with a period or other punctuation as appropriate.

> We addressed the following research questions:
>
> 1. What research methodologies are used to examine the effects of cultural competency training?
> 2. How are psychologists trained to be culturally competent?
> 3. How are training outcomes assessed?
> 4. What are the outcomes of cultural competency training?

6.52 Bulleted Lists

The use of a numbered list may connote an unwanted or unwarranted ordinal position (e.g., chronology, importance, priority) among the items. To achieve the same effect without the implication of ordinality, use bullets to identify the items in the series. Use the bulleted list function of your word-processing program to create the bulleted list; this will automatically indent the list as well. Symbols such as small circles, squares, dashes, and so forth may be used for the bullets. When an article accepted for publication is typeset, the bullet symbol will be changed to the style used by that journal.

Items That Are Complete Sentences. If bulleted list items are complete sentences, begin each sentence with a capital letter and finish it with a period or other end punctuation.

> There are several ways in which psychologists could apply social-media-driven methods to improve their work:
>
> • Social psychologists could use these methods to improve research on emotional experiences.
> • Community psychologists could use these methods to improve population assessment at the city level.
> • Clinical psychologists could use these methods to improve assessment or treatment.

Items That Are Phrases. If bulleted list items are phrases or sentence fragments (i.e., not full sentences), begin each bulleted item with a lowercase letter (for exceptions, such as proper nouns, see Sections 6.14–6.21). There are two options for punctuating a bulleted list in which the items are phrases or fragments.

Phrases Without End Punctuation. The first option is to use no punctuation after the bulleted items (including the final one), which may be better when the items are shorter and simpler.

> Some strategies used by faculty of color in the United States for survival and success on the tenure track include the following:
>
> • learning the rules of the game
> • being aware of who possesses power
> • working doubly hard
> • emphasizing one's strengths and establishing some authority
> • finding White allies (Lutz et al., 2013; Turner et al., 2011)

Phrases With End Punctuation. The second option is to insert punctuation after the bulleted items as though the bullets were not there, following the guidelines in Sections 6.3 and 6.4 for comma and semicolon usage; this option may be better when the items are longer or more complex.

> Adolescents may crave the opportunities for peer connection that social media affords because it allows them to
> - communicate privately with individuals or publicly with a larger audience,
> - seek affirmation by posting pictures or commentary and receiving likes or comments,
> - see how their numbers of friends and followers compare with those of their peers, and
> - monitor who is doing what with whom by seeing how many peers like and comment on their posts and comparing the feedback they get with what others received (Underwood & Ehrenreich, 2017).

Items That Contain Both Phrases and Sentences. When bulleted items contain both phrases and sentences (as with a list of definitions in a glossary), various formats are possible, but the presentation should be consistent and logical. One approach is to lowercase the word or phrase at the beginning of the bullet in bold, followed by a colon. If what follows the colon is a sentence fragment, lowercase the first word after the colon.

> - **creativity:** the ability to produce or develop original work, theories, techniques, or thoughts.

Use a period after a sentence fragment when an additional sentence follows the fragment; otherwise, the punctuation after the fragment is optional.

> - **goal:** the end state toward which a human or nonhuman animal is striving. It can be identified by observing that an organism ceases or changes its behavior upon attaining this state.

If what follows the colon is a complete sentence, capitalize the first word after the colon and end the sentence with a period or other end punctuation.

> - **problem solving:** Individuals use problem solving to attempt to overcome difficulties, achieve plans that move them from a starting situation to a desired goal, or reach conclusions through the use of higher mental functions, such as reasoning and creative thinking.

7

TABLES AND FIGURES

Contents

7

TABLES AND FIGURES

Tables and figures enable authors to present a large amount of information efficiently and to make their data more comprehensible. Tables usually show numerical values (e.g., means and standard deviations) or textual information (e.g., lists of stimulus words, responses from participants) arranged in an orderly display of columns and rows. A figure may be a chart, graph, photograph, drawing, or any other illustration or nontextual depiction. At times, the boundary between tables and figures may be unclear; in general, tables are characterized by a row–column structure, and any type of illustration or image other than a table is considered a figure. In this chapter, we discuss the purpose of tables and figures; principles for designing, preparing, placing, and reproducing them; and guidelines for creating and formatting tables and figures in APA Style, with examples of various types.

General Guidelines for Tables and Figures

7.1 Purpose of Tables and Figures

The primary purpose of any table or figure is to facilitate readers' understanding of the work. For example, tables and figures can be used to summarize information (e.g., a theoretical model, qualities of studies included in a meta-analysis), to present the results of exploratory data analysis or data mining techniques (e.g., a factor analysis), to estimate some statistic or function (e.g., a nomograph), or to share full trial-level data (for more on data sharing, see Section 1.14). Although tables and figures attract attention, they should not be used for mere decoration in an academic paper. Instead, every table and figure should serve a purpose.

7.2 Design and Preparation of Tables and Figures

When preparing a table or figure, first determine the purpose of the display and the relative importance of that purpose (see Section 7.1); then, select a format that supports that purpose (see Sections 7.21 and 7.36 for sample tables and figures, respectively). For example, if the purpose is to illustrate a theoretical model, a chart is most likely the best option. Sometimes, multiple approaches are possible; for example, if your goal is to present group scores, a table would allow readers to see each group's exact scores, whereas a figure would emphasize similarities or differences between groups. When possible, use a standard, or *canonical*, form for a table or figure (examples are shown in Sections 7.21 and 7.36).

Design tables and figures with readers in mind. Communicate findings clearly while also creating attractive visual displays. Prepare tables and figures with the same care as the text of the paper; changes in text often demand changes in tables and figures, and a mismatch between data presented in the text versus in tables and figures may result in the need for a correction notice for published articles or in a lower grade for student assignments if the error is not corrected before publication or submission, respectively. Use the following principles when designing tables and figures:

- Label all columns in tables.
- Label all elements in figure images (e.g., label the axes of a graph).
- Place items that are to be compared next to each other.
- Place labels next to the elements they are labeling.
- In figure images, use sans serif fonts that are large enough to be read without magnification.
- Design the table or figure so it can be understood on its own (meaning readers do not have to refer to the text to understand it). Define abbreviations used in the table or figure even if they are also defined in the text (see Section 7.15 for some exceptions).
- Tables or figures designated as supplemental materials should also contain enough information to be understood on their own.
- Avoid decorative flourishes, which are distracting and can interfere with readers' comprehension; instead, ensure that every element supports the goal of effective communication.

7.3 Graphical Versus Textual Presentation

Be selective in choosing how many tables and figures to include in your paper. Readers may lose track of your message if there are a large number of tables and figures; for example, if many tables and figures accompany a small amount of text, it can cause problems with page layout for published articles. Moreover, graphical presentation is not always optimal for effective communication. For example, the results of a single statistical significance test or a few group means and standard deviations can be presented in text.

> The one-way ANOVA, $F(1, 136) = 4.86$, $MSE = 3.97$, $p = .029$, $\eta^2 = .03$, demonstrated . . .
> Scores on the insomnia measure ($M = 4.08$, $SD = 0.22$) were . . .

A table or figure is an effective choice to present the results of multiple statistical tests or many descriptive statistics (e.g., when reporting the results of numerous analyses of variance [ANOVAs] or summarizing participant demographic data). It may also be possible to combine several smaller tables or figures with similar content into one larger table or figure. Consider how the table or figure augments or supplements the text. For example, when the components of a theoretical model are discussed in the text, a figure may help summarize the model; the value of the figure is the visual summary. However, tables or figures that are redundant with the text may be unnecessary.

7.4 Formatting Tables and Figures

Tables and figures follow the same structure: They have a table or figure number, a table or figure title, a body (for tables) or an image (for figures), and table or figure notes as needed. Tables and figures may be produced in many different file formats; publishers or instructors may limit the formats they accept.

Use the tables function of your word-processing program to create tables. If you copy and paste tables from another program (e.g., SPSS, Excel) into your word-processing program, you may need to adjust the formatting to comply with APA Style guidelines. Do not use the tab key or space bar to manually create the look of a table; this approach is prone to alignment errors and is especially problematic if the table will be typeset for publication.

Figures can be created in a variety of ways using many programs, such as Excel, PowerPoint, Photoshop, Illustrator, MATLAB, and Inkscape. Regardless of the program used to create the figure, the output should be of sufficient resolution to produce high-quality images. TIFF and EPS files are recommended for figures that are to be submitted for publication; file formats such as JPG or PNG are also acceptable for other works produced in APA Style (e.g., classroom assignments). Some types of figures require higher resolution than others; for example, line art requires finer detail than a photograph. Ensure that the format used supports the resolution needed for clear presentation of the image. Check the author guidelines for the journal or publisher to which you are submitting your work for specifications (for APA journals, see the Journal Manuscript Preparation Guidelines at http://on.apa.org/WDtxdW).

7.5 Referring to Tables and Figures in the Text

In the text, refer to every table and figure by its number—known as a *callout* (see Sections 7.10 and 7.24, respectively, for how to assign numbers for tables and figures that accompany the main text; see Section 2.14 for how to assign numbers for tables and figures that appear in appendices). When you call out a table or figure, also tell readers what to look for in that table or figure.

> As shown in Table 1, the demographic characteristics . . .
> Figure 2 shows the event-related potentials . . .
> . . . of the results of the testing (see Table 3).
> . . . of the comparisons (see Figures 4 and 7).

Do not write "the table above" (or "below") or "the figure on page 32." Page numbers often shift during the writing process, which can lead to errors. For published work, final page numbers and the placement of tables and figures on the page are determined during typesetting. Referring to tables and figures by number rather than by location on the page also helps readers who access a work using assistive technologies such as screen readers. Authors seeking publication also should not write "place Table 1 here" or "put Figure 2 here";

the typesetter will determine the position of tables and figures in relation to the callouts.

7.6 Placement of Tables and Figures

There are two options for the placement of tables and figures in a paper. The first option is to place all tables and figures on separate pages after the reference list (with each table on a separate page followed by each figure on a separate page). The second option is to embed each table and figure within the text after its first callout. Follow the specifications of the journal publisher or of the classroom assignment for the placement of tables and figures. Placing all tables and figures on separate pages after the reference list may be preferable for manuscripts being submitted for publication to facilitate copyediting; either approach is appropriate for student assignments or when the placement for tables and figures has not been specified. Dissertations and theses may have different specifications for the placement of tables and figures; for example, in some university guidelines, multiple tables or figures may be placed on the same page at the end of the document as long as they fit. When formatting your dissertation or thesis, abide by the guidelines specified by your advisor and/or university. Authors seeking publication may need to submit figures as high-resolution files separate from the manuscript regardless of where the figures are located within the manuscript.

Align all tables and figures with the left margin regardless of where they appear in the paper. When embedding a table or figure within the text, position it after a full paragraph, ideally the paragraph where it is first called out. Place the table or figure so that it fits on one page if possible (see Section 7.18 for tables longer or wider than a page). If text appears on the same page as a table or figure, add a double-spaced blank line between the text and the table or figure so that the separation between the text and table or figure is easier to see. Put a short table or small figure at the beginning or end of a page rather than in the middle.

Tables and figures that support but are not essential to the text may be placed in one or more appendices. Tables and figures may appear within an appendix that also contains text, or a table or figure may constitute a whole appendix by itself (see Section 2.14). Tables and figures can also be placed in supplemental materials when they would enrich understanding of the material presented in the article but are not essential to a basic understanding or cannot be fully displayed in print (see Section 2.15). If tables or figures are included as supplemental materials, call them out in the text but describe them only briefly (e.g., write "see Table 1 in the supplemental materials for the list of stimuli").

7.7 Reprinting or Adapting Tables and Figures

If you reprint or adapt a table or figure from another source in your paper (e.g., a table from your own published work, an image you found on the internet), you must include a copyright attribution in the table note or figure note indicating the origin of the reprinted or adapted material in addition to a reference list entry for the work. You may also need to obtain permission from the copyright holder to reprint or adapt the table or figure. Table 7.14 in Section 7.21 and Figures 7.3, 7.14, and 7.21 in Section 7.36 show copyright attributions for an adapted table when permission is not necessary, a reprinted figure when permission is not necessary, a reprinted figure in the public domain, and a figure reprinted with permission, respectively. See Sections 12.14 to 12.18 for further information on copyright and permission and for more copyright attribution formats and examples.

Tables

7.8 Principles of Table Construction

Tables should be integral to the text but designed so that they are concise and can be understood in isolation. The principle of conciseness is relevant not only for tables included with the main text but also for tables to be placed in appendices and supplemental materials. Although supplemental tables may be longer and more detailed than tables that accompany the main text, they must be directly and clearly related to the content of the article (see Section 2.15).

All tables are meant to show something specific; for example, tables that communicate quantitative data are effective only when the data are arranged so that their meaning is obvious at a glance (Wainer, 1997). Often, the same data can be arranged in different ways to emphasize different features of the data, and which arrangement is better depends on your purpose. Above all, table layout should be logical and easily grasped by readers. Table entries that are to be compared should be next to one another. In general, different indices (e.g., means, sample sizes) should be presented in different rows or columns. Place variable and condition labels close to their values to facilitate comparison. See the sample tables (Section 7.21) for examples of effective layouts.

7.9 Table Components

The basic components of a prototypical table are shown in Table 7.1 and are summarized as follows.

- **number:** The table number (e.g., Table 1) appears above the table in bold font (see Section 7.10).
- **title:** The table title appears one double-spaced line below the table number in italic title case (see Sections 6.17 and 7.11).
- **headings:** Tables may include a variety of headings depending on the nature and arrangement of the data. All tables should include column headings, including a stub heading (heading for the leftmost column). Some tables also include column spanners, decked heads, and table spanners (see Section 7.12).
- **body:** The table body includes all the rows and columns of a table (see Section 7.13). A *cell* is the point of intersection between a row and a column. The body may be single-spaced, one-and-a-half-spaced, or double-spaced.
- **notes:** Three types of notes (general, specific, and probability) appear below the table as needed to describe contents of the table that cannot be understood from the table title or body alone (e.g., definitions of abbreviations, copyright attribution). Not all tables include table notes (see Section 7.14).

See Section 7.21 for sample tables.

Table 7.1 Basic Components of a Table

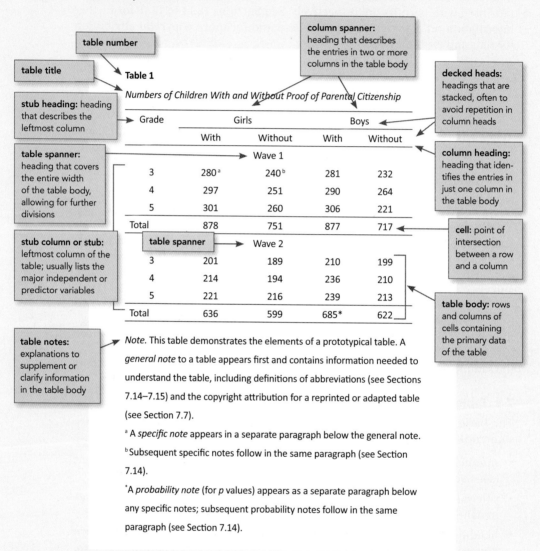

table number

table title

column spanner: heading that describes the entries in two or more columns in the table body

decked heads: headings that are stacked, often to avoid repetition in column heads

stub heading: heading that describes the leftmost column

table spanner: heading that covers the entire width of the table body, allowing for further divisions

column heading: heading that identifies the entries in just one column in the table body

stub column or stub: leftmost column of the table; usually lists the major independent or predictor variables

cell: point of intersection between a row and a column

table body: rows and columns of cells containing the primary data of the table

table notes: explanations to supplement or clarify information in the table body

Table 1

Numbers of Children With and Without Proof of Parental Citizenship

Grade	Girls		Boys	
	With	Without	With	Without
Wave 1				
3	280[a]	240[b]	281	232
4	297	251	290	264
5	301	260	306	221
Total	878	751	877	717
Wave 2				
3	201	189	210	199
4	214	194	236	210
5	221	216	239	213
Total	636	599	685*	622

Note. This table demonstrates the elements of a prototypical table. A *general note* to a table appears first and contains information needed to understand the table, including definitions of abbreviations (see Sections 7.14–7.15) and the copyright attribution for a reprinted or adapted table (see Section 7.7).

[a] A *specific note* appears in a separate paragraph below the general note.

[b] Subsequent specific notes follow in the same paragraph (see Section 7.14).

*A *probability note* (for *p* values) appears as a separate paragraph below any specific notes; subsequent probability notes follow in the same paragraph (see Section 7.14).

7.10 Table Numbers

Number all tables that are part of the main text (i.e., not part of an appendix or supplemental materials) using Arabic numerals—for example, Table 1, Table 2, and Table 3. Assign the numbers in the order in which each table is first mentioned in the text, regardless of whether a more detailed discussion of the table occurs elsewhere in the paper. Write the word "Table" and the number in bold and flush left (i.e., not indented or centered). Tables that appear in appendices follow a different numbering scheme (see Section 2.14).

7.11 Table Titles

Give every table a brief but clear and explanatory title; the basic content of the table should be easily inferred from the title. Write the table title in italic title case below the table number and double-space the table number and title. Avoid overly general and overly detailed table titles.

Title quality	Example table title	Rationale
Too general	*Relation Between College Majors and Performance*	It is unclear what data are presented in the table.
Too detailed	*Mean Performance Scores on Test A, Test B, and Test C of Students With Psychology, Physics, English, and Engineering Majors*	The title duplicates information in the headings of the table.
Effective	*Mean Performance Scores of Students With Different College Majors*	The title is specific but not redundant with headings.

Abbreviations that appear in the headings or the body of a table may be parenthetically explained in the table title.

  Hit and False-Alarm (FA) Proportions in Experiment 2

Abbreviations may also be defined in a general note to the table (see Section 7.14). Do not use a specific note to clarify an element of the title.

7.12 Table Headings

Headings establish the organization of information in the table and identify what is in each column. Column headings describe the entries below them. Table headings should be brief; if possible, the heading should be not much wider than the information in the column below it. Provide a heading for every column in a table, including the *stub column* or *stub*, which is the leftmost column of the table (see Table 7.1 for an illustration).

The stub column usually lists the major independent or predictor variables. In Table 7.1, for instance, the stub column lists the grades. For the stub column, the heading "Variable" is often used when no other heading is suitable. Write the entries in the stub column in parallel form (see Section 4.24 for guidance on parallel construction). Number entries in the stub column only in a correlation matrix (see Tables 7.10–7.11 in Section 7.21) or when they are referred to by number in the text. To show subordination within the stub column, use indentation rather than creating an additional column (see, e.g., Table 7.2, in which "Single," "Married/Partnered," etc. are indented under the heading "Marital Status").[1] Set indentation using the paragraph-formatting feature of your word-processing program rather than by using the tab key. In typeset articles, the indentation is equal to one em space; this can be approximated in draft manuscripts by setting the paragraph indentation to 0.15 in. or inserting an em space from the special characters menu of your word-processing program.

The headings above the columns to the right of the stub column identify what is in each column. A *column heading* applies to just one column; a *column spanner* is a heading that covers two or more columns, each with its own column heading. Headings stacked in this way are called *decked heads*. Often,

---

[1] Table column headings are written in sentence case in a table but in title case if they are referred to in the text.

decked heads can be used to avoid repetition of words in column headings (see Table 7.1). If possible, do not use more than two levels of decked heads. More complex tables may require *table spanners*, which are headings within the body of the table that cover the entire width of the table, allowing for further divisions within the table when the column headings remain the same (see Table 7.1). Table spanners can also be used to combine two tables, provided they have identical column headings.

Any item within a column should be syntactically as well as conceptually comparable with the other items in that column, and all items should be described by the column heading. For example, a column with the heading "%" would contain only percentages; numbers in that column would not be followed by the percent symbol because the symbol is already in the heading (see Table 7.2 in Section 7.21).

Use sentence case for all headings in a table (see Section 6.17). Center all table headings above their column(s). Stub headings, column headings, and column spanners should be singular (e.g., Measure, Item) unless they refer to a group (e.g., Children, Women), but table spanners may be singular or plural.

7.13 Table Body

The main part of the table, the *table body*, contains information organized in cells. Information in a table body may be in the form of numbers, words, or a mixture of both. The body of the table (including table headings) may be single-spaced, one-and-a-half-spaced, or double-spaced, depending on which presentation most effectively conveys information to readers (e.g., single spacing may allow a table to fit on one page). If entries are longer than one line, use a hanging indent of 0.15 in. or one em space. In the stub column of the table, center the stub heading and align the entries flush left beneath it. If entries in this column are significantly shorter than the stub heading, it is permissible to center them beneath the stub heading (e.g., single-digit numbers in the stub column; see the partial table later in this section for an example). The entries in all other cells of the table should be centered (however, aligning them flush left is acceptable if doing so improves the readability of longer entries). Use sentence case for all word entries in the table body (see Section 6.17). Numbers that appear in the table body should be written as words or numerals according to the guidelines in Sections 6.32 to 6.39; however, it is permissible to use numerals for all numbers in tables if this would be clearer or save space.

Decimal Values. Express numerical values to the number of decimal places that the precision of measurement justifies (see Section 6.36). If possible, carry all comparable values to the same number of decimal places. Numerical values should be centered in the column and may also be aligned on the decimal if desired (for the published version, the typesetter will typically center values and align on the decimal).

Empty Cells. If a cell cannot be filled because data are not applicable, leave the cell blank. Use a general or specific table note if you need to explain why the cell is blank or the element is inapplicable (see Section 7.14). If a cell cannot be filled because data were not obtained or are not reported, insert a dash in that cell and explain the use of the dash in the general note to the table (see Section 7.14). By convention, a dash in the main diagonal position of a correlation matrix (see Tables 7.10–7.11 in Section 7.21) indicates the correlation of an item with itself, which must be 1.00, and is simply replaced by the dash with no explanation needed.

Conciseness. Be selective in your presentation. Do not include columns of data that can be calculated easily from other columns. For example, the following partial table is redundant because it shows both the number of responses per trial and the total number of responses; instead, show only whichever is more important to the discussion.

	No. of responses		
Participant	First trial	Second trial	Total responses
1	5	7	12
2	6	4	10

Citations in Tables. If a table contains citations to other works, follow the formats described in Section 8.11. Use an ampersand (&) for the word "and" in all citations in tables to conserve space. Table 7.4 in Section 7.21 shows an example of a table containing citations to studies included in a meta-analysis.

7.14 Table Notes

Tables may have three kinds of notes, which are placed below the body of the table: general notes, specific notes, and probability notes. Table notes apply only to a specific table and not to any other table. If information in one table note is true for another table, repeat the information in the notes for both tables so that the tables can be understood on their own. Some tables do not require table notes at all.

General Note. A *general note* qualifies, explains, or provides information relating to the table as a whole and explains any abbreviations, symbols, special use of italics, bold, or parentheses, and the like. The general note also includes any acknowledgments that a table is reprinted or adapted from another source (see Section 7.7). General notes are designated by the word "*Note*" (italicized) followed by a period (see Table 7.1 and the sample tables in Section 7.21 for examples). Explanations of abbreviations and copyright attributions for reprinted or adapted tables appear at the end of the general note, in that order.

> *Note.* Factor loadings greater than .45 are shown in bold. M = match process; N = nonmatch process.

Specific Note. A *specific note* refers to a particular column, row, or cell. Specific notes are indicated by superscript lowercase letters (e.g., [a], [b], [c]). Do not add specific notes to a table title; instead, use a general note. Within each table that has specific notes, order the superscripts from left to right and from top to bottom, starting at the top left and beginning with the letter "a" (see, e.g., Tables 7.2, 7.10, and 7.15 in Section 7.21). The corresponding specific note below the table begins with the same superscript letter. Place a superscript space before the superscript letter in the table body (e.g., Group [a]). Place a superscript space after the superscript letter in the specific note. This space prevents specific notes from getting caught by spell-check and improves readability.

> [a] $n = 25$. [b] This participant did not complete the trials.

Probability Note. A *probability note* describes how asterisks and other symbols are used in a table to indicate p values and thus the significance of the results of statistical hypothesis testing. To report the results of significance testing, it is best to provide the exact probabilities to two or three decimal places (e.g., $p = .023$; see, e.g., Tables 7.8–7.9 in Section 7.21; see also Section 3.7 and Section 6.36). However, when p values are less than .001, it is acceptable to write the value as "<.001."

It may sometimes be difficult to report exact p values in a table because doing so would make the table difficult to read. An alternative to reporting exact p values in a table is to use the "$p <$" notation. Use this notation only in tables and figures (see Section 7.28 for more on figure notes), not in the text. In the "$p <$" notation, asterisks or daggers appear after table entries to indicate that the entries have reached the established threshold for significance; definitions of the asterisks and/or daggers appear in a corresponding probability note. Use the same number of asterisks to indicate the same p values across tables (or figures) within your paper, such as $^*p < .05$, $^{**}p < .01$, and $^{***}p < .001$ (see, e.g., Tables 7.10–7.11 in Section 7.21). In general, do not use any p value smaller than .001. Daggers are sometimes used to indicate nonsignificant trends based on the threshold established for your study (e.g., $^†p < .10$) or to distinguish between one-tailed and two-tailed tests. Use superscript formatting for asterisks and daggers. In a table body (or a figure), position asterisks and daggers immediately after the entries they belong to, with no space in between (e.g., $.02^*$). In the probability note, place asterisks and daggers immediately before the p, with no space in between (e.g., $^*p < .002$).

One-Tailed Versus Two-Tailed Tests. If you need to distinguish between one-tailed and two-tailed tests in the same table, use an asterisk for the two-tailed p values and an alternate symbol (e.g., dagger) for the one-tailed p values, and specify the convention in the probability note.

$^*p < .05$, two-tailed. $^{**}p < .01$, two-tailed. $^†p < .05$, one-tailed. $^{††}p < .01$, one-tailed.

Indicating Significant Differences Between Values. To indicate statistically significant differences between two or more table values—for example, when comparing values with post hoc tests such as Tukey's honestly significant difference (HSD) test, Bonferroni procedure, Scheffé method, Fisher's least significant difference, or Duncan's new multiple range test—use lowercase subscript letters (see Table 7.9 in Section 7.21 for an example). Explain the use of the subscripts in the table's general note, as in the following example:

Note. Means sharing a common subscript are not significantly different at $\alpha = .01$ according to Tukey's honestly significant difference procedure.

Formatting of Notes. Begin each kind of note on a new line below the table body. A general note appears first. A specific note begins on a new line under a general note; subsequent specific notes begin on the same line. A probability note begins on a new line under any general or specific notes; subsequent probability notes begin on the same line. Multiple specific or probability notes are separated from each other by a period and a space. Lengthy specific notes may be presented on separate lines if this improves readability. Double-space all table notes, and align all notes flush left (i.e., with no paragraph indentation).

Note. The responses were gathered in the laboratory.
$^a n = 25$. $^b n = 42$.
$^*p < .05$. $^{**}p < .01$. $^{***}p < .001$.

Use of Notes to Eliminate Repetition. Table notes can be useful for eliminating repetition from the body of a table. Certain types of information are appropriate either in the table body or in a note. To determine the placement of such material, remember that clearly and efficiently organized data enable readers to focus on that data. Thus, if probability values or subsample sizes are numerous, use a column rather than many notes. Conversely, if a row or column contains few entries (or the same entry), eliminate the column by adding a note to the table, as shown in the following partial tables.

Repetitive		Concise	
Group	n	Group[a]	
Anxious	15	Anxious	
Depressed	15	Depressed	
Control	15	Control	

[a] $n = 15$ for each group.

7.15 Standard Abbreviations in Tables and Figures

Use standard abbreviations and symbols for all statistics (e.g., M, SD, SE, F, df, n, p), Greek letters (e.g., α, β, χ^2), and units of measurement (see Tables 6.4–6.5) used in tables without defining them in a note. This guidance also applies to statistics, Greek letters, and units of measurement appearing in figures (see Section 7.28 for more on figure notes). The abbreviation "no." (for number) and the symbol "%" (for percent) may also be used without providing a definition. Other abbreviations used in a table or figure should be defined in the table or figure title, body, or note, even if the abbreviations are also defined in the paper (see Sections 6.25 and 6.44). Except where it makes sense to group similar abbreviations, define the abbreviations in the order that they appear in the table, starting at the top left and moving left to right, top to bottom.

7.16 Confidence Intervals in Tables

When a table includes point estimates—for example, means, correlations, or regression slopes—it should also, when possible, include confidence intervals. Report confidence intervals in tables either by using square brackets, as in the text (see Section 6.9) and in Table 7.16 in Section 7.21, or by giving lower and upper limits in separate columns, as in Table 7.17 in Section 7.21. In every table that includes confidence intervals, state the confidence level (e.g., 95% or 99%). It is usually best to use the same confidence level throughout a paper.

7.17 Table Borders and Shading

Limit the use of borders or lines in a table to those needed for clarity. In general, use a border at the top and bottom of the table, beneath column headings (including decked heads), and above column spanners. You may also use a border to separate a row containing totals or other summary information from other rows in the table (see Table 7.1 for an example). Do not use vertical borders to separate data, and do not use borders around every cell in a table. Use spacing between columns and rows and strict alignment to clarify relations among the elements in a table.

Avoid the use of shading in tables. Do not use shading for mere decoration. To emphasize the content of a particular cell or cells, use a specific or probability note; italics or bold may also be used with explanation in the table's general note. Instead of using shading, add white space or borders between rows and columns to help readers distinguish them. If shading is necessary, explain its purpose in the table's general note.

7.18 Long or Wide Tables

If a table is longer than one page, repeat the heading row on each subsequent page of the table. It is best to use the automated table-formatting tools of your word-processing program rather than manually retyping the headings. Table 7.4 in Section 7.21 shows an example of a multipage table—in this case, a table summarizing the studies included in a meta-analysis.

Wide tables may be presented in landscape orientation (it is not important if landscape orientation impacts the position of the page header). If a table in landscape format is still too wide to fit on one page, the stub column (left column) should repeat on each subsequent page. If a table is too wide and too long to fit on one page, create separate tables.

7.19 Relation Between Tables

Consider combining tables that repeat data. Ordinarily, identical columns or rows of data should not appear in two or more tables. Be consistent in the presentation of all tables within a paper to facilitate comparisons. Use similar formats, titles, and headings and the same terminology across tables whenever possible (e.g., do not use "response time" in one table and "reaction time" in another table to refer to the same concept). If multiple tables contain similar data but cannot be combined, number these tables separately (e.g., Table 1 and Table 2); do not use letters to indicate subtables (i.e., do not label two tables Table 1A and Table 1B).

7.20 Table Checklist

The table checklist may help ensure that the data in your table are effectively presented and conform to the style guidelines presented in this chapter.

7.21 Sample Tables

Some tables have certain standard, or *canonical*, forms (e.g., a correlation table). When possible, use a standard form rather than designing your own form. The advantage of using the canonical form is that readers generally already know where to look in the table for certain kinds of information. In some situations, you may want to use a form other than the canonical table form to make a specific point or to stress certain relationships. The judicious use of nonstandard forms can be effective but must always be motivated by the special circumstances of the data array. When using nonstandard forms, make certain that labeling is clear.

Sample tables are presented next; follow these samples to design basic tables. The exact contents and structure of your table will vary from the sample tables depending on the nature of the information being presented. For variations not addressed in this chapter, consult similar published articles to see examples of current standards and practices.

Table Checklist

☐ Is the table necessary?

☐ Does the table belong in the print and electronic versions of the article, or can it be placed in supplemental materials?

☐ Are all comparable tables in the paper consistent in presentation?

☐ Are all tables numbered consecutively with Arabic numerals in the order in which they are first mentioned in the text? Is the table number bold and flush left?

☐ Are all tables called out or referred to in the text?

☐ Is the table title brief but explanatory? Is it written in italic title case and flush left?

☐ Does every column have a column heading, including the leftmost (stub) column? Are all column headings centered?

☐ Are all abbreviations explained (with exceptions as noted in Section 7.15), as well as the special use of italics, bold, parentheses, dashes, and symbols?

☐ Are the table notes, if needed, in the order of general note, specific note, and probability note? Are the notes double-spaced and flush left and in the same font as the text of the paper?

☐ Are table borders correctly applied (at the top and bottom of the table, beneath column headings, above table spanners)?

☐ Is the line spacing of the table correctly applied (double-spacing for the table number, title, and notes; single-spacing, one-and-a-half-spacing, or double-spacing for the table body)?

☐ Are entries in the left column flush left beneath the centered stub heading? Are all other column headings and cell entries centered (except when aligning entries to the left would improve readability)?

☐ Are confidence intervals reported for all major point estimates? Is the confidence level—for example, 95%—stated, and is the same level of confidence used for all tables and throughout the paper?

☐ If the results of statistical significance testing are included in the table, are all p values correctly identified? Are exact p values provided? Is the "$p <$" notation used only when needed? When the "$p <$" notation is used, are asterisks or daggers attached to the appropriate table entries and defined? Are asterisks or daggers used consistently to indicate the same p value in all tables in the same paper?

☐ If all or part of a table is reprinted or adapted, is there a copyright attribution? If permission was necessary to reproduce the table, have you received written permission for its reuse (in print and electronic forms) from the copyright holder and sent a copy of that written permission with the final version of your paper?

- **demographic characteristics of study participants** (Table 7.2): Demographic data can help readers understand the generalizability of the results. The demographic data you report will depend on the nature of the study.

- **properties of study variables** (Table 7.3): Describe the properties of study variables (e.g., means, standard deviations). If reporting psychometric information, clearly state the index of reliability (or other psychometric property) being used and the sample on which the reliability was based (if different from the study sample).

- **meta-analysis summary** (Table 7.4): The qualities of the studies included in a meta-analysis can be reported in a table as a summary for readers (what information is relevant to report will depend on the nature of the study).

- **summary of complex experimental design** (Table 7.5): Complex designs can be summarized in a table, making the entire structure of the experiment(s) clear without the need for lengthy textual description.

- **descriptive statistics for study measures** (Table 7.6): Descriptive statistics include means and standard deviations. The exact statistics you should provide will depend on the nature and purpose of the analyses.

- **chi-square results** (Table 7.7): The results of individual chi-square tests are usually reported in the text only (see Section 6.43). The results of multiple chi-square tests may be summarized in a table, which typically also includes frequencies, p values, and any other relevant statistics such as effect sizes.

- **_t_-test results** (Table 7.8): When there is only one t test to report, the results should be incorporated into the text (see Section 6.43). Use a table to report the results of multiple t tests.

- **a priori or post hoc comparisons** (Table 7.9): A priori and post hoc tests (e.g., Tukey's HSD test, Bonferroni procedure, Scheffé method, Fisher's least significant difference, Duncan's new multiple range test) are used to compare specific group means in studies in which the independent variables have more than two levels. Although these results are often presented in the text rather than in a table, a table can be used to summarize comparisons. This table is similar to the table for presenting descriptive statistics (Table 7.6) with the addition of subscripts to note significantly different means.

- **correlations** (Tables 7.10–7.11): A correlation table presents correlations between study variables and may also incorporate descriptive statistics, alpha values, or other relevant statistics (Table 7.10). The perfect correlation along the diagonal is indicated by an em dash. Intercorrelations for two different groups can be presented in the same table, with correlations for one group above the diagonal and for the other group below the diagonal (Table 7.11). The variables in a correlation table should be numbered and named in the stub column, with corresponding numbers alone in the column headings to avoid repeating the variable names in the column headings.

- **analysis of variance** (Tables 7.12–7.13): The results of a single one-way ANOVA are typically reported in the text only. The results of multiple ANOVAs can be reported in a table; various presentations are possible. For example, degrees of freedom may be presented in the column heading when they are the same for all tests (Table 7.12) or in their own column when they differ (Table 7.13). Sums of squares and mean squares are not typically included in tables intended for publication.

- **factor analysis** (Table 7.14): Factor coefficients or loadings (rotated or unrotated) can be presented in a variety of ways and may be accompanied by other indices such as the percentage of variance and eigenvalues. If a rotation is used, specify the type (e.g., varimax, oblimin). Factor coefficients or loadings above a prescribed threshold are typically indicated by the use of bold; the purpose of any bolding should be explained in the table note.

- **multiple regression** (Tables 7.15–7.18): The results of multiple regression, including mediation and moderation analyses, can be presented in a variety of ways depending on the purpose of the table and need for detail. Clearly label the regression type (e.g., hierarchical) and the type of regression coefficients (raw or standardized) being reported. For hierarchical and other sequential regressions, be sure to provide the increments of change (see Section 6.43). Four options are shown in the sample tables: regression coefficients without confidence intervals (Table 7.15), regression coefficients and bracketed confidence intervals (Table 7.16), moderator analysis with confidence intervals in separate columns (Table 7.17), and hierarchical multiple regression (Table 7.18).

- **model comparisons** (Tables 7.19–7.21): Model comparison tables are used to compare different models of data (Table 7.19), including multilevel models (Table 7.20), and to report the results of confirmatory factor analyses (Table 7.21). Ensure that the competing models are clearly identified and that the comparisons are clearly specified. Comparative fit indices can be useful for readers.

- **qualitative tables** (Tables 7.22–7.23): Qualitative data can be presented in tabular form in an innumerable variety of ways depending on the purpose of the table. Qualitative tables might include descriptions of variables (as in Table 7.22), referenced studies, test items, or quotations from research participants. Quantitative data may be incorporated alongside the qualitative data (e.g., quotations might be presented alongside response frequencies, as in Table 7.23).

- **mixed methods tables** (Table 7.24): The procedures or findings of mixed methods research can be presented in tabular form in various ways depending on the purpose of the table.

Sample Tables

Table 7.2 Sample Demographic Characteristics Table

Table 1

Sociodemographic Characteristics of Participants at Baseline

Baseline characteristic	Guided self-help		Unguided self-help		Wait-list control		Full sample	
	n	%	*n*	%	*n*	%	*n*	%
Gender								
Female	25	50	20	40	23	46	68	45.3
Male	25	50	30	60	27	54	82	54.7
Marital status								
Single	13	26	11	22	17	34	41	27.3
Married/partnered	35	70	38	76	28	56	101	67.3
Divorced/widowed	1	2	1	2	4	8	6	4.0
Other	1	1	0	0	1	2	2	1.3
Children[a]	26	52	26	52	22	44	74	49.3
Cohabitating	37	74	36	72	26	52	99	66.0
Highest educational level								
Middle school	0	0	1	2	1	2	2	1.3
High school/some college	22	44	17	34	13	26	52	34.7
University or post-graduate degree	27	54	30	60	32	64	89	59.3
Employment								
Unemployed	3	6	5	10	2	4	10	6.7
Student	8	16	7	14	3	6	18	12.0
Employed	30	60	29	58	40	80	99	66.0
Self-employed	9	18	7	14	5	10	21	14.0
Retired	0	0	2	4	0	0	2	1.3
Previous psychological treatment[a]	17	34	18	36	24	48	59	39.3
Previous psychotropic medication[a]	6	12	13	26	11	22	30	20.0

use of specific note ➤ [points to "Previous psychological treatment[a]"]

Note. $N = 150$ ($n = 50$ for each condition). Participants were on average 39.5 years old ($SD = 10.1$), and participant age did not differ by condition.

[a] Reflects the number and percentage of participants answering "yes" to this question.

Table 7.3 Sample Properties of Study Variables Table

Table 1

Psychometric Properties for DLOPFQ Scales and Subscales

Scale	*M*	*SD*	Range	Cronbach's α
Identity total score	86.6	28.0	28–155	.94
Work Identity	41.6	13.3	16–76	.88
Social Identity	45.0	15.7	14–84	.91
Self-Directedness total score	91.2	26.5	34–151	.92
Work Self-Directedness	44.9	13.5	16–76	.85
Social Self-Directedness	46.3	14.3	17–80	.86
Empathy total score	101.8	15.8	48–139	.84
Work Empathy	49.9	8.2	20–72	.72
Social Empathy	51.9	8.6	28–76	.77
Intimacy total score	122.9	28.6	56–189	.91
Work Intimacy	61.7	14.3	28–94	.82
Social Intimacy	61.2	15.4	24–96	.86

Note. The *Diagnostic and Statistical Manual of Mental Disorders* (5th ed.) Levels of Personality Functioning Questionnaire (DLOPFQ) we developed had four scales (Identity, Self-Directedness, Empathy, and Intimacy), each with subscales for the work and social domains.

Table 7.4 Sample Meta-Analysis Summary Table

Table 1

Sample and Task Information for Studies Included in the Meta-Analysis

Study	Sample	Task
Barch et al. (2001)	14 with first-episode schizophrenia 12 healthy control participants	AX-CPT
Barch et al. (2008)	57 with chronic schizophrenia 37 healthy control participants	AX-CPT
Becker (2012)	49 with chronic schizophrenia 28 healthy control participants	AX-CPT
Braver et al. (1999)	16 with first-episode schizophrenia 16 healthy control participants	AX-CPT
Chung et al. (2011)	41 with chronic schizophrenia 27 healthy control participants	AX-CPT
Cohen et al. (1999)	53 with chronic schizophrenia	AX-CPT

Delawalla

Edwards e

Gold et al.

Holmes et

Jones et al

headings repeat on second page of table

Study	Sample	Task
MacDonald & Carter (2003)	17 with chronic schizophrenia 17 healthy control participants	AX-CPT
Poppe et al. (2016)	47 with chronic schizophrenia 56 healthy control participants	DPX
Reilly et al. (2017)	402 with chronic schizophrenia 304 bipolar with psychotic features 210 healthy control participants	DPX
Sheffield et al. (2014)	104 with chronic schizophrenia 132 healthy control participants	AX-CPT, DPX
Todd et al. (2014)	33 with chronic schizophrenia 58 healthy control participants	AX-CPT
Zhang et al. (2015)	339 with chronic schizophrenia 665 healthy control participants	DPX

Note. AX-CPT = AX–continuous performance task; DPX = dot–pattern expectancy task.

Table 7.5 Sample Summary of Complex Experimental Design Table

Table 1

Summary of Designs of Experiments 1–4

Group	Preexposure 1	Preexposure 2	Conditioning	Test
Experiment 1				
Compound	A– X– Y–	AX– BY–	X+	X–
Compound novel	A– X– Y–	AX– BY–	Y+	Y–
Experiment 2				
Compound A	A– X– Y–	AX– BY–	A+	A–
Compound X	A– X– Y–	AX– BY–	X+	X–
Compound novel	A– X– Y–	AX– BY–	Y+	Y–
Experiment 3				
Compound	A– X– Y–	AX– Y–	X+	X–
Element	A– X– Y–	AX– Y–	Y+	Y–
Experiment 4				
Control			A+/Y+	A–/Y–
Element A	A– X– Y–	A– X– Y–	A+	A–
Element Y	A– X– Y–	A– X– Y–	Y+	Y–

Note. A, X, Y, and B = tone, clicker, steady light, and flashing light, respectively (counterbalanced), with the constraint that A and B are drawn from one modality and X and Y from another (counterbalanced); plus sign (+) = shock to floor of rat chamber; minus sign (–) = absence of shock.

Table 7.6 Sample Descriptive Statistics for Study Measures Table

Table 1

Means and Standard Deviations of Scores on Baseline Measures

Scale	High BAS group	Moderate BAS group	*p*
BAS-T	46.17 (2.87)	37.99 (1.32)	<.001
SR	17.94 (1.88)	11.52 (1.84)	<.001
BDI	7.11 (6.50)	6.18 (6.09)	.254
ASRM	6.46 (4.01)	5.63 (3.69)	.109
M-SRM	11.05 (3.36)	11.76 (2.75)	.078

> Parenthetical values in a short table are easily read. In most tables, different indices should be presented in different rows or columns.

Note. Standard deviations are presented in parentheses. BAS = Behavioral Activation System; BAS-T = Behavioral Activation System–Total scores from the Behavioral Inhibition System/Behavioral Activation System Scales; SR = Sensitivity to Reward scores from the Sensitivity to Punishment and Sensitivity to Reward Questionnaire; BDI = Beck Depression Inventory scores; ASRM = Altman Self-Rating Mania Scale scores; M-SRM = Modified Social Rhythm Metric Regularity scores.

Table 7.7 Sample Chi-Square Analysis Table

Table 1

Frequencies and Chi-Square Results for Belief Perseverance in Attitudes Toward Celebrities (N = 201)

Source	Do not believe		Unsure		Believe		$\chi^2(2)$
	n	%	n	%	n	%	
Media reports	17	8.46	140	69.65	44	21.89	124.75*
Family reports	47	23.38	106	52.74	48	23.88	34.06*
Friends' reports	42	20.90	112	55.72	47	23.38	45.52*
Caught by media	19	9.45	82	40.80	100	49.75	54.00*
Celebrity display of behavior	12	5.97	61	30.35	128	63.68	101.22*

*$p < .001$.

Table 7.8 Sample Results of Several t Tests Table

Table 2

Results of Curve-Fitting Analysis Examining the Time Course of Fixations to the Target

> exact *p* values

Logistic parameter	9-year-olds		16-year-olds		$t(40)$	p	Cohen's d
	M	SD	M	SD			
Maximum asymptote, proportion	.843	.135	.877	.082	0.951	.347	0.302
Crossover, in ms	759	87	694	42	2.877	.006	0.840
Slope, as change in proportion per ms	.001	.0002	.002	.0002	2.635	.012	2.078

Note. For each participant, the logistic function was fit to target fixations separately. The maximum asymptote is the asymptotic degree of looking at the end of the time course of fixations. The crossover is the point in time when the function crosses the midway point between peak and baseline. The slope represents the rate of change in the function measured at the crossover. Mean parameter values for each of the analyses are shown for the 9-year-olds (*n* = 24) and the 16-year-olds (*n* = 18), as well as the results of *t* tests (assuming unequal variance) comparing the parameter estimates between the two ages.

Table 7.9 Sample a Priori or Post Hoc Comparisons Table

Table 3

Analyses for the Interaction of Professor Type and Timing of Response on Perceptions of Professor Traits

Professor trait	End of semester professor type		Start of semester professor type		F ratio	p	η^2
	Typical	Effective	Typical	Effective			
Dedicated	4.706$_b$	4.789$_b$	4.154$_c$	5.000$_a$	19.26	.001	.15
Easy to understand	3.059$_c$	4.895$_a$	3.231$_c$	4.429$_b$	5.01	.028	.03
Fair	4.000$_b$	4.263$_b$	3.731$_c$	4.667$_a$	5.75	.019	.06
Manipulative	1.471$_a$	1.632$_a$	1.731$_a$	1.238$_a$	3.92	.051	.05
Insensitive	2.059$_b$	1.526$_c$	2.538$_a$	1.143$_c$	8.12	.006	.06

exact p values

Note. Means with different subscripts differ at the $p = .05$ level by Duncan's new multiple range test.

Table 7.10 Sample Correlation Table for One Sample

Table 1

Descriptive Statistics and Correlations for Study Variables

Variable	n	M	SD	1	2	3	4	5	6	7
1. Internal–external status [a]	3,697	0.43	0.49	—						
2. Manager job performance	2,134	3.14	0.62	−.08**	—					
3. Starting salary [b]	3,697	1.01	0.27	.45**	−.01	—				
4. Subsequent promotion	3,697	0.33	0.47	.08**	−.07**	.04*	—			
5. Organizational tenure	3,697	6.45	6.62	−.29**	.09**	.01	.09**	—		
6. Unit service performance [c]	3,505	85.00	6.98	−.25**	−.39**	.24**	.08**	.01	—	
7. Unit financial performance [c]	694	42.61	5.86	.00	−.03	.12*	−.07	−.02	.16**	—

use of specific note

asterisks for p values

[a] 0 = internal hires and 1 = external hires. [b] A linear transformation was performed on the starting salary values to maintain pay practice confidentiality. The standard deviation (0.27) can be interpreted as 27% of the average starting salary for all managers. Thus, ±1 *SD* includes a range of starting salaries from 73% (i.e., 1.00 − 0.27) to 127% (i.e., 1.00 + 0.27) of the average starting salaries for all managers. [c] Values reflect the average across 3 years of data.

*$p < .05$. **$p < .01$.

Table 7.11 Sample Correlation Table for Two Samples

Table 1

Intercorrelations for Study Variables Disaggregated by Gender

Variable	1	2	3	4
1. Grade point average	—	49**	.35**	−.05
2. Academic self-concept	.35**	—	.36**	.02
3. Teacher trust	.49**	.35**	—	.20**
4. Age	.10	.21*	−.15	—

Note. The results for the female sample (*n* = 199) are shown above the diagonal. The results for the male sample (*n* = 120) are shown below the diagonal.

*p < .05. **p < .01.

asterisks for
p values

Table 7.12 Sample Analysis of Variance Table (Option 1)

Table 1

Means, Standard Deviations, and One-Way Analyses of Variance in Psychological and Social Resources and Cognitive Appraisals

Measure	Urban		Rural		$F(1, 294)$	η^2
	M	SD	M	SD		
Self-esteem	2.91	0.49	3.35	0.35	68.87***	.19
Social support	4.22	1.50	5.56	1.20	62.60***	.17
Cognitive appraisals						
Threat	2.78	0.87	1.99	0.88	56.35***	.20
Challenge	2.48	0.88	2.83	1.20	7.87***	.03
Self-efficacy	2.65	0.79	3.53	0.92	56.35***	.16

***p < .001.

Table 7.13 Sample Analysis of Variance Table (Option 2)

Table 2

Means, Standard Deviations, and Two-Way ANOVA Statistics for Study Variables

Variable	SMT		Control		ANOVA			
	M	*SD*	*M*	*SD*	Effect	*F* ratio	*df*	η^2
Psychological strain								
Time 1	0.24	0.30	0.22	0.29	G	2.82	1,151	.02
Time 2	0.16	0.27	0.27	0.32	T	0.38	2,302	.00
Time 3	0.16	0.26	0.26	0.31	G × T	4.64**	2,302	.03
Emotional exhaustion								
Time 1	2.82	1.47	2.50	1.25	G	0.32	1,151	.00
Time 2	2.55	1.31	2.47	1.28	T	6.59**	2,302	.04
Time 3	2.36	1.39	2.43	1.16	G × T	3.89*	2,302	.03
Depersonalization								
Time 1	1.20	1.09	1.12	1.05	G	0.07	1,149	.00
Time 2	1.13	1.07	1.25	1.16	T	0.67	2,302	.00
Time 3	1.00	0.93	1.24	0.93	G × T	3.04*	2,302	.02

Note. $N = 153$. ANOVA = analysis of variance; SMT = stress management training group; Control = wait-list control group; G = group; T = time.

*$p < .05$. **$p < .01$.

Table 7.14 Sample Factor Analysis Table

Table 1

Results From a Factor Analysis of the Parental Care and Tenderness (PCAT) Questionnaire

PCAT item	Factor loading		
	1	2	3
Factor 1: Tenderness—Positive			
20. You make a baby laugh over and over again by making silly faces.	**.86**	.04	.01
22. A child blows you kisses to say goodbye.	**.85**	−.02	−.01
16. A newborn baby curls its hand around your finger.	**.84**	−.06	.00
19. You watch as a toddler takes their first step and tumbles gently back down.	**.77**	.05	−.07
25. You see a father tossing his giggling baby up into the air as a game.	**.70**	.10	−.03
Factor 2: Liking			
5. I think that kids are annoying. (R)	−.01	**.95**	.06
8. I can't stand how children whine all the time. (R)	−.12	**.83**	−.03
2. When I hear a child crying, my first thought is "shut up!" (R)	.04	**.72**	.01
11. I don't like to be around babies. (R)	.11	**.70**	−.01
14. If I could, I would hire a nanny to take care of my children. (R)	.08	**.58**	−.02
Factor 3: Protection			
7. I would hurt anyone who was a threat to a child.	−.13	−.02	**.95**
12. I would show no mercy to someone who was a danger to a child.	.00	−.05	**.74**
15. I would use any means necessary to protect a child, even if I had to hurt others.	.06	.08	**.72**
4. I would feel compelled to punish anyone who tried to harm a child.	.07	.03	**.68**
9. I would sooner go to bed hungry than let a child go without food.	.46	−.03	**.36**

use of bold on factor loadings

Note. $N = 307$. The extraction method was principal axis factoring with an oblique (promax with Kaiser normalization) rotation. Factor loadings above .30 are in bold. Reverse-scored items are denoted with (R). Adapted from "Individual Differences in Activation of the Parental Care Motivational System: Assessment, Prediction, and Implications," by E. E. Buckels, A. T. Beall, M. K. Hofer, E. Y. Lin, Z. Zhou, and M. Schaller, 2015, *Journal of Personality and Social Psychology, 108*(3), p. 501 (https://doi.org/10.1037/pspp0000023). Copyright 2015 by the American Psychological Association.

example copyright attribution for an adapted table when permission is not necessary

Table 7.15 Sample Regression Table, Without Confidence Intervals

Table 2

Regression Coefficients of Leader Sleep on Charismatic Leadership

Variable	Model 1			Model 2		
	B	β	SE	B	β	SE
Constant	2.65**		.31	2.76		
Leader gender[a]	−.11	−.07	.16	−.09	−.06	.15
Leader sleep condition[b]				−.36**	−.24	.15
R^2	.09				.14	
ΔR^2					.05*	

use of specific notes

Note. N = 88. We examined the impact of leader sleep condition (control vs. sleep deprived) on ratings of charismatic leadership. In Model 1, we entered the control variables of gender and video length to predict leader charisma. In Model 2, we entered sleep condition as a predictor.

[a] Male = 1, female = 2. [b] Control condition = 0, sleep-deprived condition = 1.

*p < .05. **p < .01.

Table 7.16 Sample Regression Table, With Confidence Intervals in Brackets

Table 4

Regressions of Associations Between Marital Satisfaction and Average Levels of Marital Behavior

Variable	B	SE	t	p	95% CI
		Angry behavior			
Actor					
H → H	−98.90	40.20	−2.46	.016	[− 179.1, −18.7]
W → W	−.87.11	30.87	−2.82	.006	[−148.7, −25.6]
Partner					
W → H	−76.18	39.43	−1.93	.057	[−154.8, 2.4]
H → W	−91.80	38.16	−2.41	.019	[−167.9, −15.7]
		Disregard			
Actor					
H → H	−38.62	27.86	−1.39	.170	[−94.2, 16.9]
W → W	−47.54	26.99	−1.76	.082	[−101.4, 6.3]
Partner					
W → H	−82.81	32.01	−2.59	.012	[−146.6, −19.0]
H → W	−79.36	27.16	−2.92	.005	[−133.5, −25.2]
		Distancing			
Actor					
H → H	−47.42	24.72	−1.92	.059	[−96.7, 1.9]
W → W	3.04	23.48	0.13	.897	[−43.8, 49.8]
Partner					
W → H	−0.05	23.91	0.00	.998	[−47.7, 47.6]
H → W	−53.50	24.47	−2.19	.032	[−102.3, −4.7]

square brackets around confidence intervals

Note. CI = confidence interval; H → H = husband-as-actor effect on the husband's own marital satisfaction; W → W = wife-as-actor effect on the wife's own marital satisfaction; W → H = wife-as-partner effect on the husband's satisfaction; H → W = husband-as-partner effect on the wife's satisfaction.

Table 7.17 Sample Regression Table, With Confidence Intervals in Separate Columns

confidence intervals in separate columns

Table 3

Moderator Analysis: Types of Measurement and Study Year

Effect	Estimate	SE	95% CI		p
			LL	*UL*	
Fixed effects					
Intercept	.119	.040	.041	.198	.003
Creativity measurement[a]	.097	.028	.042	.153	.001
Academic achievement measurement[b]	−.039	.018	−.074	−.004	.03
Study year[c]	.0002	.001	−.001	.002	.76
Goal[d]	−.003	.029	−.060	.054	.91
Published[e]	.054	.030	−.005	.114	.07
Random effects					
Within-study variance	.009	.001	.008	.011	<.001
Between-study variance	.018	.003	.012	.023	<.001

Note. Number of studies = 120, number of effects = 782, total *N* = 52,578. CI = confidence interval; *LL* = lower limit; *UL* = upper limit.

[a] 0 = self-report, 1 = test. [b] 0 = test, 1 = grade point average. [c] Study year was grand centered. [d] 0 = other, 1 = yes. [e] 0 = no, 1 = yes.

Table 7.18 Sample Hierarchical Multiple Regression Table

Table 2

Hierarchical Regression Results for Well-Being

Variable	B	95% CI for B		SE B	β	R^2	ΔR^2
		LL	UL				
Step 1						.11	.11***
Constant	4.37***	3.72	5.03	0.33			
Perceived social class	0.43***	0.19	0.68	0.12	.30***		
Generation level	−0.11	−0.27	0.04	0.08	−.12		
Step 2						.23	.13***
Constant	1.78	−0.39	3.95	1.10			
Perceived social class	0.40***	0.16	0.64	0.12	.28***		
Generation level	−0.02	−0.23	0.19	0.11	−.02		
Familismo	0.33**	0.07	0.60	0.14	.21**		
Acculturation	0.09	−0.31	0.48	0.20	.04		
Enculturation	0.29	−0.04	0.61	0.17	.19		
Mex Am margin	−0.23**	−0.45	−0.01	0.11	−.17**		
Step 3						.26	.03**
Constant	2.27**	0.08	4.45	1.11			
Perceived social class	0.45***	0.21	0.69	0.12	.31***		
Generation level	−0.01	−0.21	0.20	0.10	−.01		
Familismo	0.37*	0.10	0.63	0.13	.23*		
Acculturation	0.11	−0.28	0.50	0.20	.05		
Enculturation	0.35**	0.02	0.68	0.17	.24**		
Mex Am margin	−0.23**	−0.45	−0.02	0.11	−.17**		
Masculinity ideology	−0.05**	−0.10	−0.01	0.20	−.18**		

Note. CI = confidence interval; *LL* = lower limit; *UL* = upper limit; familismo = the collective importance of family unity that emphasizes interdependence and solidarity; Mex Am margin = Mexican American marginalization.
*p < .05. **p < .01. ***p < .001.

Table 7.19 Sample Model Comparison Table

Table 1

Comparison of Fit Indices in Models Fitted to Simulated Data Across Longitudinal Mediation Model Types

Model	χ^2			RMSEA			AIC	BIC	ΔAIC	ΔBIC
	Value	df	p	Value	95% CI	p				
Simplex lagged	63.3	28	<.001	.044	[.030, .059]	.72	13,479	13,658	—	—
Simplex contemporaneous	58.0	29	.001	.040	[.024, .054]	.87	13,472	13,646	−7	−12
Latent growth	65.0	33	<.001	.039	[.025, .053]	.90	13,471	13,627	−8	−31
Modified latent change	26.2	33	.79	.000	[.000, .020]	>.99	13,432	13,588	−47	−70

Note. AIC and BIC differences are relative to the simplex lagged model. RMSEA = root-mean-square error of approximation; CI = confidence interval; AIC = Akaike information criterion; BIC = Bayesian information criterion.

Table 7.20 Sample Multilevel Model Comparison Table

Table 2

Model Parameters and Goodness of Fit for Linear and Quadratic Changes in Emotions by Behavior Type

Effect	Parameter	Positive emotions		Negative emotions	
		Model 1	Model 2	Model 1	Model 2
		Fixed effects			
Status at posttest, π_{0i}					
Intercept	γ_{00}	3.60*** (0.06)	3.34*** (0.12)	1.59*** (0.05)	1.82*** (0.11)
Prosocial behavior	γ_{02}		0.39*** (0.14)		−0.36** (0.13)
Self-focused behavior	γ_{03}		0.26 (0.17)		−0.16 (0.15)
Linear rate of change, π_{1i}					
Time	γ_{10}	−0.03 (.02)	−0.002 (0.05)	0.01 (0.02)	0.01 (0.04)
Prosocial behavior	γ_{11}		−0.06 (0.06)		0.02 (0.05)
Self-focused behavior	γ_{12}		0.001 (0.07)		−0.04 (0.06)
Quadratic rate of change, π_{2i}					
Time^2	γ_{20}	−0.02*** (0.01)	−0.001 (0.01)	0.02*** (0.01)	0.02 (0.01)
Prosocial behavior	γ_{21}		−0.03* (0.02)		0.01 (0.02)
Self-focused behavior	γ_{22}		−0.01 (0.02)		−0.01 (0.02)
		Random effects			
Variance components					
Level 1	σ_ϵ^2	0.52	0.52	0.51	0.51
Level 2	σ_0^2	1.34	1.31	1.02	1.00
	σ_1^2	0.040	0.040	.002	0.001
	σ_2^2	0.004	0.003	0.001	0.001
		Goodness of fit			
Deviance		6,703.18	6,692.50	6,424.12	6,413.91
$\Delta\chi^2$			10.68†		10.21
Δdf			6		6

Note. Standard errors are in parentheses. All *p* values in this table are two-tailed. In Model 1 (unconditional quadratic growth), the intercept parameter estimate (γ_{00}) represents the average positive or negative emotions score at posttest across the sample. In Model 2 (prosocial and self-focused behavior vs. control), the intercept parameter estimate (γ_{00}) represents the average positive or negative emotions score in the control condition at posttest, γ_{02} represents the difference at posttest between the prosocial behavior conditions and the control condition, and γ_{03} represents the difference at posttest between the self-focused behavior condition and the control condition. γ_{10} represents the average linear rate of change in the control condition, γ_{11} represents additional effects of prosocial behavior on linear rate of change, and γ_{12} represents additional effects of self-focused behavior on linear rate of change. Finally, γ_{20} represents the average quadratic rate of change in the control condition, γ_{21} represents additional effects of prosocial behavior on quadratic rate of change, and γ_{22} represents additional effects of self-focused behavior on quadratic rate of change. In all models, the intercept, linear slope (time), and quadratic slope (time^2) were free to vary.

†$p \le .10$. *$p < .05$. **$p < .10$. ***$p < .001$.

> Displaying values in parentheses sometimes saves space when they are not applicable to all portions of the table. In most tables, different indices should be presented in different rows or columns.

Table 7.21 Sample Confirmatory Factor Analysis Model Comparison Table

Table 2

Results of Confirmatory Factor Analysis for the Relationships Among Three Types of Intelligence

Model	χ^2	*df*	NFI	CFI	RMSEA
A: One-intelligence model[a]	10,994.664[***]	1539	.296	.326	.115
B: Two-intelligences model[b]	10,091.236[***]	1538	.354	.390	.109
C: Three-intelligences model[c]	8,640.066[***]	1536	.447	.494	.100

Note. Structural equation modeling was used for the analysis. NFI = normed fit index; CFI = comparative fit index; RMSEA = root-mean-square error of approximation.

[a] In Model A, all 57 items of social intelligence, emotional intelligence, and cultural intelligence were loaded onto one factor. [b] In Model B, the 21 items of social intelligence were loaded onto one factor, and the 16 items of emotional intelligence and the 20 items of cultural intelligence were loaded onto another factor. [c] In Model C, the 21 items of social intelligence were loaded onto one factor, the 16 items of emotional intelligence were loaded onto a second factor, and the 20 items of cultural intelligence were loaded onto a third factor.

[***]$p < .001$.

Table 7.22 Sample Qualitative Table With Variable Descriptions

Table 2

Master Narrative Voices: Struggle and Success and Emancipation

Discourse and dimension	Example quote
Struggle and success	
Self-actualization as a member of a larger gay community is the end goal of healthy sexual identity development, or "coming out"	"My path of gayness . . . going from denial to saying, 'well, this is it,' and then the process of coming out, and the process of just sort of looking around and seeing, well where do I stand in the world? And sort of having, uh, political feelings." (Carl, age 50)
Maintaining healthy sexual identity entails vigilance against internalization of societal discrimination	"When I'm, like, thinking of criticisms of more mainstream gay culture, I try to . . . make sure it's coming from an appropriate place and not, like, a place of self-loathing." (Patrick, age 20)
Emancipation	
Open exploration of an individually fluid sexual self is the goal of healthy sexual identity development	"[For heterosexuals] the man penetrates the woman, whereas with gay people, I feel like there is this potential for really playing around with that model a lot, you know, and just experimenting and exploring." (Orion, age 31)
Questioning discrete, monolithic categories of sexual identity	"LGBTQI, you know, and added on so many letters. It does start to raise the question about what the terms mean and whether . . . any term can adequately be descriptive." (Bill, age 50)

Table 7.23 Sample Qualitative Table Incorporating Quantitative Data

Table 1

Reasons Why Individuals Chose to Watch the Royal Wedding (N = 45)

Reason for interest	Example quote	Frequency, n (%)
Royal family and its history	"I love all things British. I studied abroad in the U.K. I also watched the weddings of Charles & Diana and Andrew & Fergie. I watched Diana's funeral. Watching William & Kate get married seemed like the natural thing to do."	16 (35.6)
	"I find the royal family and their practices and traditions fascinating. I am a big fan of tradition in any capacity (graduation ceremonies, weddings, etc.) and enjoy watching traditions older than our own country (the U.S.)."	
Fashion and pop culture	"When big pop culture things happen, I tend to want to watch so I'm 'in on it.' Also, when I was little my mom made us get up to watch Princess Diana get married, so it felt a little like tradition."	13 (28.9)
	"I was curious. Wanted to see her dress and how the other people who attended dressed. Like pomp and ceremony."	
Fairy tales and love stories	"I watched his mom and dad get married, watched him grow up. Plus I love a fairy tale that comes true. I believe in love and romance."	11 (24.4)
	"I am a romantic and think this is a great love story."	
To pass time/it was on TV	"I was at the airport and it was broadcasting on TV while I was waiting for my flight."	5 (11.1)
	"It was on CNN when I got up."	

Table 7.24 Sample Mixed Methods Table

Table 3

Integrated Results Matrix for the Effect of Topic Familiarity on Reliance on Author Expertise

Quantitative result	Qualitative result	Example quote
When the topic was more familiar (climate change) and cards were more relevant, participants placed less value on author expertise.	When an assertion was considered to be more familiar and to be general knowledge, participants perceived less need to rely on author expertise.	Participant 144: "I feel that I know more about climate, and there are several things on the climate cards that are obvious, and that if I sort of know it already, then the source is not so critical . . . whereas with nuclear energy, I don't know so much, so then I'm maybe more interested in who says what."
When the topic was less familiar (nuclear power) and cards were more relevant, participants placed more value on author expertise.	When an assertion was considered to be less familiar and not general knowledge, participants perceived more need to rely on author expertise.	Participant 3: "[Nuclear power], which I know much, much less about, I would back up my arguments more with what I trust from the professors."

Note. We integrated quantitative data (whether students selected a card about nuclear power or about climate change) and qualitative data (interviews with students) to provide a more comprehensive description of students' card selections between the two topics.

Figures

7.22 Principles of Figure Construction

All types of graphical displays other than tables are considered figures in APA Style. Ensure that all figures add substantively to readers' understanding and do not duplicate other elements of the paper. Also consider whether a figure is the best way to communicate the information. In some cases (particularly when quantitative information is being conveyed), a table may offer more precision than, say, a graph. If you focus on the principle of enhancing readers' understanding, other questions—for example, use of color, use of photographic images, or magnitude of cropping of a picture—should be relatively easy to resolve.

The standards for good figures are simplicity, clarity, continuity, and (of course) information value. A good figure

- augments rather than duplicates the text,
- conveys only essential information,
- omits visually distracting detail,
- is easy to read—its elements (e.g., type, lines, labels, symbols) are large enough to be seen and interpreted with ease,
- is easy to understand—its purpose is readily apparent,
- is carefully planned and prepared, and
- is consistent with and in the same style as similar figures in the same article.

For figures of all types, check that

- images are clear,
- lines are smooth and sharp,
- font is simple and legible,
- units of measurement are provided,
- axes are clearly labeled, and
- elements within the figure are labeled or explained.

Be certain, for instance, to distinguish between error bars and confidence intervals. When using confidence intervals, clearly specify the size of the interval (e.g., 95%); when using error bars, provide the label for the error (e.g., standard error of the mean) in the figure image or note. In addition, check all figures to ensure that

- sufficient information is given in the legend and/or note to make the figure understandable on its own (i.e., apart from the text),
- symbols are easy to differentiate, and
- the graphic is large enough for its elements to be discernible.

Even when using high-quality graphics software to construct figures, examine figures carefully and make any necessary adjustments to follow these guidelines.

7.23 Figure Components

The basic components of a prototypical figure are shown in Figure 7.1 and are summarized as follows:

- **number:** The figure number (e.g., Figure 1) appears above the figure in bold (see Section 7.24).
- **title:** The figure title appears one double-spaced line below the figure number in italic title case (see Sections 6.17 and 7.25).

Figure 7.1 Basic Components of a Figure

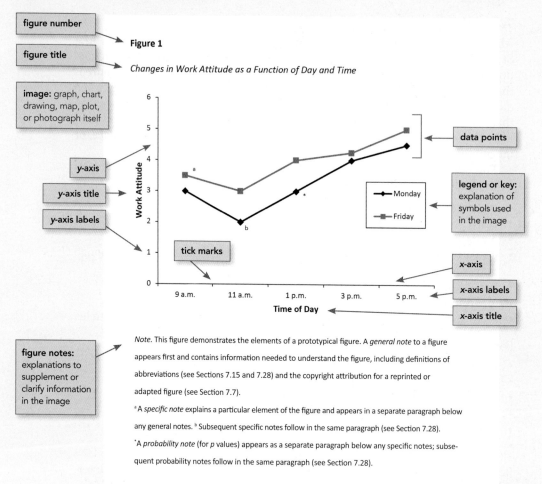

Figure 1

Changes in Work Attitude as a Function of Day and Time

[Labeled diagram with callout boxes pointing to a line graph:]

- figure number → Figure 1
- figure title → Changes in Work Attitude as a Function of Day and Time
- image: graph, chart, drawing, map, plot, or photograph itself
- y-axis
- y-axis title
- y-axis labels
- tick marks
- data points
- legend or key: explanation of symbols used in the image
- x-axis
- x-axis labels
- x-axis title
- figure notes: explanations to supplement or clarify information in the image

[Graph shows Work Attitude (y-axis, 0–6) vs Time of Day (x-axis: 9 a.m., 11 a.m., 1 p.m., 3 p.m., 5 p.m.) with lines for Monday and Friday.]

Note. This figure demonstrates the elements of a prototypical figure. A *general note* to a figure appears first and contains information needed to understand the figure, including definitions of abbreviations (see Sections 7.15 and 7.28) and the copyright attribution for a reprinted or adapted figure (see Section 7.7).

[a] A *specific note* explains a particular element of the figure and appears in a separate paragraph below any general notes. [b] Subsequent specific notes follow in the same paragraph (see Section 7.28).

[*] A *probability note* (for *p* values) appears as a separate paragraph below any specific notes; subsequent probability notes follow in the same paragraph (see Section 7.28).

- **image:** The image portion of the figure is the chart, graph, photograph, drawing, or other illustration itself (see Section 7.26).
- **legend:** A figure legend, or key, if present, should be positioned within the borders of the figure and explains any symbols used in the figure image (see Section 7.27).
- **note:** Three types of notes (general, specific, and probability) can appear below the figure to describe contents of the figure that cannot be understood from the figure title, image, and/or legend alone (e.g., definitions of abbreviations, copyright attribution). Not all figures include figure notes (see Section 7.28).

See Section 7.36 for sample figures.

7.24 Figure Numbers

Number all figures that are part of the main text (i.e., not part of an appendix or supplemental materials) using Arabic numerals—for example, Figure 1, Figure 2, and Figure 3. Assign the numbers in the order in which each figure is first mentioned in the text, regardless of whether a more detailed discussion of the figure occurs elsewhere in the paper. Write the word "Figure" and the number in bold and flush left (i.e., not indented or centered). Figures that appear in appendices follow a different numbering scheme (see Section 2.14).

7.25 Figure Titles

Give every figure a brief but clear and explanatory title; the basic content of the figure should be easily inferred from the title. Write the figure title in italic title case below the figure number and double-space the figure number and title. Avoid overly general and overly detailed figure titles (see Section 7.11).

7.26 Figure Images

The image part of the figure (e.g., graph, chart, diagram) should be saved in a resolution sufficient to allow for clear printing or viewing (see Section 7.4). Attend to the following considerations when creating images.

Size and Proportion of Elements. Each element in a figure must be large enough and sharp enough to be legible. Use a simple sans serif font (e.g., Arial, Calibri, Lucida Sans Unicode; see Section 2.19) within the image portion of the figure with enough space between letters to avoid crowding. Letters should be clear, sharp, and uniformly dark and should be sized consistently throughout the figure; the font size should be no smaller than 8 points and no larger than 14 points. As a general guideline, plot symbols should be about the size of lowercase letters that appear in a label within the figure. Also consider the weight (i.e., size, density) of each element in a figure in relation to that of every other element, and make the most important elements the most prominent. For example, curves on line graphs and outlines of bars on bar graphs should be bolder than axis labels, which should be bolder than the axes and tick marks.

Spelling, Capitalization, and Numbers Within Figure Images. Use title case for axis labels. Abbreviate the words "percentage" to "%" and "number" to "no." Words within figure images other than those on the axis labels or in the figure legend may be written in either title case or sentence case (see Section 6.17), depending on the contents of the figure. In general, labels, phrases, or words that serve as headings would be better set in title case, whereas other descriptive phrases, sentences, or paragraphs within a figure would be better set in sentence case. Numbers that appear in the image portion of a figure should be written as words or numerals according to the guidelines in Sections 6.32 to 6.39; however, it is permissible to use numerals for all numbers in a figure if this would be clearer or save space. Statistics, Greek letters, and units of measurement do not need to be defined in a figure note (see Section 7.15).

Shading. Limit the number of different shadings used in a single graphic. If different shadings are used to distinguish bars or segments of a graph, choose shadings that are distinct; for example, the best option to distinguish two sets of bars is no shading ("open") and black or gray ("solid"). If more than two shadings are needed, use patterns, again making sure that the patterns are distinct—for example, use no (open) shading, solid black or gray, and stripes for three shadings. If error bars or other information overlaps with shaded areas (e.g., double-sided error bars in a bar graph), ensure that the overlapping information can be clearly distinguished from the shading.

Color. Color can serve both communicative and decorative purposes in figures. Authors seeking publication should avoid the use of color except when it is necessary for understanding the material because of the relatively high cost of color reproduction for printed materials (authors may bear some of this cost; for APA journals guidelines, see http://on.apa.org/WDtxdW). For example, photographs, fMRI images, and gene staining results often use color. If color representation is not crucial for understanding and the article is to be published both in print and online, convert the figure to grayscale or consider placing the figure online as supplemental material. Some journals offer the option to publish a figure in color online and in grayscale in print at no cost; when using this option, ensure that the figure can still be understood even when it is printed in grayscale. It is the author's responsibility to ensure that the final representation is accurate. However, authors submitting a manuscript to an online-only journal may use color more liberally (e.g., colored bars rather than gray and white bars in a bar graph). Likewise, students preparing a figure for a course assignment may use color provided that the assignment will be delivered in a format that supports it.

When selecting colors for a figure, ensure that there is plenty of contrast so that people living with a color-vision deficiency (often referred to as "color blindness") or people who do not see color in a typical way can understand the information and tell the colors apart. Best practice is to use a contrast checker such as the free Colour Contrast Analyser (https://developer.paciellogroup.com/resources/contrastanalyser) to evaluate the contrast ratio and confirm that your content passes the standards for WCAG 2.0 AA or later.[2] Adequate contrast ratios ensure that the figure is not only accessible to readers with color-deficient vision but also understandable by all readers if the figure is printed or photocopied in grayscale. Another strategy to achieve adequate contrast is to use a pattern in combination with color so that the differentiation of elements does not rely on color alone (e.g., in a line graph, different lines may be in different colors and also of different styles, such as solid, dashed, and dotted). When many colors must be used and it is not possible to achieve high contrast among all of them, label colored areas directly in the image or use lines to connect the object to its label rather than placing the label in a legend, if possible, so that readers do not have to match colors in the figure to colors in the legend. See the APA Style website (https://apastyle.apa.org) for an example of how people with certain color-vision deficiencies see color and how the colors used in figures can be adjusted to accommodate them.

Gridlines and 3-D Effects. Avoid the use of gridlines in figures unless the gridlines will substantially aid readers in understanding the content, such as when many data points need to be compared across the x-axis. Likewise, avoid including 3-D effects for mere decoration (e.g., 3-D bar graphs) because they may make the figure more difficult to read. However, 3-D effects can be used to convey essential information (e.g., 3-D representations of stimuli).

---

[2] WCAG 2.0 refers to the Web Content Accessibility Guidelines, Version 2.0 (Web Accessibility Initiative, 2018).

Panels. The decision of whether to divide a figure into panels or create a separate figure for each panel will depend on the nature of the information being presented. Although panels help readers directly compare information, they also increase the density of the information being presented on the page; as always, prioritize clear communication when constructing any figure. If the figure includes multiple panels, it is optional to label them. If panels are unlabeled, refer to panels by their position (e.g., the top panel, the left panel, the middle panel). To label panels, assign each one a capital letter (e.g., A, B) and place the label at the top left of the panel. Refer to the panels as Panel A, Panel B, and so forth. In the main text, refer to a panel using the format "Figure 5A" or "Panel A of Figure 5." In the figure general note, explain each panel. See Figures 7.18 and 7.19 in Section 7.36 for examples of figures with labeled panels.

Citations in Figures. If a figure contains citations to other works, follow the formats described in Section 8.11. Use an ampersand (&) for the word "and" in all citations in figures to conserve space.

7.27 Figure Legends

A *legend* (also called a *key*) explains any symbols, line styles, or shading or pattern variants used in the image portion of the figure (see Figures 7.2–7.3 in Section 7.36 for examples). The legend is an integral part of the figure; therefore, its lettering should be of the same kind and proportion as that appearing in the rest of the figure. Capitalize words in the legend using title case (see Section 6.17). Only figures that have symbols, line styles, or shadings needing definition should include legends. When possible, place legends within or below the image instead of to the side to avoid having empty space around the legend.

7.28 Figure Notes

Figure notes contain information needed to clarify the contents of the figure for readers. As with tables, figures may have three kinds of notes: general, specific, and probability.

A general note should explain units of measurement, symbols, and abbreviations that are not included in the legend or defined elsewhere in the figure (see Section 7.15 for information on abbreviations and symbols that do not require definitions). Make certain that the symbols, abbreviations, and terminology in the note and legend match the symbols, abbreviations, and terminology in the figure, in other figures in the paper, and in the text. Explain the use of shading, color, and any other design element that carries meaning. Provide individual descriptions of panels for multipanel figures. If a graph includes error bars, explain in the image or general note whether they represent standard deviations, standard errors, confidence limits, or ranges; it is also helpful to provide sample sizes. Also include within the general note any acknowledgment that a figure is reprinted or adapted from another source (see Section 7.7). Place explanations of abbreviations and copyright attributions for reproduced figures last in the general note.

Position any superscripts for specific notes near the element being identified. It is preferable to report exact *p* values; however, if statistically significant values are marked with asterisks or daggers in the figure, explain them in a probability note (see Section 7.14). For guidelines on formatting figure notes, see Section 7.14.

7.29 Relation Between Figures

Similar figures or figures of equal importance should be of equal size and scale. Combine figures that are alike to facilitate comparisons between their content. For example, two line graphs with identical axes might be combined horizontally into a single figure, or multiple figures might be combined into one figure with multiple panels (see Section 7.26).

7.30 Photographs

Photographs are a type of figure with special considerations. Authors seeking publication must check publisher guidelines to ensure the photograph is submitted in the correct file type. Photographs may be printed in grayscale or in color, depending on the contents of the photograph and the venue of publication. Color photographs should include enough contrast to ensure that contents will be understandable if reproduced in grayscale. Photographs in most student papers can be in color and saved in any widely available photo format (see Section 7.26 for more information on the use of color in figures).

It is essential that photographic images be submitted at appropriate levels of resolution (as specified by the publisher). Because reproduction softens contrast and detail in photographs, starting with rich contrast and sharp detail will improve the final version of the image. The camera view and the lighting should highlight the subject and provide high contrast; a light or dark background can provide even more contrast. Photographs usually benefit from cropping to, for example, eliminate extraneous detail or center the image. However, when a photographic image has been altered in a manner beyond simple cropping and/ or adjustment for light levels, clearly indicate in a general note how the image has been altered. Ethical principles of publication forbid any intentional misrepresentation of images, just as fradulent data manipulation is forbidden. See Figure 7.17 in Section 7.36 for an example of a photograph as a figure.

If you photograph an identifiable person, obtain a signed release from that person to use the photograph in your paper (see Section 12.17); if the person is not identifiable, a release is not needed. If you took a photograph yourself, no citation or copyright attribution is required in the figure note. If you want to reprint or adapt a photograph from another source, you may need to obtain permission to use it in your paper because professional photographs are usually the property of the photographer. See Sections 12.14 to 12.18 for further information on reprinting or adapting photographs from other sources.

7.31 Considerations for Electrophysiological, Radiological, Genetic, and Other Biological Data

The presentation of electrophysiological, radiological, genetic, and other biological data presents special challenges because of the complexity of the data. Focus first on making sure your image accurately represents the data. It is essential that you identify in the general note how images were processed or enhanced and that you clearly label the images. Next, consider principles of clarity of representation, necessity for inclusion, and consistency among representations. If your figure contains more than one panel or your paper contains more than one figure, keep style and formatting elements as consistent as possible throughout (although specific features such as axis labels and scale units may vary). Biological and genetic data often must be presented in color for the information to be interpretable (see Section 7.26).

Carefully consider whether to include complex graphs and images in the main text or as supplemental materials. Use supplemental materials to present content that is better displayed online than in print or that can only be viewed online. For example, the dynamic spread of brain activation may be able to be displayed only through color video clips.

7.32 Electrophysiological Data

When presenting electrophysiological data, clear labeling of the image is essential; for example, in the presentation of event-related brain potential data, it is essential that the direction of negativity (i.e., negative up or down) be indicated as well as the scale of the response. Information that is necessary for proper interpretation of the image, such as number or placement of electrodes, should accompany the figure. See Figure 7.19 in Section 7.36 for an example of a figure presenting event-related brain potential data.

7.33 Radiological (Imaging) Data

When presenting brain images, clearly label each image and provide details needed to interpret the image in the figure note. When axial or coronal sections are being displayed, clearly label which hemisphere is the left and which is the right. When sagittal slices are displayed, clearly indicate whether each slice is of the right or the left hemisphere. When slices are shown, also present an image that indicates where in the brain the slices were taken to help orient readers. Specify the coordinate space in which the images have been normalized (e.g., Talairach, MNI).

Cutaway views of the brain that show activations interior to it can be useful if the cutaways clearly depict the tissue that has been excised. When activations are superimposed on a surface-rendered image of a brain, clear explanation of what activations are being shown should accompany the figure, particularly with regard to the depth of the activation that has been brought to the surface; the use of flattened surface images may help make the data clearer. When using color, use it consistently in all representations within the paper and clearly specify the color–scale mapping. Neuroimaging data almost always require extensive postacquisition processing, and details of the processing methods should accompany their display. Photomicrographs are often used in cell-staining and other types of imaging studies. When preparing photomicrographs, include a scale bar and staining materials information. See Figure 7.20 in Section 7.36 for an example of fMRI data in a figure.

7.34 Genetic Data

As with other displays of biological material, clear labeling of images enhances displays of genetic information (e.g., deletion patterns), be they of the physical map variety or the photographic stain variety. Present information concerning locations, distances, markers, and identification methods with the figure. Genetic data displays often contain much information; careful and circumscribed editing of the image and its legend can improve the communicative value of the figure. See Figure 7.21 in Section 7.36 for an example of a physical map of genetic material in a figure.

7.35 Figure Checklist

The figure checklist may be helpful to ensure that your figure communicates effectively and conforms to the style guidelines presented in this chapter.

Figure Checklist

☐ Is the figure necessary?

☐ Does the figure belong in the print and electronic versions of the article, or can it be placed in supplemental materials?

☐ Is the figure being submitted in a file format acceptable to the publisher?

☐ Has the file been produced at a sufficiently high resolution to allow for accurate reproduction?

☐ Are figures of equally important concepts prepared according to the same size and scale?

☐ Are all figures numbered consecutively with Arabic numerals in the order in which they are first mentioned in the text? Is the figure number bold and flush left?

☐ Are all figures called out or referred to in the text?

☐ Is the figure title brief but explanatory? Is it written in italic title case and flush left?

☐ Is the figure image simple, clear, and free of extraneous detail?

☐ Are all elements of the image clearly labeled?

☐ Are the magnitude, scale, and direction of grid elements clearly labeled?

☐ Has the figure been formatted properly? Is the font sans serif within the image portion of the figure and between 8 and 14 points in size?

☐ Are all abbreviations explained (with exceptions as noted in Section 7.15), as well as the use of special symbols?

☐ If the figure includes a legend to define symbols, line styles, or shading variants, does the legend appear within or below the image? Are words in the legend written in title case?

☐ Have all substantive modifications to photographic images been disclosed?

☐ Are the figure notes, if needed, in the order of general note, specific note, and probability note? Are the notes double-spaced and flush left and in the same font as the text of the paper?

☐ If all or part of a figure is reprinted or adapted, is there a copyright attribution? If permission was necessary to reproduce the figure, have you received written permission for reuse (in print and electronic forms) from the copyright holder and sent a copy of that written permission with the final version of your paper?

7.36 Sample Figures

Many types of figures can be used to present data to readers. The more common types of figures used in qualitative, quantitative, and mixed methods research are presented next. There are many variations and versions of each, and the distinctions among many of them are not clear. For situations not addressed here, consult similar published articles to see examples of current standards and practices and follow those examples.

- **graphs** (Figures 7.2–7.3): Graphs typically display the relationship between two quantitative indices or between a continuous quantitative variable (usually displayed on the *y*-axis) and groups of participants or subjects (usually displayed on the *x*-axis). Bar graphs (Figure 7.2) and line graphs (Figure 7.3) are two examples of graphs.
- **charts** (Figures 7.4–7.11): Charts generally display nonquantitative information with the use of enclosed boxes, squares, or circles connected with straight or curved lines or arrows. They are used to
  - show the flow of participants or subjects, such as through a study process (Figure 7.4) or in a randomized clinical trial (Figure 7.5; this is referred to as a CONSORT flow diagram; for a downloadable template, see the CONSORT website at http://www.consort-statement.org/consort-statement/flow-diagram);
  - illustrate models—for example, conceptual or theoretical models (Figure 7.6), structural equation models (Figure 7.7), confirmatory factor analysis models (Figure 7.8), and path models (Figure 7.9); and
  - illustrate qualitative (Figure 7.10) and mixed methods (Figure 7.11) research designs or frameworks.
- **drawings** (Figures 7.12–7.13): Drawings show information pictorially and can be used to illustrate, for example,
  - experimental setups (Figure 7.12) and
  - experimental stimuli (Figure 7.13).
- **maps** (Figure 7.14): Maps generally display spatial information—for example, geographic census information. This information often comes from government sources (e.g., the U.S. Census Bureau or the Centers for Disease Control and Prevention); to reprint or adapt tables or figures from these sources, see Section 12.16.
- **plots** (Figures 7.15–7.16): Plots present individual data points as a function of axis variables. Common types of plots include
  - the scatterplot (Figure 7.15), which is used to explore the relationship between two variables (e.g., a linear relationship may be indicated if the data points are clustered along the diagonal), and
  - multidimensional scaling (Figure 7.16), in which similar points or stimuli are presented close together in a multidimensional space and those that are dissimilar appear farther apart.
- **photographs** (Figure 7.17): Photographs (see Section 7.30) contain direct visual representations of information. They are often used to present infor-

mation that would be difficult to portray effectively with drawings, such as facial expressions or precise placement of stimuli in an environment.

Multipanel Figures. A multipanel figure may combine bar graphs, line graphs, histograms, and other figure types into one figure (see Figure 7.18 for an example; see also Section 7.26). Whether it is advisable to combine panels into one figure or to present panels as separate figures will depend on the size of the figures and the nature of the information being presented.

Figures for Electrophysiological, Radiological, Genetic, and Other Biological Data. A variety of figures are used to present biological data. These data include

- event-related potentials (Figure 7.19),
- fMRI data (Figure 7.20), and
- genetic maps (Figure 7.21).

Sample Figures

Figure 7.2 Sample Bar Graph

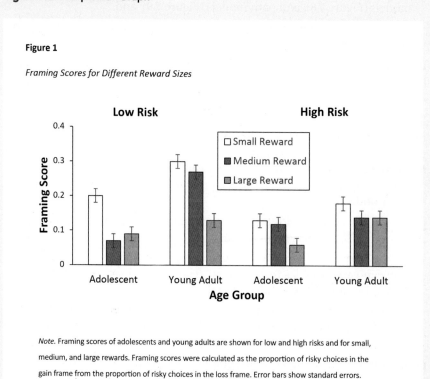

Figure 1

Framing Scores for Different Reward Sizes

Note. Framing scores of adolescents and young adults are shown for low and high risks and for small, medium, and large rewards. Framing scores were calculated as the proportion of risky choices in the gain frame from the proportion of risky choices in the loss frame. Error bars show standard errors.

Figure 7.3 Sample Line Graph

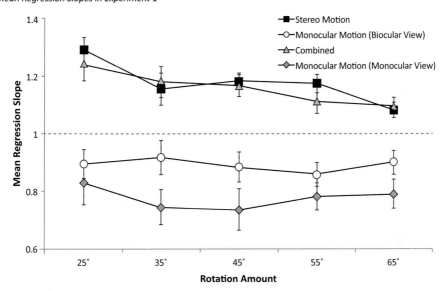

Figure 3

Mean Regression Slopes in Experiment 1

Note. Mean regression slopes in Experiment 1 are shown for the stereo motion, biocularly viewed monocular motion, combined, and monocularly viewed monocular motion conditions, plotted by rotation amount. Error bars represent standard errors. From "Large Continuous Perspective Change With Noncoplanar Points Enables Accurate Slant Perception," by X. M. Wang, M. Lind, and G. P. Bingham, 2018, *Journal of Experimental Psychology: Human Perception and Performance, 44*(10), p. 1513 (https://doi.org/10.1037/xhp0000553). Copyright 2018 by the American Psychological Association.

example copyright attribution for a reprinted figure when permission is not necessary

Figure 7.4 Sample Figure Showing the Flow of Participants Through a Study Process

Figure 1

Flowchart of Participant Decisions

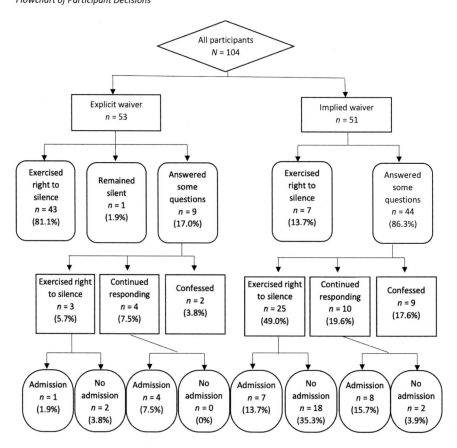

Note. Participant decisions regarding the right to silence, confessions, and admissions of incriminatory information are shown.

Figure 7.5 Sample CONSORT Flow Diagram

Figure 7.5

CONSORT Flowchart of Participants

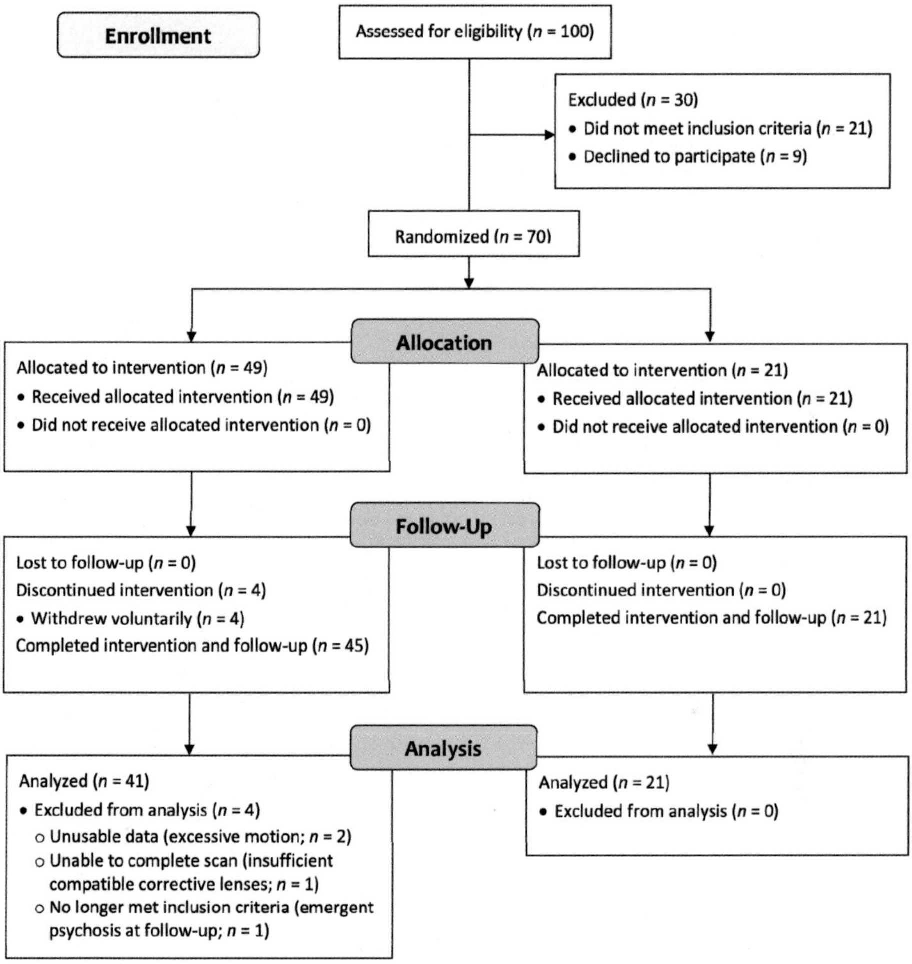

Figure 7.6 Sample Conceptual Model

Figure 2

Integrated Child and Youth Behavioral Health System

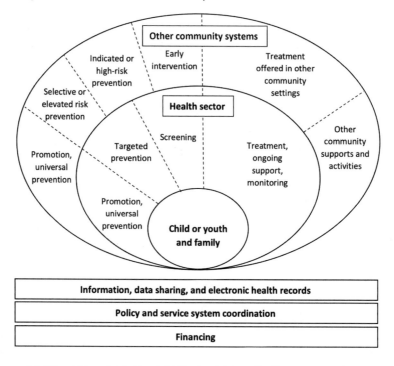

Note. This model shows that the integrated child and youth behavioral health system is centered on the child or youth and family and includes promotion; prevention; screening; and treatment, ongoing support, and monitoring both in the health sector and in other community systems. This structure is supported by information systems, policy and service system coordination, and financing, which are shown in rectangles beneath the ovals to illustrate this support.

Figure 7.7 Sample Structural Equation Model

Figure 2

Structural Equation Model Predicting Children's Cognitive Functioning

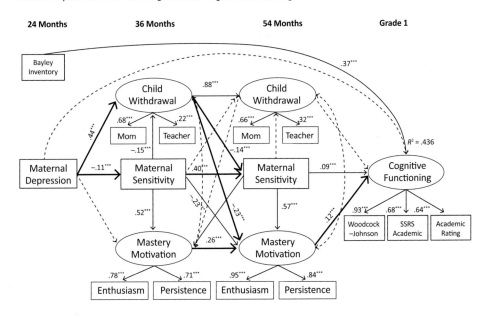

Note. This structural equation model predicts children's cognitive functioning from mothers' early depressive symptoms, with mediating effects of child withdrawal and mastery motivation. Statistics are standardized regression coefficients. Maternal depression is averaged across 6, 15, and 24 months. Dotted lines represent nonsignificant relations; bold lines represent significant indirect paths. SSRS = Social Skills Rating System.

**p < .01. ***p < .001.

Figure 7.8 Sample Confirmatory Factor Analysis Results Figure

Figure 2

Second-Order Confirmatory Factor Analysis for Study 2

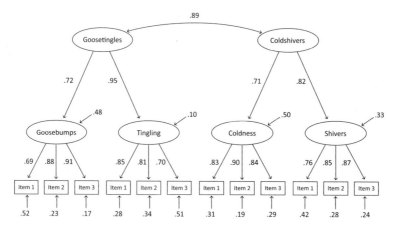

Note. Items are numbered in the order presented in the text. All modeled correlations and path coefficients are significant ($p < .05$).

Figure 7.9 Sample Path Model

Figure 1

Path Analysis Model of Associations Between ASMC and Body-Related Constructs

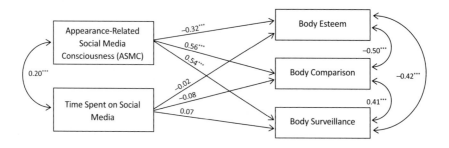

Note. The path analysis shows associations between ASMC and endogenous body-related variables (body esteem, body comparison, and body surveillance), controlling for time spent on social media. Coefficients presented are standardized linear regression coefficients.

***$p < .001$.

Figure 7.10 Sample Qualitative Research Figure

Figure 1

Organizational Framework for Racial Microaggressions in the Workplace

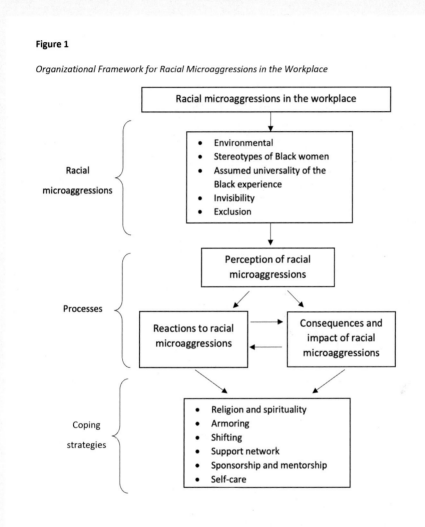

Figure 7.11 Sample Mixed Methods Research Figure

Figure 1

A Multistage Paradigm for Integrative Mixed Methods Research

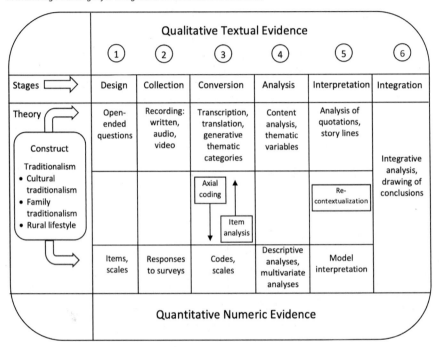

Note. Items are numbered in the order presented in the text. All modeled correlations and path coefficients are significant ($p < .05$).

Figure 7.12 Sample Illustration of Experimental Setup

Figure 7

Design of Experiment 7

Experiment 7A: Test
Who changed her choice?

Experiment 7B: Control
Who changed her choice?

Note. Children watched two puppets—one who knew about the unobservable set of stairs and one who did not—choose the tomato over the corn (high-cost choice in Experiment 7A and low-cost choice in Experiment 7B). Children then learned that one puppet changed her choice after opening the door and were asked to infer who that was.

Figure 7.13 Sample Illustration of Experimental Stimuli

Figure 4

Examples of Stimuli Used in Experiment 1

Note. Stimuli were computer-generated cartoon bees that varied on four binary dimensions, for a total of 16 unique stimuli. They had two or six legs, a striped or spotted body, single or double wings, and antennae or no antennae. The two stimuli shown here demonstrate the use of opposite values on all four binary dimensions.

Figure 7.14 Sample Map

Figure 1

Poverty Rate in the United States, 2017

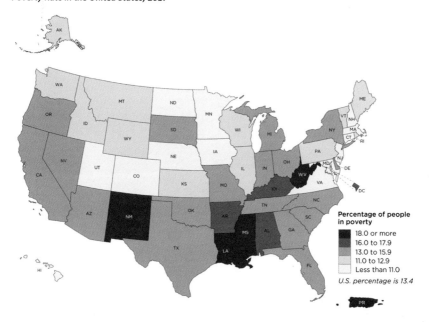

Note. The U.S. percentage does not include data for Puerto Rico. Adapted from 2017 *Poverty Rate in the United States*, by U.S.

Census Bureau, 2017 (https://www.census.gov/library/visualizations/2018/comm/acs-poverty-map.html). In the public domain.

example copyright attribution for an adapted figure in the public domain

Figure 7.15 Sample Scatterplot

Figure 2

Association Between Perceptual Speed and Empathic Pattern Accuracy for Happiness

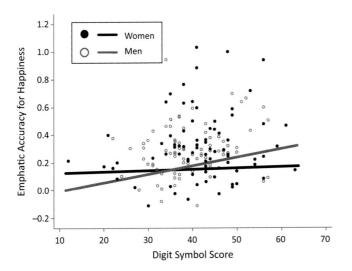

Note. Each dot represents an individual participant. Scores for empathic pattern accuracy for happiness were obtained in a zero-order multilevel model in which a target's self-reported happiness was the only predictor of a rater's perceptions (the estimate plotted on the *y*-axis is equivalent to β_{1i} in Equation 4). Among men, higher levels of digit symbol performance were associated with higher empathic pattern accuracy for happiness in daily life (gray line). Among women, the association was not significant (black line).

Figure 7.16 Sample Multidimensional Scaling Figure

Figure 3

Two-Dimensional Solution Derived From Multidimensional Scaling of Relatedness Scores

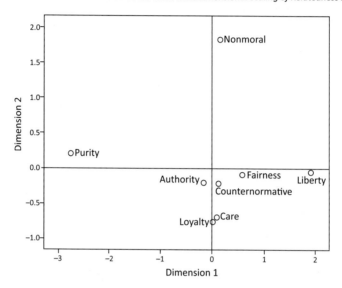

Note. Relatedness scores were defined as the mean likelihood judgment within category pairs. Violations of care, authority, fairness, and loyalty and counternormative actions are quite close to one another in the resultant two-dimensional space, whereas liberty violations, and especially purity violations and nonmoral actions, are more distant. Model stress was .08.

Figure 7.17 Sample Photograph

Figure 1

Example Scenes of Participant Response to Locations of Schema-Irrelevant Objects

Note. Top panel: A version of the kitchen scene using schema-irrelevant objects (walking boots, bath towel, and teapot) in unexpected locations (right side of the floor, rail beneath table, and stool, respectively). Middle panel: One of the possible test images (out of two) associated with the study image depicted in the top panel used in Study 1 (shift-to-expected condition). Bottom panel: Example participant response when the participant originally studied the image in the top panel in the recall task of Study 2. Schema-relevant objects in expected places at study are the metal pot and toaster; those in unexpected places are the microwave and teapot; those not present are the fruit bowl and paper towel roll.

Figure 7.18 Sample Complex Multipanel Figure

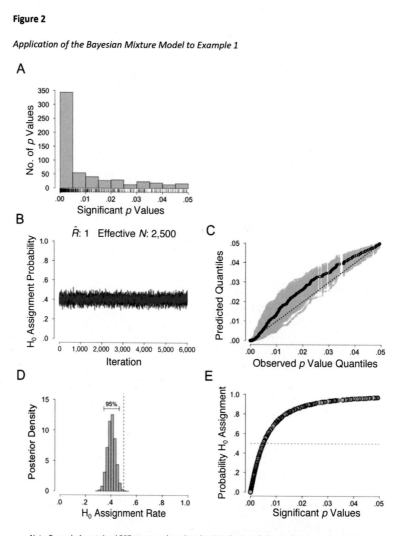

Figure 2

Application of the Bayesian Mixture Model to Example 1

Note. Example 1 contained 587 *t*-test *p* values. Panel A: Distribution of observed *p* values. Panel B: Trace plot of the Markov chain Monte Carlo chains for the H_0 assignment rate. Panel C: Q-Q plot for comparing the observed *p* value distribution with the posterior predictive distribution. Panel D: Posterior distribution of the H_0 assignment rate. Panel E: Individual H_0 assignment probabilities.

Figure 7.19 Sample Event-Related Potential Figure

Figure 1

Centroparietal Late Positive Potential as a Function of Trustworthiness

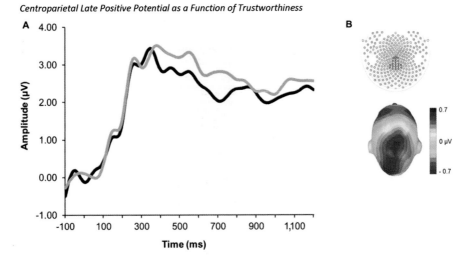

Note. Panel A: Event-related potential waveforms for untrustworthy (gray line) and trustworthy (black line) faces. Panel B: Display of the scalp topographies for untrustworthy as compared with trustworthy faces in the selected time window (500–800 ms).

Figure 7.20 Sample fMRI Figure

Figure 3

Brain Regions Sensitive to Ratings of Dehumanization, Liking, and Similarity to the Self

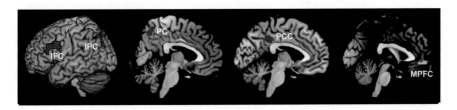

Note. Brain regions where activity is sensitive to parametric ratings of dehumanization (blue), liking (red), and similarity to the self (green) are shown. Dehumanization and liking are thresholded at $p < .05$, corrected; similarity is thresholded at $p < .001$, uncorrected. IFC = inferior frontal cortex; IPC = inferior parietal cortex; PC = precuneus; PCC = posterior cingulate cortex; MPFC = medial prefrontal cortex.

Figure 7.21 Sample Display of Genetic Material (Physical Map)

Figure 1

Microduplications Encompassing NF1 *for Subjects With Oligonucleotide Microarray Analysis*

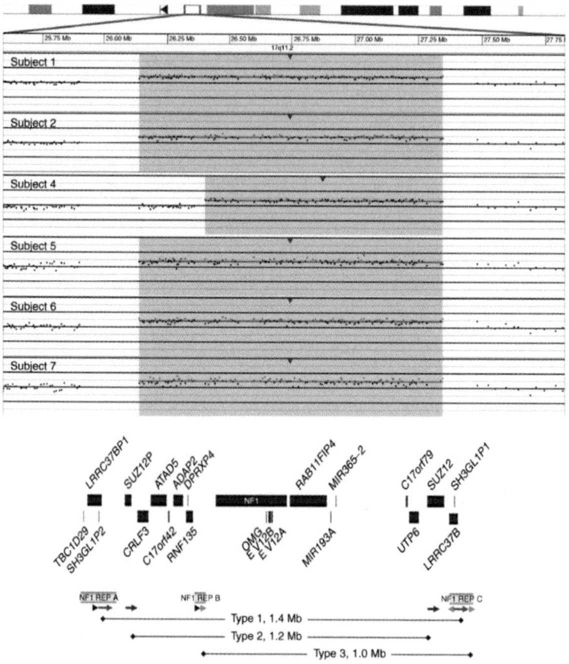

Note. Six subjects had microduplications encompassing *NF1*. For all microarray plots, probes are arranged on the *x*-axis according to physical mapping positions, with the most proximal 17q11.2 probes on the left and the most distal 17q11.2 probes on the right. Values along the *y*-axis represent log$_2$ ratios of subject: control signal intensities. Genes in the duplication region are shown underneath the plots as purple boxes. The yellow boxes represent the blocks of low-copy repeats in the region, with colored arrows corresponding to areas of homology among the low-copy repeats. Identical colors correspond to homologous regions. The sizes of the three types of *NF1* microdeletions are shown, with nonallelic homologous recombination between the red arrows leading to Type 1, brown to Type 2, and green to Type 3. From "*NF1* Microduplications: Identification of Seven Nonrelated Individuals Provides Further Characterization of the Phenotype," by K. J. Moles, G. C. Gowans, S. Gedela, D. Beversdorf, A. Yu, L. H. Seaver, R. A. Schultz, J. A. Rosenfeld, B. S. Torchia, and L. G. Shaffer, 2012, *Genetics in Medicine, 14*(5), p. 509 (https://doi.org/10.1038/gim.2011.46). Copyright 2012 by the American College of Medical Genetics and Genomics. Reprinted with permission.

8

WORKS CREDITED IN THE TEXT

Contents

8

WORKS CREDITED IN THE TEXT

Scientific knowledge represents the accomplishments of many researchers over time. A critical part of writing in APA Style is helping readers place your contribution in context by citing the researchers who influenced you.

In this chapter, we provide the ground rules for acknowledging how others contributed to your work. General guidance for in-text citation is presented first, including how to provide an appropriate level of citation and avoid plagiarism and self-plagiarism in your writing. Specific guidance for in-text citation follows, including formats for interviews, classroom and intranet sources, and personal communications; in-text citations in general; and paraphrases and direct quotations.

General Guidelines for Citation

8.1 Appropriate Level of Citation

Cite the work of those individuals whose ideas, theories, or research have directly influenced your work. The works you cite provide key background information, support or dispute your thesis, or offer critical definitions and data. Cite only works that you have read and ideas that you have incorporated into your writing. Cite primary sources when possible and secondary sources sparingly (see Section 8.6). In addition to crediting the ideas of others that you used to develop your thesis, provide documentation for all facts and figures that are not common knowledge. Both paraphrases (see Sections 8.23–8.24) and direct quotations (see Sections 8.25–8.35) require citations. If you reprint or adapt a table or figure (e.g., if you reproduce an image from the internet, even if it was free or in the Creative Commons) or reprint a long quotation or commercially copyrighted test item, you may also need to seek permission from the copyright holder and provide a copyright attribution (see Sections 12.14–12.18).

The number of sources you cite in your paper depends on the purpose of your work. For most papers, cite one or two of the most representative sources for each key point. Literature review papers, however, typically include a more exhaustive list of references, given that the purpose of the paper is to acquaint readers with everything that has been written on the topic.

Avoid both undercitation and overcitation. Undercitation can lead to plagiarism (see Section 8.2) and/or self-plagiarism (see Section 8.3). Even when sources cannot be retrieved (e.g., because they are personal communications; see Section 8.9), you still need to credit them in the text (however, avoid using online sources that are no longer recoverable; see Section 9.37). Overcitation can be distracting and is unnecessary. For example, it is considered overcitation to repeat the same citation in every sentence when the source and topic have not changed. Instead, when paraphrasing a key point in more than one sentence within a paragraph, cite the source in the first sentence in which it is relevant and do not repeat the citation in subsequent sentences as long as the source remains clear and unchanged (see Section 8.24). When the author's name appears in the narrative, the year can be omitted in repeated citations under certain circumstances (see Section 8.16). Figure 8.1 provides an example of an appropriate level of citation.

8.2 Plagiarism

Plagiarism is the act of presenting the words, ideas, or images of another as your own; it denies authors or creators of content the credit they are due. Whether deliberate or unintentional, plagiarism violates ethical standards in scholarship (see APA Ethics Code Standard 8.11, Plagiarism). Writers who plagiarize disrespect the efforts of original authors by failing to acknowledge their contributions, stifle further research by preventing readers from tracing ideas back to their original sources, and unfairly disregard those who exerted the effort to complete their own work. Writers who try to publish plagiarized work face

Figure 8.1 Example of an Appropriate Level of Citation

Humor plays an important role in everyday life, from interacting with strangers to attracting mates (Bressler & Balshine, 2006; Earleywine, 2010; Tornquist & Chiappe, 2015). Some people, however, come up with funny and witty ideas much more easily than do others. In this study, we examined the role of cognitive abilities in humor production, a topic with a long past (e.g., Feingold & Mazzella, 1991; Galloway, 1994) that has recently attracted more attention (Greengross & Miller, 2011; Kellner & Benedek, 2016). Humor production ability is measured with open-ended tasks (Earleywine, 2010), the most common of which involves asking participants to write captions for single-panel cartoons (for a review, see Nusbaum & Silvia, 2017).

Note. The authors have provided citations to representative sources for each new idea in the text. Common knowledge (here, the idea that some people come up with funny ideas more easily than do others) does not require a citation.

rejection from publication and possible censure in their place of employment. Students who plagiarize may fail the assignment or course, be placed on academic probation, or be expelled from their institution (see also Section 1.17).

To avoid plagiarism, provide appropriate credit to the source whenever you do the following:

- paraphrase (i.e., state in your own words) the ideas of others (see Sections 8.23–8.24)
- directly quote the words of others (see Sections 8.25–8.35)
- refer to data or data sets (see Section 10.9)
- reprint or adapt a table or figure, even images from the internet that are free or licensed in the Creative Commons (see Sections 12.14–12.18)
- reprint a long text passage or commercially copyrighted test item (see Sections 12.14–12.18)

For most works, appropriate credit takes the form of an author–date citation (see Section 8.10). However, according to U.S. copyright law, authors who wish to reprint or adapt tables, figures, and images or to reprint long quotations or commercially copyrighted test items (see Section 12.15) must provide more comprehensive credit in the form of a copyright attribution (see Section 12.18) and may need permission from the copyright holder to use the materials (see Section 12.17).

The necessity for credit extends to the ideas of others as well. For example, authors should credit the originators of theories they refer to in their paper. If authors model a study after one conducted by someone else, the author of the original study should be given credit. If the rationale for a study was suggested in someone else's article, that person should be given credit. Given the free exchange of ideas, which is important to the health of intellectual discourse, authors may not be able to pinpoint exactly where the idea for their study originated. They should make their best effort to find and acknowledge the source(s), including any personal communications (see Section 8.9).

Although many cases of plagiarism are straightforward (e.g., passages of text copied from another source without attribution), other cases are more challenging to evaluate. Usually, using incorrect citations (e.g., misspelling an author's name, forgetting or mistyping an element in a reference list entry, or citing a source in the text that does not have a corresponding reference list entry) is not considered plagiarism if the error is minor and attributable to an editorial oversight rather than an intentional attempt to steal someone's ideas or obfuscate the origin of the information (Cooper, 2016). However, such errors may still result in deductions on an academic assignment or a request for revision of a manuscript submitted for publication.

Publishers and educators may use plagiarism-checking software (e.g., iThenticate, Turnitin) to identify cases in which entire papers have been copied, passages of specified lengths match, or a few words have been changed but content is largely the same (the latter is known as *patchwriting*; see Merriam-Webster, n.d.-a). However, human review is often necessary to determine whether plagiarism has actually taken place. Take careful notes as you research and write to keep track of and accurately cite your sources. Check your work carefully to ensure that you acknowledge the words and ideas of others with citations in the text that have corresponding reference list entries.

Unethical writing practices other than plagiarism are also prohibited. For example, it is unethical to fabricate citations and/or reference list entries. This practice gives the appearance of properly credited sources, but the sources are fictitious or untraceable; the author may have made up the information as well as the sources, or the information may come from real works that have not been credited. Likewise, *contract cheating*, in which students hire another person to write a paper for them, is unethical. Even when the resulting work is original (i.e., not plagiarized), these students still take credit for work that they did not do themselves, which violates academic integrity policies, honor codes, and ethics codes.

8.3 Self-Plagiarism

Self-plagiarism is the presentation of your own previously published work as original; like plagiarism, self-plagiarism is unethical. Self-plagiarism deceives readers by making it appear that more information is available on a topic than really exists. It gives the impression that findings are more replicable than is the case or that particular conclusions are more strongly supported than is warranted by the evidence. It may lead to copyright violations if you publish the same work with multiple publishers (sometimes called *duplicate publication*; see Section 1.16).

Some institutions may consider it self-plagiarism if a student submits a paper written for one class to complete an assignment for another class without permission from the current instructor; using the same paper in multiple classes may violate the academic integrity policy, honor code, or ethics code of the university. However, incorporating previous classwork into one's thesis or dissertation and building on one's own existing writing may be permissible; students who wish to do this should discuss their ideas with their instructor or advisor and follow their university's honor code, ethics code, or academic policies when reusing their previous work.

In specific circumstances, authors may wish to duplicate their previously used words without quotation marks or citation (e.g., in describing the details of an instrument or an analytic approach), feeling that extensive self-referencing is undesirable or awkward and that rewording may lead to inaccuracies. When the duplicated material is limited in scope, this approach is permissible.

When the duplication is more extensive, authors should cite the source of the duplicated material. What constitutes the maximum acceptable length of duplicated material is difficult to define but must conform to legal notions of fair use (see Section 12.17). General guidelines for using an acceptable amount of duplicated material are as follows:

- Ensure that the core of the new document constitutes an original contribution to knowledge in that
  - only the amount of previously published material necessary to understand that contribution is included and
  - the material appears primarily in the discussion of theory and methodology.
- Place all duplicated material in a single paragraph or a few paragraphs, when feasible, with a citation at the beginning or end of each paragraph. Introduce the duplicated material with a phrase such as "as I have previously discussed." Do not use quotation marks or block quotation formatting around your own duplicated material.

- When you reanalyze your own previously published data, such as in a large-scale, longitudinal, or multidisciplinary project, provide sufficient information about the project so that readers can evaluate the current report but do not repeat every detail of the design and method. Find a balance that involves referring readers to the earlier work using citations.

If a manuscript will receive masked review (see Section 12.7), you may need to conceal references to your previous work until the manuscript is ready for publication. To conceal your previous work, omit the relevant entries from the reference list and indicate in the text where citations will be reinstated after the review process by including "citation omitted," or similar, in parentheses.

An exception to the prohibition against self-plagiarism is publishing a work of limited circulation in a venue of wider circulation. For example, authors may publish their doctoral dissertation or master's thesis in whole or in part in one or more journal articles. In such cases, authors would not cite their dissertation or thesis in the article text but rather acknowledge in the author note that the work was based on their dissertation or thesis (see Section 2.7). Similarly, an article based on research the authors described in an abstract published in a conference program or proceeding does not usually constitute duplicate publication; the author should acknowledge previous presentation of the research in the article's author note (see the author note of the sample professional paper in Chapter 2 as an example). Seek clarification from the journal editor or course instructor if you are concerned about duplicate publication or self-plagiarism.

8.4 Correspondence Between Reference List and Text

APA Style uses the author–date citation system (see Section 8.10), in which a brief in-text citation directs readers to a full reference list entry. Each work cited in the text must appear in the reference list, and each work in the reference list must be cited in the text. Ensure that the spelling of author names and the publication dates in the reference list entries match those in the in-text citations. The date element of a reference list entry may include the month, season, and/or day in addition to the year; however, the corresponding in-text citation includes only the year (see, e.g., Example 15 in Chapter 10).

There are a few exceptions to these guidelines:

- Personal communications, which are unrecoverable sources, are cited in the text only (see Section 8.9).
- General mentions of whole websites or periodicals (see Section 8.22) and common software and apps (see Section 10.10) in the text do not require a citation or reference list entry.
- The source of an epigraph does not usually appear in the reference list (see Section 8.35).
- Quotations from your research participants can be presented and discussed in the text but do not need citations or reference list entries (see Section 8.36).
- References included in a meta-analysis, which are marked with an asterisk in the reference list, may be cited in the text (or not) at the author's discretion (see Section 9.52).

8.5 Use of the Published Version or Archival Version

Multiple versions of the same work might coexist on the internet, and you should cite the version of the work you used. Ideally, use and cite the final, published version of a work (see Chapter 10, Examples 1–3). However, if you used the advance online version (see Chapter 10, Example 7), the in-press version (see Chapter 10, Example 8), or the final peer-reviewed manuscript accepted for publication (but before it was typeset or copyedited; see Chapter 10, Example 73), cite that version. The final peer-reviewed manuscript as accepted for publication might be available from a variety of places, including a personal website, an employer's server, an institutional repository, a reference manager, or an author social network.

Informally published works, such as those in a preprint archive (e.g., PsyArXiv) or an institutional repository or database (e.g., ERIC), can also be cited (see Chapter 10, Examples 73–74) when these are the version used. Draft manuscripts (unpublished, in preparation, or submitted) can be cited when the draft is the most current version of the work (see Chapter 10, Examples 70–72). When you cite a draft manuscript, in-press article, advance online publication, or informally published work in your paper, ensure you have the most up-to-date publication information for these works and update the reference list entry if necessary before you submit your paper. Publishers label advance online publications in various ways (e.g., "online first publication," "advance online publication," "epub ahead of print"); standardize this label to "advance online publication" for an APA Style reference list entry (see Chapter 10, Example 7).

8.6 Primary and Secondary Sources

In scholarly work, a *primary source* reports original content; a *secondary source* refers to content first reported in another source. Cite secondary sources sparingly—for instance, when the original work is out of print, unavailable, or available only in a language that you do not understand. If possible, as a matter of good scholarly practice, find the primary source, read it, and cite it directly rather than citing a secondary source. For example, rather than citing an instructor's lecture or a textbook or encyclopedia that in turn cites original research, find, read, and cite the original research directly (unless an instructor has directed you to do otherwise).

When citing a secondary source, provide a reference list entry for the secondary source that you used. In the text, identify the primary source and then write "as cited in" the secondary source that you used. If the year of publication of the primary source is known, also include it in the text. For example, if you read a work by Lyon et al. (2014) in which Rabbitt (1982) was cited, and you were unable to read Rabbitt's work yourself, cite Rabbitt's work as the original source, followed by Lyon et al.'s work as the secondary source. Only Lyon et al.'s work appears in the reference list.

(Rabbitt, 1982, as cited in Lyon et al., 2014)

If the year of the primary source is unknown, omit it from the in-text citation.

Allport's diary (as cited in Nicholson, 2003)

Works Requiring Special Approaches to Citation

8.7 Interviews

An *interview* is a dialogue or an exchange of information between people. Interviews used as sources can be classified into three categories: published interviews, personal interviews, and research participant interviews.

- **Published interviews** appear in a variety of places—for example, in a magazine, newspaper, recorded radio broadcast, podcast episode, YouTube video, TV show, or transcript of a video or audio recording. To cite a published interview, follow the format for the reference type (e.g., magazine article, podcast episode, radio broadcast; see Chapter 10, Examples 15 and 95, for interviews published in a magazine article and a digital archive, respectively). The person being interviewed will not necessarily appear in the author element of the reference; when this is case, integrate the person's name into the narrative of the sentence if desired (see Chapter 10, Example 88).

- **Personal interviews** are those you conduct as a means of obtaining information to support a key point in your paper (e.g., an email to an author inquiring about their published work). Because readers cannot recover this type of interview, cite it as a personal communication (see Section 8.9).

- **Research participant interviews** are those you conducted as part of your methodology. They do not require a citation in APA Style because you do not cite your own work in the paper in which it is being first reported. However, information gathered from research participant interviews can be presented and discussed in a paper according to the guidelines in Section 8.36.

8.8 Classroom or Intranet Resources

Some works are recoverable only by certain audiences, which determines how they are cited. For example, a student writing a paper for a course assignment might cite works from the classroom website or learning management system (LMS; e.g., Canvas, Blackboard, Brightspace, Moodle, Sakai), or an employee might cite resources from the company intranet when writing an internal company report. These sources are recoverable by the instructor and fellow students or by other employees of the company but not the general public.

When the audience you are writing for can retrieve the works you used, cite the works using the formats shown in Chapter 10, which are organized according to reference group and category. For example, to cite a recorded lecture or PowerPoint presentation available from a classroom website or LMS for a student assignment, follow the format shown in Chapter 10, Example 102. The source element of these references includes the name of the classroom website or LMS and the URL (which for sites requiring users to log in should be the homepage or login page URL). Likewise, for a report on a company intranet, follow the report formats shown in Section 10.4. However, if the work is for professional publication or intended for a wider audience who will not have access to these sources, cite the sources as personal communications (see Section 8.9).

8.9 Personal Communications

Works that cannot be recovered by readers (i.e., works without a source element; see Section 9.4) are cited in the text as *personal communications*. Personal communications include emails, text messages, online chats or direct messages, personal interviews, telephone conversations, live speeches, unrecorded classroom lectures, memos, letters, messages from nonarchived discussion groups or online bulletin boards, and so on.

Use a personal communication citation only when a recoverable source is not available. For example, if you learned about a topic via a classroom lecture, it would be preferable to cite the research on which the instructor based the lecture. However, if the lecture contained original content not published elsewhere, cite the lecture as a personal communication. When communications are recoverable only in an archive (e.g., a presidential library), cite them as archival materials (see the APA Style website at https://apastyle.apa.org for more). Do not use a personal communication citation for quotes or information from participants whom you interviewed as part of your own original research (see Section 8.36).

Citing Personal Communications in the Text. Because readers cannot retrieve the information in personal communications, personal communications are not included in the reference list; they are cited in the text only. Give the initial(s) and surname of the communicator, and provide as exact a date as possible, using the following formats:

> *Narrative citation:* E.-M. Paradis (personal communication, August 8, 2019)
> *Parenthetical citation:* (T. Nguyen, personal communication, February 24, 2020)

Citing Traditional Knowledge or Oral Traditions of Indigenous Peoples. The manner of citing Traditional Knowledge or Oral Traditions (other terms are "Traditional Stories" and "Oral Histories") of Indigenous Peoples varies depending on whether and how the information has been recorded—only certain cases use a variation of the personal communication citation. If the information has been recorded and is recoverable by readers (e.g., video, audio, interview transcript, book, article), cite it in the text and include a reference list entry in the correct format for that type of source (see Section 10.12, Example 90, for a recording on YouTube; see Section 10.13, Example 95, for a recorded interview).

Examine published works carefully (especially older works) to ensure that the information about Indigenous Peoples is accurate and appropriate to share before citing those works. Likewise, work closely with Indigenous people to ensure that material is appropriate to publish (e.g., some stories are told only at certain times of year or by certain people and may not be appropriate to publish in a journal article) and that your wording accurately mirrors and maintains the integrity of their perspectives (see Younging, 2018, for more on the nature of collaboration with Indigenous people). Likewise, because Indigenous cultural heritage belongs to Indigenous Peoples in perpetuity, matters concerning copyright and authorship may arise depending on the scope and nature of the material being presented (see Younging, 2018, for more).

Capitalize most terms related to Indigenous Peoples. These include names of specific groups (e.g., Cherokee, Cree, Ojibwe) and words related to Indigenous culture (e.g., Creation, the Creator, Elder, Oral Tradition, Traditional Knowledge, Vision Quest). The capitalization is intentional and demonstrates respect for Indigenous perspectives (for more, see *International Journal of Indigenous Health*, n.d.; Younging, 2018).

To describe Traditional Knowledge or Oral Traditions that are not recorded (and therefore are not recoverable by readers), provide as much detail in the in-text citation as is necessary to describe the content and to contextualize the origin of the information. Because there is no recoverable source, a reference list entry is not used.

If the purpose of your paper is to present the Oral History of one or more of your research participants, follow the guidelines in Section 8.36 for including quotations from research participants. If the paper is published, this Oral History then becomes part of the recorded scholarly literature and can thus be cited by others using standard formats.

If you spoke with an Indigenous person directly to learn information (but they were not a research participant), use a variation of the personal communication citation: Provide the person's full name and the nation or specific Indigenous group to which they belong, as well as their location or other details about them as relevant, followed by the words "personal communication," and the date of the communication. Provide an exact date of correspondence if available; if correspondence took place over a period of time, provide a more general date or a range of dates. (The date refers to when you consulted with the person, not to when the information originated.) Ensure that the person agrees to have their name included in your paper and confirms the accuracy and appropriateness of the information you present.

> We spoke with Anna Grant (Haida Nation, lives in Vancouver, British Columbia, Canada, personal communication, April 2019) about traditional understandings of the world by First Nations Peoples in Canada. She described . . .

If you are an Indigenous person and are sharing your own experiences or the previously unrecorded Traditional Knowledge or Oral Tradition of your people, describe yourself in the text (e.g., what nation you belong to, where you live) to contextualize the origin of the information you are sharing. Do not use a personal communication citation or provide a reference list entry because you do not need to cite personal information. It is often useful to collaborate with other Indigenous people to address any questions that may arise. For more on the terms to use when describing Indigenous Peoples, see Section 5.7.

In-Text Citations

8.10 Author–Date Citation System

Use the *author–date citation system* to cite references in the text in APA Style. In this system, each work used in a paper has two parts: an in-text citation and a corresponding reference list entry (see Figure 8.2). The in-text citation appears within the body of the paper (or in a table, figure, footnote, or appendix) and

Figure 8.2 Correspondence Between a Reference List Entry and an In-Text Citation

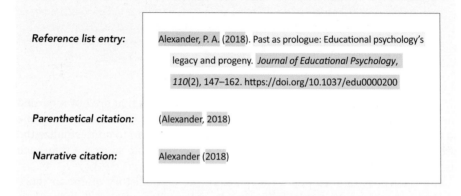

Reference list entry: Alexander, P. A. (2018). Past as prologue: Educational psychology's

legacy and progeny. *Journal of Educational Psychology,*

110(2), 147–162. https://doi.org/10.1037/edu0000200

Parenthetical citation: (Alexander, 2018)

Narrative citation: Alexander (2018)

Note. The four elements of a reference list entry include the author (in purple), the date (in blue), the title (in yellow), and the source (in green). The in-text citations that correspond to this reference include the last name of the author and year of publication, which match the information in the reference list entry.

briefly identifies the cited work by its author and date of publication. This in-text citation enables readers to locate the corresponding entry in the alphabetical reference list at the end of the paper. Each reference list entry provides the author, date, title, and source of the work cited in the paper and enables readers to identify and retrieve the work (see Chapter 9 for how to create and order reference list entries).

In an in-text citation, provide the surname(s) of the author(s) or the name(s) of the group author(s). Do not include suffixes such as "Jr." in the in-text citation. (For authors with only one name or only a username, see Section 9.8.) The list of authors in an in-text citation may be shortened in certain cases (for individual authors, see Section 8.17; for group authors, see Section 8.21). To create an in-text citation for a work with an unknown or anonymous author, see Section 8.14.

The date in the in-text citation should match the date in the reference list entry. Use only the year in the in-text citation, even if the reference list entry contains a more specific date (e.g., year, month, and day). For works with no date, use "n.d." in the in-text citation (see also Section 9.17); for works that have been accepted for publication but have not yet been published, use "in press." Do not use phrases like "in progress" for draft manuscripts; instead, use the year the draft was written (see Section 10.8).

Each in-text citation must correspond to only one reference list entry. Avoid ambiguity when abbreviating the list of authors (see Sections 8.17 and 8.21), when multiple works have the same author(s) and date (see Section 8.19), and when multiple first authors share the same surname (see Section 8.20).

8.11 Parenthetical and Narrative Citations

In-text citations have two formats: parenthetical and narrative. In parenthetical citations, the author name and publication date (or equivalent information; see Section 9.12) appear in parentheses. In narrative citations, this information is incorporated into the text as part of the sentence.

Parenthetical Citation. Both the author and the date, separated by a comma, appear in parentheses for a parenthetical citation. A parenthetical citation can appear within or at the end of a sentence. When a parenthetical citation is at the end of a sentence, put the period or other end punctuation after the closing parenthesis.

> Falsely balanced news coverage can distort the public's perception of expert consensus on an issue (Koehler, 2016).

- If other text appears with the parenthetical citation, use commas around the year.

> (see Koehler, 2016, for more detail)

- When text and a citation appear together in parentheses, use a semicolon to separate the citation from the text; do not use parentheses within parentheses.

> (e.g., falsely balanced news coverage; Koehler, 2016)

Narrative Citation. The author appears in running text and the date appears in parentheses immediately after the author name for a narrative citation.

> Koehler (2016) noted the dangers of falsely balanced news coverage.

- In rare cases, the author and date might both appear in the narrative. In this case, do not use parentheses.

> In 2016, Koehler noted the dangers of falsely balanced news coverage.

8.12 Citing Multiple Works

When citing multiple works parenthetically, place the citations in alphabetical order, separating them with semicolons. Listing both parenthetical in-text citations and reference list entries in alphabetical order helps readers locate and retrieve works because they are listed in the same order in both places.

> (Adams et al., 2019; Shumway & Shulman, 2015; Westinghouse, 2017)

- Arrange two or more works by the same authors by year of publication. Place citations with no date first, followed by works with dates in chronological order; in-press citations appear last. Give the authors' surnames once; for each subsequent work, give only the date.

> (Department of Veterans Affairs, n.d., 2017a, 2017b, 2019)
> Zhou (n.d., 2000, 2016, in press)

- In the case of multiple works in which some author names have been abbreviated to "et al." (see Section 8.17), place the citations in chronological order (regardless of the order in which they appear in the reference list).

> (Carraway et al., 2013, 2014, 2019)

- To highlight the work(s) most directly relevant to your point in a given sentence, place those citations first within parentheses in alphabetical order and then insert a semicolon and a phrase, such as "see also," before the first of the remaining citations, which should also be in alphabetical order. This strategy allows authors to emphasize, for example, the most recent or most important research on a topic, which would not be reflected by alphabetical order alone.

> (Sampson & Hughes, 2020; see also Augustine, 2017; Melara et al., 2018; Pérez, 2014)

- Readers may find a long string of citations difficult to parse, especially if they are using assistive technology such as a screen reader; therefore, include only those citations needed to support your immediate point (for more on appropriate level of citation, see Section 8.1).

- If multiple sources are cited within the narrative of a sentence, they can appear in any order.

  Suliman (2018), Gutiérrez (2012, 2017), and Medina and Reyes (2019) examined . . .

8.13 Citing Specific Parts of a Source

To cite a specific part of a source, provide an author–date citation for the work plus information about the specific part. There are many possible parts to cite, including

- pages, paragraphs, sections, tables, figures, supplemental materials, or footnotes from an article, book, report, webpage, or other work;

- chapters, forewords, or other sections of authored books;

- time stamps of videos or audiobooks; and

- slide numbers in PowerPoint presentations.

For religious and classical works with canonically numbered parts common across editions (e.g., books, chapters, verses, lines, cantos), cite the part instead of a page number (see Section 9.42).

  (Centers for Disease Control and Prevention, 2019, p. 10)
  (Shimamura, 2017, Chapter 3)
  (Armstrong, 2015, pp. 3–17)
  (Shadid, 2020, paras. 2–3)
  (Kovačič & Horvat, 2019, Table 1)
  (Thompson, 2020, Slide 7)
  (Beck Institute for Cognitive Behavior Therapy, 2012, 1:30:40)
  (*King James Bible*, 1769/2017, 1 Cor. 13:1)
  (Aristotle, ca. 350 B.C.E./1994, Part IV)
  (Shakespeare, 1623/1995, 1.3.36–37)

In the reference list, provide an entry for the entire work (not only the part that you used).

It is possible to cite a specific part of a source whether you are paraphrasing (see Sections 8.23–8.24) or directly quoting (see Sections 8.25–8.27). For further guidance on quoting works without page numbers (e.g., webpages, websites, audiovisual works) and religious and classical works with canonically numbered sections, see Section 8.28.

8.14 Unknown or Anonymous Author

When the author of a work is not named, the author may be unknown (i.e., no author is listed on the work, as with a religious work) or identified specifically as "Anonymous." For works with an unknown author (see Section 9.12), include the title and year of publication in the in-text citation (note that the title moves to the author position in the reference list entry as well). If the title of the work is italicized in the reference, also italicize the title in the in-text citation. If the title of the work is not italicized in the reference, use double quotation marks around the title in the in-text citation. Capitalize these titles in the text using title case (see Section 6.17), even though sentence case is used in the reference list entry. If the title is long, shorten it for the in-text citation.

> **Book with no author:** (*Interpersonal Skills*, 2019)
> **Magazine article with no author:** ("Understanding Sensory Memory," 2018)

When the author of a work is overtly designated as "Anonymous" (see Section 9.12), "Anonymous" takes the place of the author name in the in-text citation.

> (Anonymous, 2017)

8.15 Translated, Reprinted, Republished, and Reissued Dates

References to translated, reprinted, republished, or reissued works (see Sections 9.39–9.41) contain two dates in the in-text citation: the year of publication of the original work and the year of publication of the translation, reprint, republication, or reissue. Separate the years with a slash, with the earlier year first (see Chapter 10, Example 29).

> Freud (1900/1953)
> (Piaget, 1966/2000)

8.16 Omitting the Year in Repeated Narrative Citations

In general, include the author and date in every in-text citation. If you need to repeat a citation (see Section 8.1), repeat the entire citation; do not, for example, include only a page number (the abbreviation "ibid." is not used in APA Style). The year can be omitted from a citation only when multiple narrative citations to a work appear within a single paragraph (see Figure 8.3 for an example).

Figure 8.3 Example of Repeated Narrative Citations With the Year Omitted

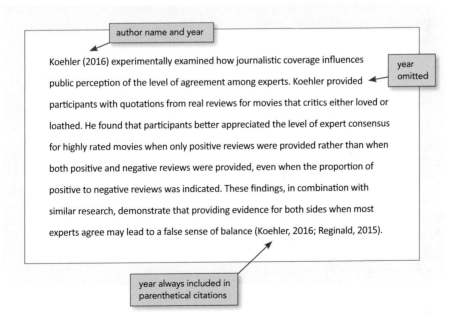

Once you have provided a narrative citation to a work in a paragraph, do not repeat the year in subsequent narrative citations in that same paragraph. Follow this guideline with each paragraph (i.e., include the year in the first narrative citation in a new paragraph). Include the year in every parenthetical citation.

However, if you cite multiple works by the same author or authors, regardless of the publication years, include the date in every in-text citation to prevent ambiguity. For example, if you cite Mohammed and Mahfouz (2017) and Mohammed and Mahfouz (2019), include the year with every citation, even when one of the references is cited multiple times in a single paragraph.

8.17 Number of Authors to Include in In-Text Citations

The format of the author element of the in-text citation changes depending on the number of authors and is abbreviated in some cases. See Table 8.1 for examples of the basic in-text citation styles.

- For a work with one or two authors, include the author name(s) in every citation.

- For a work with three or more authors, include the name of only the first author plus "et al." in every citation, including the first citation, unless doing so would create ambiguity (see Section 8.18).

In parenthetical citations, use an ampersand (&) between names for a work with two authors or before the last author when all names must be included to avoid ambiguity (see Section 8.18). In narrative citations, spell out the word "and."

(Jöreskog & Sörbom, 2007)
Eifert and Yildiz (2018)

In tables and figures, use an ampersand between names in both parenthetical and narrative citations.

The same guidelines apply when any of the authors are groups. For example, if a work is authored by three groups, the in-text citation would include the name of the first group plus "et al."

(American Educational Research Association et al., 2014)

Table 8.1 Basic In-Text Citation Styles

Author type	Parenthetical citation	Narrative citation
One author	(Luna, 2020)	Luna (2020)
Two authors	(Salas & D'Agostino, 2020)	Salas and D'Agostino (2020)
Three or more authors	(Martin et al., 2020)	Martin et al. (2020)
Group author with abbreviation First citation [a]	(National Institute of Mental Health [NIMH], 2020)	National Institute of Mental Health (NIMH, 2020)
Subsequent citations	(NIMH, 2020)	NIMH (2020)
Group author without abbreviation	(Stanford University, 2020)	Stanford University (2020)

[a] Define the abbreviation for a group author only once in the text, choosing either the parenthetical or the narrative format. Thereafter, use the abbreviation for all mentions of the group in the text (see Section 8.21).

8.18 Avoiding Ambiguity in In-Text Citations

Sometimes multiple works with three or more authors and the same publication year shorten to the same in-text citation form when the guidelines described in Section 8.17 are applied, which creates ambiguity. To avoid ambiguity, when the in-text citations of multiple works with three or more authors shorten to the same form, write out as many names as needed to distinguish the references, and abbreviate the rest of the names to "et al." in every citation. For example, two works have the following authors:

> Kapoor, Bloom, Montez, Warner, and Hill (2017)
> Kapoor, Bloom, Zucker, Tang, Köroğlu, L'Enfant, Kim, and Daly (2017)

Both these citations shorten to Kapoor et al. (2017). To avoid ambiguity when citing them both in your paper, cite them as follows:

> Kapoor, Bloom, Montez, et al. (2017)
> Kapoor, Bloom, Zucker, et al. (2017)

Because "et al." is plural (meaning "and others"), it cannot stand for only one name. When only the final author is different, spell out all names in every citation.

> Hasan, Liang, Kahn, and Jones-Miller (2015)
> Hasan, Liang, Kahn, and Weintraub (2015)

8.19 Works With the Same Author and Same Date

When multiple references have an identical author (or authors) and publication year, include a lowercase letter after the year (see Section 9.47). The year–letter combination is used in both the in-text citation and the reference list entry. Use only the year with a letter in the in-text citation, even if the reference list entry contains a more specific date.

> (Judge & Kammeyer-Mueller, 2012a)
> Judge and Kammeyer-Mueller (2012b)
> (Sifuentes, n.d.-a, n.d.-b)

8.20 Authors With the Same Surname

If the first authors of multiple references share the same surname but have different initials, include the first authors' initials in all in-text citations, even if the year of publication differs. Initials help avoid confusion within the text and help readers locate the correct entry in the reference list (see Section 9.48).

> (J. M. Taylor & Neimeyer, 2015; T. Taylor, 2014)

If the first authors of multiple references share the same surname and the same initials, cite the works in the standard author–date format.

Sometimes people publish under multiple names because of a name change (e.g., transgender authors, authors with a change in marital status). It is seldom relevant to note that two names refer to the same person. When a given name has changed, include initials with in-text citations only when the initials are different. If it is necessary to clarify that two names refer to the same person (e.g., to avoid confusion when reviewing an author's body of work), consult the person and respect their preferences in whether and how to address the name change. If it is necessary to clarify that two names refer to different people to avoid confusion, include the first name of the first author in the in-text citation: "Sarah Williams (2019) stated X, whereas Shonda Williams (2020) stated Y."

If multiple authors within a single reference share the same surname, the initials are not needed in the in-text citation; cite the work in the standard author–date format.

(Chen & Chen, 2019)

8.21 Abbreviating Group Authors

If a reference has a group author, the name of the group can sometimes be abbreviated—for example, "American Psychological Association" can be abbreviated to "APA." You are not obligated to abbreviate the name of a group author, but you can if the abbreviation is well-known, will help avoid cumbersome repetition, or will appear at least three times in the paper.

- As with other abbreviations (see Section 6.25), provide the full name of the group on first mention in the text, followed by the abbreviation.

- If the group name first appears in a narrative citation, include the abbreviation before the year in parentheses, separated with a comma.

  The American Psychological Association (APA, 2017) described . . .

- If the group name first appears in a parenthetical citation, include the abbreviation in square brackets, followed by a comma and the year.

  (American Psychological Association [APA], 2017)

- In the reference list entry, do not abbreviate the group author name. Instead, spell out the full name of the group as presented in the source.

  American Psychological Association. (2017, January). *Understanding and overcoming opioid abuse.* https://www.apa.org/helpcenter/opioid-abuse.aspx

- If several references have the same group author, introduce the abbreviation only once in the text.

- In the rare case that two different groups abbreviate to the same form (e.g., both the American Psychological Association and the American Psychiatric Association abbreviate to "APA") and you cite both groups in your paper, spell out each name every time to avoid confusion.

- If a work has three or more group authors, the in-text citation is also shortened as described in Section 8.17.

8.22 General Mentions of Websites, Periodicals, and Common Software and Apps

For a general mention of a website with no indication of particular information or a specific page from that site, no reference list entry or in-text citation is needed. Provide the name of the website in the text and include the URL in parentheses. For example, if you used a website to create a survey, mention the website in the text.

We created our survey using Qualtrics (https://www.qualtrics.com).

A variation of this technique is also used for general mentions of periodicals. For example, if you want to include the name of a journal you searched during a meta-analysis, provide the journal title (in italic) using title case.

> I searched the *Journal of Abnormal Psychology* for studies to include in the meta-analysis.

Common software and mobile apps are treated in a similar manner; in most cases, it is sufficient to mention the name of the program or app and the version used (if known) in the text, without providing an in-text citation or reference list entry (see Section 10.10). Likewise, for apparatuses, provide a reference for specialized products only (see Section 10.10).

Paraphrases and Quotations

8.23 Principles of Paraphrasing

A *paraphrase* restates another's idea (or your own previously published idea) in your own words. Paraphrasing is an effective writing strategy because it allows authors to summarize and synthesize information from one or more sources, focus on significant information, and compare and contrast relevant details. Published authors paraphrase their sources most of the time, rather than directly quoting the sources; student authors should emulate this practice by paraphrasing more than directly quoting. Use a professional tone when describing a concept, idea, or finding in your own words (see Section 4.7).

Cite the work you paraphrase in the text using either the narrative or parenthetical format (see Section 8.11).

> Avid readers of science fiction and fantasy books are more likely than readers of other genres to believe in futuristic scenarios—for example, that it will someday be possible to travel to other galaxies or power a car on solar energy (Black et al., 2018).

Although it is not required to provide a page or paragraph number in the citation for a paraphrase, you may include one in addition to the author and year when it would help interested readers locate the relevant passage within a long or complex work (e.g., a book).

> Webster-Stratton (2016) described a case example of a 4-year-old girl who showed an insecure attachment to her mother; in working with the family dyad, the therapist focused on increasing the mother's empathy for her child (pp. 152–153).

The guidelines in this section pertain to when authors read a primary source and paraphrase it themselves. If you read a paraphrase of a primary source in a published work and want to cite that source, it is best to read and cite the primary source directly if possible; if not, use a secondary source citation (see Section 8.6).

8.24 Long Paraphrases

A paraphrase may continue for several sentences. In such cases, cite the work being paraphrased on first mention. Once the work has been cited, it is not necessary to repeat the citation as long as the context of the writing makes it clear that the same work continues to be paraphrased (see Figure 8.4 for an example). The citation may be either parenthetical or narrative; if you select the narrative approach and repeat the author names in the narrative of subsequent sentences, the year of the work can often be omitted (see Section 8.16).

Figure 8.4 Example of a Long Paraphrase With a Single In-Text Citation

Velez et al. (2018) found that for women of color, sexism and racism in the workplace were associated with poor work and mental health outcomes, including job-related burnout, turnover intentions, and psychological distress. However, self-esteem, person–organization fit, and perceived organizational support mediated these effects. Additionally, stronger womanist attitudes—which acknowledge the unique challenges faced by women of color in a sexist and racist society—weakened the association of workplace discrimination with psychological distress. These findings underscore the importance of considering multiple forms of workplace discrimination in clinical practice and research with women of color, along with efforts to challenge and reduce such discrimination.

If the paraphrase continues into a new paragraph, reintroduce the citation. If the paraphrase incorporates multiple sources or switches among sources, repeat the citation so the source is clear (see Figure 8.5 for an example). Read your sentences carefully to ensure you have cited sources appropriately.

8.25 Principles of Direct Quotation

A *direct quotation* reproduces words verbatim from another work or from your own previously published work. It is best to paraphrase sources (see Sections 8.23–8.24) rather than directly quoting them because paraphrasing allows you to fit material to the context of your paper and writing style. Use direct quotations rather than paraphrasing when reproducing an exact definition (see example in Section 6.22), when an author has said something memorably or succinctly, or when you want to respond to exact wording (e.g., something someone said). Instructors, programs, editors, and publishers may establish limits on the use of direct quotations. Consult with your instructor or editor if you are concerned that you may have too much quoted material in your paper.

When quoting directly, always provide the author, year, and page number of the quotation in the in-text citation in either parenthetical or narrative format (see Section 8.11). To indicate a single page, use the abbreviation "p." (e.g., p. 25, p. S41, p. e221); for multiple pages, use the abbreviation "pp." and separate the page range with an en dash (e.g., pp. 34–36). If pages are discontinuous, use a comma between the page numbers (e.g., pp. 67, 72). If the work does not have page numbers, provide another way for the reader to locate the quotation (see Section 8.28).

Figure 8.5 Example of Repeated Citations Necessary to Clarify Sources

Play therapists can experience many symptoms of impaired wellness, including emotional exhaustion or reduced ability to empathize with others (Elwood et al., 2011; Figley, 2002), disruption in personal relationships (Elwood et al., 2011; Robinson-Keilig, 2014), decreased satisfaction with work (Elwood et al., 2011), avoidance of particular situations (Figley, 2002; O'Halloran & Linton, 2000), and feelings or thoughts of helplessness (Elwood et al., 2011; Figley, 2002; O'Halloran & Linton, 2000).

Note. In this passage, some works are cited multiple times to support multiple points. It is necessary to repeat these citations because different combinations of works support different ideas—the sources change and thus must be made clear to readers. If all ideas had the same sources, it would not be necessary to repeat the citations.

The format of a direct quotation depends on its length (fewer than 40 words vs. 40 words or more; see Sections 8.26–8.27). Regardless of quotation length, do not insert an ellipsis at the beginning and/or end of a quotation unless the original source includes an ellipsis. If you need to make changes to a direct quotation, see Sections 8.30 and 8.31. For other uses of quotation marks, such as when presenting verbatim instructions to participants or quotations from research participants, see Sections 6.7 and 8.36, respectively. To reproduce material that is already a direct quotation in the work you are citing, see Section 8.33.

8.26 Short Quotations (Fewer Than 40 Words)

If a quotation consists of fewer than 40 words, treat it as a short quotation: Incorporate it into the text and enclose it within double quotation marks. For a direct quotation, always include a full citation (parenthetical or narrative) in the same sentence as the quotation. Place a parenthetical citation either immediately after the quotation or at the end of the sentence. For a narrative citation, include the author and year in the sentence and then place the page number or other location information in parentheses after the quotation; if the quotation precedes the narrative citation, put the page number or location information after the year and a comma.

If the citation appears at the end of a sentence, put the end punctuation after the closing parenthesis for the citation. If the quotation includes citations, see Section 8.32; if the quotation includes material already in quotation marks, see Section 8.33. Place periods and commas within closing single or double quotation marks. Place other punctuation marks inside quotation marks only when they are part of the quoted material.

Short quotations can be presented in a variety of ways, as shown in Table 8.2.

Table 8.2 Examples of Direct Quotations Cited in the Text

Correct	Incorrect	Rationale
Effective teams can be difficult to describe because "high performance along one domain does not translate to high performance along another" (Ervin et al., 2018, p. 470).	Effective teams can be difficult to describe because "high performance along one domain does not translate to high performance along another." (Ervin et al., 2018, p. 470)	The period marking the end of a sentence should follow the citation, not precede it.
"Even smart, educated, emotionally stable adults believe superstitions that they recognize are not rational," as exemplified by the existence of people who knock on wood for good luck (Risen, 2016, p. 202).	"Even smart, educated, emotionally stable adults believe superstitions that they recognize are not rational (Risen, 2016, p. 202)," as exemplified by the existence of people who knock on wood for good luck.	The citation should be outside the quotation marks, not within them.
Biebel et al. (2018) noted that "incorporating the voice of students with psychiatric disabilities into supported education services can increase access, involvement, and retention" (p. 299).	Biebel et al. (2018) noted that "incorporating the voice of students with psychiatric disabilities into supported education services can increase access, involvement, and retention." (p. 299)	The period marking the end of the sentence should follow the page number, not precede it.
"Some people are hilarious, others are painfully unfunny, and most are somewhere in between," wrote Nusbaum et al. (2017, p. 231) in their exploration of humor.	"Some people are hilarious, others are painfully unfunny, and most are somewhere in between," (p. 231) wrote Nusbaum et al. (2017) in their exploration of humor.	The page number should be within the same parentheses as the year when the quotation precedes the narrative citation.
The item read, "What were the best aspects of the program for you?" (Shayden et al., 2018, p. 304).	The item read, "What were the best aspects of the program for you"? (Shayden et al., 2018, p. 304).	The question mark that ends the quotation should appear within the quotation marks.
In 2018, Soto argued that "more similar stimuli, such as those coming from the same modality, produce more configural processing" (p. 598).	In 2018, Soto argued that "more similar stimuli, such as those coming from the same modality, produce more configural processing" (Soto, 2018, p. 598).	It is not necessary to repeat the author and year within parentheses when they already appear in the narrative.

8.27 Block Quotations (40 Words or More)

If a quotation contains 40 words or more, treat it as a block quotation. Do not use quotation marks to enclose a block quotation. Start a block quotation on a new line and indent the whole block 0.5 in. from the left margin. If there are additional paragraphs within the quotation, indent the first line of each subsequent paragraph an additional 0.5 in. Double-space the entire block quotation; do not add extra space before or after it. Either (a) cite the source in parentheses after the quotation's final punctuation or (b) cite the author and year in the narrative before the quotation and place only the page number in parentheses after the quotation's final punctuation. Do not add a period after the closing parenthesis in either case.

> **Block quotation with parenthetical citation:**
> Researchers have studied how people talk to themselves:
>> Inner speech is a paradoxical phenomenon. It is an experience that is central to many people's everyday lives, and yet it presents considerable challenges to any effort to study it scientifically. Nevertheless, a wide range of methodologies and approaches have combined to shed light on the subjective experience of inner speech and its cognitive and neural underpinnings. (Alderson-Day & Fernyhough, 2015, p. 957)

Block quotation with narrative citation:

Flores et al. (2018) described how they addressed potential researcher bias when working with an intersectional community of transgender people of color:

> Everyone on the research team belonged to a stigmatized group but also held privileged identities. Throughout the research process, we attended to the ways in which our privileged and oppressed identities may have influenced the research process, findings, and presentation of results. (p. 311)

Block quotation consisting of two paragraphs:

Regarding implications for chronic biases in expectation formation,

> in order to accurately estimate whether people are likely to form positive or negative expectations on any given occasion, it is necessary to go beyond simply considering chronic individual differences and identify the factors that make people more likely to form expectations in line with one bias or the other.
>
> The present research sheds light on this issue by identifying a crucial distinction in the operation of these two trait biases in expectation formation. Specifically, people's valence weighting biases and self-beliefs about the future appear to shape expectations via qualitatively distinct processes. (Niese et al., 2019, p. 210)

If the block quotation includes citations, see Section 8.32; if the block quotation includes material already in quotation marks, see Section 8.33.

8.28 Direct Quotation of Material Without Page Numbers

Textual Works. To directly quote from written material that does not contain page numbers (e.g., webpages and websites, some ebooks), provide readers with another way of locating the quoted passage. Any of the following approaches is acceptable; use the approach that will best help readers find the quotation:

- Provide a heading or section name.

  > For people with osteoarthritis, "painful joints should be moved through a full range of motion every day to maintain flexibility and to slow deterioration of cartilage" (Gecht-Silver & Duncombe, 2015, Osteoarthritis section).

- Provide an abbreviated heading or section name in quotation marks to indicate the abbreviation if the full heading or section name is too long or unwieldy to cite in full. In the next example, the original heading was "What Can You Do to Prevent Kidney Failure?" and the items are quoted separately because they originally appeared as part of a bulleted list.

  > To prevent kidney failure, patients should "get active," "quit smoking," and "take medications as directed" (Centers for Disease Control and Prevention, 2017, "What Can You Do" section).

- Provide a paragraph number (count the paragraphs manually if they are not numbered).

  > People planning for retirement need more than just money—they also "need to stockpile their emotional reserves" to ensure adequate support from family and friends (Chamberlin, 2014, para. 1).

- Provide a heading or section name in combination with a paragraph number.

  > Music and language are intertwined in the brain such that "people who are better at rhythmic memory skills tend to excel at language skills as well" (DeAngelis, 2018, Musical Forays section, para. 4).

Do not include Kindle location numbers with in-text citations. Instead, provide the page number (which is available in many Kindle books, especially those based on print editions) or use the methods described in this section to create a page number alternative.

Note that the name of the section or other part of the work will not necessarily appear in the reference list entry for the work. For example, if you cite a particular section of a webpage or website in the text, the reference list entry should be for the page you used, not for only that section of the page.

Audiovisual Works. To directly quote from an audiovisual work (e.g., audiobook, YouTube video, TED Talk, TV show), provide a time stamp for the beginning of the quotation in place of a page number.

> People make "sweeping inferences and judgments from body language" (Cuddy, 2012, 2:12).

Works With Canonically Numbered Sections. To directly quote from material with canonically numbered sections (e.g., religious or classical works; see also Section 9.42 and Chapter 10, Examples 35–37), use the name of the book, chapter, verse, line, and/or canto instead of a page number.

> The person vowed to "set me as a seal upon thine heart" (*King James Bible*, 1769/2017, Song of Solomon 8:6).

For plays, cite the act, scene, and line(s). In the following example, "1.3.36–37" refers to Act 1, Scene 3, Lines 36 and 37.

> In *Much Ado About Nothing*, Don John said, "In the meantime / let me be that I am and seek not to alter me" (Shakespeare, 1623/1995, 1.3.36–37).

8.29 Accuracy of Quotations

Direct quotations must be accurate. Except as noted here and in Sections 8.30 and 8.31, the quotation must match the wording, spelling, and interior punctuation of the original source, even if the source is incorrect. If any incorrect spelling, punctuation, or grammar in the source might confuse readers, insert the word "[*sic*]," italicized and in brackets, immediately after the error in the quotation. (See Section 8.31 regarding the use of square brackets to clarify meaning in quotations.) A quotation that includes an error may be distracting, so consider paraphrasing instead. When quoting, always check your paper against the source to ensure that there are no discrepancies.

> Nowak (2019) wrote that "people have an obligation to care for there [*sic*] pets" (p. 52).

8.30 Changes to a Quotation Requiring No Explanation

Some changes can be made to direct quotations without alerting readers:

- The first letter of the first word in a quotation may be changed to an uppercase or a lowercase letter to fit the context of the sentence in which the quotation appears.

- Some punctuation marks at the end of a quotation may be changed to fit the syntax of the sentence in which the quotation appears, as long as meaning is not changed (e.g., it might alter meaning to change a period to a question mark, depending on how the sentence is written).

- Single quotation marks may be changed to double quotation marks and vice versa.

- Footnote or endnote number callouts can be omitted (see also Section 8.32).

Any other changes (e.g., italicizing words for emphasis or omitting words; see Section 8.31) must be explicitly indicated. For more on quoting from a bulleted list without reproducing the bullets, see the second example in Section 8.28.

8.31 Changes to a Quotation Requiring Explanation

Some changes to direct quotations require explanation, as shown in the example in Figure 8.6.

Omitting Material. Use an ellipsis to indicate that you have omitted words within a quotation (e.g., to shorten a sentence or tie two sentences together). Either type three periods with spaces around each (. . .) or use the ellipsis character created by your word-processing program when you type three periods in a row (…), with a space before and after. Do not use an ellipsis at the beginning or end of any quotation unless the original source includes an ellipsis; start or end the quotation at the point where the source's text begins or ends. Use four periods—that is, a period plus an ellipsis (. …)—to show a sentence break within omitted material, such as when a quotation includes the end of one sentence and the beginning of another sentence.

Inserting Material. Use square brackets, not parentheses, to enclose material such as an addition or explanation you have inserted in a quotation.

Adding Emphasis. If you want to emphasize a word or words in a quotation, use italics. Immediately after the italicized words, insert "emphasis added" within square brackets as follows: [emphasis added].

Figure 8.6 Example of Changes Made to a Direct Quotation

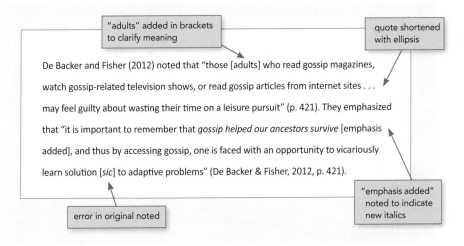

8.32 Quotations That Contain Citations to Other Works

When quoting material that contains embedded citations, include the citations within the quotation. Do not include these works in the reference list unless you cite them as primary sources elsewhere in your paper. In the following example, Panero et al. (2016) would appear in the reference list, but the Stanislavski citations would not:

> Actors "are encouraged to become immersed in a character's life (Stanislavski, 1936/1948, 1950), an activity that calls for absorption" (Panero et al., 2016, p. 234).

Footnote or endnote number callouts in the quoted material can be omitted with no explanation (see Section 8.30).

If citations appear at the end of material you want to quote, it is common practice to end the quotation before the citations and to cite only the work you read (see Figure 8.7 for an example). It is appropriate to omit the citations at the end of a quotation when the material you quote represents a new approach to or conceptualization of the ideas presented in the cited works—for example, when authors have summarized a body of work and you want to quote and cite that summary. If you want to quote the same material that was quoted in the work you are citing, see Section 8.33.

Figure 8.7 Example of Citations Omitted at the End of a Quotation

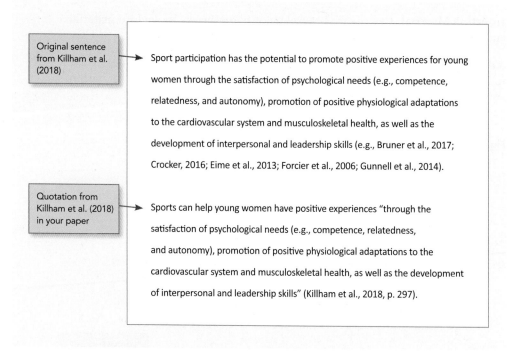

Note. In the original passage, Killham et al. (2018) summarized the results of many studies and cited their sources at the end of the sentence. To quote Killham et al.'s summary in your paper, cite Killham et al., and omit the citations at the end of the original sentence. Interested readers can consult Killham et al. for further information.

8.33 Quotations That Contain Material Already in Quotation Marks

If your source includes a direct quotation from another work, and you would like to use the same direct quotation in your paper, it is best to read and cite the original source directly. If the original source is unavailable, cite the quotation using the secondary source (see Section 8.6).

To quote material that already uses quotation marks for some other purpose (e.g., to enclose a phrase such as a coined expression or linguistic example; see Section 6.7), it may be necessary to change double quotation marks to single or vice versa in your paper depending on the number of words you are quoting.

Short Quotations. For quotations of fewer than 40 words, use single quotation marks within double quotation marks to set off material that was enclosed in double quotation marks in the original source.

> *Correct:* Bliese et al. (2017) noted that "mobile devices enabled employees in many jobs to work 'anywhere, anytime' and stay electronically tethered to work outside formal working hours" (p. 391).

> *Incorrect:* Bliese et al. (2017) noted that "mobile devices enabled employees in many jobs to work "anywhere, anytime" and stay electronically tethered to work outside formal working hours" (p. 391).

Block Quotations. Use double quotation marks around quoted material that appears within a block quotation. (If the original quotation marks were single quotation marks, as in British-style publications, change them to double quotation marks in your paper.)

> *Correct:*
> It is also worth considering the need for subjective certainty:
>> If a conjecture is just mere guess, one would not expect the same bias to occur, because it might likely come along with the metacognition of "I know I am/was just guessing," which would counteract retrospectively increased perceptions of foreseeability. (von der Beck & Cress, 2018, p. 97)

> *Incorrect:*
> It is also worth considering the need for subjective certainty:
>> If a conjecture is just mere guess, one would not expect the same bias to occur, because it might likely come along with the metacognition of 'I know I am/was just guessing,' which would counteract retrospectively increased perceptions of foreseeability. (von der Beck & Cress, 2018, p. 97)

8.34 Permission to Reprint or Adapt Lengthy Quotations

You may need written permission from the owner of a copyrighted work if you include lengthy quotations (usually more than 800 words) from it in your work. Quotations from shorter works (e.g., poems, songs) may also need permission. See Sections 12.14 to 12.18 for guidelines on citing these quotations.

8.35 Epigraphs

An epigraph is a quotation that is used to introduce an article, book, chapter, dissertation, or other work. Authors may use an epigraph to set the stage for what follows or to serve as a summary or counterpoint. The epigraph should appear before the first line of text and should be indented 0.5 in. from the left margin, like a block quotation, without quotation marks.

The source of an epigraph is not usually listed in the reference list unless the work is cited elsewhere in the text of the paper or is important within the context of the topic. If the source of the epigraph is not included in the reference list, on the line below the quotation, provide the credit line—consisting of an em dash and then the author's full name, a comma, and the title of the work in which the quotation appeared—and align it to the right.

> Research is formalized curiosity. It is poking and prying with a purpose.
> —Zora Neale Hurston, *Dust Tracks on a Road*

However, do provide a reference list entry for an epigraph from an academic source (e.g., scholarly book or journal) or a quotation used with permission. The parenthetical citation, including the author, date, and page number, appears after the end punctuation of the quotation with no line break. The example quotation comes from a republished work (see Chapter 10, Example 29).

> If life is to be sustained, hope must remain, even where confidence is wounded, trust impaired. (Erikson, 1966/2000, p. 192)

8.36 Quotations From Research Participants

Quotations from participants whom you interviewed as part of your research are treated differently than quotations from published works. When quoting research participants, use the same formatting as for other quotations: Present a quotation of fewer than 40 words in quotation marks within the text (see Section 8.26), and present a quotation of 40 words or more in a block quotation (see Section 8.27). Because quotations from research participants are part of your original research, do not include them in the reference list or treat them as personal communications; state in the text that the quotations are from participants.

When quoting research participants, abide by the ethical agreements regarding confidentiality and/or anonymity between you and your participants. Take extra care to obtain and respect participants' consent to have their information included in your report. You may need to assign participants a pseudonym, obscure identifying information, or present information in the aggregate (strategies for adequately disguising materials are further described in Sections 1.14 and 1.19; see also Section 1.15 regarding confidentiality in qualitative studies).

> Participant "Julia," a 32-year-old woman from California, described her experiences as a new mother as "simultaneously the best and hardest time of my life." Several other participants agreed, describing the beginning of parenthood as "joyful," "lonely," and "intense." Julia and the other participants completed interviews in their homes.

Agreements regarding confidentiality and/or anonymity may also extend to other sources related to your methodology (e.g., quoting a school policy document when conducting a case study at a school). These sources would not be cited in text or listed in the reference list because doing so would compromise the school's confidentiality and/or anonymity. However, it may be possible to discuss information from these sources in the text if the material is suitably disguised.

> Our study was conducted at a high school in Atlanta, Georgia. School administrators provided documents containing students' average test scores and the percentage of students receiving free or reduced-price lunch. We used these data to contextualize the impact of our intervention.

9

REFERENCE LIST

Contents

9

REFERENCE LIST

The reference list at the end of a paper provides the information necessary to identify and retrieve each work cited in the text. Choose references judiciously, and include only the works that you used in the research for and preparation of your paper. APA publications and other publishers and institutions using APA Style generally require reference lists, not bibliographies. A reference list cites works that specifically support the ideas, claims, and concepts in a paper; in contrast, a bibliography cites works for background or further reading and may include descriptive notes (e.g., an annotated bibliography; see Section 9.51).

In this chapter, we provide guidelines for creating reference list entries, with specific sections focusing on each reference element (author, date, title, source) and the format and order of an APA Style reference list. For information on crediting works in the text and formatting in-text citations, see Chapter 8; for examples of specific reference types, see Chapter 10 (these examples are cross-referenced within this chapter).

Reference Categories

9.1 Determining the Reference Category

References in the *Publication Manual* are organized by group, category, and type. *Reference groups* are textual works; data sets, software, and tests; audiovisual media; and online media. Each group contains numbered *reference categories*. For example, the textual works group contains the categories of periodicals, books and reference works, edited book chapters and reference work entries, and dissertations and theses. The online media group contains the categories of social media and webpages and websites. Within each category are different *reference types*. For example, the periodical reference category includes journal articles, magazine articles, newspaper articles, and blog posts. The social media reference category includes tweets, Facebook posts, and Instagram photos.

To create a reference list entry, first determine the reference group and category and then choose the appropriate reference type within the category and follow that example. If the work you want to cite does not match any example, choose the group, category, and type that are most similar and adapt the format using the elements shown in the relevant template. How a work was accessed or obtained (e.g., online, in print, via interlibrary loan) and how it is formatted (e.g., print, PDF, DVD, online streaming video) have little, if any, impact on the reference list entry. See Chapter 10 for reference templates and examples.

9.2 Using the Webpages and Websites Reference Category

The term "website" can cause confusion because people use it to refer to both a reference category (see Section 10.16) and a method of retrieval (i.e., online). Many types of works can be retrieved online, including articles, books, reports, and data sets, but only some works fall into the webpages and websites reference category. Use that category only when the work does not better fit within another category. First ask yourself, "What type of work is on this website?" Then choose the reference category in Chapter 10 that is most similar to the work you want to cite and follow the most relevant example. For example, to cite a report from a government website, use the reports category (Section 10.4) and follow the format for a government report (see Chapter 10, Examples 50–52). Likewise, to cite a webpage from a government website, use the webpages and websites category (Section 10.16) and follow the format for a work on a website (see Chapter 10, Examples 110–114). Note that the author of a webpage or website may be difficult to determine or may be identified through context (see Section 9.7), and webpages and websites often have unknown dates of publication (see Section 9.17).

9.3 Online and Print References

APA Style references for online and print works are largely the same. All references generally include the author, date, title, and source; differences between online and print versions are evident within the source element. The *source element* includes information about where the work came from (e.g., a periodical's title, a book's or report's publisher, a website's name). References for works with DOIs also include the DOI in the source element, and references for most online works without DOIs include the work's URL (see Section 9.34 for more on when to include DOIs and URLs). However, database information and/or database URLs are not usually included in references (see Section 9.30 for an explanation and a few exceptions). Thus, the same template can be used to create a reference for both the print and online versions of a work. Use only one template (not multiple templates) to create your reference entry.

Principles of Reference List Entries

9.4 Four Elements of a Reference

A reference generally has four elements: author, date, title, and source. Each element answers a question:

- **author:** Who is responsible for this work?
- **date:** When was this work published?
- **title:** What is this work called?
- **source:** Where can I retrieve this work?

Considering these four elements and answering these four questions will help you create a reference for any type of work, even if you do not see a specific example that matches it. See the sections on the author (Sections 9.7–9.12), date (Sections 9.13–9.17), title (Sections 9.18–9.22), and source (Sections 9.23–9.37) for more information on each element. Figure 9.1 shows an example of an article title page highlighting the locations of the reference elements and showing their placement in a reference list entry.

Sometimes reference elements are unknown or missing and the reference list entry must be adapted. See Table 9.1 for a summary of how reference elements are assembled and adjusted when information is missing.

Figure 9.1 Example of Where to Find Reference Information for a Journal Article

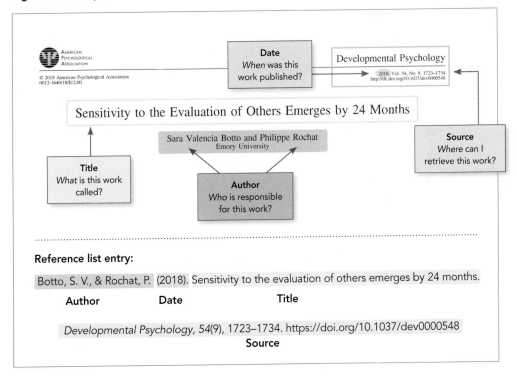

Table 9.1 How to Create a Reference When Information Is Missing

Missing element	Solution	Template	
		Reference list entry	In-text citation
Nothing—all elements are present	Provide the author, date, title, and source of the work.	Author. (Date). Title. Source.	(Author, year) Author (year)
Author	Provide the title, date, and source.	Title. (Date). Source.	(Title, year) Title (year)
Date	Provide the author, write "n.d." for "no date," and then provide the title and source.	Author. (n.d.). Title. Source.	(Author, n.d.) Author (n.d.)
Title	Provide the author and date, describe the work in square brackets, and then provide the source.	Author. (Date). [Description of work]. Source.	(Author, year) Author (year)
Author and date	Provide the title, write "n.d." for "no date," and then provide the source.	Title. (n.d.). Source.	(Title, n.d.) Title (n.d.)
Author and title	Describe the work in square brackets, and then provide the date and source.	[Description of work]. (Date). Source.	([Description of work], year) [Description of work] (year)
Date and title	Provide the author, write "n.d." for "no date," describe the work in square brackets, and then provide the source.	Author. (n.d.). [Description of work]. Source.	(Author, n.d.) Author (n.d.)
Author, date, and title	Describe the work in square brackets, write "n.d." for "no date," and then provide the source.	[Description of work]. (n.d.). Source.	([Description of work], n.d.) [Description of work] (n.d.)
Source	Cite as a personal communication (see Section 8.9) or find another work to cite (see Section 9.37).	No reference list entry	(C. C. Communicator, personal communication, month day, year) C. C. Communicator (personal communication, month day, year)

Note. This table illustrates how reference category templates change when reference elements such as the author (Section 9.12), date (Section 9.17), title (Section 9.22), and/or source (Section 9.37) are missing. Italic formatting within the title or source varies by category and is not shown here. To create a reference list entry, follow the template for the work's reference category (see Section 9.1) and adjust the information as shown here.

9.5 Punctuation Within Reference List Entries

Use punctuation marks within reference list entries to group information.

- Ensure that a period appears after each reference element—that is, after the author, date, title, and source. However, do not put a period after a DOI or URL because it may interfere with link functionality.
- Use punctuation marks (usually commas or parentheses) between parts of the same reference element. For example, in a reference for a journal article, use a comma between each author's last name and initials and between different authors' names, between the journal name and the volume number, and between the journal issue number and the page numbers. Do not use a comma between the journal volume and issue numbers; place the issue number in parentheses instead (see Section 9.25 and Chapter 10, Example 1).

- Italicize punctuation marks that appear within an italic reference element (e.g., a comma or colon within a book title). Do not italicize punctuation between reference elements (e.g., the period after an italic book title).

9.6 Accuracy and Consistency in References

Because one purpose of listing references is to enable readers to retrieve and use the cited works, reference data must be accurate and complete. The best way to ensure that information is accurate and complete is to check each reference carefully against the original publication. Authors are responsible for all information in their reference lists. Accurately prepared references help establish your credibility as a careful researcher and writer.

Consistency in reference formatting allows readers to focus on the content of your reference list, discerning both the types of works you consulted and the important reference elements (who, when, what, and where) with ease. When you present each reference in a consistent fashion, following APA Style reference guidelines, readers do not need to spend time determining how you organized the information. And when searching the literature yourself, you also save time and effort when reading reference lists in the works of others. Some works contain suggested citations; these citations often contain the information necessary to write an APA Style reference but need editing for style.

Accuracy and consistency of references are also important for ensuring that other researchers can find and access the works in your reference list. For example, in the online version of an article, publishers use computer algorithms to link in-text citations to reference list entries within the article, link the reference list entries to the works they cite, and compile lists of works that have cited each source. If reference elements are out of order or incomplete, the algorithm may not recognize them, lowering the likelihood that the reference will be captured for indexing. When in doubt, place reference elements in the order of author, date, title, and source.

Reference Elements

Author

The following sections describe the definition, format, and spelling of author names (Sections 9.7–9.9); the identification of specialized author roles, such as editor or director (Section 9.10); and how to handle group authors (Section 9.11) and works without an author (Section 9.12).

9.7 Definition of Author

In a reference, the *author* refers broadly to the person(s) or group responsible for a work. This element includes not only author(s) of articles, books, reports, and other works but also others who played primary roles in the creation of a work, such as the editor(s) of a book, the director of a film, the principal investigator of a grant, a podcast host, and so on.

An author may be

- an individual,
- multiple people,
- a group (institution, government agency, organization; see Section 9.11), or
- a combination of people and groups.

Sometimes the author of a work is not listed in a traditional byline but can be determined from context. For instance, the author of an annual report is usually the organization that produced it, unless otherwise specified in the report. Thus, in the reference list entry for that annual report, the organization would be listed as the author. Likewise, in the reference for a page from an organizational or government agency website, the organization or government agency itself is considered the author, unless otherwise specified. The author of a webpage or website may also be located on an "about us" or acknowledgments page. When you cannot determine who the author is, treat the work as having no author (see Section 9.12).

9.8 Format of the Author Element

Follow these guidelines to format the author element.

- Invert all individual authors' names, providing the surname first, followed by a comma and the initials: Author, A. A.

- Use a comma to separate an author's initials from additional author names, even when there are only two authors; use an ampersand (&) before the final author's name: Author, A. A., & Author, B. B.

- Do not use a comma to separate two group authors: American Psychological Association & National Institutes of Health.

- Use a serial comma before the ampersand (&) with three or more authors.

- Provide surnames and initials for up to and including 20 authors. When there are two to 20 authors, use an ampersand before the final author's name: Author, A. A., Author, B. B., & Author, C. C.

- When there are 21 or more authors, include the first 19 authors' names, insert an ellipsis (but no ampersand), and then add the final author's name (see Chapter 10, Example 4).

- Use one space between initials.

- When given names are hyphenated, retain the hyphen and include a period after each initial but no space (e.g., Xu, A.-J., for Ai-Jun Xu). When the second element of a hyphenated name is lowercase, treat it as a single name (e.g., Raboso, L., for Lee-ann Raboso).

- Use commas to separate initials and suffixes such as Jr. and III: Author, A. A., Jr., & Author, B. B.

- If nonprimary authors are credited using the word "with" (e.g., on a book cover), include them in the reference list entry in parentheses: Meyers, K. (with Long, W. T.). The in-text citation, however, refers to the primary author only: (Meyers, 2019).

- If an author has only one name (e.g., some celebrities, some authors from Indonesia, ancient Greek and Roman authors, some group or corporate authors); an inseparable multipart name (e.g., Malcolm X, Lady Gaga); an essential title, in rare cases (Queen Elizabeth II); or a username (or screen name) only, provide the full name or username without abbreviation in both the reference list and the in-text citation. That is, cite Plato, Sukarno, or Lady Gaga; do not abbreviate these names to P.; S.; or Gaga, L. In the reference list entry, add a period after the author's name: Plato. (2017).

- Do not include titles, positions, ranks, or academic achievements with names in reference list entries (e.g., Reverend, President, General, PhD, LCSW). A few reference types include an author's role in parentheses, when needed (e.g., film director; see Chapter 10, Example 84).

- If both an author's username and real name are known, such as for some individual and group social media authors, provide the real name of the individual (in inverted format) or group, followed by the username in square brackets (see examples in Section 10.15). This approach allows the reference to be grouped with any other works by that author in the reference list and will aid readers in identifying and retrieving the cited work.

- When the @ symbol is part of a username, include that symbol with the username in brackets (see Chapter 10, Examples 103–108).

9.9 Spelling and Capitalization of Author Names

Follow these guidelines for proper spelling and capitalization of author names.

- Write the author's surname exactly as it appears in the published work, including hyphenated surnames (e.g., Santos-García) and two-part surnames (e.g., Velasco Rodríguez; see also Chapter 10, Example 25).

- If uncertain about the proper format for a name, consult other works that cite that author, bibliographic database records, or the author's website or curriculum vitae (CV) to determine the appropriate format. This will help avoid mistaking, for example, a two-part surname for a middle name and surname or vice versa. Follow the most common presentation if any ambiguity remains.

- Retain the author's preferred capitalization (e.g., hooks, b., for bell hooks) in both the reference list and the in-text citation.

9.10 Identification of Specialized Roles

People in roles other than author who contributed substantially to the creation of a work are recognized for a variety of reference types. See the examples in Chapter 10 for instances when a specialized role is credited in the reference. In these references, the role is placed in parentheses after the inverted surname and initials. Put a period at the end of the author element.

- Use the abbreviation "(Ed.)" for one editor and the abbreviation "(Eds.)" for multiple editors. In the case of multiple editors, include the role once.

Schulz, O. P. (Ed.).
Wong, C. T., & Music, K. (Eds.).

- When a reference includes more than one type of specialized role (e.g., both writers and a director), and different individuals played different roles, identify each role separately. If an individual played multiple roles, combine the roles using an ampersand (&).

  Park, O. (Writer), Gunnarsson, N. (Writer), & Botha, V. N. (Director).
  Lutz, T. (Writer & Director).

In some cases, a specialized role is identified later in the reference (e.g., an editor of a book for an edited book chapter, see Chapter 10, examples in Section 10.3; a symposium chair, see Chapter 10, Example 63; a TV series producer, see Chapter 10, Example 87).

9.11 Group Authors

Group authors may include government agencies, associations, nonprofit organizations, businesses, hospitals, task forces, and study groups (see Chapter 10, Examples 50, 53–55, 90, and 111). A group may author a publication on its own or in combination with individuals or other groups (see Chapter 10, Example 5).

- Spell out the full name of a group author in the reference list entry, followed by a period: National Institute of Mental Health.

- An abbreviation for the group author can be used in the text (see Section 8.21); however, do not include an abbreviation for a group author in a reference list entry.

- When numerous layers of government agencies are listed as the author of a work, use the most specific agency as the author in the reference (e.g., use "National Institute of Nursing Research" rather than "U.S. Department of Health and Human Services, National Institutes of Health, National Institute of Nursing Research"). The names of parent agencies not present in the group author name appear in the source element as the publisher. This presentation aids in identifying the agency responsible for the work and in creating concise in-text citations. However, if using only the most specific responsible agency as the author would cause confusion (e.g., if you are citing both U.S. and Canadian versions of an agency and they have the same name), then include the parent agencies in the author element to differentiate them. When there are multiple layers of agencies, the parent body precedes the subdivision (e.g., The White House, Office of the Press Secretary). Agencies listed in the author element are not repeated in the source element of the reference.

- Sometimes it can be difficult to know whether to credit a group author or the individuals who wrote on behalf of that group; for example, the individuals who wrote a government agency report may be credited in an acknowledgments section. To confirm, consult the cover or title page of the work. If the cover or title page lists only the name of the group (and no names of individuals), treat the reference as having a group author (see Chapter 10, Examples 50 and 53–55). If the cover or title page lists the names of individuals, treat the reference as having individual authors, and include the name of the group as part of the source element (see Chapter 10, Examples 51–52). When a document includes a suggested reference, the author names included in that reference indicate who should be credited (note that the format of the suggested reference may need to be adjusted for APA Style).

9.12 No Author

A work is treated as having no author when its author is unknown or cannot reasonably be determined. In this case, move the title of the work to the author position (followed by a period), before the date of publication (see Chapter 10, Example 49).

> Generalized anxiety disorder. (2019).

If, and only if, the work is signed "Anonymous," use "Anonymous" as the author.

> Anonymous. (2017).

See Section 8.14 for how to format the in-text citation for a work with no author. See Section 9.49 for how to order works with no authors in the reference list.

Date

The following sections describe the definition and format of the date element (Sections 9.13–9.14) and how to handle online works that are updated or reviewed (Section 9.15) or that need a retrieval date (Section 9.16), as well as works with no date (Section 9.17).

9.13 Definition of Date

In a reference, the *date* refers to the date of publication. The date may take one of the following forms:

- year only;
- year, month, and day (i.e., an exact date);
- year and month;
- year and season; or
- range of dates (e.g., range of years, range of exact dates).

For books, use the copyright date shown on the work's copyright page as the date of publication in the reference, even if the copyright date is different than the release date (e.g., 2020 would be the date in the reference for a book released in December 2019 with a copyright date of 2020). For a journal article reference, use the year of the volume, even if it is different than the copyright year.

When citing webpages and websites (see Section 10.16), ensure that the copyright date applies to the content you are citing. Do not use a copyright date from a webpage or website footer because this date may not indicate when the content on the site was published. If a note indicates the "last updated" date of the page, use that date if it applies to the content you are citing (see Section 9.15). If no separate date of publication is indicated for the work on the webpage, treat the work as having no date (see Section 9.17).

9.14 Format of the Date Element

Follow the date format and examples shown in each reference category (see Chapter 10). Use more specific dates for works that are published more frequently (e.g., year, month, and day for newspaper articles and blog posts). Most references include only the year of publication.

- Enclose the date of publication in parentheses, followed by a period: (2020).
- For works from a reference category that includes the month, day, and/or season along with the year, put the year first, followed by a comma, and then the month and date or season:

(2020, August 26).
(2020, Spring/Summer).

- For unpublished, informally published, or in-progress works, provide the year the work was produced (see Section 10.8). Do not use "in progress" or "submitted for publication" in the date element of a reference.
- If a work has been accepted for publication but is not yet published, use the term "in press" instead of a year (see Chapter 10, Example 8). Do not provide a date in the reference until the work has been published.
- If a work is an advance online publication, use the year of the advance online publication in the reference (see Chapter 10, Example 7).
- If a work includes both an advance online publication date and a final publication date, use the final publication date in the reference.
- When the date of original publication is approximate, use the abbreviation "ca." (which stands for "circa"; see Chapter 10, Example 36).

9.15 Updated or Reviewed Online Works

Some online works note when a work was last updated. If this date is available and is clearly attributable to the specific content you are citing rather than the overall website, use the updated date in the reference (see Chapter 10, Example 14, for a source retrieved from the UpToDate database).

Do not include a date of last review in a reference because content that has been reviewed has not necessarily been changed. If a date of last review is noted on a work, ignore it for the purposes of the reference.

9.16 Retrieval Dates

Although most online sources can be updated, some are inherently designed to change (e.g., dictionary entry, Twitter profile, Facebook page; see Chapter 10, Examples 33, 47, 104, and 106) or reflect information that changes over time (e.g., UpToDate article, map generated by Google Maps, work on a website that updates frequently; see Chapter 10, Examples 14, 100, and 113). Provide a retrieval date in the source element when citing an unarchived (i.e., not stable) work that is likely or meant to change. Including this date indicates to readers that the version of the work they retrieve may be different from the version you used.

For works that may change over time but have archived versions (e.g., Cochrane reviews or *Wikipedia* articles), a retrieval date is not needed because the archived version of the page is stable and can be retrieved (e.g., via a permalink; see Chapter 10, Examples 13 and 49). The majority of references do not include retrieval dates; the types that might are noted in the applicable reference examples in Chapter 10. The retrieval date, when needed, appears before the URL.

Retrieved October 11, 2020, from https://xxxxx

9.17 No Date

Sometimes the publication date of a work is unknown or cannot be determined. For works with no date, write "n.d." (which stands for "no date") in parentheses. Put a period after the "n" and after the "d" with no space between the letters.

Gagnon, R. (n.d.).

The date also appears as "n.d." in the corresponding in-text citation.

(Gagnon, n.d.)   *or*   Gagnon (n.d.)

Title

The following sections describe the definition and format of the title element (Sections 9.18–9.19) and how to handle series and multivolume works (Section 9.20), use bracketed descriptions (Section 9.21), and account for works without a title (Section 9.22).

9.18 Definition of Title

In a reference, the *title* refers to the title of the work being cited. Titles fall into two broad categories: works that stand alone (e.g., whole books, reports, gray literature, dissertations and theses, informally published works, data sets, videos, films, TV series, podcasts, social media, and works on websites) and works that are part of a greater whole (e.g., periodical articles, edited book chapters, and TV and podcast episodes). When a work stands alone (e.g., a report), the title of that work appears in the title element of the reference. When a work is part of a greater whole (e.g., a journal article or edited book chapter), the title of the article or chapter appears in the title element of the reference and the title of the greater whole (the journal or edited book) appears in the source element (see Sections 9.25 and 9.28, respectively).

9.19 Format of the Title Element

Follow these guidelines to format the title element.

- For works that are part of a greater whole (e.g., journal articles, edited book chapters), do not italicize the title or use quotation marks, and capitalize it using sentence case (see Section 6.17).

  The virtue gap in humor: Exploring benevolent and corrective humor.

- For works that stand alone (e.g., books, reports, webpages and websites), italicize the title, and capitalize it using sentence case (see Section 6.17).

  Adoption-specific therapy: A guide to helping adopted children and their families thrive.

- For book and report references, enclose in parentheses after the title any additional information given in the publication for its identification and retrieval (e.g., edition, report number, volume number). Do not add a period between the title and the parenthetical information, and do not italicize the parenthetical information. If both edition and volume information are included, separate these elements with a comma, placing the edition number first.

  Nursing: A concept-based approach to learning (2nd ed., Vol. 1).

- If a numbered volume has its own title, the volume number and title are included as part of the main title, rather than in parentheses (see Chapter 10, Examples 30 and 45).

- Finish the title element with a period. However, if the title ends with a question mark or exclamation point, that punctuation mark replaces the period.

- See Section 6.17 for how to format titles that appear in the text.

9.20 Series and Multivolume Works

For a book that is part of a multivolume work, such as a handbook comprising three volumes, include the series title in the reference list entry. For examples of titled and untitled volumes, see Chapter 10, Example 30.

When a book is part of a series of conceptually related but separate works (e.g., popular book series such as Harry Potter or the Chronicles of Narnia), include only the book title, not the series title, in the reference. Depending on the publisher and the series, the series name may be either prominent or hard to find; therefore, we recommend omitting it to avoid confusion (see Chapter 10, Example 31).

9.21 Bracketed Descriptions

To help identify works outside the peer-reviewed academic literature (i.e., works other than articles, books, reports, etc.), provide a description of the work in square brackets after the title and before the period. The description aids readers in identifying and retrieving the work. Examples of works that include bracketed descriptions are some audiobooks, gray literature (e.g., press releases), audiovisual works (e.g., films, YouTube videos, photographs), software and mobile apps, data sets, manuscripts in preparation, and dissertations and theses. Bracketed descriptions are also used in social media references to indicate attached links or images. Capitalize the first letter of the description, but do not italicize the description.

> *Comprehensive meta-analysis* (Version 3.3.070) [Computer software].

The examples in Chapter 10 include bracketed descriptions where they are needed. When in doubt, include a description. Back-to-back brackets (e.g., when a translated title is followed by a description) are acceptable in references. Consistency of wording is helpful (see Section 9.6), but you may alter the wording shown in the examples to best convey the information readers need. Use succinct descriptions, as shown in the examples in Chapter 10.

9.22 No Title

For works without a title, include a description of the work in square brackets instead.

- When possible, specify the medium in the description of the untitled work (e.g., a map) rather than including two bracketed descriptions.

> [Map showing the population density of the United States as of the year 2010].

- For untitled comments on periodical articles, include up to the first 20 words of the comment or post in addition to a description (see Chapter 10, Example 18).

- For untitled social media posts, include up to the first 20 words of the comment or post (in italic) in addition to a bracketed description (see Chapter 10, Examples 103, 105, 107, and 108).

Source

The following sections describe the definition and format of the source element (Sections 9.23–9.24). Then guidelines for handling specific kinds of sources are presented, including periodicals (Sections 9.25–9.27); edited book chapters and reference work entries (Section 9.28); publishers (Section 9.29); databases and archives (Section 9.30); works with specific locations, such as conferences (Section 9.31); social media (Section 9.32); and webpages and websites (Section 9.33). Works that have a DOI or URL (Sections 9.34–9.36) and works without a source (Section 9.37) are also addressed.

9.23 Definition of Source

In a reference, the *source* indicates where readers can retrieve the cited work. As with titles (see Section 9.18), sources fall into two broad categories: works that are part of a greater whole and works that stand alone.

- The source for a work that is part of a greater whole (e.g., journal article, edited book chapter) is that greater whole (i.e., the journal [see Section 9.25] or edited book [see Section 9.28]), plus any applicable DOI or URL (see Sections 9.34–9.36).

- The source for a work that stands alone (e.g., whole book, report, dissertation, thesis, film, TV series, podcast, data set, informally published work, social media, webpage) is the publisher of the work (see Section 9.29), database or archive (see Section 9.30), social media site (see Section 9.32), or website (see Section 9.33), plus any applicable DOI or URL (see Sections 9.34–9.36).

- Works associated with a specific location (e.g., conference presentations) include location information in the source (see Section 9.31) and, depending on the work, may also include a DOI or URL (see Sections 9.34–9.36).

General guidelines on the source element are provided in the following sections; see Chapter 10 for templates and examples of source components to include for each reference category.

9.24 Format of the Source Element

The source element of a reference has one or two parts, depending on the reference category. For example, the source for a print book without a DOI has one part: the book publisher. However, the source for a journal article with a DOI has two parts: the periodical information (the journal title, volume number, issue number, and page range or article number) and the DOI.

Information in the source may be omitted from the reference to avoid repetition. Namely, when the author and publisher or site name of a book, report, webpage, or website are the same, the publisher or site name is omitted from the source element. See Sections 9.25 to 9.33 for guidance on formatting the source for particular reference categories.

9.25 Periodical Sources

When a periodical (i.e., journal, magazine, newspaper, newsletter, or blog) is the source, provide the periodical title, volume number, issue number, and page range or article number (see Chapter 10, Examples 1–6, 9–12, 15, and 16).

   Psychology of Popular Media Culture, 5(2), 101–118.

- Capitalize the title of a periodical using title case (see Section 6.17), italicize it, and place a comma (not italicized) after it.

- Reproduce periodical titles as shown on the cited work. If the periodical's official title includes an abbreviation, reproduce that abbreviated title in the reference (e.g., *PLOS ONE, JAMA Pediatrics*). However, do not abbreviate periodical titles yourself (e.g., do not abbreviate *The New England Journal of Medicine* to *N Engl J Med*). Likewise, do not reproduce abbreviated titles from other reference lists or databases (e.g., if you find an article from *JAMA Pediatrics* in PubMed Central, use *JAMA Pediatrics* in the reference, not PubMed Central's abbreviation of *JAMA Pediatr*).

- Italicize the volume number.

- Include the issue number for all periodicals that have issue numbers. Place the issue number immediately after the volume number (with no space in between), and enclose the issue number in parentheses. Place a comma after the closing parenthesis. Do not italicize the issue number, the parentheses, or the comma after the issue number.

- Write the page range (or article number; see Section 9.27) after a comma and the issue number, without italics. Separate page numbers in a range by an en dash, followed by a period. Separate discontinuous page numbers by commas.
  39–47, 50.

- Finish the periodical information part of the source element with a period, followed by a DOI or URL as applicable (see Sections 9.34–9.36).

9.26 Online Periodicals With Missing Information

Many online periodicals (e.g., newspapers, blogs) publish articles without volume, issue, and/or page numbers or article numbers. Omit these elements from the reference if they are not present in the cited work. For example, for an online newspaper article or blog post, only the title of the periodical (i.e., of the newspaper or blog) may be present (see Chapter 10, Examples 16, 17, and 68).

   The New York Times.

9.27 Article Numbers

For articles with article numbers (which may be called "eLocators" or another term), write the word "Article" (capitalized) and then provide the article number instead of the page range (see Chapter 10, Example 6).

   PLOS ONE, 11(7), Article e0158474.

If an article with an article number also has numbered pages (such as in a PDF), those page numbers may be used for in-text citations (see Sections 8.23 and 8.25) but do not appear in the reference list entry.

9.28 Edited Book Chapter and Reference Work Entry Sources

For edited book chapters and entries in reference works (e.g., dictionary definitions), the source is the edited book or the whole reference work (see Chapter 10, Examples 38–48).

- For works with editors, in the source element of the reference, write the word "In" followed by the initials and surnames (not inverted) of the editors. If there is one editor, follow that editor's name with "(Ed.)." If there are two or more editors, follow the final editor's name with "(Eds.)." Then add a comma, the title of the whole book or reference work in italic sentence case (see Section 6.17), the page (abbreviated "p.") or page range (abbreviated "pp.") of the chapter or entry in parentheses without italics, and a period. Then provide the name of the publisher (see Section 9.29).

  In E. E. Editor (Ed.), *Title of book* (pp. xx–xx). Publisher.

- If the edited book or reference work has edition or volume information in addition to page numbers, include them in the same parentheses in the following order: edition, volume number, and page numbers (separated by commas).

  Title of book (2nd ed., Vol. 3, pp. xx–xx).

- If a numbered book volume has its own title, include the volume number and title after the main title of the book. A colon follows the main title, "Volume" is abbreviated "Vol.," and a period follows the volume number, after which the volume title appears.

  Main title of book: Vol. 2. Volume title (2nd ed., pp. xx–xx).

- For a reference work (e.g., *Merriam-Webster's Dictionary*, *APA Dictionary of Psychology*, mobile app reference work) with a group author, do not repeat the group author name in the source element when the publisher is the same as the author. Simply write "In" and the name of the reference work in italics (see Chapter 10, Examples 47 and 80).

- TV episodes, podcast episodes, and songs from albums follow the same pattern as edited book chapters and entries from reference works (see Chapter 10, Examples 87, 92, and 94).

- Finish the source element with a period, followed by a DOI or URL as applicable (see Section 9.34).

9.29 Publisher Sources

The name of the publisher is provided in the source element for a number of reference categories, including whole books, edited book chapters, reports, computer software and mobile apps, and data sets. Do not include the publisher location in the reference. Online search makes a work easily discoverable without it, and it may be unclear what location to provide for publishers with offices worldwide or online-only publishers that do not readily disclose their location.

- Write the publisher name as shown on the work, followed by a period. Do not abbreviate the publisher name unless it is shown in abbreviated form on the work.

> *Note:* Some publishers may prefer to abbreviate publisher names (e.g., "John Wiley & Sons" to "Wiley") to save space in reference list entries; this is acceptable as part of a house style. If you intend to publish your work, consult the policies of the publisher to determine whether to follow this practice.

- The format of publisher names may vary over time and across works (e.g., SAGE Publishing vs. Sage Publications); use the spelling and capitalization of the publisher name as shown on the work you used. It is not necessary to standardize the presentation of a publisher's name if it appears in multiple entries in a reference list.

- If the work is published by an imprint or division, use the imprint or division as the publisher (e.g., Magination Press, which is an imprint of the American Psychological Association, would be used as the publisher).

- Do not include designations of business structure (e.g., Inc., Ltd., LLC) in the publisher name.

- If two or more publishers are listed on the copyright page, include all of them in the order shown on the work, separated by semicolons (see Chapter 10, Example 24).

  Guilford Press; Basic Books.

- When the author is the same as the publisher (such as with an annual report written and published by the same company, a reference book published by a professional organization, or a work from an organizational website), omit the publisher from the reference to avoid repetition (see Chapter 10, Examples 32, 50, 54, and 55).

- Finish the publisher information component of the source element with a period, followed by a DOI or URL as applicable (see Sections 9.34–9.36).

9.30 Database and Archive Sources

Database and archive information is seldom needed in reference list entries. The purpose of a reference list entry is to provide readers with the details they will need to perform a search themselves if necessary, not to replicate the path the author of the work personally used. Most periodical and book content is available through a variety of databases or platforms, and different readers will have different methods or points of access. Additionally, URLs from databases or library-provided services usually require a login and/or are session specific, meaning they will not be accessible to most readers and are not suitable to include in a reference list.

- Provide database or other online archive information in a reference only when it is necessary for readers to retrieve the cited work from that exact database or archive.

- – Provide the name of the database or archive when it publishes original, proprietary works available only in that database or archive (e.g., Cochrane Database of Systematic Reviews or UpToDate; see Chapter 10, Examples 13–14). References for these works are similar to journal article references; the name of the database or archive is written in italic title case in the source element, the same as a periodical title.
- – Provide the name of the database or archive for works of limited circulation, such as
  - ▷ dissertations and theses published in ProQuest Dissertations and Theses Global,
  - ▷ works in a university archive,
  - ▷ manuscripts posted in a preprint archive like PsyArXiv (see Chapter 10, Example 73),
  - ▷ works posted in an institutional or government repository, and
  - ▷ monographs published in ERIC or primary sources published in JSTOR (see Chapter 10, Example 74).

  These references are similar to report references; the name of the database or archive is provided in the source element (in title case without italics), the same as a publisher name.

- Do not include database information for works obtained from most academic research databases or platforms because works in these resources are widely available. Examples of academic research databases and platforms include APA PsycNET, PsycINFO, Academic Search Complete, CINAHL, Ebook Central, EBSCO*host*, Google Scholar, JSTOR (excluding its primary sources collection because these are works of limited distribution), MEDLINE, Nexis Uni, Ovid, ProQuest (excluding its dissertations and theses databases, because dissertations and theses are works of limited circulation), PubMed Central (excluding authors' final peer-reviewed manuscripts because these are works of limited circulation), ScienceDirect, Scopus, and Web of Science. When citing a work from one of these databases or platforms, do not include the database or platform name in the reference list entry unless the work falls under one of the exceptions.

- If you are in doubt as to whether to include database information in a reference, refer to the template for the reference type in question (see Chapter 10).

- Finish the database or archive component of the source element with a period, followed by a DOI or URL as applicable (see Sections 9.34–9.36).

9.31 Works With Specific Locations

For works associated with a specific location, such as conference presentations (see Chapter 10, Examples 60–63; for more, see the Source Variations list at the beginning of Chapter 10), include the location in the source element of the reference to help with retrieval. Provide the city; state, province, or territory as applicable; and country. Use the two-letter postal code abbreviations for U.S. states and the analogous abbreviations (if any) for states, provinces, or territories in other countries.

New York, NY, United States   Istanbul, Turkey
Vancouver, BC, Canada   Lima, Peru
Sydney, NSW, Australia   London, England

9.32 Social Media Sources

Use social media as a source only when the content was originally published there (e.g., an original Instagram post). If you found a link to content via social media (e.g., a pin on Pinterest), cite the content you used directly and do not mention that you originally discovered it through a link on social media, except as necessary in describing your research methodology.

- When social media is the source (e.g., Instagram photo, tweet, Facebook post), provide the social media site name (in title case without italics) in the source element (see Section 6.17): Twitter.

- Include a period after the social media site name, followed by the URL (see Sections 9.34–9.36).

9.33 Website Sources

When a website is the source for a webpage (see Section 9.2), follow these guidelines to format the website source.

- Provide the website name (in title case without italics) in the source element (see Section 6.17): BBC News.

- Include a period after the the website name, followed by the URL (see Sections 9.34–9.36).

- When the author of the work is the same as the website name, omit the site name from the source element to avoid repetition (see Chapter 10, Examples 111 and 114). In this case, the source element will consist of only the URL of the work.

9.34 When to Include DOIs and URLs

The DOI or URL is the final component of the reference list entry. Because so much scholarship is available and/or retrieved online, most reference list entries end with either a DOI or a URL. A DOI, or *digital object identifier*, is a unique alphanumeric string that identifies content and provides a persistent link to its location on the internet. It is typically located on the first page of an article near the copyright notice, and it starts with "https://doi.org/" or "http://dx.doi.org" or "DOI:" and is followed by a string of letters and numbers. DOIs begin with the number 10 and contain a prefix and a suffix separated by a slash. The prefix is a unique number of four or more digits assigned to the organization by the International DOI Foundation (https://www.doi.org/); the suffix is assigned by the publisher and was designed to be flexible with publisher identification standards. The publisher assigns a DOI to a work when it is published, and many publishers have retroactively assigned DOIs to works published prior to the implementation of the DOI system in 2000. Registration agencies, such as Crossref, use DOIs to provide reference-linking services to the scientific publishing sector. DOIs can also be found in database records and the reference lists of published works. A URL, or *uniform resource locator*, specifies the location of digital information on the internet and can be found in the address bar of your internet browser.

URLs in references should link directly to the cited work when possible. For example, when citing a comment on an online newspaper article, the URL in the reference should link to the comment itself rather than to the article or the newspaper's home page (direct links to comments may be available if you click the comment's time stamp and copy the URL for the comment that appears in your browser).

Follow these guidelines for including DOIs and URLs in references:

- Include a DOI for all works that have a DOI, regardless of whether you used the online version or the print version.

- If a print work does not have a DOI, do not include any DOI or URL in the reference.

- If an online work has both a DOI and a URL, include only the DOI.

- If an online work has a URL but no DOI, include the URL in the reference as follows:

  - For works without DOIs from websites (not including databases), provide a URL in the reference (as long as the URL will work for readers).

  - For works without DOIs from most academic research databases, do not include a URL or database information in the reference because these works are widely available (see Section 9.30). The reference should be the same as the reference for a print version of the work.

  - For works from databases that publish works of limited circulation (such as the ERIC database) or original, proprietary material available only in that database (such as the UpToDate database), include the name of the database or archive and the URL of the work (see Section 9.30). If the URL requires a login or is session specific, meaning it will not resolve for readers, provide the URL of the database or archive home page or login page instead of the URL for the work.

  - If the URL is no longer working or no longer provides readers access to the content you intend to cite, follow the guidance for works with no source (see Section 9.37).

- Other alphanumeric identifiers such as the International Standard Book Number (ISBN) and the International Standard Serial Number (ISSN) are not included in APA Style references.

9.35 Format of DOIs and URLs

Follow these guidelines to format DOIs and URLs.

- Present both DOIs and URLs as hyperlinks (i.e., beginning with "http://" or "https://"). Because a hyperlink leads readers directly to the content, it is not necessary to include the words "Retrieved from" or "Accessed from" before a DOI or URL.

- It is acceptable to use either the default display settings for hyperlinks in your word-processing program (e.g., usually blue font, underlined) or plain text that is not underlined.

- Links should be live if the work is to be published or read online.

- Follow the current recommendations of the International DOI Foundation to format DOIs in the reference list, which as of this publication is as follows:

  https://doi.org/xxxxx

Here, "https://doi.org/" is a way of presenting a DOI as a link, and "xxxxx" refers to the DOI number. The preferred format of the DOI has changed over time; although older works use previous formats (e.g., "http://dx.doi.org/" or "doi:" or "DOI:" before the DOI number), in your reference list, standardize DOIs into the current preferred format for all entries. For example, use https://doi.org/10.1037/a0040251 in your reference even though that article, published in 2016, presented the number in an older format.

> **Why use the new DOI format?** The current DOI format presents the DOI as a direct link to the work rather than as an unlinked number or a link through a proxy server. It simplifies and standardizes retrieval.

- See Chapter 10, Sections 10.1 to 10.3, 10.7, and 10.9, for examples of references that include DOIs.

- Copy and paste the DOI or URL from your web browser directly into your reference list to avoid transcription errors. Do not change the capitalization or punctuation of the DOI or URL. Do not add line breaks manually to the hyperlink; it is acceptable if your word-processing program automatically adds a break or moves the hyperlink to its own line. If your work is published, the typesetter may break hyperlinks after punctuation to improve page flow.

- Do not add a period after the DOI or URL because it may interfere with link functionality.

9.36 DOI or URL Shorteners

When a DOI or URL is long or complex, you may use shortDOIs or shortened URLs if desired. Use the shortDOI service provided by the International DOI Foundation (http://shortdoi.org/) to create shortDOIs. A work can have only one DOI and only one shortDOI; the shortDOI service will either produce a new shortDOI for a work that has never had one or retrieve an existing shortDOI.

Some websites provide their own branded shortened URLs, and independent URL shortening services are available as well. Any shortened URL is acceptable in a reference as long as you check the link to ensure that it takes you to the correct location. See Examples 4 and 18 in Chapter 10 for a shortDOI and a shortened URL, respectively, used in a reference.

9.37 No Source

A reference without a recoverable source cannot be included in the reference list because readers cannot retrieve the work. In most cases, nonrecoverable sources such as personal emails, classroom lectures, and intranet sources should be cited only in the text as personal communications (see Section 8.9).

Online works that are no longer accessible are considered nonrecoverable sources. Before submitting a paper, test the URLs in your reference list to ensure that they work and update them as necessary. Do not include broken URLs in your paper. If the content you cited is no longer available online, search for an archived version of the page on the Internet Archive (https://archive.org/) and use the archived URL. If no archived version of the URL is available, delete the reference list entry and substitute another reference if possible.

Reference Variations

Some works may be in another language or translated, reprinted, reissued, or republished. For each of these reference variations, additional information about the work and/or its publication history is included in the reference list entry.

9.38 Works in Another Language

Multilingual authors may cite works published in a language other than the language in which they are writing. For example, an author who understands both English and Spanish may write a paper in English and cite both English and Spanish works. From the perspective of readers of that paper, the language in which the paper is written (in this example, English) is considered the main language and any other language in the paper (in this example, Spanish) is considered "another language."

To cite a work that is in another language, provide the author, date, title, and source of the work in the original language as well as a translation of the title in square brackets after the title and before the period (see Chapter 10, Examples 9, 27, and 85). In the case of a work that is part of a greater whole (e.g., an edited book chapter), translate only the title of the work being cited (e.g., the chapter title; see Chapter 10, Example 41); it is not necessary to translate the title of the greater whole (e.g., the book title). So, for example, if you are writing in English and cite a Spanish work, provide the author, date, title, and source in the original Spanish in the reference list, and also provide the title of the work translated into English in square brackets. The translation does not have to be literal; the purpose of including the translation is to give readers a sense of what the work is about. Use appropriate grammar and punctuation in the translated title. Authors writing in any language can implement these guidelines.

If the other language uses a different alphabet from the one you are writing in, transliterate the alphabet into the Roman alphabet. For example, Dutch, English, French, German, Spanish, and Swahili use the Roman alphabet, whereas Amharic, Arabic, Farsi, Hebrew, Hindi, Japanese, Korean, Mandarin, and Russian use other alphabets. If transliteration is not possible or advisable, it is acceptable to reproduce the original alphabet in the paper. In that case, use your judgment about where to alphabetize the reference list entry—let the order of reference list entries found in other published articles serve as a guide—or place the entry at the end of the list. In any case, provide a translation of the title of the work in square brackets after the title, before the period (see Chapter 10, Example 27).

9.39 Translated Works

Cite translated works in the language in which the translation was published. For example, if a French article was translated into English and you read the English translation, your reference list entry should be in English. Credit the translator in the reference for a translated work (see Chapter 10, Examples 10,

28, 29, 35, 36, and 42). For all translated works, also provide the year the work was originally published in its original language at the end of the reference in parentheses in the following format:

(Original work published 1955)

See Section 8.15 for how to write the in-text citation for a translated work.

9.40 Reprinted Works

A reprinted work is one that has been published in two places and is available in both (e.g., a journal article that was reprinted as an edited book chapter). The reference list entry includes information about both publications to avoid the appearance of duplicate publication (see Section 1.16). In the reference list entry for a reprinted work, first provide the information for the work that you read. Then, in parentheses, provide information about the original publication. In Chapter 10, see Example 11 for a journal article reprinted in another journal, Example 43 for a journal article reprinted as a chapter in an edited book, and Example 44 for a chapter in an edited book reprinted in another book. See Section 8.15 for how to write the in-text citation for a reprinted work.

9.41 Republished or Reissued Works

A republished work is one that went out of print (i.e., was no longer available) and then was published again; this is common for older works. The term "reissued" is used in the music industry to refer to the same concept. When an anthology consists of works that were published previously (as opposed to new works), the works in that anthology are treated as being republished rather than reprinted. To cite a republished or reissued work (e.g., a work republished in an anthology), provide the details of the new publication that you used, followed by the year the work was originally published in parentheses at the end of the reference in the following format:

(Original work published 1922)

In Chapter 10, see Example 10 for an example of a republished journal article; Examples 28, 29, and 42 for examples of republished books; and Example 46 for an example of a work republished in an anthology. See Section 8.15 for how to write the in-text citation for a republished work.

9.42 Religious and Classical Works

Religious works (e.g., Bible, Qur'an, Torah, Bhagavad Gita), classical works (e.g., ancient Greek and Roman works), and classical literature (e.g., by Shakespeare) are all cited like books (see Section 10.2).

- Religious works (see Chapter 10, Example 35) are usually treated as having no author (see Section 9.12). However, an annotated version of a religious work would be treated as having an editor.

- The year of original publication of a religious work may be unknown or in dispute and is not included in the reference in those cases. However, versions of religious works such as the Bible may be republished; these republished dates are included in the reference (see Section 9.41 and Chapter 10, Example 35).

- For translated religious and classical works, include the translator's name in the reference (see Section 9.39 and Chapter 10, Example 28).

- Classical works (e.g., ancient Greek and Roman works; see Chapter 10, Example 36) and works of classical literature (e.g., by Shakespeare; see Chapter 10, Example 37) are treated as republished works (see Section 9.41).

- When the date of original publication for a classical work is ancient, use the abbreviation "B.C.E." (which stands for "before the common era"), and if that date is approximate, use the abbreviation "ca." (which stands for "circa"; see Chapter 10, Example 36). Dates in the common era do not need to be noted as "C.E." ("common era") or "A.D." ("anno Domini").

- If a religious or classical work has canonically numbered parts common across editions (e.g., books, chapters, verses, lines, cantos), use these numbers instead of page numbers when referring to a specific part of the work (see Section 8.13) or directly quoting the work (see Section 8.28).

See Section 8.28 for how to format the in-text citation for these works.

Reference List Format and Order

9.43 Format of the Reference List

The following guidelines will help you properly format your reference list in APA Style:

- Begin the reference list on a new page after the text.
- Place the section label "References" in bold at the top of the page, centered.
- Order the reference list entries alphabetically by author, as described in Sections 9.44 to 9.48.
- Double-space the entire reference list (both within and between entries).
- Apply a hanging indent of 0.5 in. to each reference list entry, meaning that the first line of the reference is flush left and subsequent lines are indented 0.5 in. from the left margin. Use the paragraph-formatting function of your word-processing program to apply the hanging indent.

9.44 Order of Works in the Reference List

Works are listed in alphabetical order in the reference list by the first word of the reference list entry, according to the following principles:

- Arrange entries in alphabetical order by the surname of the first author followed by the initials of the author's given name(s). In APA Style for alphabetizing names, "nothing precedes something": Loft, V. H. precedes Loftus, E. F., even though "u" precedes "v" in the alphabet.

- When alphabetizing names, disregard any spaces or punctuation marks (e.g., apostrophes, hyphens) in two-word surnames. Also disregard anything in parentheses (e.g., roles like "Eds.") or square brackets (e.g., usernames).

- Alphabetize entries by authors who have the same given name and surname with suffixes indicating birth order chronologically, oldest first.

Figure 9.2 Examples of the Order of Works in a Reference List

Benjamin, A. S., *precedes* ben Yaakov, D.

Denzin, N. K., *precedes* de Onís, C., *precedes* Devlin, J. T.

Girard, J.-B., *precedes* Girard-Perregaux, A. S.

Ibn Abdulaziz, T., *precedes* Ibn Nidal, A. K. M.

López, M. E., *precedes* López de Molina, G.

MacCallum, T., II, *precedes* MacCallum, T., III

MacNeil, E., *precedes* McAdoo, Z. C. E., *precedes* M'Carthy, L. L.

Olson, S. R., *precedes* O'Neil, U., *precedes* Oppenheimer, R.

Partridge, F., *precedes* Plato

San Martin, Q. E., *precedes* Santa Maria, M., *precedes* Santayana, F. E.

Santiago, J., Sr., *precedes* Santiago, J., Jr.

Villafuerte, S. A., *precedes* Villa-Lobos, J.

See Figure 9.2 for examples of how to order works in the reference list. For further examples, review the reference lists of published articles or the sample papers on the APA Style website (https://apastyle.apa.org).

9.45 Order of Surname and Given Name

Naming practices for the order of given name and surname vary by culture; in some cultures, the given name appears before the surname, whereas in others, the surname appears first. If you are uncertain of which name order you are reading, check the author's preferred form (e.g., by visiting their website or their institution's website or by reading their bio or CV), or consult the author's previous publications to see how their name was presented there. For example, an author may publish as "Zhang Yi-Chen" in China but as "Yi-Chen Zhang" in the United States; in either case, according to APA Style, this author would be listed as "Zhang, Y.-C.," in the reference list. See Section 9.9 for more.

9.46 Order of Multiple Works by the Same First Author

When ordering multiple works by the same first author in the reference list, include the author's name in every entry.

- One-author entries should be arranged by year of publication, the earliest first. References with no date precede references with dates, and in-press references are listed last.

  Patel, S. N. (n.d.).
  Patel, S. N. (2016).
  Patel, S. N. (2020a).
  Patel, S. N. (2020b, April).
  Patel, S. N. (in press).

- One-author entries should precede multiple-author entries beginning with the same first author, even if the multiple-author work was published earlier.

    Davison, T. E. (2019).
    Davison, T. E., & McCabe, M. P. (2015).

- Multiple-author entries in which all authors appear in the same order should be arranged by the year of publication (the same as one-author entries).

    Costa, P. T., Jr., & McCrae, R. R. (2013).
    Costa, P. T., Jr., & McCrae, R. R. (2014).

- Multiple-author entries with the same first author and different subsequent authors should be arranged alphabetically by the surname of the second author or, if the second author is the same, the surname of the third author, and so forth.

    Jacobson, T. E., Duncan, B., & Young, S. E. (2019).
    Jacobson, T. E., & Raymond, K. M. (2017).
    Pfeiffer, S. J., Chu, W.-W., & Park, S. H. (2018).
    Pfeiffer, S. J., Chu, W.-W., & Wall, T. L. (2018).

9.47 Order of Works With the Same Author and Same Date

Ambiguity can arise when multiple works cited in a paper have the same author and date (i.e., the same author[s] in the same order and the same year of publication) because the same in-text citation would then correspond to multiple reference list entries. To differentiate references with the same author and year, put a lowercase letter after the year in both the in-text citation and the reference list entry.

- The letter format for references with years is "2020a," "2020b."
- The letter format for references with no date is "n.d.-a," "n.d.-b."
- The letter format for in-press references is in "in press-a," "in press-b."

Assigning the letters is a two-step process. First, compare the dates. References with only a year precede those with more specific dates, and specific dates are placed in chronological order.

    Azikiwe, H., & Bello, A. (2020a).
    Azikiwe, H., & Bello, A. (2020b, March 26).
    Azikiwe, H., & Bello, A. (2020c, April 2).

Second, if the references have identical dates, alphabetize the references by title (disregarding the words "A," "An," and "The" at the beginning of a reference title). The following are examples of references in the proper order.

    Judge, T. A., & Kammeyer-Mueller, J. D. (2012a). General and specific measures in organizational behavior research: Considerations, examples, and recommendations for researchers. *Journal of Organizational Behavior, 33*(2), 161–174. https://doi.org/10.1002/job.764

    Judge, T. A., & Kammeyer-Mueller, J. D. (2012b). On the value of aiming high: The causes and consequences of ambition. *Journal of Applied Psychology, 97*(4), 758–775. https://doi.org/10.1037/a0028084

However, if references with the same author and date are identified as articles in a series (e.g., Part 1 and Part 2), order the references in the series order, regardless of the titles' alphabetical order.

For citing works with the same author and date in text, see Section 8.19.

9.48 Order of Works by First Authors With the Same Surname

Arrange works by first authors with the same surname and different initials alphabetically by first initial(s).

> Taylor, J. M., & Neimeyer, G. J. (2015).
> Taylor, T. (2014).

The in-text citations for these references also include the initials of the first author (see Section 8.20). These guidelines apply to only the first author in each reference.

    If multiple first authors share the same surname and the same initials, order the works as described in Sections 9.46 and 9.47. This guideline applies regardless of whether the authors are different people or the same person with a name change. For guidance on the corresponding in-text citations, see Section 8.20.

9.49 Order of Works With No Author or an Anonymous Author

Before treating a work as though it has no author, consider whether a group or organization is the author (see Section 9.11). If, and only if, the work is signed "Anonymous," begin the entry with the word "Anonymous," and alphabetize the entry as if Anonymous were a true name.

    If there is no author and the work is not signed "Anonymous," the reference begins with the work's title (see Section 9.12); alphabetize the entry by the first significant word of the title (i.e., ignoring the words "A," "An," and "The" at the beginning of the title).

    Alphabetize numerals as though they were spelled out (e.g., alphabetize 22 as though it were "twenty-two"). Thus, "Top 100 business schools" precedes "Top 10 nursing specialties" because when spelled out, "one hundred" appears alphabetically before "ten." Likewise, "Theological studies" precedes "200 years" because "theological" precedes "two hundred."

    For citing works with no author in text, see Section 8.14.

9.50 Abbreviations in References

Some parts of books, reports, and other publications are abbreviated in the reference list to save space, including the following examples. Many, but not all, reference abbreviations are capitalized.

Abbreviation	Book or publication part
ed.	edition
Rev. ed.	revised edition
2nd ed.	second edition
Ed. (Eds.)	editor (editors)
Trans.	translator(s)
Narr. (Narrs.)	narrator (narrators)
n.d.	no date
p. (pp.)	page (pages)
para. (paras.)	paragraph (paragraphs)
Vol. (Vols.)	volume (volumes)
No.	number

Abbreviation	Book or publication part
Pt.	part
Tech. Rep.	technical report
Suppl.	supplement

9.51 Annotated Bibliographies

An *annotated bibliography* is a type of student paper in which reference list entries are followed by short descriptions of the work called *annotations*. Annotated bibliographies can also constitute one element of a research paper in fields that require bibliographies rather than reference lists. Most APA Style guidelines are applicable to annotated bibliographies. For guidance on paper margins, font, and line spacing, see Chapter 2. This chapter provides guidelines for creating and properly ordering references in an annotated bibliography. For templates and examples of reference list entries, see Chapter 10. When writing the text of your annotations, consult the writing style and grammar guidelines in Chapter 4, the bias-free language guidelines in Chapter 5, and the mechanics of style guidelines in Chapter 6. In general, it is not necessary to cite the work being annotated in the annotation because the origin of the information is clear through context. However, do include in-text citations (see Chapter 8) if you refer to multiple works within an annotation to clarify the source.

Instructors generally set all other requirements for annotated bibliographies (e.g., number of references to include, length and focus of each annotation). In the absence of other guidance, format an annotated bibliography as follows:

- Format and order references in an annotated bibliography in alphabetical order, the same as you would order entries in a reference list (see Sections 9.43–9.44).

- Each annotation should be a new paragraph below its reference entry. Indent the entire annotation 0.5 in. from the left margin, the same as you would a block quotation (see Section 8.27). Do not indent the first line of the annotation.

- If the annotation spans multiple paragraphs, indent the first line of the second and any subsequent paragraphs an additional 0.5 in., the same as you would a block quotation with multiple paragraphs.

See Figure 9.3 for an example of an annotated bibliography.

9.52 References Included in a Meta-Analysis

Studies included in a meta-analysis (see Sections 3.12 and 3.17) should be incorporated alphabetically into the reference list for the paper; the meta-analysis references should not be presented in a separate list. Place an asterisk at the beginning of each reference that was included in the meta-analysis. On the first page of the reference list, below the "References" section label, insert the following statement (indented as a new paragraph) describing the purpose of the asterisks: "References marked with an asterisk indicate studies included in the meta-analysis." See Figure 9.4 for an example.

References included in the meta-analysis do not have to be cited in the text. However, they can be cited at the author's discretion (e.g., in a table for comparison; see Chapter 7, Table 7.4). In-text citations do not include asterisks.

Figure 9.3 Sample Annotated Bibliography

2

Workplace Stress: Annotated Bibliography

Barber, L. K., Grawitch, M. J., & Maloney, P. W. (2016). Work–life balance: Contemporary perspectives.

In M. J. Grawitch & D. W. Ballard (Eds.), *The psychologically healthy workplace: Building a win–*

win environment for organizations and employees (pp. 111–133). American Psychological

Association. https://doi.org/10.1037/14731-006

This book chapter provides an overview of the psychosociological concept of work–life balance.

The authors discuss findings from studies showing harmful effects of work–life conflict on

psychological and behavioral health as well as beneficial effects of work–life facilitation, wherein

one role makes a positive contribution to the other. The chapter concludes with a description of

work–life balance initiatives that organizations have adopted to help employees manage their

dual work and nonwork obligations and some of the key factors influencing their effectiveness.

Carlson, D. S., Thompson, M. J., & Kacmar, K. M. (2019). Double crossed: The spillover and crossover

effects of work demands on work outcomes through the family. *Journal of Applied Psychology,*

104(2), 214–228. https://doi.org/10.1037/apl0000348

Carlson et al. (2019) conducted an empirical study to examine the multiple paths through which

work and family variables can affect work outcomes. Whereas Barber et al. (2016) explored how

work obligations can increase stress or enhance fulfillment at home, Carlson et al. viewed work

demands as raising family stress, with potential negative consequences on work performance.

Results supported a model in which direct effects of work demands and spillover effects of work

demands to work-to-family conflict led to lower job satisfaction and affective commitment, as

well as crossover effects of work-to-family conflict, spousal stress transmission, and later family-

to-work conflict on organizational citizenship and absenteeism. Overall, the study demonstrated

a link from work demands to work outcomes when considering the family, but those paths

differed depending on whether attitudinal or behavioral work outcomes were examined.

Figure 9.4 Use of Asterisks to Indicate Studies Included in a Meta-Analysis

35

References

References marked with an asterisk indicate studies included in the meta-analysis.

*Angel, L., Bastin, C., Genon, S., Balteau, E., Phillips, C., Luxen, A., Maquet, P., Salmon, E., &

Collette, F. (2013). Differential effects of aging on the neural correlates of

recollection and familiarity. *Cortex, 49*(6), 1585–1597.

https://doi.org/10.1016/j.cortex.2012.10.002

Finley, J. R., Tullis, J. G., & Benjamin, A. S. (2010). Metacognitive control of learning and

remembering. In M. S. Khine & I. M. Saleh (Eds.), *New science of learning: Cognition,*

computers and collaboration in education (pp. 109–131). Springer.

https://doi.org/10.1007/978-1-4419-5716-0_6

*Hanaki, R., Abe, N., Fujii, T., Ueno, A., Nishio, Y., Hiraoka, K., Shimomura, T., Iizuka, O.,

Shinohara, M., Hirayama, K., & Mori, E. (2011). The effects of aging and Alzheimer's

disease on associative recognition memory. *Neurological Sciences, 32*(6), 1115–

1122. https://doi.org/10.1007/s10072-011-0748-4

Hargis, M. B., & Castel, A. D. (2018). Younger and older adults' associative memory for

medication interactions of varying severity. *Memory, 26*(8), 1151–1158.

https://doi.org/10.1080/09658211.2018.1441423

10

REFERENCE EXAMPLES

Contents

10

REFERENCE EXAMPLES

Appropriately crediting the contributions of scholars on which your research and writing are based is a hallmark of scholarly discourse. These contributions must be cited accurately and consistently so that future scholars can identify and retrieve the works cited in the text.

In this chapter, we provide examples of references in APA Style and their corresponding in-text citations. The reference examples are organized first by group, then by category, and then by type, as follows:

- The **textual works group** (Sections 10.1–10.8) contains the categories of periodicals, books and reference works, edited book chapters and reference work entries, reports and gray literature, conference sessions and presentations, dissertations and theses, reviews of other works, and unpublished and informally published works. Within those categories are examples by type (e.g., journal article, edited book chapter, government report, dissertation).

- The **data sets, software, and tests group** (Sections 10.9–10.11) contains the categories of data sets; computer software, mobile apps, apparatuses, and equipment; and tests, scales, and inventories. Within those categories are examples by type (e.g., unpublished raw data, entry in a mobile reference work, test scoring manual).

- The **audiovisual media group** (Sections 10.12–10.14) contains the categories of audiovisual works, audio works, and visual works. Within those categories are examples by type (e.g., YouTube video, speech audio recording, podcast episode, PowerPoint slides).

- The **online media group** (Sections 10.15–10.16) contains the categories of social media and webpages and websites. Within those categories are examples by type (e.g., Instagram photo, tweet, webpage on a news website).

As described in Chapter 9, the key elements of a reference are the author (who), date (when), title (what), and source (where; see also Figure 9.1). For each reference category, a corresponding template illustrates the order and format in which these elements should appear, and examples of the most common reference types follow. If you do not see an example that matches the work you want to cite, use the template for the applicable reference category as a starting point for writing the reference list entry. Then select the appropriate option from each column of the template to write the reference. Mix and match elements within a template; it is not necessary to use multiple templates. When in doubt, provide more information rather than less. For every reference, the in-text citation contains the first two parts of the reference—usually the "who" (author) and the "when" (date; see Section 8.11), although this can change if reference information is missing (see Table 9.1).

Most legal references (e.g., court cases and laws) are formatted in a legal reference style, which is different in several ways from the author–date–title–source pattern of other APA Style references. Legal references are presented in Chapter 11. Additional reference examples, including references to archival documents, are available on the APA Style website (https://apastyle.apa.org) and on the APA Style blog (https://apastyle.apa.org/blog).

The following index of reference examples is organized by variations in each reference element. The numbers after each index entry refer to the numbered reference examples in this chapter.

Author Variations

Date Variations

Title Variations

Source Variations

Textual Works

10.1 Periodicals

Periodicals are generally published on a continuous basis and include journals, magazines, newspapers, newsletters, and even blogs and other online platforms that publish articles. Sometimes the distinctions between periodical types are ambiguous—for example, a blog that is hosted on a newspaper website. Regardless of where the work appears, its reference list entry follows the same pattern. The date element is presented in different formats for journal, magazine, and newspaper articles and blog posts (see Examples 1, 15, 16, and 17, respectively). When periodical information (e.g., volume number, issue number, page range) is missing, omit it from the reference. For online news websites, see Section 10.16 and Example 110. Use the template shown next to construct references for periodical articles.

Author	Date	Title	Source	
			Periodical information	**DOI or URL**
Author, A. A., & Author, B. B. Name of Group. Author, C. C. [username]. Username.	(2020). (2020, January). (2020, February 16).	Title of article.	*Title of Periodical, 34*(2), 5–14. *Title of Periodical, 2*(1–2), Article 12. *Title of Periodical.*	https://doi.org/xxxx https://xxxxx

1. Journal article with a DOI

McCauley, S. M., & Christiansen, M. H. (2019). Language learning as language use: A cross-linguistic model of child language development. *Psychological Review, 126*(1), 1–51. https://doi.org/10.1037/rev0000126

Parenthetical citation: (McCauley & Christiansen, 2019)
Narrative citation: McCauley and Christiansen (2019)

2. Journal article without a DOI, with a nondatabase URL

Ahmann, E., Tuttle, L. J., Saviet, M., & Wright, S. D. (2018). A descriptive review of ADHD coaching research: Implications for college students. *Journal of Postsecondary Education and Disability, 31*(1), 17–39. https://www.ahead.org/professional-resources/publications/jped/archived-jped/jped-volume-31

Parenthetical citation: (Ahmann et al., 2018)
Narrative citation: Ahmann et al. (2018)

3. Journal, magazine, or newspaper article without a DOI, from most academic research databases or print version

Anderson, M. (2018). Getting consistent with consequences. *Educational Leadership, 76*(1), 26–33.

Goldman, C. (2018, November 28). The complicated calibration of love, especially in adoption. *Chicago Tribune.*

Parenthetical citations: (Anderson, 2018; Goldman, 2018)
Narrative citations: Anderson (2018) and Goldman (2018)

- Do not include the database name or URL. See Section 9.30 for more on excluding or including database information in references.

4. Journal article with a DOI, 21 or more authors

Kalnay, E., Kanamitsu, M., Kistler, R., Collins, W., Deaven, D., Gandin, L., Iredell, M., Saha, S., White, G., Woollen, J., Zhu, Y., Chelliah, M., Ebisuzaki, W., Higgins, W., Janowiak, J., Mo, K. C., Ropelewski, C., Wang, J., Leetmaa, A., . . . Joseph, D. (1996). The NCEP/NCAR 40-year reanalysis project. *Bulletin of the American Meteorological Society, 77*(3), 437–471. http://doi.org/fg6rf9

Parenthetical citation: (Kalnay et al., 1996)
Narrative citation: Kalnay et al. (1996)

- Because the original DOI was long and complex, a shortDOI is used (see Section 9.36). Either the long or short form of the DOI is acceptable.

5. Journal article with a DOI, combination of individual and group authors

De Vries, R., Nieuwenhuijze, M., Buitendijk, S. E., & the members of Midwifery Science Work Group. (2013). What does it take to have a strong and independent profession of midwifery? Lessons from the Netherlands. *Midwifery, 29*(10), 1122–1128. https://doi.org/10.1016/j.midw.2013.07.007

Parenthetical citation: (De Vries et al., 2013)
Narrative citation: De Vries et al. (2013)

- Write the name of the group author as shown on the source (see Section 9.11). This byline included the wording "the members of."

6. Journal article with an article number or eLocator

Burin, D., Kilteni, K., Rabuffetti, M., Slater, M., & Pia, L. (2019). Body ownership increases the interference between observed and executed movements. *PLOS ONE, 14*(1), Article e0209899. https://doi.org/10.1371/journal.pone.0209899

Parenthetical citation: (Burin et al., 2019)
Narrative citation: Burin et al. (2019)

- Capitalize the word "Article" before the article number or eLocator.

7. Journal article, advance online publication

Huestegge, S. M., Raettig, T., & Huestegge, L. (2019). Are face-incongruent voices harder to process? Effects of face–voice gender incongruency on basic cognitive information processing. *Experimental Psychology.* Advance online publication. https://doi.org/10.1027/1618-3169/a000440

Parenthetical citation: (Huestegge et al., 2019)
Narrative citation: Huestegge et al. (2019)

- See Section 8.5 for further information on which version of an article to cite.

8. Journal article, in press

Pachur, T., & Scheibehenne, B. (in press). Unpacking buyer–seller differences in valuation from experience: A cognitive modeling approach. *Psychonomic Bulletin & Review.*

Parenthetical citation: (Pachur & Scheibehenne, in press)
Narrative citation: Pachur and Scheibehenne (in press)

9. Journal article, published in another language

Chaves-Morillo, V., Gómez Calero, C., Fernández-Muñoz, J. J., Toledano-Muñoz, A., Fernández-Huete, J., Martínez-Monge, N., Palacios-Ceña, D., & Peñacoba-Puente, C. (2018). La anosmia neurosensorial: Relación entre subtipo, tiempo de reconocimiento y edad [Sensorineural anosmia: Relationship between subtype, recognition time, and age]. *Clínica y Salud, 28*(3), 155–161. https://doi.org/10.1016/j.clysa.2017.04.002

Parenthetical citation: (Chaves-Morillo et al., 2018)
Narrative citation: Chaves-Morillo et al. (2018)

- When an article is in a different language than your paper, include a translation of the article title in square brackets (see Section 9.38).

10. Journal article, republished in translation

Piaget, J. (1972). Intellectual evolution from adolescence to adulthood (J. Bliss & H. Furth, Trans.). *Human Development, 15*(1), 1–12. https://doi.org/10.1159/000271225 (Original work published 1970)

Parenthetical citation: (Piaget, 1970/1972)
Narrative citation: Piaget (1970/1972)

- For more on translated works, see Section 9.39.

11. Journal article, reprinted from another source

Shore, M. F. (2014). Marking time in the land of plenty: Reflections on mental health in the United States. *American Journal of Orthopsychiatry, 84*(6), 611–618. https://doi.org/10.1037/h0100165 (Reprinted from "Marking time in the land of plenty: Reflections on mental health in the United States," 1981, *American Journal of Orthopsychiatry, 51*[3], 391–402, https://doi.org/10.1111/j.1939-0025.1981.tb01388.x)

Parenthetical citation: (Shore, 1981/2014)
Narrative citation: Shore (1981/2014)

- Provide information for the reprinted version that you used; then provide in parentheses the original article title (even if the title did not change), year, and source information (see Section 9.40).
- Place the original issue number in square brackets rather than in parentheses to avoid nested parentheses.

12. Special section or special issue in a journal

Lilienfeld, S. O. (Ed.). (2018). Heterodox issues in psychology [Special section]. *Archives of Scientific Psychology*, *6*(1), 51–104.

McDaniel, S. H., Salas, E., & Kazak, A. E. (Eds.). (2018). The science of teamwork [Special issue]. *American Psychologist*, *73*(4).

Parenthetical citations: (Lilienfeld, 2018; McDaniel et al., 2018)
Narrative citations: Lilienfeld (2018) and McDaniel et al. (2018)

- List the editor(s) of the special section or issue in the author position and the title of the special section or issue in the title position.
- Provide the page range for a special section. Do not provide a page range for a special issue.
- Some publishers include an "S" in issue numbers for special issues. In the reference, write the issue number exactly as shown in the publication.
- For an article within a special section or special issue, follow the format for a journal article (see Examples 1–3), in which case the title of the special section or issue does not appear in the reference.

13. Article from the Cochrane Database of Systematic Reviews

Mehrholz, J., Pohl, M., Platz, T., Kugler, J., & Elsner, B. (2018). Electromechanical and robot-assisted arm training for improving activities of daily living, arm function, and arm muscle strength after stroke. *Cochrane Database of Systematic Reviews.* https://doi.org/10.1002/14651858.CD006876.pub5

Parenthetical citation: (Mehrholz et al., 2018)
Narrative citation: Mehrholz et al. (2018)

- Articles in the Cochrane Database of Systematic Reviews are available only in that database (see Section 9.30). In the reference list, format Cochrane articles like periodical articles. Do not italicize the database name if it appears in text.

14. Article from the UpToDate database

Morey, M. C. (2019). Physical activity and exercise in older adults. *UpToDate*. Retrieved July 22, 2019, from https://www.uptodate.com/contents/physical-activity-and-exercise-in-older-adults

Parenthetical citation: (Morey, 2019)
Narrative citation: Morey (2019)

- Articles in the UpToDate database are available only in that database (see Section 9.30) and have information that changes over time. In the reference list, format UpToDate articles like periodical articles. Do not italicize the database name if it appears in text.
- Use the year of last update in the date element (see Section 9.15).
- Include a retrieval date because the content is designed to change over time and versions of the page are not archived (see Section 9.16).

15. Magazine article

Bergeson, S. (2019, January 4). Really cool neutral plasmas. *Science, 363*(6422), 33–34. https://doi.org/10.1126/science.aau7988

Bustillos, M. (2013, March 19). On video games and storytelling: An interview with Tom Bissell. *The New Yorker.* https://www.newyorker.com/books/page-turner/on-video-games-and-storytelling-an-interview-with-tom-bissell

Weir, K. (2017, January). Forgiveness can improve mental and physical health. *Monitor on Psychology, 48*(1), 30.

> *Parenthetical citations:* (Bergeson, 2019; Bustillos, 2013; Weir, 2017)
> *Narrative citations:* Bergeson (2019), Bustillos (2013), and Weir (2017)

16. Newspaper article

Guarino, B. (2017, December 4). How will humanity react to alien life? Psychologists have some predictions. *The Washington Post.* https://www.washingtonpost.com/news/speaking-of-science/wp/2017/12/04/how-will-humanity-react-to-alien-life-psychologists-have-some-predictions

Hess, A. (2019, January 3). Cats who take direction. *The New York Times,* C1.

> *Parenthetical citations:* (Guarino, 2017; Hess, 2019)
> *Narrative citations:* Guarino (2017) and Hess (2019)

- To cite articles from online news websites (vs. online newspapers as shown here), see Example 110.

17. Blog post

Klymkowsky, M. (2018, September 15). Can we talk scientifically about free will? *Sci-Ed.* https://blogs.plos.org/scied/2018/09/15/can-we-talk-scientifically-about-free-will/

> *Parenthetical citation:* (Klymkowsky, 2018)
> *Narrative citation:* Klymkowsky (2018)

18. Comment on an online periodical article or post

KS in NJ. (2019, January 15). From this article, it sounds like men are figuring something out that women have known forever. I know of many [Comment on the article "How workout buddies can help stave off loneliness"]. *The Washington Post.* https://wapo.st/2HDToGJ

> *Parenthetical citation:* (KS in NJ, 2019)
> *Narrative citation:* KS in NJ (2019)

- Credit the person who left the comment as the author using the format that appears with the comment (i.e., a real name or a username).
- Provide the comment title or up to the first 20 words of the comment; then write "Comment on the article" and the title of the article on which the comment appeared (in quotation marks and sentence case, enclosed within square brackets).
- Link to the comment itself if possible (see Sections 9.33–9.34).
- Because the comment URL was long and complex, it has been shortened (see Section 9.36). Either the long or the short form of the URL is acceptable.

19. Editorial

Cuellar, N. G. (2016). Study abroad programs [Editorial]. *Journal of Transcultural Nursing, 27*(3), 209. https://doi.org/10.1177/1043659616638722

> *Parenthetical citation:* (Cuellar, 2016)
> *Narrative citation:* Cuellar (2016)

- Use the reference format for the publication in which the editorial was published. This example shows an editorial from a journal; editorials also appear in magazines, newspapers, and other publications.
- Include the notation "Editorial" in square brackets after the title (except when the word "Editorial" is included in the title).
- If the editorial is unsigned, follow the guidelines in Sections 8.14 and 9.12 for the in-text citation and reference list entry, respectively.

10.2 Books and Reference Works

The books category includes authored books, edited books, anthologies, religious works, and classical works. The reference works category includes dictionaries, encyclopedias (including *Wikipedia*), and diagnostic manuals. For ebooks, the format, platform, or device (e.g., Kindle) is not included in the reference. For audiobooks, include the narrator and audiobook notation only in specific cases (see Examples 22 and 29). For a chapter in an authored book, create a reference for the whole book (see Examples 20–23) and provide the chapter number with the in-text citation only (see Section 8.13). Use the template shown next to construct references for books and reference works.

Author or editor	Date	Title	Source Publisher information	Source DOI or URL
Author, A. A., & Author, B. B. Name of Group. Editor, E. E. (Ed.). Editor, E. E., & Editor, F. F. (Eds.).	(2020).	*Title of book.* *Title of book* (2nd ed., Vol. 4). *Title of book* [Audiobook]. *Title of book* (E. E. Editor, Ed.). *Title of book* (T. Translator, Trans.; N. Narrator, Narr.).	Publisher Name. First Publisher Name; Second Publisher Name.	https://doi.org/xxxx https://xxxxx

20. Authored book with a DOI

Brown, L. S. (2018). *Feminist therapy* (2nd ed.). American Psychological Association. https://doi.org/10.1037/0000092-000

Parenthetical citation: (Brown, 2018)
Narrative citation: Brown (2018)

21. Authored book without a DOI, from most academic research databases or print version

Burgess, R. (2019). *Rethinking global health: Frameworks of power.* Routledge.

Parenthetical citation: (Burgess, 2019)
Narrative citation: Burgess (2019)

- See Section 9.30 for more on including database information in references.

22. Authored ebook (e.g., Kindle book) or audiobook without a DOI, with a nondatabase URL

Cain, S. (2012). *Quiet: The power of introverts in a world that can't stop talking* (K. Mazur, Narr.) [Audiobook]. Random House Audio. http://bit.ly/2G0Bpbl

Christian, B., & Griffiths, T. (2016). *Algorithms to live by: The computer science of human decisions.* Henry Holt and Co. http://a.co/7qGBZAk

Parenthetical citations: (Cain, 2012; Christian & Griffiths, 2016)
Narrative citations: Cain (2012) and Christian and Griffiths (2016)

- It is not necessary to note when you used an audiobook versus a book or an ebook when the content is the same, even if the format is different. However, do note that the work is an audiobook in the title element when the content is different (e.g., abridged), if you want to note something special about the audiobook (e.g., the impact of the narration on the listener), or if you quote from the audiobook (see Section 8.28).
- If the audiobook was released in a different year from the text version of the book, treat the work as republished (see Example 29).

23. Authored book with editor credited on the book cover

Meadows, D. H. (2008). *Thinking in systems: A primer* (D. Wright, Ed.). Chelsea Green Publishing.

Parenthetical citation: (Meadows, 2008)
Narrative citation: Meadows (2008)

- When an editor is credited on the cover of an authored book, provide the editor's name in parentheses after the book title with "Ed." or "Eds." in parentheses (see Section 9.10).

24. Edited book with a DOI, with multiple publishers

Schmid, H.-J. (Ed.). (2017). *Entrenchment and the psychology of language learning: How we reorganize and adapt linguistic knowledge.* American Psychological Association; De Gruyter Mouton. https://doi.org/10.1037/15969-000

Parenthetical citation: (Schmid, 2017)
Narrative citation: Schmid (2017)

- Separate multiple publisher names using semicolons.

25. Edited book without a DOI, from most academic research databases or print version

Hacker Hughes, J. (Ed.). (2017). *Military veteran psychological health and social care: Contemporary approaches.* Routledge.

Parenthetical citation: (Hacker Hughes, 2017)
Narrative citation: Hacker Hughes (2017)

- See Section 9.30 for more on including database information in references.

26. Edited ebook (e.g., Kindle book) or audiobook without a DOI, with a nondatabase URL

Pridham, K. F., Limbo, R., & Schroeder, M. (Eds.). (2018). *Guided participation in pediatric nursing practice: Relationship-based teaching and learning with parents, children, and adolescents.* Springer Publishing Company. http://a.co/0IAiVgt

Parenthetical citation: (Pridham et al., 2018)
Narrative citation: Pridham et al. (2018)

- An ebook example is shown. See Example 22 for information about when a notation is needed after an audiobook title.

27. Book in another language

Amano, N., & Kondo, H. (2000). *Nihongo no goi tokusei* [Lexical characteristics of Japanese language] (Vol. 7). Sansei-do.

Piaget, J., & Inhelder, B. (1966). *La psychologie de l'enfant* [The psychology of the child]. Quadrige.

Parenthetical citations: (Amano & Kondo, 2000; Piaget & Inhelder, 1966)
Narrative citations: Amano and Kondo (2000) and Piaget and Inhelder (1966)

- When a book is in a different language than your paper, include a translation of the book title in square brackets (see Section 9.38).

28. Book republished in translation

Piaget, J., & Inhelder, B. (1969). *The psychology of the child* (H. Weaver, Trans.; 2nd ed.). Basic Books. (Original work published 1966)

Parenthetical citation: (Piaget & Inhelder, 1966/1969)
Narrative citation: Piaget and Inhelder (1966/1969)

- For more on translated works, see Section 9.39.

29. Republished book, ebook, or audiobook

Freud, S. (2010). *The interpretation of dreams: The complete and definitive text* (J. Strachey, Ed. & Trans.). Basic Books. (Original work published 1900)

Rowling, J. K. (2015). *Harry Potter and the sorcerer's stone* (J. Dale, Narr.) [Audiobook]. Pottermore Publishing. http://bit.ly/2TcHchx (Original work published 1997)

Parenthetical citations: (Freud, 1900/2010; Rowling, 1997/2015)
Narrative citations: Freud (1900/2010) and Rowling (1997/2015)

- If the new version has been edited and/or translated from the original, provide the name(s) of the editor(s) and/or translator(s) after the title in parentheses.
- If an audiobook was released in a different year than the text version of the book, treat the audiobook as republished (see also Example 22 and Section 9.41).

30. One volume of a multivolume work

Fiske, S. T., Gilbert, D. T., & Lindzey, G. (2010). *Handbook of social psychology* (5th ed., Vol. 1). John Wiley & Sons. https://doi.org/10.1002/9780470561119

Travis, C. B., & White, J. W. (Eds.). (2018). *APA handbook of the psychology of women: Vol. 1. History, theory, and battlegrounds.* American Psychological Association. https://doi.org/10.1037/0000059-000

Parenthetical citations: (Fiske et al., 2010; Travis & White, 2018)
Narrative citations: Fiske et al. (2010) and Travis and White (2018)

- If the volume has both series editors (or editors-in-chief) and volume editors, only the volume editors appear in the author element.
- If the volume does not have its own title, include the volume number in parentheses without italics (as in the Fiske et al. example).
- If the volume has its own title, include the volume number and title after the main title in italics (as in the Travis & White example).

31. Book in a series

Madigan, S. (2019). *Narrative therapy* (2nd ed.). American Psychological Association. https://doi.org/10.1037/0000131-000

Parenthetical citation: (Madigan, 2019)
Narrative citation: Madigan (2019)

REFERENCE EXAMPLES

- For a series of conceptually related titles, the series title is not included in the reference (this book is part of the Theories of Psychotherapy Series; see Section 9.20).

32. Diagnostic manual (*DSM, ICD*)

American Psychiatric Association. (2013). *Diagnostic and statistical manual of mental disorders* (5th ed.). https://doi.org/10.1176/appi.books.9780890425596

World Health Organization. (2019). *International statistical classification of diseases and related health problems* (11th ed.). https://icd.who.int/

Parenthetical citation with abbreviation included:
Diagnostic and Statistical Manual of Mental Disorders (5th ed.; *DSM-5*; American Psychiatric Association, 2013)

International Statistical Classification of Diseases and Related Health Problems (11th ed.; *ICD-11*; World Health Organization, 2019)

Narrative citation with abbreviation included:
American Psychiatric Association's (2013) *Diagnostic and Statistical Manual of Mental Disorders* (5th ed.; *DSM-5*)

World Health Organization's (2019) *International Statistical Classification of Diseases and Related Health Problems* (11th ed.; *ICD-11*)

Subsequent parenthetical citations: (American Psychiatric Association, 2013; World Health Organization, 2019)
Subsequent narrative citations: American Psychiatric Association (2013) and World Health Organization (2019)

- When the author and publisher are the same, omit the publisher from the source element.
- It is common, but not required, to identify the title (and edition) of a diagnostic manual in the text. Group authors and manual titles can be abbreviated in the text (with a few exceptions) but not the reference list (see Sections 6.25 and 8.21).
- Generally, include a citation for a manual the first time it is mentioned in the text. If the first mention appears in a heading, do not cite the manual in the heading; rather, cite it within the first paragraph of that section or soon thereafter.
- Do not repeat the citation for a subsequent general mention of a manual. Repeat a citation only when it directly supports a statement (e.g., quoting, paraphrasing).
- Additional examples and guidance for citing other editions of and entries in the *DSM* and *ICD* are available on the APA Style website.

33. Dictionary, thesaurus, or encyclopedia

American Psychological Association. (n.d.). *APA dictionary of psychology*. Retrieved June 14, 2019, from https://dictionary.apa.org/

Merriam-Webster. (n.d.). *Merriam-Webster.com dictionary*. Retrieved May 5, 2019, from https://www.merriam-webster.com/

Zalta, E. N. (Ed.). (2019). *The Stanford encyclopedia of philosophy* (Summer 2019 ed.). Stanford University. https://plato.stanford.edu/archives/sum2019/

Parenthetical citations: (American Psychological Association, n.d.; Merriam-Webster, n.d.; Zalta, 2019)
Narrative citations: American Psychological Association (n.d.), Merriam-Webster (n.d.), and Zalta (2019)

- When a stable or archived version of the work is cited (as shown for the Zalta example), a retrieval date is not needed.

- When an online reference work is continuously updated (see Section 9.15) and the versions are not archived (as with the *APA Dictionary of Psychology* and the *Merriam-Webster.com Dictionary* examples), use "n.d." as the year of publication and include a retrieval date (see Section 9.16).

34. Anthology

Gold, M. (Ed.). (1999). *The complete social scientist: A Kurt Lewin reader.* American Psychological Association. https://doi.org/10.1037/10319-000

Parenthetical citation: (Gold, 1999)
Narrative citation: Gold (1999)

- Provide the editor(s) of the anthology in the author position of the reference.
- The date refers to the year the anthology was published (for a work included in an anthology, see Example 46).

35. Religious work

King James Bible. (2017). King James Bible Online. https://www.kingjamesbibleonline.org/ (Original work published 1769)

The Qur'an (M. A. S. Abdel Haleem, Trans.). (2004). Oxford University Press.

The Torah: The five books of Moses (3rd ed.). (2015). The Jewish Publication Society. (Original work published 1962)

Parenthetical citations: (*King James Bible*, 1769/2017; *The Qur'an*, 2004; *The Torah*, 1962/2015)
Narrative citations: *King James Bible* (1769/2017), *The Qur'an* (2004), and *The Torah* (1962/2015)

- For more on citing religious works, see Section 9.42; to cite a specific book or verse, see Section 8.13; to quote a passage, see Section 8.28.
- Additional examples of religious texts are available on the APA Style website.

36. Ancient Greek or Roman work

Aristotle. (1994). *Poetics* (S. H. Butcher, Trans.). The Internet Classics Archive. http://classics.mit.edu/Aristotle/poetics.html (Original work published ca. 350 B.C.E.)

Parenthetical citation: (Aristotle, ca. 350 B.C.E./1994)
Narrative citation: Aristotle (ca. 350 B.C.E./1994)

- For ancient Greek or Roman works, include the copyright date of the version used in the date element and the date of the original (ancient) publication in parentheses at the end of the entry. When the date of original publication is approximate, use the abbreviation "ca." (which stands for "circa").
- For more on citing classical works, see Section 9.42; to cite a canonically numbered part of a classical work, see Section 8.13; to quote a passage, see Section 8.28.

37. Shakespeare

Shakespeare, W. (1995). *Much ado about nothing* (B. A. Mowat & P. Werstine, Eds.). Washington Square Press. (Original work published 1623)

Parenthetical citation: (Shakespeare, 1623/1995)
Narrative citation: Shakespeare (1623/1995)

- For more on citing Shakespeare and other works of classical literature, see Section 9.42; to cite a specific act, scene, or line, see Section 8.13; to quote a passage, see Section 8.28.

10.3 Edited Book Chapters and Entries in Reference Works

The edited book chapter category includes chapters of edited books and works in anthologies. The entries in reference works category includes dictionary, thesaurus, and encyclopedia entries. For ebook chapters or entries, the format, platform, or device (e.g., Kindle) is not included in the reference. For audiobook chapters or entries, include the narrator and audiobook notation only in specific cases (see Example 22). For a chapter in an authored book, create a reference for the whole book (see Examples 20–23) and provide the chapter number with the in-text citation only (see Section 8.13). Use the template shown next to construct references for edited book chapters and entries in reference works.

Chapter author	Date	Chapter title	Source	
			Edited book information	**DOI or URL**
Author, A. A., & Author, B. B. Name of Group.	(2020).	Title of chapter.	In E. E. Editor (Ed.), *Title of book* (pp. 3–13). Publisher Name. In E. E. Editor & F. F. Editor (Eds.), *Title of book* (3rd ed., Vol. 2, pp. 212–255). Publisher Name.	https://doi.org/ xxxx https://xxxxx

38. Chapter in an edited book with a DOI

Balsam, K. F., Martell, C. R., Jones, K. P., & Safren, S. A. (2019). Affirmative cognitive behavior therapy with sexual and gender minority people. In G. Y. Iwamasa & P. A. Hays (Eds.), *Culturally responsive cognitive behavior therapy: Practice and supervision* (2nd ed., pp. 287–314). American Psychological Association. https://doi.org/ 10.1037/0000119-012

Parenthetical citation: (Balsam et al., 2019)
Narrative citation: Balsam et al. (2019)

39. Chapter in an edited book without a DOI, from most academic research databases or print version

Weinstock, R., Leong, G. B., & Silva, J. A. (2003). Defining forensic psychiatry: Roles and responsibilities. In R. Rosner (Ed.), *Principles and practice of forensic psychiatry* (2nd ed., pp. 7–13). CRC Press.

Parenthetical citation: (Weinstock et al., 2003)
Narrative citation: Weinstock et al. (2003)

• See Section 9.30 for more on including database information in references.

40. Chapter in an edited ebook (e.g., Kindle book) or audiobook without a DOI, with nondatabase URL

Tafoya, N., & Del Vecchio, A. (2005). Back to the future: An examination of the Native American Holocaust experience. In M. McGoldrick, J. Giordano, & N. Garcia-Preto (Eds.), *Ethnicity and family therapy* (3rd ed., pp. 55–63). Guilford Press. http://a. co/36xRhBT

Parenthetical citation: (Tafoya & Del Vecchio, 2005)
Narrative citation: Tafoya and Del Vecchio (2005)

• See Examples 22 and 29 for further information about audiobooks.

41. Chapter in an edited book in another language

Carcavilla González, N. (2015). Terapia sensorial auditiva: Activación cerebral por medio de la música [Auditory sensory therapy: Brain activation through music]. In J. J. García Meilán (Ed.), *Guía práctica de terapias estimulativas en el Alzhéimer* (pp. 67–86). Editorial Síntesis. https://www.sintesis.com/guias-profesionales-203/guia-practica-de-terapias-estimulativas-en-el-alzheimer-libro-1943.html

Parenthetical citation: (Carcavilla González, 2015)
Narrative citation: Carcavilla González (2015)

- When a chapter is in a different language than your paper, include a translation of the chapter title in square brackets (see Section 9.38 for more).

42. Chapter in an edited book, republished in translation

Heidegger, M. (2008). On the essence of truth (J. Sallis, Trans.). In D. F. Krell (Ed.), *Basic writings* (pp. 111–138). Harper Perennial Modern Thought. (Original work published 1961)

Parenthetical citation: (Heidegger, 1961/2008)
Narrative citation: Heidegger (1961/2008)

- For more on translated works, see Section 9.39.

43. Chapter in an edited book, reprinted from a journal article

Sacchett, C., & Humphreys, G. W. (2004). Calling a squirrel a squirrel but a canoe a wigwam: A category-specific deficit for artefactual objects and body parts. In D. A. Balota & E. J. Marsh (Eds.), *Cognitive psychology: Key readings in cognition* (pp. 100–108). Psychology Press. (Reprinted from "Calling a squirrel a squirrel but a canoe a wigwam: A category-specific deficit for artefactual objects and body parts," 1992, *Cognitive Neuropsychology*, 9[1], 73–86, http://doi.org/d4vb59)

Parenthetical citation: (Sacchett & Humphreys, 1992/2004)
Narrative citation: Sacchett and Humphreys (1992/2004)

- Provide information for the reprinted version you used, then provide in parentheses the original article title (even if the title did not change), year, and source information (see Section 9.40 for more).
- Place the original journal article issue number in square brackets rather than parentheses to avoid nested parentheses.

44. Chapter in an edited book, reprinted from another book

Bronfenbrenner, U. (2005). The social ecology of human development: A retrospective conclusion. In U. Bronfenbrenner (Ed.), *Making human beings human: Bioecological perspectives on human development* (pp. 27–40). SAGE Publications. (Reprinted from *Brain and intelligence: The ecology of child development*, pp. 113–123, by F. Richardson, Ed., 1973, National Educational Press)

Parenthetical citation: (Bronfenbrenner, 1973/2005)
Narrative citation: Bronfenbrenner (1973/2005)

- Provide information for the reprinted version you used, then provide in parentheses the original book title, page range, author or editor name (including "Ed." for an editor), year, and publisher (see Section 9.40 for more).

45. Chapter in a volume of a multivolume work

Goldin-Meadow, S. (2015). Gesture and cognitive development. In L. S. Liben & U. Mueller (Eds.), *Handbook of child psychology and developmental science: Vol. 2. Cognitive processes* (7th ed., pp. 339–380). John Wiley & Sons. https://doi.org/10.1002/9781118963418.childpsy209

Parenthetical citation: (Goldin-Meadow, 2015)
Narrative citation: Goldin-Meadow (2015)

- If the volume has both series editors (or editors-in-chief) and volume editors, only the volume editors appear in the reference.
- The volume in this example has its own title. See Example 30 for how to include untitled volume information in parentheses after the book title.

46. Work in an anthology

Lewin, K. (1999). Group decision and social change. In M. Gold (Ed.), *The complete social scientist: A Kurt Lewin reader* (pp. 265–284). American Psychological Association. https://doi.org/10.1037/10319-010 (Original work published 1948)

Parenthetical citation: (Lewin, 1948/1999)
Narrative citation: Lewin (1948/1999)

- Works that have been published elsewhere before appearing in an anthology are treated as being republished (see Section 9.41) rather than reprinted.

47. Entry in a dictionary, thesaurus, or encyclopedia, with group author

American Psychological Association. (n.d.). Positive transference. In *APA dictionary of psychology*. Retrieved August 31, 2019, from https://dictionary.apa.org/positive-transference

Merriam-Webster. (n.d.). Self-report. In *Merriam-Webster.com dictionary*. Retrieved July 12, 2019, from https://www.merriam-webster.com/dictionary/self-report

Parenthetical citations: (American Psychological Association, n.d.; Merriam-Webster, n.d.)
Narrative citations: American Psychological Association (n.d.) and Merriam-Webster (n.d.)

- When an online reference work is continuously updated (see Section 9.15) and the versions are not archived, use "n.d." as the year of publication and include a retrieval date (see Section 9.16).

48. Entry in a dictionary, thesaurus, or encyclopedia, with individual author

Graham, G. (2019). Behaviorism. In E. N. Zalta (Ed.), *The Stanford encyclopedia of philosophy* (Summer 2019 ed.). Stanford University. https://plato.stanford.edu/archives/sum2019/entries/behaviorism/

Parenthetical citation: (Graham, 2019)
Narrative citation: Graham (2019)

- This example is structured similarly to the reference for a chapter in an edited book because the entry has an individual author, the encyclopedia has an editor, and the whole work has a publisher.
- Because this version of the entry is archived, a retrieval date is not needed.

49. *Wikipedia* entry

List of oldest companies. (2019, January 13). In *Wikipedia.* https://en.wikipedia.org/w/index.php?title=List_of_oldest_companies&oldid=878158136

Parenthetical citation: ("List of Oldest Companies," 2019)
Narrative citation: "List of Oldest Companies" (2019)

- Cite the archived version of the page so that readers can retrieve the version you used. Access the archived version on *Wikipedia* by selecting "View history" and then the time and date of the version you used. If a wiki does not provide permanent links to archived versions of the page, include the URL for the entry and the retrieval date.

10.4 Reports and Gray Literature

There are many kinds of reports, including government reports, technical reports, and research reports. These reports, like journal articles, usually cover original research, but they may or may not be peer reviewed. They are part of a body of literature sometimes referred to as *gray literature*. The category of gray literature includes press releases, codes of ethics, grants, policy briefs, issue briefs, and so forth. It is optional—but often helpful—to describe these less common types of gray literature in square brackets after the title. Reports themselves sometimes include a suggested reference format; this reference usually contains the information necessary to write an APA Style reference (author, date, title, and source), but you may need to adjust the order of the elements and other formatting to conform to APA Style. When the publisher is the same as the author, which is often the case for group authors (see Examples 50 and 54), omit the publisher from the source element. Use the template shown next to construct references for reports and gray literature.

Author	Date	Title	Source	
			Publisher information	DOI or URL
Author, A. A., & Author, B. B.	(2020).	*Title of report.*	Publisher Name.	https://doi.org/xxxx
Name of Group.	(2020, May 2).	*Title of report* (Report No. 123).		https://xxxxx
		Title of gray literature [Description].		

50. Report by a government agency or other organization

Australian Government Productivity Commission & New Zealand Productivity Commission. (2012). *Strengthening trans-Tasman economic relations.* https://www.pc.gov.au/inquiries/completed/australia-new-zealand/report/trans-tasman.pdf

Canada Council for the Arts. (2013). *What we heard: Summary of key findings: 2013 Canada Council's Inter-Arts Office consultation.* http://publications.gc.ca/collections/collection_2017/canadacouncil/K23-65-2013-eng.pdf

National Cancer Institute. (2018). *Facing forward: Life after cancer treatment* (NIH Publication No. 18-2424). U.S. Department of Health and Human Services, National Institutes of Health. https://www.cancer.gov/publications/patient-education/life-after-treatment.pdf

Parenthetical citations: (Australian Government Productivity Commission & New Zealand Productivity Commission, 2012; Canada Council for the Arts, 2013; National Cancer Institute, 2018)

Narrative citations: Australian Government Productivity Commission and New Zealand Productivity Commission (2012), Canada Council for the Arts (2013), and National Cancer Institute (2018)

- See Section 9.11 for how to treat the names of group authors.
- The names of parent agencies not present in the group author name appear in the source element as the publisher (see Section 9.11).
- If multiple agencies authored a report together, join the names with an ampersand, using commas to separate the names of three or more agencies.

51. Report by individual authors at a government agency or other organization

Fried, D., & Polyakova, A. (2018). *Democratic defense against disinformation.* Atlantic Council. https://www.atlanticcouncil.org/images/publications/Democratic_Defense_Against_Disinformation_FINAL.pdf

Segaert, A., & Bauer, A. (2015). *The extent and nature of veteran homelessness in Canada.* Employment and Social Development Canada. https://www.canada.ca/en/employment-social-development/programs/communities/homelessness/publications-bulletins/veterans-report.html

> *Parenthetical citations:* (Fried & Polyakova, 2018; Segaert & Bauer, 2015)
> *Narrative citations:* Fried and Polyakova (2018) and Segaert and Bauer (2015)

52. Report by individual authors at a government agency, published as part of a series

Blackwell, D. L., Lucas, J. W., & Clarke, T. C. (2014). *Summary health statistics for U.S. adults: National Health Interview Survey, 2012* (Vital and Health Statistics Series 10, Issue 260). Centers for Disease Control and Prevention. https://www.cdc.gov/nchs/data/series/sr_10/sr10_260.pdf

> *Parenthetical citation:* (Blackwell et al., 2014)
> *Narrative citation:* Blackwell et al. (2014)

53. Report by a task force, working group, or other group

British Cardiovascular Society Working Group. (2016). *British Cardiovascular Society Working Group report: Out-of-hours cardiovascular care: Management of cardiac emergencies and hospital in-patients.* British Cardiovascular Society. http://www.bcs.com/documents/BCSOOHWP_Final_Report_05092016.pdf

> *Parenthetical citation:* (British Cardiovascular Society Working Group, 2016)
> *Narrative citation:* British Cardiovascular Society Working Group (2016)

- Capitalize the name of the task force or working group wherever it appears in the reference because it is a proper noun.

54. Annual report

U.S. Securities and Exchange Commission. (2017). *Agency financial report: Fiscal year 2017.* https://www.sec.gov/files/sec-2017-agency-financial-report.pdf

> *Parenthetical citation:* (U.S. Securities and Exchange Commission, 2017)
> *Narrative citation:* U.S. Securities and Exchange Commission (2017)

55. Code of ethics

American Counseling Association. (2014). *2014 ACA code of ethics.* https://www.counseling.org/knowledge-center

American Nurses Association. (2015). *Code of ethics for nurses with interpretive statements.* https://www.nursingworld.org/coe-view-only

American Psychological Association. (2017). *Ethical principles of psychologists and code of conduct* (2002, amended effective June 1, 2010, and January 1, 2017). https://www.apa.org/ethics/code/index.aspx

Parenthetical citations: (American Counseling Association, 2014; American Nurses Association, 2015; American Psychological Association, 2017)

Narrative citations: American Counseling Association (2014), American Nurses Association (2015), and American Psychological Association (2017)

56. Grant

Blair, C. B. (Principal Investigator). (2015–2020). *Stress, self-regulation and psychopathology in middle childhood* (Project No. 5R01HD081252-04) [Grant]. Eunice Kennedy Shriver National Institute of Child Health & Human Development. https://projectreporter.nih.gov/project_info_details.cfm?aid=9473071&icde=40092311

Parenthetical citation: (Blair, 2015–2020)
Narrative citation: Blair (2015–2020)

- List the principal investigator as the author with their role in parentheses, the project start and end year(s) as the date, the project title as the title, and the funding agency as the source.
- The National Institutes of Health (NIH) refers to grant numbers as *project numbers*; use the appropriate terminology for the grant in your reference, and include the number in parentheses after the title.
- A grant application is not a recoverable source and should be discussed as part of the methodology but not included in the reference list.

57. Issue brief

Lichtenstein, J. (2013). *Profile of veteran business owners: More young veterans appear to be starting businesses* (Issue Brief No. 1). U.S. Small Business Administration, Office of Advocacy. https://www.sba.gov/sites/default/files/Issue%20Brief%201,%20Veteran%20Business%20Owners.pdf

Parenthetical citation: (Lichtenstein, 2013)
Narrative citation: Lichtenstein (2013)

- Issue briefs are typically numbered; identify the number of the issue brief in parentheses after the title.
- If a number is not provided, identify the work as an issue brief in square brackets following the title.

58. Policy brief

Harwell, M. (2018). *Don't expect too much: The limited usefulness of common SES measures and a prescription for change* [Policy brief]. National Education Policy Center. https://nepc.colorado.edu/publication/SES

Parenthetical citation: (Harwell, 2018)
Narrative citation: Harwell (2018)

59. Press release

U.S. Food and Drug Administration. (2019, February 14). *FDA authorizes first interoperable insulin pump intended to allow patients to customize treatment through their individual diabetes management devices* [Press release]. https://www.fda.gov/NewsEvents/Newsroom/PressAnnouncements/ucm631412.htm

Parenthetical citation: (U.S. Food and Drug Administration, 2019)
Narrative citation: U.S. Food and Drug Administration (2019)

10.5 Conference Sessions and Presentations

Conference sessions and presentations include paper presentations, poster sessions, keynote addresses, and symposium contributions. Include a label in square brackets after the title that matches how the presentation was described at the conference; include all authors listed as contributing to the presentation (even if they were not physically present). The date should match the date(s) of the full conference to help readers find the source, even though a session or presentation likely occurred on only one day. Include the location of the conference to help with retrieval (see Section 9.31 for the format of locations). Conference proceedings published in a journal or book follow the same format as for a journal article (see Example 1), edited book (see Examples 24–26 and 30), or edited book chapter (see Examples 38–42 and 45).

Use the template shown next to construct references for conference sessions and presentations.

			Source	
Author	**Date**	**Title**	**Conference information**	**DOI or URL**
Presenter, A. A., & Presenter, B. B	(2020, September 18–20). (2020, October 30–November 1).	*Title of contribution* [Type of contribution].	Conference Name, Location.	https://doi.org/ xxxx https://xxxxx

Use the template shown next to construct references for symposium contributions.

			Source	
Author	**Date**	**Contribution title**	**Conference information**	**DOI or URL**
Contributor, A. A., & Contributor, B. B.	(2020, September 18–20). (2020, October 30–November 1).	Title of contribution.	In C. C. Chairperson (Chair), *Title of symposium* [Symposium]. Conference Name, Location.	https://doi. org/xxxxx https://xxxxx

60. Conference session

Fistek, A., Jester, E., & Sonnenberg, K. (2017, July 12–15). *Everybody's got a little music in them: Using music therapy to connect, engage, and motivate* [Conference session]. Autism Society National Conference, Milwaukee, WI, United States. https://asa.con-fex.com/asa/2017/webprogramarchives/Session9517.html

Parenthetical citation: (Fistek et al., 2017)
Narrative citation: Fistek et al. (2017)

61. Paper presentation

Maddox, S., Hurling, J., Stewart, E., & Edwards, A. (2016, March 30–April 2). *If mama ain't happy, nobody's happy: The effect of parental depression on mood dysregulation in children* [Paper presentation]. Southeastern Psychological Association 62nd Annual Meeting, New Orleans, LA, United States.

Parenthetical citation: (Maddox et al., 2016)
Narrative citation: Maddox et al. (2016)

62. Poster presentation

Pearson, J. (2018, September 27–30). *Fat talk and its effects on state-based body image in women* [Poster presentation]. Australian Psychological Society Congress, Sydney, NSW, Australia. http://bit.ly/2XGSThP

Parenthetical citation: (Pearson, 2018)
Narrative citation: Pearson (2018)

63. Symposium contribution

De Boer, D., & LaFavor, T. (2018, April 26–29). The art and significance of successfully identifying resilient individuals: A person-focused approach. In A. M. Schmidt & A. Kryvanos (Chairs), *Perspectives on resilience: Conceptualization, measurement, and enhancement* [Symposium]. Western Psychological Association 98th Annual Convention, Portland, OR, United States.

Parenthetical citation: (De Boer & LaFavor, 2018)
Narrative citation: De Boer and LaFavor (2018)

10.6 Dissertations and Theses

References for doctoral dissertations and master's and undergraduate theses are divided by whether they are unpublished or published; unpublished works generally must be retrieved directly from the college or university in print form, whereas published works are available from a database (e.g., the ProQuest Dissertations and Theses Global database), a university archive, or a personal website. Thus, for unpublished dissertations and theses, the university name appears in the source element of the reference, whereas for published dissertations and theses, the university name appears in square brackets after the title.

Use the template shown next to construct references for unpublished dissertations and theses.

Author	Date	Title	Source
Author, A. A.	(2020).	*Title of dissertation* [Unpublished doctoral dissertation]. *Title of thesis* [Unpublished master's thesis].	Name of Institution Awarding the Degree.

Use the template shown next to construct references for published dissertations and theses.

Author	Date	Title	Source Database or archive name	URL
Author, A. A.	(2020).	*Title of dissertation* [Doctoral dissertation, Name of Institution Awarding the Degree]. *Title of thesis* [Master's thesis, Name of Institution Awarding the Degree].	Database Name. Archive Name.	https://xxxxx

64. Unpublished dissertation or thesis

Harris, L. (2014). *Instructional leadership perceptions and practices of elementary school leaders* [Unpublished doctoral dissertation]. University of Virginia.

> *Parenthetical citation:* (Harris, 2014)
> *Narrative citation:* Harris (2014)

65. Dissertation or thesis from a database

Hollander, M. M. (2017). *Resistance to authority: Methodological innovations and new lessons from the Milgram experiment* (Publication No. 10289373) [Doctoral dissertation, University of Wisconsin–Madison]. ProQuest Dissertations and Theses Global.

> *Parenthetical citation:* (Hollander, 2017)
> *Narrative citation:* Hollander (2017)

66. Dissertation or thesis published online (not in a database)

Hutcheson, V. H. (2012). *Dealing with dual differences: Social coping strategies of gifted and lesbian, gay, bisexual, transgender, and queer adolescents* [Master's thesis, The College of William & Mary]. William & Mary Digital Archive. https://digitalarchive.wm.edu/bitstream/handle/10288/16594/HutchesonVirginia2012.pdf

> *Parenthetical citation:* (Hutcheson, 2012)
> *Narrative citation:* Hutcheson (2012)

10.7 Reviews

Reviews of books, films, TV shows, albums, and other entertainment are published in a variety of outlets, including journals, magazines, newspapers, websites, and blogs. The reference format for a review should be the same as the format for the type of content appearing within that source, with the addition of information about the item being reviewed in square brackets after the review title. Within the square brackets, write "Review of the" and then the type of work being reviewed (e.g., film, book, TV series episode, video game); its title (in sentence case, described in Section 6.17; see also Section 9.19 for whether to format the title in italics or quotation marks); and its author or editor, director, writer, and so forth, with a designation of role for all except regular authors of books. Use the template shown next to construct references for reviews.

		Title		Source	
		Review title	Details of reviewed work	Periodical information	
Author	Date				DOI or URL
Reviewer, A. A.	(2020). (2020, February 3).	Title of review	[Review of the book *Book title*, by A. A. Author].	*Periodical Title, 34*(2), 14–15.	https://doi.org/xxxxx
			[Review of the book *Book title*, by E. E. Editor, Ed.].	*Blog Title.*	https://xxxxxx
			[Review of the film *Film title*, by D. D. Director, Dir.].		
			[Review of the TV series episode "Episode title," by W. W. Writer, Writer, & D. D. Director, Dir.].		

67. Film review published in a journal

Mirabito, L. A., & Heck, N. C. (2016). Bringing LGBTQ youth theater into the spotlight [Review of the film *The year we thought about love*, by E. Brodsky, Dir.]. *Psychology of Sexual Orientation and Gender Diversity*, *3*(4), 499–500. https://doi.org/10.1037/sgd0000205

Parenthetical citation: (Mirabito & Heck, 2016)
Narrative citation: Mirabito and Heck (2016)

68. Book review published in a newspaper

Santos, F. (2019, January 11). Reframing refugee children's stories [Review of the book *We are displaced: My journey and stories from refugee girls around the world*, by M. Yousafzai]. *The New York Times*. https://nyti.ms/2HIgjk3

Parenthetical citation: (Santos, 2019)
Narrative citation: Santos (2019)

69. TV series episode review published on a website

Perkins, D. (2018, February 1). The good place *ends its remarkable second season with irrational hope, unexpected gifts, and a smile* [Review of the TV series episode "Somewhere else," by M. Schur, Writer & Dir.]. A.V. Club. https://www.avclub.com/the-good-place-ends-its-remarkable-second-season-with-i-1822649316

Parenthetical citation: (Perkins, 2018)
Narrative citation: Perkins (2018)

- The title is italicized because this work is a webpage on a website (see Example 112). In the reference, the title of the show appears in reverse italics (see Section 6.23) and sentence case.

10.8 Unpublished Works and Informally Published Works

Unpublished works include work that is in progress, has been completed but not yet submitted for publication, and has been submitted but not yet accepted for publication. Informally published works include work that is available from a preprint archive or repository such as PsyArXiv, an electronic archive such as ERIC, an institutional archive, a government archive, a personal website, and so forth. Refer to the final published version of your sources when possible (see Section 8.5); remember to update your references prior to publication of your work or submission for a classroom assignment to ensure they contain the most up-to-date publication information.

For an unpublished or informally published work, the date should be the year the work was completed or the year the draft was written. Do not use the words "in preparation," "submitted," or "submitted for publication" in the date element of the reference. After the title, describe the status of the work (e.g., unpublished, in preparation, submitted for publication) using the appropriate descriptor for the work (e.g., manuscript, report) in square brackets. When the source of the unpublished work is known (e.g., a university or university department), include it in the source element of the reference. Include a DOI or URL when available for informally published works.

Use the template shown next to construct references for unpublished works.

Author	Date	Title	Source	
			University information	**URL**
Author, A. A., & Author, B. B.	(2020).	*Title of the work* [Unpublished manuscript]. *Title of work* [Manuscript in preparation]. *Title of work* [Manuscript submitted for publication].	Department Name, University Name.	https://xxxxx

Use the template shown next to construct references for informally published works.

Author	Date	Title	Source	
			Database or archive information	**DOI or URL**
Author, A. A., & Author B. B.	(2020).	*Title of the work.* *Title of the work* (Publication No. 123).	Name of Database. Name of Archive.	https://doi.org/ xxxxx https://xxxxxx

70. Unpublished manuscript

Yoo, J., Miyamoto, Y., Rigotti, A., & Ryff, C. (2016). *Linking positive affect to blood lipids: A cultural perspective* [Unpublished manuscript]. Department of Psychology, University of Wisconsin–Madison.

Parenthetical citation: (Yoo et al., 2016)
Narrative citation: Yoo et al. (2016)

- An unpublished manuscript is only in the authors' possession. Treat a manuscript available online as informally published (see Examples 73–74).
- Include the department and institution where the work was produced, if possible.

71. Manuscript in preparation

O'Shea, M. (2018). *Understanding proactive behavior in the workplace as a function of gender* [Manuscript in preparation]. Department of Management, University of Kansas.

Parenthetical citation: (O'Shea, 2018)
Narrative citation: O'Shea (2018)

- A manuscript in preparation is only in the authors' possession. Treat a manuscript available online as informally published (see Examples 73–74).
- Include the department and institution where the work was produced, if possible.

72. Manuscript submitted for publication

Lippincott, T., & Poindexter, E. K. (2019). *Emotion recognition as a function of facial cues: Implications for practice* [Manuscript submitted for publication]. Department of Psychology, University of Washington.

Parenthetical citation: (Lippincott & Poindexter, 2019)
Narrative citation: Lippincott and Poindexter (2019)

- Do not list the name of the journal to which the work was submitted. Once the manuscript has been accepted for publication, cite it as an in-press article (see Example 8).
- A manuscript submitted for publication is not available to the public. If the manuscript is available online, treat it as informally published (see Examples 73–74).

73. Informally published work, from a preprint archive or an institutional repository

Leuker, C., Samartzidis, L., Hertwig, R., & Pleskac, T. J. (2018). *When money talks: Judging risk and coercion in high-paying clinical trials.* PsyArXiv. https://doi.org/10.17605/OSF.IO/9P7CB

Stults-Kolehmainen, M. A., & Sinha, R. (2015). *The effects of stress on physical activity and exercise.* PubMed Central. https://www.ncbi.nlm.nih.gov/pmc/articles/PMC3894304

Parenthetical citations: (Leuker et al., 2018; Stults-Kolehmainen & Sinha, 2015)
Narrative citations: Leuker et al. (2018) and Stults-Kolehmainen and Sinha (2015)

- The informally published work may not be peer reviewed (as with Leuker et al.'s preprint article from PsyArXiv), or it may be the author's final, peer-reviewed manuscript as accepted for publication (as with Stults-Kolehmainen & Sinha's manuscript from PubMed Central). See Section 8.5 for more on use of an archival version.

74. Informally published work, from ERIC database

Ho, H.-K. (2014). *Teacher preparation for early childhood special education in Taiwan* (ED545393). ERIC. https://files.eric.ed.gov/fulltext/ED545393.pdf

Parenthetical citation: (Ho, 2014)
Narrative citation: Ho (2014)

- ERIC assigns document numbers to the works in the database. Include this number in parentheses after the title of the work.

Data Sets, Software, and Tests

10.9 Data Sets

Citing data supports their discovery and reuse, leading to better science through the validation of results. It also recognizes data as an essential part of the scientific record and acknowledges data creators for their contributions. We recommend that authors include an in-text citation and a reference list entry for a data set when they have either (a) conducted secondary analyses of publicly archived data or (b) archived their own data being presented for the first time in the current work (see also Section 1.14 on data retention and sharing).

The date for published data is the year of publication and for unpublished data is the year(s) of collection. When a version number exists, include it in parentheses after the title. The bracketed description is flexible (e.g., data set, data set and code book). In the source element of the reference, for published data, provide the name of the organization that has published, archived, produced, or distributed the data set; for unpublished data, provide the source (e.g., a university), if known. Include a retrieval date only if the data set is designed to change over time (e.g., if data are still undergoing collection; see Section 9.16 for more on retrieval dates). Use the template shown next to construct references for data sets.

Author	Date	Title	Source	
			Publisher	**DOI or URL**
Author, A. A., & Author, B. B.	(2020). (2015–	*Title of data set* (Version 1.2) [Data set].	Publisher Name.	https://doi.org/ xxxxx
Name of Group.	2019).	*Title of data set* [Unpublished raw data].	Source of Unpublished	https://xxxxxx
		[Description of untitled data set] [Unpublished raw data].	Data.	Retrieved October 21, 2020, from https://xxxxx

75. Data set

D'Souza, A., & Wiseheart, M. (2018). *Cognitive effects of music and dance training in children* (ICPSR 37080; Version V1) [Data set]. ICPSR. https://doi.org/10.3886/ICPSR37080.v1

National Center for Education Statistics. (2016). *Fast Response Survey System (FRSS): Teachers' use of educational technology in U.S. public schools, 2009* (ICPSR 35531; Version V3) [Data set and code book]. National Archive of Data on Arts and Culture. https://doi.org/10.3886/ICPSR35531.v3

Pew Research Center. (2018). *American trends panel Wave 26* [Data set]. https://www.pewsocialtrends.org/dataset/american-trends-panel-wave-26/

Parenthetical citations: (D'Souza & Wiseheart, 2018; National Center for Education Statistics, 2016; Pew Research Center, 2018)

Narrative citations: D'Souza and Wiseheart (2018), National Center for Education Statistics (2016), and Pew Research Center (2018)

76. Unpublished raw data

Baer, R. A. (2015). [Unpublished raw data on the correlations between the Five Facet Mindfulness Questionnaire and the Kentucky Inventory of Mindfulness Skills]. University of Kentucky.

Oregon Youth Authority. (2011). *Recidivism outcomes* [Unpublished raw data].

Parenthetical citations: (Baer, 2015; Oregon Youth Authority, 2011)
Narrative citations: Baer (2015) and Oregon Youth Authority (2011)

- For an untitled data set, provide a description in square brackets of the publication status and focus of the data.
- When the source of unpublished raw data is known (e.g., a university or a university department), include it at the end of the reference.

10.10 Computer Software, Mobile Apps, Apparatuses, and Equipment

Common software and mobile apps mentioned in text, but not paraphrased or quoted, do not need citations, nor do programming languages. "Common" is relative to your field and audience—examples of software or apps that do not require citations include Microsoft Office (e.g., Word, Excel, PowerPoint), social media apps (e.g., Facebook, Instagram, Twitter), survey software (e.g., Qualtrics, Survey Monkey), Adobe products (e.g., Adobe Reader, Photoshop, Adobe Acrobat), Java, and statistical programs (e.g., R, SPSS, SAS). If you used common software or mobile apps during your research, simply give the proper name of the software or app along the with version number in the text, if relevant.

Data were analyzed with IBM SPSS Statistics (Version 25).
Clients had installed the Facebook app on their mobile devices.

However, include reference list entries and in-text citations if you have paraphrased or quoted from any software or app. Also provide reference list entries and in-text citations when mentioning software, apps, and apparatuses or equipment of limited distribution—meaning your audience is unlikely to be familiar with them. The date of a computer software or mobile app reference is the year of publication of the version used. The titles of software and apps should be italicized in the reference list entry but not italicized in the text. To cite content on a social media app, see Section 10.15. Use the template shown next to construct references for software and mobile apps of limited distribution and for apparatuses or equipment.

Author	Date	Title	Source	
			Publisher	**URL**
Author, A. A., & Author, B. B. Name of Group.	(2020).	*Title of work* (Version 1.2) [Computer software]. *Title of work* (Version 4.6) [Mobile app]. *Name of apparatus* (Model number) [Apparatus]. *Name of equipment* (Model number) [Equipment].	Publisher. App Store. Google Play Store.	https://xxxxxx

Use the template shown next to construct references for entries in mobile app reference works. The format for an entry in a mobile app reference work is similar to that for a chapter in an edited book. The most common case, in which the same author is responsible for the whole work and all entries, is shown here.

Author	Date	Entry title	Source	
			Mobile app information	**URL**
Author, A. A., & Author, B. B. Name of Group.	(2020).	Title of entry.	In *Title of work* (Version 1.2) [Mobile app]. Publisher Name or App Store.	https://xxxxxx

77. Software

Borenstein, M., Hedges, L., Higgins, J., & Rothstein, H. (2014). *Comprehensive meta-analysis* (Version 3.3.070) [Computer software]. Biostat. https://www.meta-analysis.com/

Parenthetical citation: (Borenstein et al., 2014)
Narrative citation: Borenstein et al. (2014)

78. Apparatus or equipment

SR Research. (2016). *Eyelink 1000 plus* [Apparatus and software]. https://www.sr-research.com/eyelink1000plus.html

Tactile Labs. (2015). *Latero tactile display* [Apparatus]. http://tactilelabs.com/products/haptics/latero-tactile-display/

Parenthetical citations: (SR Research, 2016; Tactile Labs, 2015)
Narrative citations: SR Research (2016) and Tactile Labs (2015)

- If the apparatus or equipment comes with software, list both in the description.
- If the apparatus or equipment has a model number that is not included in the title, include the number after the title in parentheses.
- Because the author and publisher are the same, omit the publisher.

79. Mobile app

Epocrates. (2019). *Epocrates medical references* (Version 18.12) [Mobile app]. App Store. https://itunes.apple.com/us/app/epocrates/id281935788?mt=8

Parenthetical citation: (Epocrates, 2019)
Narrative citation: Epocrates (2019)

80. Entry in a mobile app reference work

Epocrates. (2019). Interaction check: Aspirin + sertraline. In *Epocrates medical references* (Version 18.12) [Mobile app]. Google Play Store. https://play.google.com/store/apps/details?id=com.epocrates&hl=en_US

Parenthetical citation: (Epocrates, 2019)
Narrative citation: Epocrates (2019)

10.11 Tests, Scales, and Inventories

To cite a test, scale, or inventory, provide a citation for its supporting literature (e.g., its manual, which may be an authored or an edited book, or the journal article in which it was published; see Example 81). If supporting literature is not available, it is also possible to cite the test itself (see Example 82) and/or a database record for a test (see Example 83). The title of a test, a scale, or an inventory should be capitalized using title case whenever it appears in a paper. Although the test title may be italicized in a reference (e.g., in the name of a manual or when the test itself is cited), in the text, the title of a test should appear in title case in standard (nonitalic) type. A test database name (e.g., PsycTESTS, ETS TestLink) is included only for test database records (see Example 83). Use the template shown next to construct references for tests, scales, inventories, or test database records.

Author	Date	Title	Source	
			Database	URL
Author, A. A., & Author, B. B.	(2020).	*Title of the Test.* *Title of the Test Database Record* [Database record].	Test Database Name.	https://xxxxxx

81. Manual for a test, scale, or inventory

Tellegen, A., & Ben-Porath, Y. S. (2011). *Minnesota Multiphasic Personality Inventory–2 Restructured Form (MMPI-2-RF): Technical manual.* Pearson.

Parenthetical citation: (Tellegen & Ben-Porath, 2011)
Narrative citation: Tellegen and Ben-Porath (2011)

82. Test, scale, or inventory itself

Project Implicit. (n.d.). *Gender–Science IAT.* https://implicit.harvard.edu/implicit/takeatest.html

Parenthetical citation: (Project Implicit, n.d.)
Narrative citation: Project Implicit (n.d.)

- Cite the test, scale, or inventory itself only if a manual or other supporting literature is not available to cite; if a manual is available for a test, cite the manual, not the test (see Example 81).

83. Database record for a test

Alonso-Tapia, J., Nieto, C., Merino-Tejedor, E., Huertas, J. A., & Ruiz, M. (2018). *Situated Goals Questionnaire for University Students (SGQ-U, CMS-U)* [Database record]. PsycTESTS. https://doi.org/10.1037/t66267-000

Cardoza, D., Morris, J. K., Myers, H. F., & Rodriguez, N. (2000). *Acculturative Stress Inventory (ASI)* (TC022704) [Database record]. ETS TestLink.

Parenthetical citations: (Alonso-Tapia et al., 2018; Cardoza et al., 2000)
Narrative citations: Alonso-Tapia et al. (2018) and Cardoza et al. (2000)

- Test database records (e.g., records from PsycTESTS, the ETS TestLink collection, or the CINAHL database) typically provide unique descriptive and administrative information about tests; cite the database record if you use this unique information. Otherwise, cite the test's supporting literature, if available.

Audiovisual Media

Audiovisual media may have both visual and audio components (e.g., films, TV shows, YouTube videos; see Section 10.12), audio components only (e.g., music, speech recordings; see Section 10.13), or visual components only (e.g., artwork, PowerPoint slides, photographs; see Section 10.14). The reference examples that follow are divided into those categories as an aid to readers of this manual; however, they follow the same formats, so the guidance is presented together here.

The formats for audiovisual references follow a pattern based on whether the work stands alone (e.g., films, whole TV series, podcasts, webinars, music albums, artwork, YouTube videos) or is part of a greater whole (e.g., TV series episodes, podcast episodes, songs from a music album).

The author of an audiovisual work is determined by media type, as shown next.

Media type	Include as the author
Film	Director
TV series	Executive producer(s)
TV series episode	Writer and director of episode
Podcast	Host or executive producer
Podcast episode	Host of episode
Webinar	Instructor
Classical music album or song	Composer
Modern music album or song	Recording artist
Artwork	Artist
Online streaming video	Person or group who uploaded the video
Photograph	Photographer

Describe the audiovisual work in square brackets—for example, "[Film]," "[TV series]," "[Audio podcast episode]," "[Song]," "[Painting]," and so forth in the title element of the reference. In the source element of the reference, provide the name of the production company for films, TV series, or podcasts; the label for music albums; the museum name and location for artwork; or the name of the streaming video site that hosts a streaming video. To cite a direct quotation from an audiovisual work (e.g., from a film), see Section 8.28; for interviews, see Section 8.7. If you want to reproduce an audiovisual work (e.g., a photograph or clip art) rather than just cite it, you may need to seek permission from the copyright owner and/or provide a copyright attribution per the terms of the image license (see Section 12.15 for more).

Use the template shown next to construct references for audiovisual media that stand alone.

Author	Date	Title	Source	
			Publisher	**URL**
Director, D. D. (Director).	(2020).	*Title of work* [Description].	Production Company.	https://xxxxxx
Producer, P. P. (Executive Producer).	(1989–present). (2013–2019).		Label.	
Host, H. H. (Host).	(2019, July 21).		Museum Name, Museum Location.	
Artist, A. A.			Department Name, University Name.	
Uploader, U. U.				

Use the template shown next to construct references for audiovisual media that are part of a greater whole.

Author	Date	Title	Source	
			Publisher	**URL**
Writer, W. W. (Writer), & Director, D. D. (Director).	(2020). (2020, March 26).	Title of episode (Season No., Episode No.) [Description].	In P. P. Producer (Executive Producer), *Title of TV series.* Production Company.	https://xxxxxx
Host, H. H. (Host).		Title of song [Description].	In *Title of podcast.* Production Company.	
Producer, P. P. (Producer).			On *Title of album.* Label.	
Composer, C. C.				
Artist, A. A.				

10.12 Audiovisual Works

84. Film or video

Forman, M. (Director). (1975). *One flew over the cuckoo's nest* [Film]. United Artists.

Fosha, D. (Guest Expert), & Levenson, H. (Host). (2017). *Accelerated experiential dynamic psychotherapy (AEDP) supervision* [Film; educational DVD]. American Psychological Association. https://www.apa.org/pubs/videos/4310958.aspx

Jackson, P. (Director). (2001). *The lord of the rings: The fellowship of the ring* [Film; four-disc special extended ed. on DVD]. WingNut Films; The Saul Zaentz Company.

Parenthetical citations: (Forman, 1975; Fosha & Levenson, 2017; Jackson, 2001)
Narrative citations: Forman (1975), Fosha and Levenson (2017), and Jackson (2001)

- The director should be credited as the author of a film. However, if the director is unknown (as with the Fosha & Levenson example), someone in a similar role can be credited instead to aid readers in retrieving the work; the description of role in this case matches what is on the work and is flexible.
- It is not necessary to specify how you watched a film (e.g., in a theater, on DVD, streaming online). However, the format or other descriptive information may be included—within the square brackets, following the word "Film" and a semi-colon—when you need to specify the version used (e.g., when the film's DVD release includes a commentary or special feature that you used, or when the film is a limited-release educational video or DVD). Adjust this wording as needed.

85. Film or video in another language

Malle, L. (Director). (1987). *Au revoir les enfants* [Goodbye children] [Film]. Nouvelles Éditions de Films.

> *Parenthetical citation:* (Malle, 1987)
> *Narrative citation:* Malle (1987)

- When a film title is in a different language than your paper, include a translation of the title in square brackets (see Section 9.38).

86. TV series

Simon, D., Colesberry, R. F., & Kostroff Noble, N. (Executive Producers). (2002–2008). *The wire* [TV series]. Blown Deadline Productions; HBO.

> *Parenthetical citation:* (Simon et al., 2002–2008)
> *Narrative citation:* Simon et al. (2002–2008)

- When the series spans multiple years, separate the years with an en dash. If the series is still airing, replace the second year with the word "present": (2015–present).

87. TV series episode or webisode

Barris, K. (Writer & Director). (2017, January 11). Lemons (Season 3, Episode 12) [TV series episode]. In K. Barris, J. Groff, A. Anderson, E. B. Dobbins, L. Fishburne, & H. Sugland (Executive Producers), *Black-ish*. Wilmore Films; Artists First; Cinema Gypsy Productions; ABC Studios.

Oakley, B. (Writer), Weinstein, J. (Writer), & Lynch, J. (Director). (1995, May 21). Who shot Mr. Burns? (Part one) (Season 6, Episode 25) [TV series episode]. In D. Mirkin, J. L. Brooks, M. Groening, & S. Simon (Executive Producers), *The Simpsons*. Gracie Films; Twentieth Century Fox Film Corporation.

> *Parenthetical citations:* (Barris, 2017; Oakley et al., 1995)
> *Narrative citations:* Barris (2017) and Oakley et al. (1995)

- Include writer(s) and the director for the episode. Include the contributor roles in parentheses after each contributor's name. "Writer" and "Director" are shown here, but "Executive Director" or other role descriptions might also be used.
- Provide the season number and episode number after the title in parentheses.

88. TED Talk

Giertz, S. (2018, April). *Why you should make useless things* [Video]. TED Conferences. https://www.ted.com/talks/simone_giertz_why_you_should_make_useless_things

TED. (2012, March 16). *Brené Brown: Listening to shame* [Video]. YouTube. https://www.youtube.com/watch?v=psN1DORYYV0

> *Parenthetical citations:* (Giertz, 2018; TED, 2012)
> *Narrative citations:* Giertz (2018) and TED (2012)

- When the TED Talk comes from TED's website (as with the Giertz example), use the name of the speaker as the author. When the TED Talk is on YouTube, list the owner of the YouTube account (here, TED) as the author to aid in retrieval.
- When the speaker is not listed as the author, integrate their name into the narrative if desired: "Brown discussed shame as a human experience (TED, 2012)."
- To cite a quotation from a TED Talk, see Section 8.28.

89. Webinar, recorded

Goldberg, J. F. (2018). *Evaluating adverse drug effects* [Webinar]. American Psychiatric Association. https://education.psychiatry.org/Users/ProductDetails.aspx?ActivityID=6172

Parenthetical citation: (Goldberg, 2018)
Narrative citation: Goldberg (2018)

- Use this format only for recorded, retrievable webinars.
- Cite unrecorded webinars as personal communications (see Section 8.9).

90. YouTube video or other streaming video

Cutts, S. (2017, November 24). *Happiness* [Video]. Vimeo. https://vimeo.com/244405542

Fogarty, M. [Grammar Girl]. (2016, September 30). *How to diagram a sentence (absolute basics)* [Video]. YouTube. https://youtu.be/deiEY5Yq1ql

University of Oxford. (2018, December 6). *How do geckos walk on water?* [Video]. YouTube. https://www.youtube.com/watch?v=qm1xGfOZJc8

Parenthetical citations: (Cutts, 2017; Fogarty, 2016; University of Oxford, 2018)
Narrative citations: Cutts (2017), Fogarty (2016), and University of Oxford (2018)

- The person or group who uploaded the video is credited as the author for retrievability, even if they did not create the work. Note the contributions of others who appear in the video in the text narrative if desired (see Example 88).
- See Section 9.8 for how to present usernames. To cite a quotation from a YouTube or other streaming video, see Section 8.28.

10.13 Audio Works

See the introduction to the Audiovisual Media section for templates for audio works.

91. Music album

Bach, J. S. (2010). *The Brandenburg concertos: Concertos BWV 1043 & 1060* [Album recorded by Academy of St Martin in the Fields]. Decca. (Original work published 1721)

Bowie, D. (2016). *Blackstar* [Album]. Columbia.

Parenthetical citations: (Bach, 1721/2010; Bowie, 2016)
Narrative citations: Bach (1721/2010) and Bowie (2016)

- For a recording of a classical work, provide the composer as the author, and note (in square brackets) following the title the individual or group who recorded the version you used. Provide the publication date for the version you used, and then provide the year of original composition in parentheses at the end of the reference.
- For all other recordings, provide the name of the recording artist or group as the author.
- It is not usually necessary to specify how you listened to an album (e.g., streaming on Spotify, iTunes, Amazon Music, Pandora, Tidal; on CD). However, the format

or other descriptive information may be included—in square brackets, following the word "Album" and a semicolon—when you need to specify the version you used (e.g., when a version of an album includes special tracks or features you accessed). Adjust this wording as needed.

- Include a URL in the reference if that location is the only means of retrieval (e.g., for artists who provide music in only one location, such as SoundCloud or their website).

92. Single song or track

Beethoven, L. van. (2012). Symphony No. 3 in E-flat major [Song recorded by Staats-kapelle Dresden]. On *Beethoven: Complete symphonies*. Brilliant Classics. (Original work published 1804)

Beyoncé. (2016). Formation [Song]. On *Lemonade*. Parkwood; Columbia.

Childish Gambino. (2018). This is America [Song]. mcDJ; RCA.

Lamar, K. (2017). Humble [Song]. On *Damn*. Aftermath Entertainment; Interscope Records; Top Dawg Entertainment.

> *Parenthetical citations:* (Beethoven, 1804/2012; Beyoncé, 2016; Childish Gambino, 2018; Lamar, 2017)
> *Narrative citations:* Beethoven (1804/2012), Beyoncé (2016), Childish Gambino (2018), and Lamar (2017)

- If the song has no associated album (as in the Childish Gambino example), omit that part of the reference.
- Include a URL in the reference if that location is the only means of retrieval (e.g., for artists who provide music in only one location, such as SoundCloud or on their website).

93. Podcast

Vedantam, S. (Host). (2015–present). *Hidden brain* [Audio podcast]. NPR. https://www.npr.org/series/423302056/hidden-brain

> *Parenthetical citation:* (Vedantam, 2015–present)
> *Narrative citation:* Vedantam (2015–present)

- List the host of the podcast as the author. Alternatively, provide the executive producers, if known. In either case, include their role in parentheses.
- Specify the type of podcast (audio or video) in square brackets.
- If the URL of the podcast is unknown (e.g., if accessed via an app), omit the URL.

94. Podcast episode

Glass, I. (Host). (2011, August 12). Amusement park (No. 443) [Audio podcast episode]. In *This American life*. WBEZ Chicago. https://www.thisamericanlife.org/radio-archives/episode/443/amusement-park

> *Parenthetical citation:* (Glass, 2011)
> *Narrative citation:* Glass (2011)

- List the host of the podcast as the author and include their role in parentheses.
- Provide the episode number after the title in parentheses. If the podcast does not number episodes, omit the number from the reference.
- Specify the type of podcast (audio or video) in square brackets.
- If the URL of the podcast is unknown (e.g., if accessed via an app), omit the URL.

REFERENCE EXAMPLES

95. Radio interview recording in a digital archive

de Beauvoir, S. (1960, May 4). *Simone de Beauvoir discusses the art of writing* [Interview]. Studs Terkel Radio Archive; The Chicago History Museum. https://studsterkel.wfmt.com/programs/simone-de-beauvoir-discusses-art-writing

Parenthetical citation: (de Beauvoir, 1960)
Narrative citation: de Beauvoir (1960)

- For interviews that are housed in digital or physical archives (whether in audio or audiovisual form), credit the interviewee as the author. For more on interviews, see Section 8.7.

96. Speech audio recording

King, M. L., Jr. (1963, August 28). *I have a dream* [Speech audio recording]. American Rhetoric. https://www.americanrhetoric.com/speeches/mlkihaveadream.htm

Parenthetical citation: (King, 1963)
Narrative citation: King (1963)

10.14 Visual Works

See the introduction to the Audiovisual Media section for templates for visual works.

97. Artwork in a museum or on a museum website

Delacroix, E. (1826–1827). *Faust attempts to seduce Marguerite* [Lithograph]. The Louvre, Paris, France.

Wood, G. (1930). *American gothic* [Painting]. Art Institute of Chicago, Chicago, IL, United States. https://www.artic.edu/aic/collections/artwork/6565

Parenthetical citations: (Delacroix, 1826–1827; Wood, 1930)
Narrative citations: Delacroix (1826–1827) and Wood (1930)

- Use this format to cite all types of museum artwork, including paintings, sculptures, photographs, prints, drawings, and installations; always include a description of the medium or format in square brackets after the title.
- For untitled art, include a description in square brackets in place of a title.

98. Clip art or stock image

GDJ. (2018). *Neural network deep learning prismatic* [Clip art]. Openclipart. https://openclipart.org/detail/309343/neural-network-deep-learning-prismatic

Parenthetical citation: (GDJ, 2018)
Narrative citation: GDJ (2018)

- Use this format to cite (but not reproduce) most clip art or stock images. To reproduce clip art or stock images, permission and/or a copyright attribution may be necessary in addition to the reference. No citation, permission, or copyright attribution is necessary for clip art from programs like Microsoft Word or PowerPoint (see Section 12.15).

99. Infographic

Rossman, J., & Palmer, R. (2015). *Sorting through our space junk* [Infographic]. World Science Festival. https://www.worldsciencefestival.com/2015/11/space-junk-infographic/

Parenthetical citation: (Rossman & Palmer, 2015)
Narrative citation: Rossman and Palmer (2015)

- Use this format to cite (but not reproduce) an infographic. To reproduce an infographic, permission and/or a copyright attribution may be necessary in addition to the reference (see Section 12.15).

100. Map

Cable, D. (2013). *The racial dot map* [Map]. University of Virginia, Weldon Cooper Center for Public Service. https://demographics.coopercenter.org/Racial-Dot-Map

Google. (n.d.). [Google Maps directions for driving from La Paz, Bolivia, to Lima, Peru]. Retrieved February 16, 2020, from https://goo.gl/YYE3GR

Parenthetical citations: (Cable, 2013; Google, n.d.)
Narrative citations: Cable (2013) and Google (n.d.)

- Because dynamically created maps (e.g., Google Maps) do not have a title, describe the map in square brackets, and include a retrieval date.

101. Photograph

McCurry, S. (1985). *Afghan girl* [Photograph]. National Geographic. https://www.nationalgeographic.com/magazine/national-geographic-magazine-50-years-of-covers/#/ngm-1985-jun-714.jpg

Rinaldi, J. (2016). [Photograph series of a boy who finds his footing after abuse by those he trusted]. The Pulitzer Prizes. https://www.pulitzer.org/winners/jessica-rinaldi

Parenthetical citations: (McCurry, 1985; Rinaldi, 2016)
Narrative citations: McCurry (1985) and Rinaldi (2016)

- Use this format to cite (but not reproduce) photographs or other artwork not connected to a museum (for museum artwork, see Example 97). To reproduce a photograph, permission and/or a copyright attribution may be necessary in addition to the reference (see Section 12.15).
- The source is the name of the site from which the photograph was retrieved.
- For an untitled photograph, include a description in square brackets in place of a title.

102. PowerPoint slides or lecture notes

Canan, E., & Vasilev, J. (2019, May 22). [Lecture notes on resource allocation]. Department of Management Control and Information Systems, University of Chile. https://uchilefau.academia.edu/ElseZCanan

Housand, B. (2016). *Game on! Integrating games and simulations in the classroom* [PowerPoint slides]. SlideShare. https://www.slideshare.net/brianhousand/game-on-iagc-2016/

Mack, R., & Spake, G. (2018). *Citing open source images and formatting references for presentations* [PowerPoint slides]. Canvas@FNU. https://fnu.onelogin.com/login

Parenthetical citations: (Canan & Vasilev, 2019; Housand, 2016; Mack & Spake, 2018)
Narrative citations: Canan and Vasilev (2019), Housand (2016), and Mack and Spake (2018)

- If the slides come from a classroom website, learning management system (e.g., Canvas, Blackboard), or company intranet and you are writing for an audience with access to that resource, provide the name of the site and its URL (use the login page URL for sites requiring login; see Section 8.8).

Online Media

10.15 Social Media

Cite only original content from social media sites such as Twitter, Facebook, Reddit, Instagram, Tumblr, LinkedIn, and so forth. That is, if you used social media to discover content (e.g., you found a link to a blog post on Pinterest or Twitter) and you want to cite the content, cite it directly—it is not necessary to mention that you found it through a link on social media.

Social media posts may contain text only, text with audiovisuals (e.g., photos, videos), or audiovisuals alone. Include the text of a social media post up to the first 20 words. Note the presence of audiovisuals (in square brackets) after the text of the post (see Example 105).

Social media posts might also contain nonstandard spelling and capitalization, hashtags, links, and emojis. Do not alter the spelling and capitalization in a social media reference. Retain hashtags and links. Replicate emojis, if possible. If you are not able to create the emoji, provide the emoji's name in square brackets, for example, "[face with tears of joy emoji]" for 😂. The full list of emoji names can be found on the Unicode Consortium's website (http://unicode.org/emoji/charts/index.html). When calculating the number of words in your paper, count an emoji as one word.

Use the template shown next to construct references to social media content.

			Source	
			Social media site name	URL
Author	Date	Title		
Twitter and Instagram: Author, A. A. [@username]. Name of Group [@username]. Facebook and others: Author, A. A. Name of Group. Name of Group [Username]. Username.	(n.d.). (2019, August 8).	*Content of the post up to the first 20 words.* *Content of the post up to the first 20 words* [Description of audiovisuals]. [Description of audiovisuals].	Site Name.	https://xxxxxx Retrieved August 27, 2020, from https://xxxxxx

103. Tweet

APA Education [@APAEducation]. (2018, June 29). *College students are forming mental-health clubs—and they're making a difference @washingtonpost* [Thumbnail with link attached] [Tweet]. Twitter. https://twitter.com/apaeducation/status/1012810490530140161

Badlands National Park [@BadlandsNPS]. (2018, February 26). *Biologists have identified more than 400 different plant species growing in @BadlandsNPS #DYK #biodiversity* [Tweet]. Twitter. https://twitter.com/BadlandsNPS/status/968196500412133379

White, B. [@BettyMWhite]. (2018, June 21). *I treasure every minute we spent together #koko* [Image attached] [Tweet]. Twitter. https://twitter.com/BettyMWhite/status/1009951892846227456

Parenthetical citations: (APA Education, 2018; Badlands National Park, 2018; White, 2018)

Narrative citations: APA Education (2018), Badlands National Park (2018), and White (2018)

- If the tweet includes images (including animated gifs), videos, thumbnail links to outside sources, links to other tweets (as in a retweet with comment), or a poll, indicate that in square brackets. For tweet replies, do not include the "replying to" information; if that is important to note, do so within the in-text citation.
- Replicate emojis if possible (see the introduction to Section 10.15 for more).

104. Twitter profile

APA Style [@APA_Style]. (n.d.). *Tweets* [Twitter profile]. Twitter. Retrieved November 1, 2019, from https://twitter.com/APA_Style

Parenthetical citation: (APA Style, n.d.)
Narrative citation: APA Style (n.d.)

- Provide a retrieval date because the contents of the page can change over time.
- A Twitter profile has several tabs ("Tweets" is the default). To create a reference to one of the other tabs (e.g., "Lists" or "Moments"), substitute that tab name for "Tweets" in the reference.
- Include the notation "Twitter profile" in square brackets.

105. Facebook post

Gaiman, N. (2018, March 22). *100,000+ Rohingya refugees could be at serious risk during Bangladesh's monsoon season. My fellow UNHCR Goodwill Ambassador Cate Blanchett is* [Image attached] [Status update]. Facebook. http://bit.ly/2JQxPAD

National Institute of Mental Health. (2018, November 28). *Suicide affects all ages, genders, races, and ethnicities. Check out these 5 Action Steps for Helping Someone in Emotional Pain* [Infographic]. Facebook. http://bit.ly/321Qstq

News From Science. (2018, June 26). *These frogs walk instead of hop: https://scim. ag/2KlriwH* [Video]. Facebook. https://www.facebook.com/ScienceNOW/videos/10155508587605108/

Parenthetical citations: (Gaiman, 2018; National Institute of Mental Health, 2018; News From Science, 2018)

Narrative citations: Gaiman (2018), National Institute of Mental Health (2018), and News From Science (2018)

- This format can be used for posts to other social media services, including Tumblr, LinkedIn, and so forth.
- If a status update includes images, videos, thumbnail links to outside sources, or content from another Facebook post (such as when sharing a link), indicate that in square brackets.
- Replicate emojis if possible (see the introduction to Section 10.15 for more).

106. Facebook page

Smithsonian's National Zoo and Conservation Biology Institute. (n.d.). *Home* [Facebook page]. Facebook. Retrieved July 22, 2019, from https://www.facebook.com/nationalzoo

Parenthetical citation: (Smithsonian's National Zoo and Conservation Biology Institute, n.d.)
Narrative citation: Smithsonian's National Zoo and Conservation Biology Institute (n.d.)

- Use the page title in the reference (e.g., "Timeline," "Home," "Photos," "About").
- Include the notation "Facebook page" in square brackets.

- This format can be used or adapted for references to other platform or profile pages, including YouTube, Instagram, Tumblr, LinkedIn, and so forth.

107. Instagram photo or video

Zeitz MOCAA [@zeitzmocaa]. (2018, November 26). *Grade 6 learners from Parkfields Primary School in Hanover Park visited the museum for a tour and workshop hosted by* [Photographs]. Instagram. https://www.instagram.com/p/BqpHpjFBs3b/

Parenthetical citation: (Zeitz MOCAA, 2018)
Narrative citation: Zeitz MOCAA (2018)

108. Instagram highlight

The New York Public Library [@nypl]. (n.d.). *The raven* [Highlight]. Instagram. Retrieved April 16, 2019, from https://bitly.com/2FV8bu3

Parenthetical citation: (The New York Public Library, n.d.)
Narrative citation: The New York Public Library (n.d.)

- Use "n.d." for the date; although each story within a highlight is dated, the highlight itself is not dated and may include stories from multiple dates.
- Because a highlight can change at any time, include the retrieval date.
- Because the URL was long and complex, it has been shortened (see Section 9.36). Either the long or the short form of the URL is acceptable.

109. Online forum post

National Aeronautics and Space Administration [nasa]. (2018, September 12). *I'm NASA astronaut Scott Tingle. Ask me anything about adjusting to being back on Earth after my first spaceflight!* [Online forum post]. Reddit. https://www.reddit.com/r/IAmA/comments/9fagqy/im_nasa_astronaut_scott_tingle_ask_me_anything/

Parenthetical citation: (National Aeronautics and Space Administration, 2018)
Narrative citation: National Aeronautics and Space Administration (2018)

- For more on formatting usernames, see Section 9.8.

10.16 Webpages and Websites

Use the webpages and websites category if there is no other reference category that fits and the work has no parent or overarching publication (e.g., journal, blog, conference proceedings) other than the website itself (see Section 9.2). If you cite multiple webpages from a website, create a reference for each. To mention a website in general, do not create a reference list entry or an in-text citation. Instead, include the name of the website in the text and provide the URL in parentheses (see Section 8.22 for an example).

For help in determining the author of a webpage or website reference, including how the author can be inferred from context or found on an "about us" or acknowledgments page, see Example 113 as well as Section 9.7. Provide the most specific date possible (see Section 9.15 for information on how to handle updated dates or reviewed dates)—for example, a year, month, and day; year and month; or year only. When the author name and the site name are the same, omit the site name from the source element. Include a retrieval date only when the content is designed to change over time and the page is not archived (see Section 9.16).

Use the template shown next to construct references for webpages or websites.

Author	Date	Title	Source	
			Website name	URL
Author, A. A., & Author, B. B. Name of Group.	(2020). (2020, August). (2020, September 28). (n.d.).	*Title of work.*	Site Name.	https://xxxxxx Retrieved December 22, 2020, from https://xxxxx

110. Webpage on a news website

Avramova, N. (2019, January 3). *The secret to a long, happy, healthy life? Think age-positive.* CNN. https://www.cnn.com/2019/01/03/health/respect-toward-elderly-leads-to-long-life-intl/index.html

Bologna, C. (2018, June 27). *What happens to your mind and body when you feel homesick?* HuffPost. https://www.huffingtonpost.com/entry/what-happens-mind-body-homesick_us_5b201ebde4b09d7a3d77eee1

Parenthetical citations: (Avramova, 2019; Bologna, 2018)
Narrative citations: Avramova (2019) and Bologna (2018)

• Use this format for articles published in online news sources (e.g., BBC News, Bloomberg, CNN, HuffPost, MSNBC, Reuters, Salon, Vox). To cite articles from online magazines or newspapers, see Examples 15 and 16.

111. Webpage on a website with a group author

Centers for Disease Control and Prevention. (2018, January 23). *People at high risk of developing flu-related complications.* https://www.cdc.gov/flu/about/disease/high_risk.htm

World Health Organization. (2018, March). *Questions and answers on immunization and vaccine safety.* https://www.who.int/features/qa/84/en/

Parenthetical citations: (Centers for Disease Control and Prevention, 2018; World Health Organization, 2018)
Narrative citations: Centers for Disease Control and Prevention (2018) and World Health Organization (2018)

• When the author and site name are the same, omit the site name from the source element.

112. Webpage on a website with an individual author

Martin Lillie, C. M. (2016, December 29). *Be kind to yourself: How self-compassion can improve your resiliency.* Mayo Clinic. https://www.mayoclinic.org/healthy-lifestyle/adult-health/in-depth/self-compassion-can-improve-your-resiliency/art-20267193

Parenthetical citation: (Martin Lillie, 2016)
Narrative citation: Martin Lillie (2016)

113. Webpage on a website with no date

Boddy, J., Neumann, T., Jennings, S., Morrow, V., Alderson, P., Rees, R., & Gibson, W. (n.d.). *Ethics principles.* The Research Ethics Guidebook: A Resource for Social Scientists. http://www.ethicsguidebook.ac.uk/EthicsPrinciples

National Nurses United. (n.d.). *What employers should do to protect nurses from Zika.* https://www.nationalnursesunited.org/pages/what-employers-should-do-to-protect-rns-from-zika

Parenthetical citations: (Boddy et al., n.d.; National Nurses United, n.d.)
Narrative citations: Boddy et al. (n.d.) and National Nurses United (n.d.)

- In the Boddy et al. example, the authors are listed on the acknowledgments page of the site (see Section 9.7 for more on determining the author).
- When the author and site name are the same, omit the site name from the source element.

114. Webpage on a website with a retrieval date

U.S. Census Bureau. (n.d.). *U.S. and world population clock.* U.S. Department of Commerce. Retrieved July 3, 2019, from https://www.census.gov/popclock/

Parenthetical citation: (U.S. Census Bureau, n.d.)
Narrative citation: U.S. Census Bureau (n.d.)

- When the author and site name are the same, omit the site name from the source element.
- Include a retrieval date because the contents of the page are designed to change over time and the page itself is not archived (see Section 9.16).

11

LEGAL REFERENCES

Contents

11

LEGAL REFERENCES

In APA Style, most legal materials are cited in the standard legal citation style used for legal references across all disciplines. However, legal style has notable differences from the APA Style references outlined in Chapter 10.

In this chapter, we provide information on how APA Style references differ from legal style references; general guidelines for creating APA Style legal references; in-text citation forms for legal materials; and examples of common legal references used in APA Style papers, including court decisions, statutes, legislative materials, administrative and executive materials, patents, constitutions and charters, and treaties and international conventions. For the sake of brevity, only United States and United Nations legal examples are provided in this chapter. For more information on preparing these and other kinds of legal references, consult *The Bluebook: A Uniform System of Citation* (*Bluebook*, 2015).

General Guidelines for Legal References

11.1 APA Style References Versus Legal References

Existing legal references are usually already written in legal style and require few, if any, changes for an APA Style reference list entry. Note that some court decisions are reported in multiple places, which is called *parallel citation* (see Example 6). When a work has parallel citations, include all the citations in your reference list entry. Existing legal citations generally include the parallel citations already, so you should not need to do additional research to find them. The in-text citation for a legal work is created from the reference list entry (see Section 11.3).

Ensure that your legal references are accurate and contain all of the information necessary to enable readers to locate the work being referenced. If you have questions beyond what is covered in this chapter, consult the *Bluebook*, a law librarian, or a law school website for help. For example, the Legal Information Institute at Cornell Law School provides free guidance on legal citations (https://www.law.cornell.edu). These resources will help you verify that your legal references (a) contain the information necessary for retrieval and (b) reflect the current status of the legal authority cited to avoid the possibility of relying on a case that has been overturned on appeal or on legislation that has been significantly amended or repealed. Table 11.1 summarizes key differences between APA Style references and legal style references.

11.2 General Forms

A general form is provided for each of the legal reference types in the sections that follow. Each reference form usually includes a popular or formal title or name of the legislation and the reference information, which is called the *citation*.

> *Note:* The term "citation" is used differently for legal references than it is in standard APA Style. In this chapter, the legal reference sense of the word "citation" is meant when it appears without the modifier "in-text."

Refer to the published statutory compilation of legislative materials where the legislation is codified (e.g., a specific numbered section of a specific volume of the *United States Code*), including the compilation's publication date in parentheses, if the legislation has been codified. If the legislation has not yet been codified, provide the identifying label for the legislation assigned by the enacting body during the particular legislative session (e.g., a specific section of an act identified by its public law number).

For both legislation and court decisions, the reference may be followed by certain additional descriptive information that pertains to the content of the legislation or court decision, the history of the legislation or court decision (e.g., later appeals of court decisions or later amendments to legislation), or other sources from which the legislation or court citation may be retrieved. Consult the *Bluebook* for the proper format for such additional information.

Table 11.1 Key Differences Between APA Style References and Legal References

Difference	APA Style	Legal style
Order of elements in the reference list entry	Usually the author, date, title, and source, in that order	Usually the title, source, and date, in that order
In-text citation	Usually the author and year	Usually the title and year
Version of work being referenced	The exact version used	The version of record as published in an official legal publication such as the *United States Code* or the *Federal Register*, plus a URL (optional) for the version used
Use of standard abbreviations	Used for parts of a work (e.g., "2nd ed." for a second edition)	Used for common legal entities and publications (e.g., "S." for the Senate and "H.R." for the House of Representatives)

Table 11.2   Common Legal Reference Abbreviations

Word or phrase	Abbreviation
Part of government	
Congress	Cong.
House of Representatives	H.R.
Senate	S.
Type of legal material	
Regulation	Reg.
Resolution	Res.
Section of legal material	
Section	§
Sections	§§
Number	No.
And following	*et seq.*
Reporter (source) of federal legal material	
United States Reports	U.S.
Federal Reporter	F.
Federal Reporter, Second Series	F.2d
Federal Reporter, Third Series	F.3d
Federal Supplement	F. Supp.
Federal Supplement, Second Series	F. Supp. 2d
Federal Supplement, Third Series	F. Supp. 3d
United States Code	U.S.C.
Congressional Record	Cong. Rec.
Federal Register	F.R.

Because legal references may include a great deal of information (e.g., a citation to a case may include information about appeals), legal reference style uses abbreviations to make references shorter. See Table 11.2 for some examples of the more common legal abbreviations that appear in APA Style papers.

11.3 In-Text Citations of Legal Materials

Although the reference formats for legal materials differ from those of other kinds of works cited in APA publications, in-text citations are formed in approximately the same way and serve the same purpose. Most legal reference entries begin with the title of the work; as a result, most in-text citations consist of the title and year (e.g., Americans With Disabilities Act, 1990; *Brown v. Board of Education*, 1954). If the title is long (e.g., for federal testimony), shorten it for the in-text citation (see Example 11), but give enough information in the in-text citation to enable readers to locate the entry in the reference list. Examples of in-text citations and reference entries for legal materials are given in the sections that follow.

Legal Reference Examples

11.4 Cases or Court Decisions

A reference for a case or court decision includes the following information:

- **title or name of the case**, usually one party versus another (e.g., *Brown v. Board of Education*);

- **citation**, usually to a volume and page of one of the various sets of books where published cases can be found called *reporters*, which typically contain decisions of courts in particular political divisions, which are called *jurisdictions* (e.g., *Federal Reporter, Second Series*);

- **precise jurisdiction of the court writing the decision** (e.g., Supreme Court, New York Court of Appeals), in parentheses;

- **date of the decision**, in parentheses (in the same set of parentheses as the jurisdiction if both are present); and

- **URL** from which you retrieved the case information (optional; this is not strictly required for legal citations but may aid readers in retrieval).

To create a reference list entry for the case you want to cite, first identify the court that decided the case and then follow the relevant example. Often, the document about the case will have the relevant citation included, or it can easily be retrieved by searching the internet for the name of the court decision and the word "citation." When a reference list entry for a case or court decision includes a page number, provide only the first page number. Do not provide the page range for the whole case or decision.

> *Note:* Unlike other reference types, the title or name of a case is written in standard type in the reference list entry and in italic type in the in-text citation.

Federal Court Decisions. The United States has both federal and state court systems. Within federal courts there are multiple levels of authority, and decisions from these courts are published in different publications.

- **U.S. Supreme Court:** Decisions from the U.S. Supreme Court, the highest federal court, are published in the *United States Reports* (other reporters may also publish Supreme Court decisions). The template for Supreme Court decisions is as follows:

  Reference list: Name v. Name, Volume U.S. Page (Year). URL
  Parenthetical citation: (*Name v. Name*, Year)
  Narrative citation: *Name v. Name* (Year)

- **U.S. Circuit Court:** Decisions from the U.S. Circuit Court are published in the *Federal Reporter.* The template for U.S. Circuit Court decisions is as follows:

  Reference list: Name v. Name, Volume F. [*or* F.2d, F.3d] Page (Court Year). URL
  Parenthetical citation: (*Name v. Name*, Year)
  Narrative citation: *Name v. Name* (Year)

- **U.S. District Court:** Decisions from the U.S. District Court are published in the *Federal Supplements.* The template for U.S. District Court decisions is as follows:

  Reference list: Name v. Name, Volume F. Supp. Page (Court Year). URL
  Parenthetical citation: (*Name v. Name*, Year)
  Narrative citation: *Name v. Name* (Year)

State Court Decisions. At the state level, courts also operate at different levels of authority, although different states have different names for the levels. These levels are as follows:

- **State supreme court:** The state supreme court is generally the highest state court (the state of New York is one exception; the court of appeals is the highest court in that state).

- **State appellate court:** The state court of appeals, also called appellate court, is the intermediate court wherein precedent begins to be established.

- **State trial court:** The state trial court is the lowest court of the state. State trial court decisions are seldom cited because they do not establish precedent, and they are not reported in the prominent legal databases Nexis Uni (formerly LexisNexis Academic) or WestLaw.

The template for state court decisions is as follows:

Reference list: Name v. Name, Volume Reporter Page (Court Year). URL
Parenthetical citation: (Name v. Name, Year)
Narrative citation: Name v. Name (Year)

1. U.S. Supreme Court case, with a page number

Brown v. Board of Education, 347 U.S. 483 (1954). https://www.oyez.org/cases/1940-1955/347us483

Parenthetical citation: (Brown v. Board of Education, 1954)
Narrative citation: Brown v. Board of Education (1954)

- U.S. Supreme Court decisions are published in the *United States Reports* (abbreviated "U.S." in the reference). For example, the decision to eliminate racial segregation in public schools, *Brown v. Board of Education*, was published in Volume 347 of the *United States Reports*, on page 483, in the year 1954. Cite Supreme Court decisions as published in the *United States Reports* whenever possible; cite the *Supreme Court Reporter* for cases that have not yet been published in *United States Reports*.

2. U.S. Supreme Court case, without a page number

Obergefell v. Hodges, 576 U.S. ___ (2015). https://www.supremecourt.gov/opinions/14pdf/14-556_3204.pdf

Parenthetical citation: (Obergefell v. Hodges, 2015)
Narrative citation: Obergefell v. Hodges (2015)

- The court decision to legalize same-sex marriage in the United States, *Obergefell v. Hodges*, occurred in 2015 and was published in Volume 576 of the *United States Reports*. However, as of the printing of this *Publication Manual*, the paginated volumes of the *United States Reports* have been published only for decisions through the 2012 Supreme Court term. For cases that have not been assigned a page number (like *Obergefell v. Hodges*), include three underscores instead of the page number in the reference list entry.

3. U.S. circuit court case

Daubert v. Merrell Dow Pharmaceuticals, Inc., 951 F.2d 1128 (9th Cir. 1991). https://openjurist.org/951/f2d/1128/william-daubert-v-merrell-dow-pharmaceuticals

Parenthetical citation: (Daubert v. Merrell Dow Pharmaceuticals, Inc., 1991)
Narrative citation: Daubert v. Merrell Dow Pharmaceuticals, Inc. (1991)

- This court decision regarding birth defects resulting from medication use during pregnancy appeared in Volume 951 of the *Federal Reporter, Second Series*, on page 1128, and was decided by the 9th Circuit Court in the year 1991.

4. U.S. district court case

Burriola v. Greater Toledo YMCA, 133 F. Supp. 2d 1034 (N.D. Ohio 2001). https://law.justia.com/cases/federal/district-courts/FSupp2/133/1034/2293141/

Parenthetical citation: (*Burriola v. Greater Toledo YMCA*, 2001)
Narrative citation: *Burriola v. Greater Toledo YMCA* (2001)

- This court decision stating that children with special needs should receive accommodations for services at public after-school-care providers under the Americans With Disabilities Act of 1990 appeared in Volume 133 of the *Federal Supplement, Second Series*, on page 1034. It was decided by the U.S. District Court for the Northern District of Ohio in the year 2001.

5. U.S. district court case with appeal

Durflinger v. Artiles, 563 F. Supp. 322 (D. Kan. 1981), *aff'd*, 727 F.2d 888 (10th Cir. 1984). https://openjurist.org/727/f2d/888/durflinger-v-artiles

Parenthetical citation: (*Durflinger v. Artiles*, 1981/1984)
Narrative citation: *Durflinger v. Artiles* (1981/1984)

- This court decision regarding whether third parties should be protected from involuntarily committed psychiatric patients in state custody was rendered by the federal district court for the District of Kansas in the year 1981. On appeal, the decision was affirmed by the federal-level 10th Circuit Court of Appeals in 1984. Information about both the original decision and the appealed decision appears in the reference list entry.
- If on appeal the decision is affirmed, the abbreviation "*aff'd*" is used between the two components, in italics and set off by commas; if the decision is overturned or reversed, the abbreviation "*rev'd*" is used, in italics and set off by commas.
- Consult the *Bluebook* for the proper forms of the various stages in a case's history.

6. State supreme court case

Tarasoff v. Regents of the University of California, 17 Cal.3d 425, 131 Cal. Rptr. 14, 551 P.2d 334 (1976). https://www.casebriefs.com/blog/law/torts/torts-keyed-to-dobbs/the-duty-to-protect-from-third-persons/tarasoff-v-regents-of-university-of-california

Parenthetical citation: (*Tarasoff v. Regents of the University of California*, 1976)
Narrative citation: *Tarasoff v. Regents of the University of California* (1976)

- This court decision held that mental health professionals have a duty to protect individuals who are being threatened with bodily harm by a patient. It was decided by the Supreme Court of the State of California in the year 1976.
- The court decision was reported in three places, which are all included in the parallel citation (see Section 11.1), shown here separated with commas. These three sources are Volume 17 of the *California Reports, Third Series* (Cal.3d), page 425; Volume 131 of the *California Reporter* (Cal. Rptr.), page 14; and Volume 551 of the *Pacific Reporter, Second Series* (P.2d), page 334. All three report locations are generally reported together, so no additional research is needed to find them.

7. State appellate court case

Texas v. Morales, 826 S.W.2d 201 (Tex. Ct. App. 1992). https://www.leagle.com/decision/19921027826sw2d20111010

Parenthetical citation: (*Texas v. Morales*, 1992)
Narrative citation: *Texas v. Morales* (1992)

- This court decision found that the equal protection and due process components of the Texas Constitution prohibit the criminalization of consensual same-sex activity among adults in private. It was published in Volume 826 of the *South Western Reporter, Second Series,* page 201, decided by the Texas State Court of Appeals in the year 1992.

11.5 Statutes (Laws and Acts)

A *statute* is a law or act passed by a legislative body. As with court decisions, statutes exist on both the federal and state levels, such as an act passed by Congress or by a state government.

Federal statutes are published in the *United States Code* (U.S.C.). The U.S.C. is divided into sections called *titles*—for example, Title 42 refers to public health and welfare. New laws are then added to the appropriate title as a way of keeping the law organized. State statutes are published in state-specific compilations; for example, statutes pertaining to the state of Florida are published in the *Florida Statutes.* State statutes are also typically organized into titles.

In the reference list entry for a federal or state statute, include the name of the act; the title, source (abbreviated as specified in the *Bluebook*), and section number of the statute; and, in parentheses, the publication date of the statutory compilation you used (e.g., the U.S.C. or a state-specific compilation). You may include the URL from which you retrieved the statute after the year. This is not strictly required for legal citations but may aid readers in retrieval.

In the in-text citation, give the popular or official name of the act (if any) and the year of the act. Determining the year for the statute can be confusing because there is often a year when the statute was first passed, a year when it was amended, and a year when it was supplemented. The year in the reference list entry and in-text citation should refer to the year in which the statute was published in the source being cited. This date may be different from the year in the name of the act.

The template for federal or state statutes is as follows:

Reference list: Name of Act, Title Source § Section Number (Year). URL
Parenthetical citation: (Name of Act, Year)
Narrative citation: Name of Act (Year)

The format for state statutes may differ depending on the state but generally follows the same format as for federal statutes. Consult the *Bluebook* or another legal resource for further information on your particular state. For example, a few states use chapter or article numbers instead of section numbers; for a reference to a statute from one of these states, use the chapter or article number in the reference in place of the section number. Use abbreviations or symbols as shown in the *Bluebook.*

To cite a federal statute (i.e., a law or act), cite the statute as it was codified in the *United States Code.* You may see a public law number on the act as well; this number is used in the reference list entry when the act is codified in scattered sections (see Example 9) or to refer to an act before it is codified (see Example 11). However, if a statute has been codified in the *United States Code* in a single section or range of sections (see Example 8), it is not necessary to include the public law number in the reference.

Next are several examples of acts commonly cited in APA Style papers. Citations to other federal statutes follow the same format.

8. Federal statute, Americans With Disabilities Act of 1990

Americans With Disabilities Act of 1990, 42 U.S.C. § 12101 *et seq.* (1990). https://www.ada.gov/pubs/adastatute08.htm

> *Parenthetical citation:* (Americans With Disabilities Act, 1990)
> *Narrative citation:* Americans With Disabilities Act (1990)

- This act can be located beginning at Section 12101 of Title 42 of the *United States Code* and was codified in the year 1990. The phrase "*et seq.*" is Latin for "and what follows" and is a shorthand way of showing that the act covers not only the initial section cited but also others that follow.

9. Federal statute, Civil Rights Act of 1964

Civil Rights Act of 1964, Pub. L. No. 88-352, 78 Stat. 241 (1964). https://www.govinfo.gov/content/pkg/STATUTE-78/pdf/STATUTE-78-Pg241.pdf

> *Parenthetical citation:* (Civil Rights Act, 1964)
> *Narrative citation:* Civil Rights Act (1964)

- The Civil Rights Act of 1964 is codified in the *United States Code* in three scattered sections: 2 U.S.C., 28 U.S.C., and 42 U.S.C. To cite the entire act, use the public law number as shown in the example.

10. Federal statute, Every Student Succeeds Act

Every Student Succeeds Act, 20 U.S.C. § 6301 (2015). https://www.congress.gov/114/plaws/publ95/PLAW-114publ95.pdf

> *Parenthetical citation:* (Every Student Succeeds Act, 2015)
> *Narrative citation:* Every Student Succeeds Act (2015)

- The Every Student Succeeds Act pertains to educational policy for students in public primary and secondary schools. It was codified in Title 20 of the *United States Code* in Section 6301 in the year 2015.

11. Federal statute, Lilly Ledbetter Fair Pay Act of 2009

Lilly Ledbetter Fair Pay Act of 2009, Pub. L. No. 111-2, 123 Stat. 5 (2009). https://www.govinfo.gov/content/pkg/PLAW-111publ2/pdf/PLAW-111publ2.pdf

> *Parenthetical citation:* (Lilly Ledbetter Fair Pay Act, 2009)
> *Narrative citation:* Lilly Ledbetter Fair Pay Act (2009)

- The Lilly Ledbetter Fair Pay Act of 2009 amended Title VII of the Civil Rights Act (1964) and other acts and pertains to fair wage compensation. Because it was not codified in the *United States Code*, cite the public law number. It was published in Volume 123 of the *United States Statutes at Large* (abbreviated "Stat.") beginning on page 5 in the year 2009.

12. Federal statute, Title IX (Patsy Mink Equal Opportunity in Education Act)

Patsy Mink Equal Opportunity in Education Act, 20 U.S.C. § 1681 *et seq.* (1972). https://www.justice.gov/crt/title-ix-education-amendments-1972

> *Parenthetical citation:* (Patsy Mink Equal Opportunity in Education Act, 1972)
> *Narrative citation:* Patsy Mink Equal Opportunity in Education Act (1972)

- The Patsy Mink Equal Opportunity in Education Act, commonly known as Title IX, prohibits discrimination on the basis of sex in federally funded educational programs such as sports. It was published in Volume 20 of the *United States Code*, beginning at Section 1681, in the year 1972. Note that "Title IX" refers to part of the Education Amendments of 1972, not Title 9 of the *United States Code*.

13. State statute in state code

Florida Mental Health Act, Fla. Stat. § 394 (1971 & rev. 2009). http://www.leg.state.fl.us/statutes/index.cfm?App_mode=Display_Statute&URL=0300-0399/0394/0394.html

> *Parenthetical citation:* (Florida Mental Health Act, 1971/2009)
> *Narrative citation:* Florida Mental Health Act (1971/2009)

- This Florida act can be found in the *Florida Statutes*, Section 394. It was first codified in the year 1971 and then revised in 2009. Both years appear in the in-text citation, separated by a slash.
- Consult the *Bluebook* for formats for other states.

11.6 Legislative Materials

Legislative materials include federal testimony, hearings, bills, resolutions, reports, and related documents. Bills and resolutions that have been passed by both houses of Congress and signed by the president become law and should be cited as statutes (see Section 11.5). To cite an unenacted bill or resolution (i.e., one that was not passed by both houses of Congress) or an enacted bill or resolution that was not signed into law, follow the forms in this section. When a URL for the material is available, it is optional to include it at the end of the reference list entry.

14. Federal testimony

> *Template:*
> *Title of testimony,* xxx Cong. (Year) (testimony of Testifier Name). URL

> *Example:*
> *Federal real property reform: How cutting red tape and better management could achieve billions in savings,* U.S. Senate Committee on Homeland Security and Governmental Affairs, 114th Cong. (2016) (testimony of Norman Dong). http://www.gsa.gov/portal/content/233107

> *Parenthetical citation:* (*Federal Real Property Reform*, 2016)
> *Narrative citation:* *Federal Real Property Reform* (2016)

- For the title of federal testimony, include the title as it appears on the work and the subcommittee and/or committee name (if any), separated by a comma. Then provide the number of the Congress, the year in parentheses, and "testimony of" followed by the name of the person who gave the testimony in separate parentheses. When the testimony is available online, also include a URL.

LEGAL REFERENCES

15. Full federal hearing

Template:

Title of hearing, xxx Cong. (Year). URL

Example:

Strengthening the federal student loan program for borrowers: Hearing before the U.S. Senate Committee on Health, Education, Labor & Pensions, 113th Cong. (2014). https://www.help.senate.gov/hearings/strengthening-the-federal-student-loan-program-for-borrowers

> *Parenthetical citation:* (*Strengthening the Federal Student Loan Program*, 2014)
> *Narrative citation:* *Strengthening the Federal Student Loan Program* (2014)

- For the title of a full federal hearing, include the name of the hearing and the subcommittee name. Provide the number of the Congress and year. When a video or other information about the hearing is available online, include its URL.

16. Unenacted federal bill or resolution

Template:

Title [if relevant], H.R. or S. bill number, xxx Cong. (Year). URL
Title [if relevant], H.R. or S. Res. resolution number, xxx Cong. (Year). URL

Example:

Mental Health on Campus Improvement Act, H.R. 1100, 113th Cong. (2013). https://www.congress.gov/bill/113th-congress/house-bill/1100

> *Parenthetical citation:* (Mental Health on Campus Improvement Act, 2013)
> *Narrative citation:* Mental Health on Campus Improvement Act (2013)

- The number should be preceded by "H.R." (House of Representatives) or "S." (Senate), depending on the source of the unenacted bill or resolution.

17. Enacted simple or concurrent federal resolution

Template for Senate:

S. Res. xxx, xxx Cong., Volume Cong. Rec. Page (Year) (enacted). URL

Template for House of Representatives:

H.R. Res. xxx, xxx Cong., Volume Cong. Rec. Page (Year) (enacted). URL

Example:

S. Res. 438, 114th Cong., 162 Cong. Rec. 2394 (2016) (enacted). https://www.congress.gov/congressional-record/2016/04/21/senate-section/article/S2394-2

> *Parenthetical citation:* (S. Resolution 438, 2016)
> *Narrative citation:* Senate Resolution 438 (2016)

- Use this format to cite enacted simple or concurrent resolutions from Congress. These resolutions are reported in the *Congressional Record* (abbreviated "Cong. Rec.").

- Enacted bills and joint resolutions are laws and should be cited as statutes (see Section 11.5).

- In the example, the Senate designated September 2016 as National Brain Aneurysm Awareness Month. The resolution is numbered 438 and is reported in Volume 162 of the *Congressional Record* on page 2394.

18. Federal report

Template for Senate:

S. Rep. No. xxx-xxx (Year). URL

Template for House of Representatives:
H.R. Rep. No. xxx-xxx (Year). URL

Example:
H.R. Rep. No. 114-358 (2015). https://www.gpo.gov/fdsys/pkg/CRPT-114hrpt358/pdf/CRPT-114hrpt358.pdf

Parenthetical citation: (H.R. Rep. No. 114-358, 2015)
Narrative citation: House of Representatives Report No. 114-358 (2015)

- This report was submitted to the House of Representatives by the Committee on Veterans' Affairs concerning the Veterans Employment, Education, and Healthcare Improvement Act.

- For reports submitted to the Senate, use the abbreviation "S. Rep. No." in the reference list entry and "Senate Report No." in the in-text citation.

11.7 Administrative and Executive Materials

Administrative and executive materials include rules and regulations, advisory opinions, and executive orders.

19. Federal regulation, codified

Template:
Title or Number, Volume C.F.R. § xxx (Year). URL

Example:
Protection of Human Subjects, 45 C.F.R. § 46 (2009). https://www.hhs.gov/ohrp/sites/default/files/ohrp/policy/ohrpregulations.pdf

Parenthetical citation: (Protection of Human Subjects, 2009)
Narrative citation: Protection of Human Subjects (2009)

- Official federal regulations are published in the *Code of Federal Regulations*. In the reference, provide the title or number of the regulation, the volume number in which the regulation appears in the *Code of Federal Regulations*, the abbreviation "C.F.R.," the section number, and the year in which the regulation was codified. If the regulation is available online, provide the URL.

20. Federal regulation, not yet codified

Template:
Title or Number, Volume F.R. Page (proposed Month Day, Year) (to be codified at Volume C.F.R. § xxx). URL

Example:
Defining and Delimiting the Exemptions for Executive, Administrative, Professional, Outside Sales and Computer Employees, 81 F.R. 32391 (proposed May 23, 2016) (to be codified at 29 C.F.R. § 541). https://www.federalregister.gov/articles/2016/05/23/2016-11754/defining-and-delimiting-the-exemptions-for-executive-administrative-professional-outside-sales-and

Parenthetical citation: (Defining and Delimiting, 2016)
Narrative citation: Defining and Delimiting (2016)

- If the regulation has not yet been codified in the *Code of Federal Regulations*, it will appear in the *Federal Register* first. Indicate this by the abbreviation "F.R." instead of "C.F.R." Instead of the year codified, provide the date of proposal. Also include the section of the *Code of Federal Regulations* where the proposed rule will be codified.

21. Executive order

Template:

Exec. Order No. xxxxx, 3 C.F.R. Page (Year). URL

Example:

Exec. Order No. 13,676, 3 C.F.R. 294 (2014). https://www.govinfo.gov/content/pkg/CFR-2015-title3-vol1/pdf/CFR-2015-title3-vol1-eo13676.pdf

> *Parenthetical citation:* (Exec. Order No. 13,676, 2014)
> *Narrative citation:* Executive Order No. 13,676 (2014)

- Executive orders are reported in Title 3 of the *Code of Federal Regulations*, so "3 C.F.R." is always included in the reference list entry for an executive order.

- The executive order in the example addressed how to combat antibiotic-resistant bacteria. It was published in the *Code of Federal Regulations*, on page 294, in the year 2014.

11.8 Patents

Patent references look more like typical APA Style references because the elements of author (inventor), year, title and patent number, and source are included in that order.

> *Reference list:* Inventor, A. A. (Year Patent Issued). *Title of patent* (U.S. Patent No. x,xxx, xxx). U.S. Patent and Trademark Office. URL
> *Parenthetical citation:* (Inventor, Year)
> *Narrative citation:* Inventor (Year)

The URL of the patent is optional but may be included in the reference list entry if available.

22. Patent

> Hiremath, S. C., Kumar, S., Lu, F., & Salehi, A. (2016). *Using metaphors to present concepts across different intellectual domains* (U.S. Patent No. 9,367,592). U.S. Patent and Trademark Office. http://patft.uspto.gov/netacgi/nph-Parser?patentnumber=9367592

> *Parenthetical citation:* (Hiremath et al., 2016)
> *Narrative citation:* Hiremath et al. (2016)

- This patent was issued in 2016 to the inventors Hiremath et al., who worked for the computer company IBM. The patent number is a unique identifying code given to every patent. The year refers to the year the patent was issued, not the year the patent was applied for.

11.9 Constitutions and Charters

To cite a whole federal or state constitution, a citation is not necessary. Simply refer to the constitution in text.

> The U.S. Constitution has 26 amendments.
> The Massachusetts Constitution was ratified in 1780.

Create reference list entries and in-text citations for citations to articles and amendments of constitutions. In the reference list and in parenthetical citations, abbreviate U.S. Constitution to "U.S. Const." and use the legal state abbreviation for a state constitution (e.g. "Md. Const." for the Maryland Constitution; see a list of state abbreviations for legal references at the Legal Information

Institute at https://www.law.cornell.edu/citation/4-500). In the narrative, use either "U.S." or "United States" for the U.S. Constitution, and spell out the name of the state for a state constitution—for example, "the Wisconsin Constitution." U.S. Constitution article and amendment numbers are Roman numerals. State constitution article numbers are also Roman numerals, but state constitution amendment numbers are Arabic numerals. URLs are not necessary for the reference. Additional information about the cited source can be included in the narrative, if desired.

23. Article of the U.S. Constitution

Template:
U.S. Const. art. xxx, § x.

Example:
U.S. Const. art. I, § 3.

Parenthetical citation: (U.S. Const. art. I, § 3)
Narrative citation: Article I, Section 3, of the U.S. Constitution

24. Article of a state constitution

Template:
State Const. art. xxx, § x.

Example:
S.C. Const. art. XI, § 3.

Parenthetical citation: (S.C. Const. art. IX, § 3)
Narrative citation: Article IX, Section 3, of the South Carolina Constitution

25. Amendment to the U.S. Constitution

Template:
U.S. Const. amend. xxx.

Example:
U.S. Const. amend. XIX.

Parenthetical citation: (U.S. Const. amend. XIX)
Narrative citation: Amendment XIX to the U.S. Constitution

- Amendments to state constitutions are cited in the same way as amendments to the U.S. Constitution.

- No date is needed in the reference unless the amendment has been repealed (see Example 27).

26. Repealed amendment to the U.S. Constitution

Template:
U.S. Const. amend. xxx (repealed Year).

Example:
U.S. Const. amend. XVIII (repealed 1933).

Parenthetical citation: (U.S. Const. amend. XVIII, repealed 1933)
Narrative citation: Amendment XVIII to the U.S. Constitution was repealed in 1933

- Because the amendment was repealed, a year is included in the reference.

- Repealed amendments to state constitutions are cited in the same way as repealed amendments to the U.S. Constitution.

27. U.S. Bill of Rights

U.S. Const. amend. I–X.

Parenthetical citation: (U.S. Const. amend. I–X)
Narrative citation: Amendments I–X to the U.S. Constitution

- The first 10 amendments to the U.S. Constitution are collectively referred to as the Bill of Rights. The citation is the same as that for an amendment to the constitution, except that the range of amendments is included in the citation.

28. Charter of the United Nations

Template:
U.N. Charter art. xx, para. xx.

Example:
U.N. Charter art. 1, para. 3.

Parenthetical citation: (U.N. Charter art. 1, para. 3)
Narrative citation: Article 1, paragraph 3, of the United Nations Charter

- A citation to the charter of the United Nations should include the name of the agreement, the article number, and the paragraph number. To cite an entire article, omit the paragraph number.

11.10 Treaties and International Conventions

References for treaties or international conventions should include the name of the treaty, convention, or other agreement; the signing or approval date; and a URL if available. In text, provide the name of the treaty or convention and the year.

Reference list: Name of Treaty or Convention, Month Day, Year, URL
Parenthetical citation: (Name of Treaty or Convention, Year)
Narrative citation: Name of Treaty or Convention (Year)

29. United Nations convention

United Nations Convention on the Rights of the Child, November 20, 1989, https://www.ohchr.org/en/professionalinterest/pages/crc.aspx

Parenthetical citation: (United Nations Convention on the Rights of the Child, 1989)
Narrative citation: United Nations Convention on the Rights of the Child (1989)

12

PUBLICATION PROCESS

Contents

12

PUBLICATION PROCESS

Authors, editors, reviewers, and publishers share responsibility for the ethical and efficient handling of a manuscript, beginning when the editor receives the manuscript and extending through the life of the published article.

In this chapter, we provide authors with guidance on preparing for publication, including how to adapt a dissertation or thesis into a journal article, prepare a manuscript for submission, select an appropriate and reputable journal for publication, and navigate the editorial publication process. Following are sections on copyright and permission guidelines for reprinting or adapting certain kinds of copyrighted works, the format for writing copyright attributions, and the steps to take during and after publication.

Preparing for Publication

12.1 Adapting a Dissertation or Thesis Into a Journal Article

A dissertation or thesis often provides the foundation for a new researcher's first published work. This original research can be reformatted for journal submission following one of two general strategies.

The quickest strategy for "flipping" a dissertation or thesis into a published article or articles is to structure the work using a multiple-paper format, wherein the final product submitted to fulfill the requirements for a degree consists of a paper or a series of papers that are formatted for journal submission (or close to it). These papers are usually conceptually similar (and often come from the same overarching project) but can stand alone as independent research reports. Benefits of this strategy include having your paper already formatted for and at a length consistent with journal guidelines, thereby saving time and effort in preparing for publication. In fact, you may even include manuscripts that are coauthored and under review, in press, or published

elsewhere in your dissertation or thesis, provided that all policies regarding article copyright are met (see Section 12.20). Talk to your university's editorial office beforehand to confirm that this is an acceptable format and to obtain the specific guidelines for writing and structuring the dissertation or thesis.

A second strategy to convert a dissertation or thesis into a journal article after completing your defense is to reformat the work to fit the scope and style of a journal article. This often requires adjustments to the following elements (see the APA Style website at https://apastyle.apa.org for more):

- **length:** Shorten the overall paper length by eliminating text within sections, eliminating entire sections, or separating distinct research questions into individual papers (but see Section 1.16). If the work examined several distinct research questions, narrow the focus to a specific topic for each paper. Consult the journal article reporting standards in Chapter 3 to learn more about essential information to report in quantitative, qualitative, and mixed methods research.

- **references:** Include only the most pertinent references (i.e., theoretically important or recent), especially in the introduction and literature review, rather than providing an exhaustive list. Ensure that the works you cite contribute to readers' knowledge of the specific topic and to the understanding and contextualization of your current research.

- **introduction section:** Eliminate extraneous content or sections that do not directly contribute to readers' knowledge or understanding of the specific research question(s) under investigation. End with a clear description of the questions, aims, or hypotheses that informed your research.

- **Method section:** Provide enough information to allow readers to understand how the data were collected and evaluated (following the journal article reporting standards in Chapter 3); full details about every step or the rationale behind it are unnecessary. Instead, refer readers to previous works that informed the current study's methods or to supplemental materials.

- **Results and Discussion sections:** Report the most relevant results and adjust the discussion accordingly. Ensure that the results directly contribute to answering your original research questions or hypotheses; check that your interpretation and application of the findings are appropriate.

- **tables and figures:** Make sure that tables or figures are essential (see Chapter 7) and do not reproduce content provided in the text.

Students seeking to prepare their dissertation or thesis for publication are advised to look at articles in the field and in relevant journals to see what structure and focus are appropriate for their work. To gain insight into how journal articles look and what they have and do not have, students might also consider reviewing an article submitted to a journal alongside their advisor (with permission from the journal editor) or serving as a reviewer for a student competition. Doing so offers firsthand insight into how authors are evaluated when undergoing peer review (see Section 12.7). Additionally, advisors or other colleagues may be coauthors on manuscripts that are based on a dissertation or thesis; students should request and consider the input of these coauthors during the conversion process (see Section 1.22 on the order of authors).

12.2 Selecting a Journal for Publication

Selecting a journal for publication should be an integral and early step of the writing process because the choice of journal can shape the form of the manuscript. For example, journals vary in their length requirements; some journals publish brief reports in addition to articles, whereas others publish only longer articles. Likewise, some journals reach a wide array of readers, whereas others are more specialized. Additional considerations are the journal's topical areas, open access policy, impact factor, time to publication, and citation style. The characteristics of a journal and its intended audience should inform your journal selection process.

If you are unsure about how to select a journal for publication, take a look at your reference list as you write: What journals do you cite repeatedly? What themes do you see reflected in the articles published in that journal? You can also look at the reference lists of published articles that are similar to yours to get an idea of where researchers in your field are publishing. Also ask coauthors or colleagues for recommendations. Follow up on possible leads by contacting the journal editor to make sure that your topic is within the scope of the journal and would be of interest to its audience. Editors may be able to immediately tell you that the article topic is outside the purview of their journal and even suggest a more suitable journal. Through this process, you will begin to form a list of potential journals for publication.

The next step is to narrow this list down to one or two possible journals by assessing two factors: appropriateness and prestige.

Appropriateness. Because all journals specialize in certain kinds of research, it is important that your research be appropriate for the venue you choose. One of the most common reasons editors reject a manuscript is because the research is not appropriate for the journal. To learn about a journal's scope, peruse past issues and read the journal's description on its website. Also consult the journal's manuscript submission guidelines and author instructions to identify the journal's disciplinary and methodological boundaries. Look for similarities with your paper in the following areas:

- **populations:** Consider factors such as demographic characteristics, diagnosis, and setting (e.g., naturalistic vs. laboratory).
- **methods:** Consider the use of quantitative, qualitative, review, meta-analytic, mixed methods, and other approaches (see Sections 1.1–1.9).
- **themes:** Consider the themes that unite the articles published in the journal.
- **article features:** Consider features such as length (e.g., brief reports vs. long reviews), complexity, citation style, and so forth.

Prestige. Publication in a prestigious journal will be a boon to your career and your work. When it comes to selecting a journal for publication, it is important to keep in mind that more than one high-quality journal may be an appropriate fit for your article. The prestige of a journal can be assessed in many ways; one way is by consulting indices such as the impact factor, rejection rate, and number of citations to articles in the journal. Prestigious journals are peer reviewed, have an editorial board composed of distinguished researchers in the field, and are included in trusted abstracting and indexing research databases in your field as an indication of the journals' reach to their key audiences.

PUBLICATION PROCESS

12.3 Prioritizing Potential Journals

Publication is not a matter simply of submitting to the most prestigious journal possible but rather of identifying a set of the most appropriate journals for your research and then selecting one that is well regarded. We suggest that you choose two journals to which to submit your research: your preferred choice and a backup. Remember that in the social sciences, you can submit a manuscript to only one journal at a time, so prioritize the journals accordingly. Preselecting two potential journals will help alleviate the burden of reviewing journals again should your manuscript be rejected by the first.

If you are unable to decide between options, prioritize appropriateness over prestige. The goal of publication is to share your research with your academic community; thus, if you publish in a prestigious journal but not an appropriate one, it will be harder for interested readers to find your work. Researchers typically subscribe to certain journals to keep apprised of new and relevant research and to receive alerts when new material is published. Therefore, choosing an appropriate and well-regarded journal for publication allows your work to be noticed by researchers well acquainted with your discipline and to better contribute to the growth of knowledge in the field. Other considerations that may inform your decision are the time to first response or to publication (which may be relevant to graduate students looking to publish articles from their dissertation or thesis before graduation), publishing costs (which may be relevant to researchers without grant funding), whether it is a journal for which you or your colleagues have been a reviewer, international scope or readership, and open access status.

12.4 Avoiding Predatory Journals

This section provides cautionary guidance for editors and authors. In the same way that authors are obligated to abide by ethical and professional standards when conducting research, journal editorial offices and publishers are expected to be rigorous in evaluating the articles they publish. Unfortunately, there are journals and publishers that engage in *predatory* or *deceptive practices*, involving any number of unethical or negligent means of soliciting, evaluating, and/or publishing articles.

Predatory journals (also called *deceptive journals*) are those whose publishers aggressively solicit manuscripts to be published and charge fees to do so without providing services to justify those fees. This practice is also called *deceptive publishing*. Open access journals that charge author fees for publication are not inherently predatory, but predatory journals commonly use this model. These journals often have the following characteristics:

- **informal solicitation:** The journal may solicit publication via an email that is informal (e.g., containing many exclamation points), poorly written, and signed by an editorial assistant as opposed to the editor. If the editor is identified in the email or journal website, check the editor's website or CV to confirm that the journal editorship is listed.

- **hidden publisher or website:** The journal's website or publisher may be purposefully excluded from communications to avoid scrutiny, particularly if the journal's name might be mistaken for the name of a leading journal in the field. If the only links in the email are to the online peer review system and a generic editor email (e.g., JournalEditor@[publisher].com), search for the journal online and review its website.

- **lack of rigorous evaluation:** The journal may not use rigorous evaluation standards; for example, it may omit peer review or use only a cursory peer review process and may lack editing, archiving, and/or indexing services (Bowman, 2014), resulting in low-quality papers.

- **lack of transparency:** The journal's website may make it difficult to locate information about the editorial process or publishing operations (e.g., publishing fees, editorial staff; Masten & Ashcraft, 2017).

- **poor reputation:** The journal's publisher may not have a good (or any) reputation. Its website, if one exists, may look unprofessional and lack contact information (e.g., email, postal address, working telephone number). Impact factor or other journal evaluation criteria may come with an asterisk indicating that they are "informal estimates" rather than real data.

- **nonstandard submission processes:** The journal may use a generic (e.g., not labeled with a journal or organization's name) online peer review system or allow manuscript submission via email.

- **lack of indexing in databases:** The journal and other journals by the same publisher may not be indexed in PsycINFO or other trusted research databases. Although inclusion in major research databases is not an ironclad guarantee of journal or publisher good practice, database publishers usually have processes in place to evaluate and monitor the journals they cover. Be sure to search for the title of the journal exactly as it is provided in the email; some predatory journals have titles deceptively similar to those of reputable journals.

> **Reputable journals are usually indexed in research databases.** PsycINFO's journal coverage list, which includes publisher information, is publicly available online (https://on.apa.org/2TRvolj).

Despite sharing one or more of these general characteristics, predatory journals are not identical in their practices. Just as charging publishing fees or having an open access model are not universal markers of a predatory journal, the absence of these practices does not guarantee that the journal abides by high standards of rigor and evaluation. Ultimately, it is the author's responsibility to be diligent and to critically evaluate the standards used by potential journals.

High-quality periodicals typically have digital object identifiers (DOIs) for their articles and an ISSN for the periodical (Beaubien & Eckard, 2014). Such journals usually have a well-defined scope that is aligned with the content of the articles they publish; clearly described processes for peer review, correction, and retraction; and an identified publisher and editorial board composed of individuals who are competent in their fields (Shamseer et al., 2017). If article processing or publishing fees are levied, these fees are clearly posted on the journal's website and are appropriate to cover the services rendered.

Resources are available to help authors vet journals and discern potentially predatory ones. For instance, the World Association of Medical Editors (Laine &

PUBLICATION PROCESS

Winker, 2017) has published guidance to help editors, researchers, funders, academics, and other stakeholders distinguish predatory journals from legitimate ones. Shamseer et al. (2017) used empirical data to develop a set of evidence-based standards for identifying potentially predatory journals; these indicators provide a starting point for evaluating journal quality. Both the Directory of Open Access Journals (DOAJ; https://doaj.org) and the Quality Open Access Market (QOAM; https://www.qoam.eu) maintain white lists of reputable open access, peer-reviewed journals. Authors can visit the Think. Check. Submit. website (https://thinkchecksubmit.org), which provides a checklist and additional free resources to assist in identifying trusted journals. The Open Scholarship Initiative (OSI, 2019) also provides valuable information about predatory or deceptive publishing.

If you have questions or concerns, contact your university librarian, who can help ensure that the journal you choose is a legitimate one. The most important step you can take to protect the integrity of your research is to be diligent in evaluating a potential journal before deciding whether to submit your article for publication.

Understanding the Editorial Publication Process

12.5 Editorial Publication Process

The editorial publication process begins when an author submits a manuscript to a journal for consideration. The flowchart in Figure 12.1 describes the potential paths that the manuscript can take from submission to publication. It is important to understand this process in context: Scholarly journal articles are original, primary publications, which means that they have not been previously published, contribute to the body of scientific knowledge, and have been reviewed by a panel of peers. Work that has been peer reviewed and appears in a journal with an ISSN or as a standalone work with an ISBN is considered published (see Section 1.16 for more on duplicate publication). Although it is possible to informally publish by posting versions of a paper online (e.g., on a preprint server), this alone does not constitute publication (see Section 12.23 for more on sharing your article).

The peer-reviewed literature in a field is built by individual contributions that together represent the accumulated knowledge of the field. To ensure the quality of each contribution—that the work is original, rigorous, and significant—scholars in the subspecialties of a field carefully review submitted manuscripts. By submitting a manuscript to a journal that is peer reviewed, an author implicitly consents to the circulation and discussion of the manuscript among the reviewers. During the review process, the manuscript is considered a confidential and privileged document; however, publisher policies differ, so check the journal's manuscript submission guidelines and instructions to authors (see Sections 1.20 and 1.23 for more on ethical standards for manuscript reviewers).

12.6 Role of the Editors

Publication decisions for a journal rest in the hands of editors who are responsible for the quality and content of the journal. Journal editors look for manuscripts that (a) contribute significantly to the content area covered by the journal, (b) communicate with clarity and conciseness, and (c) follow the jour-

Figure 12.1 Flowchart of Manuscript Progression From Submission to Publication

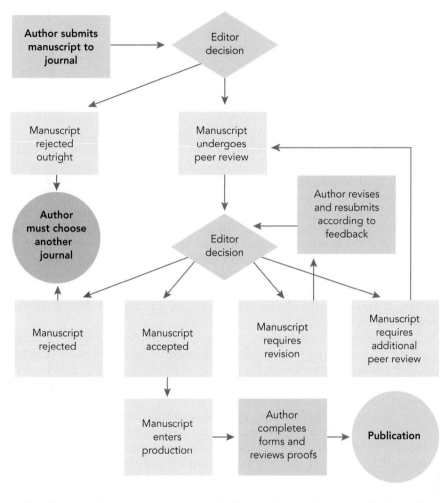

nal's style guidelines. Understanding the hierarchy of editors can help you know what to expect as an author and how to correspond during the submission and publication process.

The journal lead editor, or *editor-in-chief,* has final editorial authority on decisions regarding manuscripts. They are often assisted by *associate editors,* who assume responsibility for a specific content area of the journal or for a portion of the manuscripts submitted to the journal. For some journals, an associate editor may act as the editor at all stages of consideration of a manuscript (i.e., as an *action editor*) and may communicate with authors regarding acceptance, invited revision, or rejection of a manuscript. *Consulting* and *advisory editors* and *ad hoc reviewers* review manuscripts and make recommendations to editors or to associate editors concerning the disposition of manuscripts. Editors often seek associate, consulting, or advisory editors to advise them on manuscripts describing methods that are less familiar to them (e.g., qualitative, mixed methods) and to assist them in evaluating conflicting reviews in light of the logic of the approaches of inquiry in use (see Section 3.4). As an author, you should address interim correspondence to the editor with whom you have been in communication. However, the lead editor or editor-in-chief may make a decision other than that recommended by the reviewers or associate editor.

12.7 Peer Review Process

Just as understanding the role of editors helps you know what to expect during the submission process, so will understanding the peer review process.

Reviewer Role. An action editor usually seeks the assistance of several reviewers who are scholars in the content area of the submitted manuscript in arriving at an editorial decision. An action editor may solicit reviews from particular reviewers for any number of reasons, including familiarity with the research topic or the methodological approach, familiarity with a particular controversy, and a desire for a balance of perspectives. If reviewers do not have the knowledge to competently review a given manuscript, they are expected to identify these limitations within their review or in communication with the editor.

Reviewers provide scholarly input into the editorial decision, but the decision of whether to accept a manuscript for publication ultimately rests with the action editor or editor-in-chief. Readers interested in learning more about the peer review process or serving as a reviewer should consult APA's online peer review resources (https://on.apa.org/2KCTE6O) and the APA Reviewer Resource Center (https://on.apa.org/2F6MNn0).

When you submit a manuscript, you may be prompted to provide a list of potential reviewers along with their contact information (see Section 12.10 for more about online submission to a journal). Consider your choice of reviewers carefully and with an eye to researchers whose own research is consistent with the topic of your paper, whose area of study is similar to yours, and whose work has been cited in your manuscript. You may also consider potential reviewers' establishment in the field (e.g., recent graduates may not have much of a scholarly record, whereas renowned scholars field many requests to review and may not be available). Editors may not pick all (or any) of the reviewers you recommend. It is generally considered inappropriate to suggest reviewers who are colleagues with whom you directly work because their familiarity with you and your work may bias the review process, particularly if the journal does not participate in masked review.

Masked Review. Journal editors, either routinely or at the authors' request, may use *masked review* in which the identities of the authors of a manuscript are concealed from reviewers during the review process. Authors' names are not revealed to reviewers without the consent of the authors until the review process is complete. The names of reviewers can also be masked, although a reviewer may choose to reveal their identity by including their name in the review itself. Thus, journals can mask review in both directions (both authors' and reviewers' names masked), mask review in one direction (either authors' or reviewers' names masked), or unmask the review (all names revealed).

Consult the author guidelines to determine whether the journal to which you are submitting routinely uses masked review or offers masked review to authors who request it. Authors are responsible for concealing their identities in manuscripts that will receive masked review; for example, they should format their manuscripts so their identities as document creators are not easily revealed and describe the locations of their studies and participants in general terms (e.g., "students at a small, Midwestern U.S. liberal arts college").

Timing of Peer Review. The time required to complete a peer review varies depending on the length and complexity of the manuscript and the number of reviewers asked to evaluate it. If the journal editor determines that the manuscript is within the purview of the journal and has no major flaws or limitations (e.g., an article that exceeds prescribed page limits often is not considered for publication until revised), they will send it either directly to reviewers or to an associate editor who then serves as the action editor. Associate editors, on the basis of the reviews received, then make a recommendation to the journal editor. It is extremely rare that editors accept a paper for publication without formal peer review; exceptions might include an introduction to a special section or an editorial.

In general, the review process takes approximately 2 to 3 months, during which authors can typically view the status of their manuscript (e.g., with the editor, sent out to reviewers) through the journal's manuscript submission portal. After that time, authors can expect to be notified about a decision on their manuscript. It would be appropriate for an author to contact the editor if no communication regarding a decision has been received after more than 3 months.

12.8 Manuscript Decisions

Reviewers provide the editor with evaluations of a manuscript on the basis of their assessment of the scholarly quality of the manuscript, the importance of the contribution the work might provide, and the appropriateness of the work for the particular journal. The decision to accept a manuscript, to invite a revision, or to reject it is the responsibility of the editor; the editor's decision may differ from the recommendation of any or all of the reviewers.

Acceptance. Once a manuscript is accepted, it enters the production phase of publication, in which it is copyedited and typeset. During this phase, authors may not make significant changes to content (e.g., adding a new section of analysis or a table) other than those recommended by the copyeditor. Authors are responsible for the completion of all associated paperwork (e.g., signing copyright transfers, submitting disclosures, securing permissions for any reprinted or adapted tables and figures). Failure to complete all required paperwork may result in retraction of the acceptance of a manuscript. After the manuscript is typeset, authors receive proofs that they are encouraged to review for typesetting errors and to which they can make minor revisions (see Section 12.19 for more on reviewing article proofs).

Invitation to Revise and Resubmit. Manuscripts that are evaluated to have potential for eventual publication in the journal but that are not yet ready for final acceptance receive an invitation to revise and resubmit. Manuscripts in this category range from those that the editor has judged to need substantial reworking (including the possibility that additional empirical data need to be gathered, that entirely new experiments need to be added, that analyses need to be modified, or that the manuscript needs to be significantly shortened) to those that need only a small number of specific modifications. Some journals use a category called *conditional acceptance* for this latter level of revision; in this case, the editor indicates that the article will be published in the journal pending completion of specified changes. Invitation to revise and resubmit does not guarantee eventual publication of the paper by that journal. In addition, the invitation may be time bound; it may not extend past a designated date or across changes in editors.

Most manuscripts need to be revised, and some manuscripts need to be revised more than once (revision does not guarantee acceptance). Revisions to a manuscript may reveal to the author or to the editor and reviewers deficiencies that were not apparent in the original manuscript, and the editor may request further revision to correct those deficiencies. During the review process, an editor may ask an author to supply material that supplements the manuscript (e.g., raw data, complex statistical tables, instructions to participants). As the manuscript moves through the review process, editors are free to solicit reviews from reviewers who were not among the initial set of reviewers. Additional reviewers might be selected if their expertise is needed or if a previous reviewer is no longer available.

If the editor returns a manuscript to the author for revision, the editor explains why the revisions are required. The editor does not have to provide the reviewers' comments to the author but frequently chooses to do so. Editors do not undertake major editorial revision of a manuscript. Authors are expected to attend to editors' and reviewers' recommendations for revision; however, the content and style of the article remain the sole responsibility of the authors.

Authors should respond to reviewers' recommendations thoughtfully and judiciously. Frequently, authors are required to resubmit a version of their original manuscript with tracked changes that reflect revisions made on the basis of reviewer feedback. When resubmitting a revised manuscript, authors are also encouraged to enclose a cover letter thanking editors and reviewers for their feedback, accompanied by a document explaining how they have responded to all of the reviewers' comments (regardless of whether they agreed or disagreed with the comments). Often referred to as a *response to reviewers*, this file specifies how the authors addressed each critique made by a reviewer (e.g., by adding text or data) and where the revision can be found in the revised manuscript. Authors are not required to make every change suggested by a reviewer, but the response should explain the rationale behind the authors' decisions, including decisions not to make a change. Providing a response to reviewers facilitates the timeliness of the review process by reducing the number of follow-up questions and ultimately helps the editor decide whether to publish the article. For a sample response to reviewers, see the APA Style website (https://apastyle.apa.org).

Some journals offer authors the opportunity to revise their paper into a brief report; the journal's policies will indicate whether this option exists. For such journals, authors may also submit a brief report initially. Articles of this type generally describe a study of limited scope, contain novel or provocative findings that need further replication, or represent replications and extensions of prior published work. Research published in this format generally cannot be resubmitted as a longer research article somewhere else (see Section 1.16 on duplicate publication).

Rejection. A manuscript is usually rejected because the work (a) is seen as falling outside the coverage domain of the journal; (b) contains such severe flaws of design, methodology, analysis, or interpretation that the editor questions the validity of the findings; or (c) is judged as making a limited contribution to the field, given the standards of the journal. At times, editors reject good manuscripts simply because they lack the space to publish all of the high-quality manuscripts that are submitted to the journal.

Editors may *desk reject* a manuscript outright—that is, after an initial review but before review by an associate editor or by reviewers—in two cases. The first is when the editor determines that the manuscript is not appropriate for the specific journal because either the content or the format is not in keeping with the journal's mission. The second is when the editor determines that it is unlikely that the paper will be evaluated favorably during the peer review process. Both decisions allow for a more efficient and effective review process. Similarly, an *editorial reject* might occur when initial review of the manuscript reveals formatting flaws such as exceeding the prescribed page limits.

A manuscript that has been rejected by a journal may not be revised and resubmitted to that same journal without invitation from the editor. If a manuscript is rejected on the basis of the peer review, the editor explains why it was rejected and may provide feedback from the reviewers. Authors who believe a pertinent point was overlooked or misunderstood by the reviewers may contact the editor to appeal the decision. Those who feel that their manuscript was unfairly rejected should consult the journal or publisher website regarding the appeals process. Authors are free to submit the rejected manuscript to another journal. Reviewers may provide feedback that authors find useful when revising their manuscript; authors should give careful attention to these comments and suggestions from peers and incorporate them to improve the scientific rigor and overall quality of the paper.

Manuscript Preparation

12.9 Preparing the Manuscript for Submission

This section summarizes the steps to follow in preparing a manuscript for submission to a journal. First, follow APA Style guidelines as described in this manual when formatting and writing the paper. In particular, consult Chapter 3 to become acquainted with the reporting standards for the type of research you have conducted. Also, check whether the journal to which you are submitting your manuscript has a checklist or specific guidelines for manuscript submission. Manuscript preparation and submission guidelines for APA journals can be found on the APA website (https://on.apa.org/2E0FPOT).

Many publishers, including APA, offer a suite of author services and support that provide help with writing, translation, figure creation, and so forth. Authors are encouraged to use these services to ensure that the manuscript they submit to the publisher is in the best form possible. These guidelines and services are continually updated; authors should follow the most current guidelines for the publisher to which they are submitting their work (for APA journals, see the Journal Manuscript Preparation Guidelines at https://on.apa.org/2P0ll9j).

12.10 Using an Online Submission Portal

You will most likely submit your article electronically through an online manuscript submission portal. For APA journals, each journal has its own submission portal accessed via its website. Review the instructions for using the submission portal and understand the format for saving all files before beginning the submission process. Guidance on navigating the Editorial Manager system used by all APA journals can be found on the APA website (https://on.apa.org/2FLydBA).

Upon submission of your manuscript, you will be asked to upload at least two files—a manuscript file and a cover letter. Additional files may be needed depending on the publisher's requirements.

Manuscript File. The manuscript file consists of your manuscript, including the title page, abstract, text (body), and reference list, as well as tables and figures, footnotes, and appendices, if applicable. Whereas some journals accept all sections as a single file, others require authors to upload separate files (e.g., the title page in a separate file for masked review, all figures in separate files).

If you are submitting supplemental materials with your manuscript, check the journal's website to determine the preferred format (see Section 2.15). Keep in mind that if your manuscript is accepted, your supplemental materials most likely will not be copyedited and thus will be made available to readers in the exact format in which you submit them. Be sure to review all supplemental materials carefully for content and proper format prior to submission.

Cover Letter File. Authors often must submit a cover letter as a separate file to accompany their manuscript. Check the journal's website for the current editor's name and for specific instructions on submission. See Section 12.11 for guidance on what to include in the cover letter to the journal editor.

Additional Information. Finally, you may need to supply additional information via the submission portal, including the following:

- article title and abstract
- byline, affiliation, contact information, and order of authors
- article word count or page count
- number of tables and figures
- keywords
- names of potential reviewers (see Section 12.7)

Requirements for additional information are specific to each journal and publisher. Follow instructions as prompted by the manuscript submission portal to ensure that you enter or upload all the requested information.

12.11 Writing a Cover Letter

When writing a cover letter requesting consideration of your manuscript for publication, include the information requested by the journal. Cover letters often include the following:

- specific details about the manuscript (e.g., title and authors)
- assurances that all authors agree with the content of the manuscript and with the order of authorship (see Sections 1.21–1.22)
- assurances that the corresponding author will take responsibility for informing coauthors in a timely manner of editorial decisions, reviews received, changes made in response to editorial review, and content of revisions (if the manuscript is accepted, all the authors will need to certify authorship)

- information about the existence of any closely related manuscripts that have been submitted for simultaneous consideration to the same or to another journal (see Section 1.16 on piecemeal publication and exceptions)
- notice of any conflicts of interest or activities that might be seen as influencing the research (e.g., financial interests in a test or procedure, funding by a pharmaceutical company for drug research)
- a request for masked review, if that is an option for the journal and you choose to use it (see Section 12.7)
- verification that the treatment of human participants or nonhuman animal subjects was in accordance with established ethical standards (see Sections 1.18 and 12.13)
- a copy of any permissions granted to reproduce copyrighted material or a notice that permissions are pending (see Sections 12.14–12.18; the publisher must have copies of all granted permissions before your work can be published)
- the telephone number, email address, and mailing address of the corresponding author for future correspondence

Some journals have an author agreement checklist that authors must submit along with or in lieu of a cover letter. Check the specific policies of the journal to which you are submitting your manuscript and follow those policies. Nonadherence to submission instructions can delay the review process. For sample cover letters, see the APA Style website (https://apastyle.apa.org).

12.12 Corresponding During Publication

While a manuscript is under consideration, it is the responsibility of the authors to inform the editor of any substantive corrections needed, any changes in contact information, and so forth. In all correspondence during the publication process, include the complete manuscript title, the authors' names, and the manuscript number (assigned when the manuscript was first received). Any author may correspond with the editor or editorial staff during the submission and publication process. Most often, however, correspondence is handled by the corresponding author.

Following publication, the corresponding author serves as the main point of contact and responds to questions about the published article. All authors should decide prior to submission who will serve as the corresponding author. Although any author can serve as the corresponding author, the corresponding author often has taken the lead in executing a study or heads the lab in which the data were collected. See Section 2.7 for how to present the corresponding author's information in the author note.

12.13 Certifying Ethical Requirements

In Chapter 1 (Sections 1.11 and 1.18), we noted that authors are responsible for demonstrating that they have complied with the ethical standards that govern both the conduct of research and its scholarly publication (see Standard 8, Research and Publication, of the APA Ethics Code; APA, 2017a). When you submit a manuscript to a journal, you may be asked to provide proof of compliance with these standards. You are also expected to comply with legal standards of fair use when reprinting or adapting the work of others and to comply with the publication policies established by the journal publisher. The forms APA requires for journal publication and the instructions for the forms can be found on the APA website (https://on.apa.org/2zuMDk2).

Ethical Compliance. When you submit your manuscript, you may be asked to verify that you have complied with ethical standards in the conduct of your research. This includes whether your study has been evaluated and approved by an institutional review board (IRB) or an institutional animal care and use committee (IACUC), if such approval is required. Authors conducting research outside the United States should describe the process of ethical review their study underwent if it differs from an IRB evaluation. Authors submitting to APA journals are also required to submit the Certificate of Compliance With APA Ethical Principles Form (https://on.apa.org/2NrGSsY) if the research included human participants or nonhuman animal subjects.

Conflict of Interest. As discussed in Chapter 1 (Section 1.20), authors must disclose activities and relationships that, if known to others, might be viewed as potential conflicts of interest—for example, financial agreements or affiliations with or potential bias against any product or service used or discussed in the paper. Authors with no known conflict of interest must state this explicitly. Such disclosures should appear in the author note (see Section 2.7). For APA journals, all authors are required to submit the Full Disclosure of Interests Form (https://on.apa.org/2E0FlIr). For more information on conflicts of interest and ethical principles in research, please see APA Ethics Code Standard 3.06, Conflict of Interest.

Plagiarism Detection. Most publishers, including APA, now routinely submit manuscripts to plagiarism detection software that compares the submitted work against millions of scholarly documents as well as content appearing on the open web. This allows journal editors to check submissions for potential overlap with previously published material and to evaluate whether the overlap is reasonable or problematic. See Sections 1.17, 8.2, and 8.3 for further information on plagiarism and self-plagiarism.

Copyright and Permission Guidelines

12.14 General Guidelines for Reprinting or Adapting Materials

Most of the time, authors need to provide only an author–date in-text citation and a reference list entry to properly credit the words or ideas of other authors (see Chapters 8–11). However, according to U.S. copyright law, reprinting or adapting certain kinds of works (e.g., figures published in journal articles, images from websites, lengthy quotations) requires a more comprehensive acknowledgment of the copyright status of the reprinted or adapted work in the form of a *copyright attribution,* a brief statement providing details of the original work and naming the copyright holder (see Section 12.18 for formatting guidance).

Reprinting means reproducing material exactly as it appeared originally, without modifications, in the way in which it was intended. *Adapting* refers to modifying material so that it is suitable for a new purpose (e.g., using part of a table or figure in a new table or figure in your paper). A copyright attribution is used instead of an author–date in-text citation to credit these works; each work also should appear in the reference list. For a subset of cases (see Section 12.17), authors need to seek and obtain explicit written permission from the copyright holder to reprint or adapt the material, a process that can take substantial time and comes with no guarantee that the copyright holder will consent to the use. Because these policies are a matter of law, not specifically of APA Style, all writers—even students whose work will not be formally published—should follow them.

The remainder of this section guides authors through the process of

- understanding what types of material require a copyright attribution;
- identifying the copyright status of the material and understanding its implications for the intended use;
- determining whether permission is necessary to reproduce the material on the basis of its copyright status and the legal concept of fair use;
- securing permission (if necessary) to reproduce the material; and
- writing the copyright attribution in APA Style.

12.15 Materials That Require a Copyright Attribution

The following are examples of materials that authors often want to reprint or adapt that may require a copyright attribution; they may also require permission (see Section 12.17). Other materials may also require a copyright attribution and permission before they can be reprinted or adapted, such as songs, poetry, and art.

- **figures, tables, and other images:** Most types of visual displays require a copyright attribution to reprint or adapt, including tables and figures published in journal articles, books, reports, webpages and websites, and other works, as well as images from the internet such as illustrations, infographics, photographs, screen shots, and most clip art. Depending on the work's place of publication and copyright status, permission may or may not be required. Copyright ownership and permission status can be particularly difficult to establish for images downloaded from the internet, but journals cannot publish them without full documentation. There is no need to seek permission or to write a copyright attribution for images taken from a database whose purpose is the open dissemination of stimuli for academic research (e.g., the International Affective Picture System); for these, an author–date citation suffices.
- **data:** Published or unpublished data from another source require a copyright attribution and permission to directly reproduce. Data that have been reconfigured or reanalyzed to produce different numbers do not require permission or a copyright attribution; cite these data with a regular author–date citation instead (see Section 10.9).
- **test and scale items, questionnaires, vignettes, and so forth:** Items reprinted or adapted from copyrighted and commercially available tests or scales (e.g., Minnesota Multiphasic Personality Inventory–2, Wechsler Adult Intelligence Scale, Stanford–Binet Intelligence Scales) require a copyright attribution and permission. Obtaining these permissions can be difficult and time consuming, and a preferable alternative to reproducing the exact items in your man-

uscript may be to instead reword or paraphrase those items. Permission is required, and may be denied, to reproduce even one item from such instruments. Furthermore, many test and scale developers ask authors to submit a request (typically through their website or email) to use their measure prior to the authors administering it to participants in their study and to inform them of any publications that may result from its use. Likewise, the developers should be consulted before you make any changes to a measure (e.g., adaptations for different age groups, translation of specific items). Authors should also consider whether reprinting or adapting test materials could threaten the materials' integrity and security, as described in APA Ethics Code Standard 9.11, Maintaining Test Security.

- **long quotations:** Although most quotations taken from a published work need only an author–date citation, you should seek permission and provide a copyright attribution to reproduce a long quotation, the definition of which varies by copyright holder. It is the author's responsibility to determine the policy of each copyright holder; large publishers usually provide their permission policies on their websites. For APA's policy, see Section 12.17.

Two special cases of material with copyright requirements are commercial stock photography and clip art. If you find photos, clip art, and other images via an online search engine, the guidelines in this section apply to those search results, too.

- **commercial stock photography:** Unless a stock image has a Creative Commons license (see Section 12.16) or is in the public domain, it is not permissible to reproduce it without purchasing a license from the vendor. Commonly used vendors of stock images are Getty Images, Shutterstock, and iStock. A license usually allows the license holder to reproduce the image without a copyright attribution; however, without your own license, you cannot reproduce the image.

- **clip art:** Most clip art does not require permission to reproduce, but it may require a copyright attribution. For clip art included with a computer program (e.g., Microsoft Word), purchase of the program provides a license for that clip art, and you can use it in an academic paper or scholarly article without a copyright attribution or author–date citation. If the clip art comes from a free clip art website, check the copyright status of the image to determine whether a copyright attribution or citation is needed (see Section 12.16). See Example 98 in Chapter 10 for a reference list entry for clip art when a reference is needed.

12.16 Copyright Status

The copyright status of a work determines how you are allowed to use it in your own paper. Copyright is usually indicated on the first page of an article, on the copyright page of a book or report, below an image published online, or in the footer of a website.

The following are some common copyright statuses:

- **standard copyright:** Copyright is often indicated simply by the word "copyright" or the copyright symbol.

Sometimes determining who holds a copyright can be a challenge, particularly for older works, because publishers may merge and copyrights may change hands. Materials described in Section 12.15 require a copyright attribution, and permission may be required as well.

- **Creative Commons copyright:** Creative Commons licenses are indicated by "Creative Commons" or "CC." Most Creative Commons licenses allow you to reprint and/or adapt a work (including images) without permission from the copyright holder as long as you give credit to the original author in the form of a copyright attribution, note the license type, and indicate whether you have adapted the original. The specific terms of Creative Commons licenses vary, so check the license associated with the work you want to reproduce to determine what you are allowed to do and what specific copyright attributions, if any, are required.

- **public domain:** Works that are not bound by copyright are considered to be in the public domain. This means that you can reprint them and/or adapt them however you want, so long as you credit the original author in the form of a copyright attribution. Assume that a work is under copyright unless you see the words "public domain" on it or the work was produced by the U.S. government (in which case it is automatically in the public domain). Although copyright does expire with time—meaning that works that were once copyrighted may now be in the public domain—the laws governing this process are complex and vary by country; consult a librarian if you have questions regarding expired copyrights.

- **no copyright indicated:** If no copyright is indicated, treat the material as copyrighted. U.S. copyright law states that a work is copyrighted as soon as it is fixed in tangible form (e.g., when you can see it on a computer screen or on paper), even if the work does not have the word "copyright" or the copyright symbol on it, and even if it is not widely distributed or professionally published. For example, students automatically own the copyright to their classroom assignments.

12.17 Permission and Fair Use

Determining Whether Permission Is Necessary. Permission is not required to reprint or adapt a work (see Section 12.15 for examples) when it has a Creative Commons license or is in the public domain; however, a copyright attribution is still required in most cases. For works that are copyrighted (or for which the copyright status is unknown), permission is not always required to reprint or adapt the work. The nature of the original publication (i.e., an academic work vs. a commercial publication) and the concept of fair use govern whether permission is needed.

Scholarly Works. The journal publisher typically owns the copyright on material published in its journals. Many scientific, technical, and medical publishers (including APA) do not require written permission or fees to reproduce content under the following circumstances:

- The purpose of the use is scholarly comment, noncommercial research, or educational.

- Full credit is given to the author and the publisher as copyright holders through a complete and accurate copyright attribution.
- A maximum total of three figures or tables are being reprinted or adapted from a journal article or book chapter.
- Single text extracts being reprinted are fewer than 400 words, or a series of text extracts being reprinted totals fewer than 800 words. For quotations under these thresholds, use an author–date citation (permission and copyright attributions are not required).

All publishers have their own permission policies, which may differ from guidelines provided here and may cover cases not described in this section (e.g., reproducing whole articles or chapters). Check with the publisher of the material to determine whether permission is necessary.

Fair Use. You may be able to reprint or adapt a copyrighted work as described in Section 12.15 without permission if your use is considered "fair." *Fair use* is a loosely defined and complex legal concept (for a summary, see U.S. Copyright Office, 2019) but, in general, means that under certain circumstances it is permissible to reprint or adapt a copyrighted table, figure, image, test item, questionnaire, or long quotation without obtaining permission as long as you credit the work with a copyright attribution. If in doubt, check with the copyright holder to determine what they consider fair use, especially for items from measures, questionnaires, scales, tests, or instruments. However, the use is probably fair if it meets the following criteria:

- It is for use in an academic work and not for profit (e.g., paper for a class, article in a scholarly journal).
- It represents facts or data (e.g., a chart or diagram) rather than creative self-expression (e.g., artwork, although some famous works of art are in the public domain and thus do not require permission).
- It is small in relation to the entire work (e.g., a chart within a report) and not the whole work or the heart of the work (e.g., a whole cartoon).
- Reproducing the work will not hurt the market or potential market for the original.

Permission for Photographs of Identifiable People. If you photographed a person who is identifiable in the photograph, you must submit a signed release from that person for the photograph to be published. The release should specify that both electronic and print permissions are granted. This is not a matter of copyright but rather of permission from the individual to have their likeness reproduced. It is not necessary to mention the release in the paper or to write a copyright attribution for such a photograph. No release is necessary if the photograph is of one of the authors of the paper.

Securing Permission. When permission is required, you must request permission to reproduce the material in all formats (e.g., both print and electronic) from the copyright holder. Permission extends in some cases to all subsequent editions and to foreign-language editions as well. Permission policies vary among organizations; always check with the publisher about whether permission is required for subsequent or foreign-language editions of a publication.

Many publishers provide a way for authors to request permission on their websites (e.g., to request permission to reprint or adapt material published by APA, see https://on.apa.org/2Aswon8). Permission can also be secured via email, fax, or mail. The permission request should specify the details about the material (e.g., title of the work, year of publication, page number) and the nature of the reuse (e.g., in a journal article). Some publishers also require that you obtain permission from the author of the original work. Publishers normally grant permission contingent on the inclusion of a copyright attribution and payment of a fee per table, figure, or page.

Allow ample time (several weeks) to secure permission. Once permission is granted, you need to

- obtain that permission in writing;
- include copies of permission letters with the accepted manuscript (if submitting for publication; otherwise, provide them when submitting an assignment);
- complete the Permissions Alert Form for APA Journal Authors (if publishing in an APA journal); and
- include a copyright attribution in the manuscript, following the wording and format described in Section 12.18 or specific wording provided by the copyright holder.

Most publishers will not allow your manuscript to enter the production stage until all print and electronic permissions are secured and documentation has been provided.

12.18 Copyright Attribution Formats

An APA Style copyright attribution contains information from the reference list entry of the work, but in a different order than in the reference entry, and with additional information about the material's copyright and permission status. To write a copyright attribution,

- state whether the material was reprinted or adapted (use "From" for reprintings and "Adapted from" for adaptations);
- provide the title, author, year of publication, and source of the material;
- indicate the material's copyright status, which will be the copyright year and the name of the copyright holder, a statement that the work is licensed in the Creative Commons, or a statement that the work is in the public domain; and
- provide the permission statement as requested by the copyright holder if permission was sought and obtained.

Place the copyright attribution as follows:

- For a reprinted or adapted table, figure, or other image (including reproduced [but not reanalyzed] data in a table), place the copyright attribution at the end of the general note for the table or figure (see Sections 7.14 and 7.28).
- For reproduced test items, questionnaires, or long quotations, place the copyright attribution in a footnote to the reproduced text (see Section 2.13).

PUBLICATION PROCESS

Table 12.1 Copyright Attribution Templates

Source [a]	Reprinted or adapted status	Source information	Copyright status	Permission statement [b]
Journal, magazine, newspaper, or blog	From *or* Adapted from	"Title of Article," by A. A. Author and B. B. Author, year, *Title of Periodical, Volume*(Issue), p. xx (DOI or URL).	Copyright year by Name of Copyright Holder. *or* In the public domain. *or* CC BY-NC. [c]	Reprinted with permission. *or* Adapted with permission.
Authored book or report		*Title of Book or Report* (p. xx), by A. A. Author and B. B. Author, year, Publisher (DOI or URL).		
Edited book chapter		"Title of Chapter," by A. A. Author and B. B. Author, in E. E. Editor and F. F. Editor (Eds.), *Title of Book* (any edition or volume number, p. xx), year, Publisher (DOI or URL).		
Webpage or website		*Title of Webpage*, by A. A. Author and B. B. Author, year, Site Name (DOI or URL). *or* *Title of Webpage*, by Group Author Same as Site Name, year (DOI or URL). [d]		

[a] For works not listed here, provide the title, author, year, and source information for the work as appropriate. [b] Include a permission statement only if permission has been sought and obtained. [c] For Creative Commons licenses (e.g., CC BY-NC, CC BY 4.0), use the specified abbreviation for the type of license associated with the material you are reprinting or adapting; "CC BY-NC" is just one example. [d] For webpages or websites, omit the site name when the site name and author are the same, which is often the case with group authors.

See Table 12.1 for copyright attribution templates and Table 12.2 for examples. See Chapter 7 for examples in context, including

- an adapted table that does not require permission (Table 7.14 in Section 7.21),
- a reprinted figure that does not require permission (Figure 7.3 in Section 7.36),
- a reprinted figure in the public domain (Figure 7.14 in Section 7.36), and
- a figure reproduced with permission (Figure 7.21 in Section 7.36).

When you use a copyright attribution, also provide a reference list entry for the work. However, the copyright attribution is used instead of an in-text citation; it is not necessary to include both.

During and After Publication

12.19 Article Proofs

After your manuscript has been accepted, but prior to its publication, you will be contacted by the journal's editorial staff to review the article proofs. Proofs are usually handled via an annotation website. Through the site, you will be able to make changes or annotations directly to the proofs to correct minor style or

Table 12.2 Example Copyright Attributions for Reprinted or Adapted Tables and Figures

Work from which the table or figure was reproduced	Example copyright attribution
Journal article, if copyrighted and if no permission needed	From "Romantic Relationship Development: The Interplay Between Age and Relationship Length," by A. Lantagne and W. Furman, 2017, *Developmental Psychology, 53*(9), p. 1744 (https://doi.org/10.1037/dev0000363). Copyright 2017 by the American Psychological Association.
Journal article, if Creative Commons license	Adapted from "Comprehensive Overview of Computer-Based Health Information Tailoring: A Systematic Scoping Review," by A. K. Ghalibaf, E. Nazari, M. Gholian-Aval, and M. Tara, 2019, *BMJ Open, 9*, p. 6 (https://doi.org/cz6h). CC BY-NC.
Whole book, if copyrighted and if no permission needed	Adapted from *Managing Therapy-Interfering Behavior: Strategies From Dialectical Behavior Therapy* (p. 172), by A. L. Chapman and M. Z. Rosenthal, 2016, American Psychological Association (https://doi.org/10.1037/14752-000). Copyright 2016 by the American Psychological Association.
Edited book chapter, if copyrighted and if permission needed	From "Pharmacokinetics," by V. Yellepeddi, in K. Whalen (Ed.), *Pharmacology* (6th ed., p. 2), 2015, Wolters Kluwer. Copyright 2015 by Wolters Kluwer. Reprinted with permission.
Webpage or website, if in the public domain	From *What Parents Can Expect in Behavior Therapy*, by Centers for Disease Control and Prevention, 2017 (https://www.cdc.gov/ncbddd/adhd/infographics/what-parents-expect.html). In the public domain.
Data from the U.S. Census Bureau, in the public domain	Data are from "Annual Estimates of the Resident Population for the United States, Regions, States, and Puerto Rico: April 1, 2010 to July 1, 2018 (NST-EST2018-01)," by the U.S. Census Bureau, 2018 (http://bit.ly/2v0bucA). In the public domain.

Note. This table shows examples of copyright attributions you would include when reprinting or adapting a table or figure from another work in an academic paper. Place the copyright attribution for a reprinted or adapted table or figure at the end of the table or figure general note (see, e.g., Table 7.14 and Figure 7.3). See Sections 12.14 to 12.18 to determine when a copyright attribution (and possibly also permission) is necessary. You may need to use different wording than shown here depending on the requirements of the copyright holder.

formatting errors. It is also where you will receive and be asked to respond to specific questions posed by copyeditors or editorial staff. Keep in mind that the proof stage is your last chance to change your article. This is not, however, the time to rewrite text or to add new analyses, citations, or interpretation. Any major revisions to the text or analyses made in the proofs may require review by the editor.

Review the proofs carefully. Be alert for changes in meaning that may have inadvertently occurred during copyediting, and be attentive to levels of heading and formatting of statistics, equations, tables, and so forth. Copyeditors correct errors, ensure consistency of style, and clarify expression; you should compare the proofs with your original manuscript to confirm that any changes are consistent with the meaning you intended to convey. Limit changes to fixing spelling or grammar, correcting copyediting or typesetting errors, and updating references (e.g., to update in-press citations, to fix DOIs and URLs that no longer work). If you request changes, be explicit, because the typesetter will have only your written instructions to work from and thus will need clear direction to implement the changes correctly. In addition, be sure to check the following:

- Have you answered all copyeditor queries fully?
- Are author names and affiliations correct and consistent with prior publications?
- Is the hierarchy of headings and subheadings correct?
- Are all numbers and symbols in text, tables, and mathematical and statistical copy correct?
- Are tables correct? Are all columns aligned as expected, and do superscripts correspond to table notes? Are all table notes correct?
- Are figures correct? Are labels properly spelled? Do symbols in the legend match those in the figure? Are photographs reproduced successfully? Are all figure notes correct?

If coauthors participate in reviewing the proofs, the corresponding author is responsible for consolidating necessary changes and incorporating them into the proofs. It is important to submit your requested changes to the publisher within the established deadline so that publication of your article is not delayed.

Once you have submitted all proof corrections to the production office, your article will soon be made available. Often, publishers publish the final, typeset article online first, referred to as *advance online publication*, with the print version to follow (see Section 8.5). This is the point of official publication, and your article may now be discovered and cited.

12.20 Published Article Copyright Policies

Until publication, the copyright of a manuscript belongs to the author(s). At publication, however, it is common for the copyright of the work to change. Two of the most common scenarios are transfer of copyright to the publisher and entry into the public domain.

Transfer of Copyright to the Publisher. When a manuscript is accepted for publication, authors typically transfer copyright of their manuscript to the publisher. By transferring copyright, authors permit publishers to (a) widely distribute the article, (b) monitor and control republication of the article (in whole or in part) by others, and (c) handle the paperwork involved in copyright registration and administration. The publisher in turn represents the authors' interests and permits authors to freely reuse their own article (in whole or in part) in several ways. By law, publishers own the copyright on their journal articles for 95 years from the time of publication. The copyright transfer includes both print and electronic rights to the article to allow the publisher to disseminate the work as broadly as possible. APA journals use the APA Publications Rights Form (see https://on.apa.org/32psDvX) to complete the transfer of copyright.

Public Domain Copyright for Employees of the U.S. Government. If the primary authors are employees of the U.S. government and its departments (e.g., Veterans Affairs) and the work was performed within the scope of their employment, the work is considered in the public domain (i.e., not copyrighted by the authors or publisher; see Section 12.16). In the case of work performed under

U.S. government contract, the publisher may retain the copyright (meaning it is not in the public domain) but grant the U.S. government royalty-free permission to reproduce all or portions of the article and authorize others to do so for U.S. government purposes; authors who want to reprint or adapt material from such a work should provide a copyright attribution and determine whether permission is necessary. APA journals use the APA Publications Rights Form (see https://on.apa.org/32psDvX) to document when work has been produced by employees of the U.S. government.

12.21 Open Access Deposit Policies

Many funders and institutions around the world mandate that the work they sponsor be made freely available—or deposited in *open access* repositories—to the public upon publication, the idea being that sponsored research findings should be in the public domain to accelerate human progress. In practice, open access can take several forms, and funders and institutions outline the format(s) they accept or require. For example, some require a prepublication copy of the final manuscript as accepted for publication to be posted to a designated repository. Others require that the final journal article be made freely available immediately upon publication—rather than limited by journal subscription access—with minimal or no barriers to reuse (i.e., readers can disseminate and build on open access work without the traditional constraints of copyright on academic publications). Publishers usually support the open access publication model through article processing charges paid by the authors using funder or institutional resources designated for this purpose.

As you decide where to submit your article, check your funder and institutional guidelines on open access and compare these to the options supported by different publishers. If you are considering an open access APA journal, consult the APA Journals website (https://on.apa.org/2vJ3oGq).

12.22 Writing a Correction Notice

As described in Section 1.13, errors sometimes occur in published journal articles. If you detect an error in your published article (including the advance online publication) and think that a correction is warranted, submit a correction notice to the journal editor and publisher. A formal correction tells readers (a) exactly what the error was, (b) what the correct information is, and (c) whether some or all versions of the original article have been corrected (i.e., no longer contain the error). Because it is not the purpose of corrections to place blame for mistakes, correction notices do not identify the source of the error (e.g., unintentional oversight, mathematical errors).

It is not necessary to formally correct every error found in a published article. Minor typographical errors do not need to be called out as part of the public record of science. The following are examples of errors that need formal, public correction:

- adding an author or rearranging the order of authorship
- completely changing the affiliation (e.g., because the affiliation on the published work does not reflect where the author worked when the study was conducted)

- replacing an entry in the reference list with a completely different reference
- altering the data in a way that may or may not change the significance of the results
- substituting one word for another or rewriting a sentence or paragraph in a way that substantially impacts the meaning

A correction notice should contain the following:

- journal title and year, volume number, issue number, DOI, and inclusive page numbers of the article being corrected (as applicable)
- complete article title and names of all authors, exactly as they appear in the published article
- precise location of the error (e.g., page, column, line)
- an exact quotation of the error or, in the case of a lengthy error or an error in a table or figure, an accurate paraphrasing of the error
- a concise, unambiguous wording of the correction or, in the case of an error in a table or figure, a replacement version of the table or figure

Once the proposed correction has been reviewed by the editor and publisher, a decision is made to either move forward with a correction notice or leave the error within the published article as is. When a correction is approved, the publisher uses the information provided by the author to compile the correction notice in an official template. Correction notices are usually published with a DOI, like published articles, and appear in print and online. If the article being corrected has already appeared in print, the correction notice is published in the next available issue of the journal. If the article being corrected has not yet appeared in print, the correction notice is published within the same issue as the article. If the article being corrected has been published only online and will remain so after the next issue of the journal, an online version of the correction notice is published to amend the article while the article and correction notice await placement in a print issue. See the APA Style website for sample correction notices (https://apastyle.apa.org).

12.23 Sharing Your Article Online

Certain rights are linked to copyright ownership, including the exclusive right to reproduce and distribute the copyrighted work. Journals are committed to publishing original scholarship and distributing peer-reviewed articles, in both print and electronic formats, that serve as the version of record. Thus, many publishers have policies delineating the terms under which authors may post an article on the internet.

Many publishers, including APA, allow authors to post a version of their manuscript online—for example, in a preprint archive or repository such as PsyArXiv, in an electronic archive such as ERIC, in an institutional archive, on a personal website, on their employer's server, in their institution's repository, in a reference manager such as Mendeley, and on an author's social network. However, a number of conditions apply. For example, usually the manuscript must be a prepublication copy of the final manuscript accepted for publication, not the final typeset version. Additionally, the posted prepublication copy of the manuscript must carry a copyright notice and include a link to the final article on the publisher's website using the article's DOI. For articles published in APA journals, use the following statement:

> © American Psychological Association, [Year]. This paper is not the copy of record and may not exactly replicate the authoritative document published in the APA journal. Please do not copy or cite without the author's permission. The final article is available, upon publication, at https://doi.org/[Article DOI]

APA's guidelines for internet posting are available on the APA website (https://on.apa.org/2r7Eptq), along with general resources and FAQs on manuscript postacceptance procedures and dissemination (https://on.apa.org/2KEBBgn). If your article is published via an open access deposit policy, a version is also made available freely online (see Section 12.21).

12.24 Promoting Your Article

Authors are encouraged to promote their article after its publication. One way they may do so is to develop short summaries describing their work in plain language and share these along with the article DOI through their social media networks. A journal may also ask for a public health significance statement or impact statement as part of the article; authors can use this statement as a foundation for communicating their work and its broader impact to the public. The name of this section and whether it is required depend on the journal, but the goal is to make the research more accessible to the public. Guidance on writing public health significance or impact statements can be found on the APA website (https://on.apa.org/2DKj1lH). Similarly, organizations or universities where the author is employed may ask for text to include in a press release to disseminate key findings from the study. These materials are typically brief, so make sure that the language is clear and that findings are reported accurately and appropriately.

Communicating your research in plain language to the public is important for reaching a wide array of readers who might otherwise be unaware of your work and its potential significance. Many publishers offer various tools to assist authors in promoting their work and tracking its impact. Advice on promoting your article, including how to work with the media, write social media posts, and track readership of your article, can be found on the APA website (https://on.apa.org/2KEsnR6). The publication of your work represents a significant achievement, but in many ways publication is only the beginning of its impact on the greater public.

PUBLICATION PROCESS

CREDITS FOR ADAPTED TABLES, FIGURES, AND PAPERS

Many tables and figures, as well as the professional sample paper, presented in the *Publication Manual* were adapted from published works. The copyright attributions for those works are noted here in order of appearance. The APA Style team created all other tables and figures and the student sample paper.

Figure 2.1: Adapted from "The Role of Compulsive Texting in Adolescents' Academic Functioning," by K. M. Lister-Landman, S. E. Domoff, and E. F. Dubow, 2017, *Psychology of Popular Media Culture*, *6*(4), p. 311 (https://doi.org/10.1037/ppm0000100). Copyright 2015 by the American Psychological Association.

Figure 2.5: Adapted from "Age and Gender Differences in Self-Esteem—A Cross-Cultural Window," by W. Bleidorn, R. C. Arslan, J. J. A. Denissen, P. J. Rentfrow, J. E. Gebauer, J. Potter, and S. D. Gosling, 2016, *Journal of Personality and Social Psychology*, *111*(3), pp. 396–410 (https://doi.org/10.1037/pspp0000078). Copyright 2015 by the American Psychological Association.

Professional Sample Paper: Adapted from "A Comparison of Student Evaluations of Teaching With Online and Paper-Based Administration," by C. J. Stanny and J. E. Arruda, 2017, *Scholarship of Teaching and Learning in Psychology*, *3*(3), pp. 198–207 (https://doi.org/10.1037/stl0000087). Copyright 2017 by the American Psychological Association.

Table 3.1: Adapted from "Journal Article Reporting Standards for Quantitative Research in Psychology: The APA Publications and Communications Board Task Force Report," by M. Appelbaum, H. Cooper, R. B. Kline, E. Mayo-Wilson, A. M. Nezu, and S. M. Rao, 2018, *American Psychologist*, *73*(1), pp. 6–8 (https://doi.org/10.1037/amp0000191). Copyright 2018 by the American Psychological Association.

Table 3.2: Adapted from "Journal Article Reporting Standards for Qualitative Primary, Qualitative Meta-Analytic, and Mixed Methods Research in Psychology: The APA Publications and Communications Board Task Force Report," by H. M. Levitt, M. Bamberg, J. W. Creswell, D. M. Frost, R. Josselson, and C. Suárez-Orozco, 2018, *American Psychologist*, *73*(1), pp. 34–37 (https://doi.org/10.1037/amp0000151). Copyright 2018 by the American Psychological Association.

Table 3.3: Adapted from "Journal Article Reporting Standards for Qualitative Primary, Qualitative Meta-Analytic, and Mixed Methods Research in Psychology: The APA Publications and Communications Board Task Force Report," by H. M. Levitt, M. Bamberg, J. W. Creswell, D. M. Frost, R. Josselson, and C. Suárez-Orozco, 2018, *American Psychologist*, *73*(1), pp. 41–43 (https://doi.org/10.1037/amp0000151). Copyright 2018 by the American Psychological Association.

Figure 3.1: Adapted from "Journal Article Reporting Standards for Quantitative Research in Psychology: The APA Publications and Communications Board Task Force Report," by M. Appelbaum, H. Cooper, R. B. Kline, E. Mayo-Wilson, A. M. Nezu, and S. M. Rao, 2018, *American Psychologist*, *73*(1), p. 5 (https://doi.org/10.1037/amp0000191). Copyright 2018 by the American Psychological Association.

Table 7.2: Adapted from "Internet-Based Cognitive–Behavior Therapy for Procrastination: A Randomized Controlled Trial," by A. Rozental, E. Forsell, A. Svensson, G. Andersson, and P. Carlbring, 2015, *Journal of Consulting and Clinical Psychology*, *83*(4), p. 815 (https://doi.org/10.1037/ccp0000023). Copyright 2015 by the American Psychological Association.

Table 7.3: Adapted from "Introduction of the *DSM-5* Levels of Personality Functioning Questionnaire," by S. K. Huprich, S. M. Nelson, K. B. Meehan, C. J. Siefert, G. Haggerty, J. Sexton, V. B. Dauphin, M. Macaluso, J. Jackson, R. Zackula, and L. Baade, 2018, *Personality Disorders: Theory, Research, and Treatment*, *9*(6), p. 557 (https://doi.org/10.1037/per0000264). Copyright 2017 by the American Psychological Association.

Table 7.4: Adapted from "A Meta-Analysis of Context Integration Deficits Across the Schizotypy Spectrum Using AX-CPT and DPX Tasks," by C. A. Chun, L. Ciceron, and T. R. Kwapil, 2018, *Journal of Abnormal Psychology*, *127*(8), pp. 795–797 (https://doi.org/10.1037/abn0000383). Copyright 2018 by the American Psychological Association.

Table 7.5: Adapted from "A Further Assessment of the Hall–Rodriguez Theory of Latent Inhibition," by H. T. Leung, A. S. Killcross, and R. F. Westbrook, 2013, *Journal of Experimental Psychology: Animal Behavior Processes*, *39*(2), p. 119 (https://doi.org/10.1037/a0031724). Copyright 2013 by the American Psychological Association.

Table 7.6: Adapted from "Low Social Rhythm Regularity Predicts First Onset of Bipolar Spectrum Disorders Among At-Risk Individuals With Reward Hypersensitivity," by L. B. Alloy, E. M. Boland, T. H. Ng, W. G. Whitehouse, and L. Y. Abramson, 2015, *Journal of Abnormal Psychology*, *124*(4), p. 946 (https://doi.org/10.1037/abn0000107). Copyright 2015 by the American Psychological Association.

Table 7.7: Adapted from "I Don't Believe It! Belief Perseverance in Attitudes Toward Celebrities," by N. H. Bui, 2014, *Psychology of Popular Media Culture*, *3*(1), p. 43 (https://doi.org/10.1037/a0034916). Copyright 2013 by the American Psychological Association.

Table 7.8: Adapted from "The Slow Developmental Time Course of Real-Time Spoken Word Recognition," by H. Rigler, A. Farris-Trimble, L. Greiner, J. Walker, J. B Tomblin, and B. McMurray, 2015, *Developmental Psychology*, *51*(12), p. 1697 (https://doi.org/10.1037/dev0000044). Copyright 2015 by the American Psychological Association.

Table 7.9: Adapted from "Students' Implicit Theories of University Professors," by J. Yermack and D. R. Forsyth, 2016, *Scholarship of Teaching and Learning in Psychology*, *2*(3), p. 176 (https://doi.org/10.1037/stl0000067). Copyright 2016 by the American Psychological Association.

Table 7.10: Adapted from "Build or Buy? The Individual and Unit-Level Performance of Internally Versus Externally Selected Managers Over Time," by P. S. DeOrtentiis, C. H. Van Iddekinge, R. E. Ployhart, and T. D. Heetderks, 2018, *Journal of Applied Psychology*, *103*(8), p. 922 (https://doi.org/10.1037/

apl0000312). Copyright 2018 by the American Psychological Association.

Table 7.11: Adapted from "Academic Disidentification in Black College Students: The Role of Teacher Trust and Gender," by S. McClain and K. Cokley, 2017, *Cultural Diversity and Ethnic Minority Psychology*, *23*(1), p. 128 (https://doi.org/10.1037/cdp0000094). Copyright 2016 by the American Psychological Association.

Table 7.12: Adapted from "Living in a Continuous Traumatic Reality: Impact on Elderly Persons Residing in Urban and Rural Communities," by I. Regev and O. Nuttman-Shwartz, 2016, *American Journal of Orthopsychiatry*, *86*(6), p. 656 (https://doi.org/10.1037/ort0000165). Copyright 2016 by the Global Alliance for Behavioral Health and Social Justice. Reprinted with permission.

Table 7.13: Adapted from "Work-Related Self-Efficacy as a Moderator of the Impact of a Worksite Stress Management Training Intervention: Intrinsic Work Motivation as a Higher Order Condition of Effect," by J. Lloyd, F. W. Bond, and P. E. Flaxman, 2017, *Journal of Occupational Health Psychology*, *22*(1), p. 121 (https://doi.org/10.1037/ocp0000026). Copyright 2016 by the American Psychological Association.

Table 7.14: Adapted from "Individual Differences in Activation of the Parental Care Motivational System: Assessment, Prediction, and Implications," by E. E. Buckels, A. T. Beall, M. K. Hofer, E. Y. Lin, Z. Zhou, and M. Schaller, 2015, *Journal of Personality and Social Psychology*, *108*(3), p. 501 (https://doi.org/10.1037/pspp0000023). Copyright 2015 by the American Psychological Association.

Table 7.15: Adapted from "Too Tired to Inspire or Be Inspired: Sleep Deprivation and Charismatic Leadership," by C. M. Barnes, C. L. Guarana, S. Nauman, and D. T. Kong, 2016, *Journal of Applied Psychology*, *101*(8), p. 1195 (https://doi.org/10.1037/apl0000123). Copyright 2016 by the American Psychological Association.

Table 7.16: Adapted from "I Just Want to Be Left Alone: Daily Overload and Marital Behavior," by M. S. Sears, R. L. Repetti, T. F. Robles, and B. M. Reynolds, 2016, *Journal of Family Psychology*, *30*(5), p. 576 (https://doi.org/10.1037/fam0000197). Copyright 2016 by the American Psychological Association.

Table 7.17: Adapted from "Creativity and Academic Achievement: A Meta-Analysis," by A. Gajda, M. Karwowski, and R. A. Beghetto, 2017, *Journal of Educational Psychology*, *109*(2), p. 286 (https://doi.org/10.1037/edu0000133). Copyright 2016 by the American Psychological Association.

Table 7.18: Adapted from "The Role of Social Class, Ethnocultural Adaptation, and Masculinity Ideology on Mexican American College Men's Well-Being," by L. Ojeda and B. Piña-Watson, 2016, *Psychology of Men & Masculinity*, *17*(4), p. 376 (https://doi.org/10.1037/men0000023). Copyright 2016 by the American Psychological Association.

xge0000345). Copyright 2017 by the American Psychological Association.

Figure 7.13: Adapted from "The Limits of Learning: Exploration, Generalization, and the Development of Learning Traps," by A. S. Rich and T. M. Gureckis, 2018, *Journal of Experimental Psychology: General*, *147*(11), p. 1560 (https://doi.org/10.1037/xge0000466). Copyright 2018 by the American Psychological Association.

Figure 7.14: Adapted from *2017 Poverty Rate in the United States*, by the U.S. Census Bureau, 2017 (https://www.census.gov/library/visualizations/2018/comm/acs-poverty-map.html). In the public domain.

Figure 7.15: Adapted from "Empathic Accuracy for Happiness in the Daily Lives of Older Couples: Fluid Cognitive Performance Predicts Pattern Accuracy Among Men," by G. Hülür, C. A. Hoppmann, A. Rauers, H. Schade, N. Ram, and D. Gerstorf, 2016, *Psychology and Aging*, *31*(5), p. 550 (https://doi.org/10.1037/pag0000109). Copyright 2016 by the American Psychological Association.

Figure 7.16: Adapted from "An Empirically-Derived Taxonomy of Moral Concepts," by J. F. Landy and D. M. Bartels, 2018, *Journal of Experimental Psychology: General*, *147*(11), p. 1752 (https://doi.org/10.1037/xge0000404). Copyright 2018 by the American Psychological Association.

Figure 7.17: Adapted from "Out of Place, Out of Mind: Schema-Driven False Memory Effects for Object-Location Bindings," by A. R. Lew and M. L. Howe, *Journal of Experimental Psychology: Learning, Memory, and Cognition*, *43*(3), p. 405 (https://doi.org/10.1037/xlm0000317). Copyright 2016 by the American Psychological Association.

Figure 7.18: Adapted from "Bayesian Mixture Modeling of Significant p Values: A Meta-Analytic Method to Estimate the Degree of Contamination From H_0," by Q. F. Gronau, M. Duizer, M. Bakker, and E.-J. Wagenmakers, 2017, *Journal of Experimental Psychology: General*, *146*(9), p. 1227 (https://doi.org/10.1037/xge0000324). Copyright 2017 by the American Psychological Association.

Figure 7.19: Adapted from "Enhanced Processing of Untrustworthiness in Natural Faces With Neutral Expressions," by A. Lischke, M. Junge, A. O. Hamm, and M. Weymar, 2018, *Emotion*, *18*(2), p. 185 (https://doi.org/10.1037/emo0000318). Copyright 2017 by the American Psychological Association.

Figure 7.20: Adapted from "Denying Humanity: The Distinct Neural Correlates of Blatant Dehumanization," by E. Bruneau, N. Jacoby, N. Kteily, and R. Saxe, 2018, *Journal of Experimental Psychology: General*, *147*(7), p. 1087 (https://doi.org/10.1037/xge0000417). Copyright 2018 by the American Psychological Association.

Figure 7.21: Adapted from "*NF1* Microduplications: Identification of Seven Nonrelated Individuals Provides Further Characterization of the Phenotype," by K. J. Moles, G. C. Gowans, S. Gedela, D. Beversdorf, A. Yu, L. H. Seaver, R. A. Schultz, J. A. Rosen-

feld, B. S. Torchia, and L. G. Shaffer, 2012, *Genetics in Medicine*, *14*, p. 509 (https://doi.org/10.1038/gim.2011.46). Copyright 2012 by the American College of Medical Genetics and Genomics. Reprinted with permission.

Figure 8.1: Adapted from "Clever People: Intelligence and Humor Production Ability," by A. P. Christensen, P. J. Silvia, E. C. Nusbaum, and R. E. Beaty, 2018, *Psychology of Aesthetics, Creativity, and the Arts*, *12*(2), p. 136 (https://doi.org/10.1037/aca0000109). Copyright 2018 by the American Psychological Association.

Figure 8.3: Adapted from "Can Journalistic 'False Balance' Distort Public Perception of Consensus in Expert Opinion?" by D. J. Koehler, 2016, *Journal of Experimental Psychology: Applied*, *22*(1), pp. 24–38 (https://doi.org/10.1037/xap0000073). Copyright 2016 by the American Psychological Association.

Figure 8.4: Adapted from "Discrimination, Work Outcomes, and Mental Health Among Women of Color: The Protective Role of Womanist Attitudes," by B. L. Velez, R. Cox Jr., C. J. Polihronakis, and B. Moradi, 2018, *Journal of Counseling Psychology*, *65*(2), pp. 178, 193 (https://doi.org/10.1037/cou0000274). Copyright 2018 by the American Psychological Association.

Figure 8.5: Adapted from "Play Therapists' Perceptions of Wellness and Self-Care Practices," by K. K. Meany-Walen, A. Cobie-Nuss, E. Eittreim, S. Teeling, S. Wilson, and C. Xander, 2018, *International Journal of Play Therapy*, *27*(3), p. 177 (https://doi.org/10.1037/pla0000067). Copyright 2018 by the American Psychological Association.

Figure 8.6: Adapted from "Tabloids as Windows Into Our Interpersonal Relationships: A Content Analysis of Mass Media Gossip From an Evolutionary Perspective," by C. J. S. De Backer and M. L. Fisher, 2012, *Journal of Social, Evolutionary, and Cultural Psychology*, *6*(3), p. 421 (https://doi.org/10.1037/h0099244). Copyright 2012 by the American Psychological Association.

Figure 8.7: Adapted from "Women Athletes' Self-Compassion, Self-Criticism, and Perceived Sport Performance," by M. E. Killham, A. D. Mosewich, D. E. Mack, K. E. Gunnell, and L. J. Ferguson, 2018, *Sport, Exercise, and Performance Psychology*, *7*(3), p. 297 (https://doi.org/10.1037/spy0000127). Copyright 2018 by the American Psychological Association.

Figure 9.1: Adapted from "Sensitivity to the Evaluation of Others Emerges by 24 Months," by S. V. Botto and P. Rochat, 2018, *Developmental Psychology*, *54*(9), p. 1723 (https://doi.org/10.1037/dev0000548). Copyright 2018 by the American Psychological Association.

Figure 9.4: Adapted from "Aging and Recognition Memory: A Meta-Analysis," by S. H. Fraundorf, K. L. Hourihan, R. A. Peters, and A. S. Benjamin, 2019, Psychological Bulletin, 145(4), pp. 359–368 (https://doi.org/10.1037/bul0000185). Copyright 2019 by the American Psychological Association.

REFERENCES

Accord Alliance. (n.d.). *Learn about DSD*. http://www.accordalliance.org/learn-about-dsd/

American Educational Research Association, American Psychological Association, & National Council on Measurement in Education. (2014). *Standards for educational and psychological testing.* https://www.apa.org/science/programs/testing/standards.aspx

American Psychological Association. (n.d.-a). *Definitions related to sexual orientation and gender diversity in APA documents.* https://www.apa.org/pi/lgbt/resources/sexuality-definitions.pdf

American Psychological Association. (n.d.-b). *Task force on statistical inference.* https://www.apa.org/science/leadership/bsa/statistical/

American Psychological Association. (2010). *Publication manual of the American Psychological Association* (6th ed.).

American Psychological Association. (2012a). *Guidelines for ethical conduct in the care and use of nonhuman animals in research.* https://www.apa.org/science/leadership/care/care-animal-guidelines.pdf

American Psychological Association. (2012b). Guidelines for psychological practice with lesbian, gay, and bisexual clients. *American Psychologist, 67*(1), 10–42. https://doi.org/10.1037/a0024659

American Psychological Association. (2012c). Guidelines for the evaluation of dementia and age-related cognitive change. *American Psychologist, 67*(1), 1–9. https://doi.org/10.1037/a0024643

American Psychological Association. (2014). Guidelines for psychological practice with older adults. *American Psychologist, 69*(1), 34–65. https://doi.org/10.1037/a0035063

American Psychological Association. (2015a). Guidelines for psychological practice with transgender and gender nonconforming people. *American Psychologist, 70*(9), 832–864. https://doi.org/10.1037/a0039906

American Psychological Association. (2015b). *Key terms and concepts in understanding gender diversity and sexual orientation among students.* https://www.apa.org/pi/lgbt/programs/safe-supportive/lgbt/key-terms.pdf

American Psychological Association. (2017a). *Ethical principles of psychologists and code of conduct* (2002, amended effective June 1, 2010, and January 1, 2017). https://www.apa.org/ethics/code/index.aspx

American Psychological Association. (2017b). *Multicultural guidelines: An ecological approach to context, identity, and intersectionality.* https://www.apa.org/about/policy/multicultural-guidelines.aspx

American Psychological Association. (2018). *APA resolution for the use of the term* patient *in American Psychological Association policies, rules, and public relations activities when referring to the health-related and scientific activities of health service psychologists and scientists in health care services and settings.* https://www.apa.org/about/policy/resolution-term-patient.pdf

American Psychological Association of Graduate Students. (2015). *Proud and prepared: A guide for LGBT students navigating graduate training.* American Psychological Association. https://www.apa.org/apags/resources/lgbt-guide.aspx

APA Publications and Communications Board Working Group on Journal Article Reporting Standards. (2008). Reporting standards for research in psychology: Why do we need them? What might they be? *American Psychologist, 63*(9), 839–851. https://doi.org/10.1037/0003-066X.63.9.839

Appelbaum, M., Cooper, H., Kline, R. B., Mayo-Wilson, E., Nezu, A. M., & Rao, S. M. (2018). Journal article reporting standards for quantitative research in psychology: The APA Publications and Communications Board Task Force report. *American Psychologist, 73*(1), 3–25. https://doi.org/10.1037/amp0000191

The Asexual Visibility & Education Network. (n.d.). *General FAQ: Definitions.* https://www.asexuality.org/?q=general.html#def

Beaubien, S., & Eckard, M. (2014). Addressing faculty publishing concerns with open access journal quality indicators. *Journal of Librarianship and Scholarly Communication, 2*(2), Article eP1133. https://doi.org/10.7710/2162-3309.1133

Bentley, M., Peerenboom, C. A., Hodge, F. W., Passano, E. B., Warren, H. C., & Washburn, M. F. (1929). Instructions in regard to preparation of manuscript. *Psychological Bulletin, 26*(2), 57–63. https://doi.org/10.1037/h0071487

Blackless, M., Charuvastra, A., Derryck, A., Fausto-Sterling, A., Lauzanne, K., & Lee, E. (2000). How sexually dimorphic are we? Review and synthesis. *American Journal of Human Biology, 12*(2), 151–166. http://doi.org/bttkh4

The bluebook: A uniform system of citation (20th ed.). (2015). Harvard Law Review Association.

Bowleg, L. (2008). When Black + woman + lesbian ≠ Black lesbian woman: The methodological challenges of quantitative and qualitative intersectionality research. *Sex Roles, 59*(5–6), 312–325. https://doi.org/10.1007/s11199-008-9400-z

Bowman, J. D. (2014). Predatory publishing, questionable peer review, and fraudulent conferences. *American Journal of Pharmaceutical Education, 78*(10), Article 176. https://doi.org/10.5688/ajpe7810176

Brown, L. (n.d.). *Identity-first language.* Autistic Self Advocacy Network. https://autisticadvocacy.org/home/about-asan/identity-first-language (Original work published 2011)

Brueggemann, B. J. (2013). Disability studies/disability culture. In M. L. Wehmeyer (Ed.), *The Oxford handbook of positive psychology and disability* (pp. 279–299). Oxford University Press. https://doi.org/10.1093/oxfordhb/9780195398786.013.013.0019

Cooper, H. (2016, May 12). Principles of good writing: Avoiding plagiarism. *APA Style.* https://blog.apastyle.org/apastyle/2016/05/avoiding-plagiarism.html

Cooper, H. (2018). *Reporting quantitative research in psychology: How to meet APA Style journal article reporting standards* (2nd ed.). American Psychological Association. https://doi.org/10.1037/0000103-000

Copyright Act of 1976, 17 U.S.C. §§ 101–810 (1976).

Crenshaw, K. W. (1989). Demarginalizing the intersections of race and sex: A Black feminist critique of antidiscrimination doctrine, feminist theory, and antiracist politics. *University of Chicago Legal Forum, 1989*(1), Article 8. https://chicagounbound.uchicago.edu/uclf/vol1989/iss1/8/

Creswell, J. W. (2015). *A concise introduction to mixed methods research.* SAGE Publications.

Creswell, J. W., & Plano Clark, V. L. (2017). *Designing and conducting mixed methods research* (3rd ed.). SAGE Publications.

Creswell, J. W., & Poth, C. N. (2018). *Qualitative inquiry and research design: Choosing among five approaches* (4th ed.). SAGE Publications.

Data Sharing Working Group. (2015). *Data sharing: Principles and considerations for policy development.* American Psychological Association. https://www.apa.org/science/leadership/bsa/data-sharing-report.pdf

de Onís, C. M. (2017). What's in an "x"? An exchange about the politics of "Latinx." *Chiricú Journal: Latina/o Literatures, Arts, and Cultures, 1*(2), 78–91. https://doi.org/10.2979/chiricu.1.2.07

Diemer, M. A., Mistry, R. S., Wadsworth, M. E., López, I., & Reimers, F. (2013). Best practices in conceptualizing and measuring social class in psychological research. *Analyses of Social Issues and Public Policy, 13*(1), 77–113. https://doi.org/10.1111/asap.12001

DuBois, J. M., Walsh, H., & Strait, M. (2018). It is time to share (some) qualitative data: Reply to Guishard (2018), McCurdy and Ross (2018), and Roller and Lavrakas (2018). *Qualitative Psychology, 5*(3), 412–415. https://doi.org/10.1037/qup0000092

Dunn, D. S., & Andrews, E. E. (n.d.). *Choosing words for talking about disability.* American Psychological Association. https://www.apa.org/pi/disability/resources/choosing-words.aspx

Dunn, D. S., & Andrews, E. E. (2015). Person-first *and* identity-first language: Developing psychologists' cultural competence using disability language. *American Psychologist, 70*(3), 255–264. https://doi.org/10.1037/a0038636

Fine, M. (2013). Echoes of Bedford: A 20-year social psychology memoir on participatory action research hatched behind bars. *American Psychologist, 68*(8), 687–698. https://doi.org/10.1037/a0034359

Fisher, C. B. (2017). *Decoding the ethics code: A practical guide for psychologists* (4th ed.). SAGE Publications.

Gastil, J. (1990). Generic pronouns and sexist language: The oxymoronic character of masculine generics. *Sex Roles, 23*(11–12), 629–643. https://doi.org/10.1007/BF00289252

Greene, J. C. (2007). *Mixed methods in social inquiry*. Jossey-Bass.

Guishard, M. A. (2018). Now's not the time! Qualitative data repositories on tricky ground: Comment on DuBois et al. (2018). *Qualitative Psychology, 5*(3), 402–408. https://doi.org/10.1037/qup0000085

Guishard, M. A., Halkovic, A., Galletta, A., & Li, P. (2018). Toward epistemological ethics: Centering communities and social justice in qualitative research. *Forum: Qualitative Social Research, 19*(3), Article 27. https://doi.org/10.17169/fqs-19.3.3145

Hallock, R. M., & Dillner, K. M. (2016). Should title lengths really adhere to the American Psychological Association's twelve word limit? *American Psychologist, 71*(3), 240–242. https://doi.org/10.1037/a0040226

Hegarty, P., & Buechel, C. (2006). Androcentric reporting of gender differences in APA journals: 1965–2004. *Review of General Psychology, 10*(4), 377–389. https://doi.org/10.1037/1089-2680.10.4.377

Hill, C. E. (Ed.). (2012). *Consensual qualitative research: A practical resource for investigating social science phenomena*. American Psychological Association.

Howard, J. A., & Renfrow, D. G. (2014). Intersectionality. In J. D. McLeod, E. J. Lawler, & M. Schwalbe (Eds.), *Handbook of the social psychology of inequality* (pp. 95–121). Springer. https://doi.org/10.1007/978-94-017-9002-4

International Committee on Standardized Genetic Nomenclature for Mice & Rat Genome and Nomenclature Committee. (2018). *Guidelines for nomenclature of genes, genetic markers, alleles, and mutations in mouse and rat*. Mouse Genome Informatics. http://www.informatics.jax.org/mgi-home/nomen/gene.shtml

International Journal of Indigenous Health. (n.d.). *Defining Aboriginal Peoples within Canada*. https://journals.uvic.ca/journalinfo/ijih/IJIHDefiningIndigenousPeoplesWithinCanada.pdf

Intersex Society of North America. (n.d.). *How common is intersex?* http://www.isna.org/faq/frequency

Jamali, H. R., & Nikzad, M. (2011). Article title type and its relation with the number of downloads and citations. *Scientometrics, 88*(2), 653–661. https://doi.org/10.1007/s11192-011-0412-z

Knatterud, M. E. (1991). Writing with the patient in mind: Don't add insult to injury. *American Medical Writers Association Journal, 6*(1), 10–17.

Laine, C., & Winker, M. A. (2017). Identifying predatory or pseudo-journals. *Biochemia Medica, 27*(2), 285–291. https://doi.org/10.11613/BM.2017.031

Levitt, H. M. (2019). *Reporting qualitative research in psychology: How to meet APA Style journal article reporting standards*. American Psychological Association. https://doi.org/10.1037/0000121-000

Levitt, H. M., Bamberg, M., Creswell, J. W., Frost, D. M., Josselson, R., & Suárez-Orozco, C. (2018). Journal article reporting standards for qualitative primary, qualitative meta-analytic, and mixed methods research in psychology: The APA Publications and Communications Board Task Force report. *American Psychologist, 73*(1), 26–46. https://doi.org/10.1037/amp0000151

Levitt, H. M., Motulsky, S. L., Wertz, F. J., Morrow, S. L., & Ponterotto, J. G. (2017). Recommendations for designing and reviewing qualitative research in psychology: Promoting methodological integrity. *Qualitative Psychology, 4*(1), 2–22. https://doi.org/10.1037/qup0000082

Lindland, E., Fond, M., Haydon, A., & Kendall-Taylor, N. (2015). *Gauging aging: Mapping the gaps between expert and public understandings of aging in America*. FrameWorks Institute. https://frameworksinstitute.org/assets/files/aging_mtg.pdf

Lundebjerg, N. E., Trucil, D. E., Hammond, E. C., & Applegate, W. B. (2017). When it comes to older adults, language matters: *Journal of the American Geriatrics Society* adopts modified American Medical Association Style. *Journal of the American Geriatrics Society, 65*(7), 1386–1388. https://doi.org/10.1111/jgs.14941

Masten, Y., & Ashcraft, A. (2017). Due diligence in the open-access explosion era: Choosing a reputable journal for publication. *FEMS Microbiology Letters, 364*(21), Article fnx206. https://doi.org/10.1093/femsle/fnx206

McCurdy, S. A., & Ross, M. W. (2018). Qualitative data are not just quantitative data with text but data with context: On the dangers of sharing some qualitative data: Comment on DuBois et al (2018). *Qualitative Psychology, 5*(3), 409–411. https://doi.org/10.1037/qup0000088

Merriam, S. B., & Tisdell, E. J. (2016). *Qualitative research: A guide to design and implementation* (4th ed.). Jossey-Bass.

Merriam-Webster. (n.d.-a). *Words we're watching: 'Patchwriting': Paraphrasing in a cut-and-paste world.* https://www.merriam-webster.com/words-at-play/words-were-watching-patchwriting

Merriam-Webster. (n.d.-b). *Words we're watching: Singular 'they': Though singular 'they' is old, 'they' as a nonbinary pronoun is new—and useful.* https://www.merriam-webster.com/words-at-play/singular-nonbinary-they

Morrow, S. L. (2005). Quality and trustworthiness in qualitative research in counseling psychology. *Journal of Counseling Psychology, 52*(2), 250–260. https://doi.org/10.1037/0022-0167.52.2.250

Morse, J. M. (2008). "What's your favorite color?" Reporting irrelevant demographics in qualitative research. *Qualitative Health Research, 18*(3), 299–300. https://doi.org/10.1177/1049732307310995

Moulton, J., Robinson, G. M., & Elias, C. (1978). Sex bias in language use: "Neutral" pronouns that aren't. *American Psychologist, 33*(11), 1032–1036. https://doi.org/10.1037/0003-066X.33.11.1032

National Academies of Sciences, Engineering, and Medicine. (2019). *Reproducibility and replicability in science.* The National Academies Press. https://doi.org/10.17226/25303

National Institutes of Health. (n.d.). *NIH data sharing policies.* U.S. Department of Health & Human Services, U.S. National Library of Medicine. https://www.nlm.nih.gov/NIHbmic/nih_data_sharing_policies.html

Neimeyer, R. A., Hogan, N. S., & Laurie, A. (2008). The measurement of grief: Psychometric considerations in the assessment of reactions to bereavement. In M. S. Stroebe, R. O. Hansson, H. Schut, & W. Stroebe (Eds.), *Handbook of bereavement research and practice: Advances in theory and intervention* (pp. 133–161). American Psychological Association. https://doi.org/10.1037/14498-007

Open Scholarship Initiative. (2019, March 19). *OSI brief: Deceptive publishing.* http://osiglobal.org/2019/03/19/osi-brief-deceptive-publishing/

Parker, I. (2015). *Psychology after discourse analysis: Concepts, methods, critique.* Routledge.

Ponterotto, J. G. (2005). Qualitative research in counseling psychology: A primer on research paradigms and philosophy of science. *Journal of Counseling Psychology, 52*(2), 126–136. https://doi.org/10.1037/0022-0167.52.2.126

Rappaport, J. (1977). *Community psychology: Values, research and action.* Holt, Rinehart, & Winston.

Shamseer, L., Moher, D., Maduekwe, O., Turner, L., Barbour, V., Burch, R., Clark, J., Galipeau, J., Roberts, J., & Shea, B. J. (2017). Potential predatory and legitimate biomedical journals: Can you tell the difference? A cross-sectional comparison. *BMC Medicine, 15*(1), Article 28. https://doi.org/10.1186/s12916-017-0785-9

Singh, A. A. (2017). Understanding trauma and supporting resilience with LGBT people of color. In K. L. Eckstrand & J. Potter (Eds.), *Trauma, resilience, and health promotion in LGBT patients: What every healthcare provider should know* (pp. 113–119). Springer.

Solomon, A. (2012). *Far from the tree: Parents, children, and the search for identity.* Scribner.

Stiles, W. B. (1993). Quality control in qualitative research. *Clinical Psychology Review, 13*(6), 593–618. https://doi.org/10.1016/0272-7358(93)90048-Q

Stout, J. G., & Dasgupta, N. (2011). When *he* doesn't mean *you:* Gender-exclusive language as ostracism. *Personality and Social Psychology Bulletin, 37*(6), 757–769. https://doi.org/10.1177/0146167211406434

Sweeney, L., Crosas, M., & Bar-Sinai, M. (2015, October 16). Sharing sensitive data with confidence: The datatags system. *Technology Science.* https://techscience.org/a/2015101601/

Sweetland, J., Volmert, A., & O'Neil, M. (2017). *Finding the frame: An empirical approach to reframing aging and ageism.* FrameWorks Institute. http://frameworksinstitute.org/assets/files/aging_elder_abuse/aging_research_report_final_2017.pdf

Tashakkori, A., & Teddlie, C. (Eds.). (2010). *SAGE handbook of mixed methods in social & behavioral research* (2nd ed.). SAGE Publications. https://doi.org/10.4135/9781506335193

Tuck, E., & Yang, K. W. (2014). Unbecoming claims: Pedagogies of refusal in qualitative research. *Qualitative Inquiry, 20*(6), 811–818. https://doi.org/10.1177/1077800414530265

University of Kansas, Research and Training Center on Independent Living. (2013). *Guidelines: How to write and report about people with disabilities* (8th ed.). https://rtcil.drupal.ku.edu/sites/rtcil.drupal.ku.edu/files/images/galleries/Guidelines%208th%20edition.pdf

U.S. Copyright Office. (2017). *Copyright basics* (Circular 1). Copyright.gov. https://www.copyright.gov/circs/circ01.pdf

U.S. Copyright Office. (2019). *More information on fair use.* Copyright.gov. https://www.copyright.gov/fair-use/more-info.html

Wain, H. M., Bruford, E. A., Lovering, R. C., Lush, M. J., Wright, M. W., & Povey, S. (2002). Guidelines for human gene nomenclature. *Genomics, 79*(4), 464–470. https://doi.org/10.1006/geno.2002.6748

Wainer, H. (1997). Improving tabular displays, with NAEP tables as examples and inspirations. *Journal of Educational and Behavioral Statistics*, *22*(1), 1–30. https://doi.org/10.2307/1165236

Web Accessibility Initiative. (2018). *Web content accessibility guidelines (WCAG) overview*. https://www.w3.org/WAI/standards-guidelines/wcag

Wilkinson, L., & the Task Force on Statistical Inference. (1999). Statistical methods in psychology journals: Guidelines and explanations. *American Psychologist*, *54*(8), 594–604. https://doi.org/10.1037/0003-066X.54.8.594

World Health Organization. (2001). *International classification of functioning, disability and health (ICF)*. https://www.who.int/classifications/icf/en/

World Health Organization. (2011). *World report on disability*. https://www.who.int/disabilities/world_report/2011/en/

Younging, G. (2018). *Elements of Indigenous style: A guide for writing by and about Indigenous Peoples*. Brush Education.

Zell, E., Krizan, Z., & Teeter, S. R. (2015). Evaluating gender similarities and differences using metasynthesis. *American Psychologist*, *70*(1), 10–20. https://doi.org/10.1037/a0038208

INDEX

Numbers in **bold** refer to section numbers.